DEFENDING YOUR LIFE

*HOW CHRISTIANS MAY DEFEND
THEMSELVES AGAINST ATTACK*

A BIBLICAL HANDBOOK

DONALD E. JONES, PHD

J & A Book Publishers
www.jabookpublishers.com

(C) 2021 Donald E. Jones, PhD

Printed in the United States of America

All rights reserved. No part of this book may be reproduced in any form without permission in writing from the author, except in the case of brief quotations embodied in critical articles or reviews.

All Scripture quotations are from the World English Bible. This version was selected, because it is in the public domain and can be quoted without limit. A personal translation of a verse or passage will be designated with (DEJ).

ISBN-13:978-1946368133
ISBN-10:194636813X

DEDICATION

I want to dedicate this book to my wonderful wife Carol who has supported me in this ministry with sacrifice, enthusiasm, encouragement, and accountability. Most of all, she has been a constant blessing because of her willingness to listen. I was always sharing with her the truths God had been teaching me as I studied His word and wrote this book. It consumed many hours. Thank you, Carol and I deeply love you.

Also, I want to dedicate this book to my children, Krista, Matt, Greg, and Kara for their constant support of my ministries, love for Christ and His Word, and their willingness to live for Him. I love you all.

THE COMPANION BOOK

Standing Your Ground

The Persecution of the Saints
And How to Overcome It

A Biblical Handbook.

By Donald E. Jones, PhD

Contents

Introduction	1
Chapter - 1. The Sinful Necessity	5
Chapter - 2. The Divine Demand	31
Chapter - 3. The World's Preservation	99
Chapter - 4. The Defensive Structure	119
Chapter - 5. The Scriptural Understanding	143
Chapter - 6. The Divine Expression	181
Chapter - 7. The Human Expectation	233
Chapter - 8. The Natural Inclination	279
Chapter - 9. The Protective Judgments	303
Chapter - 10. The Legal Allowance	325
Chapter - 11. The Son's Instruction	343
Chapter - 12. The Lord's Directive	389
Chapter - 13. The Certain Urgency	465
Chapter - 14. The Biblical Significance	517
Chapter - 15. The Equal Access	549
Chapter - 16. The Scriptural Consistency	569
Conclusion	643

Introduction

The purpose of this book is to provide a complete picture of what the Bible says concerning self-defense This was no small task to research and study. I did not read any books on self-defense before or during my study. It was only after the initial study that I looked at any resources that are available. I basically read through the Bible verse by verse identifying the truths that I found therein and categorized each passage which addressed self-defense or the defend of others in some way. These biblical categories were built from the individual verses, rather than a set or group of preconceived structures, beliefs, or different ideas. Each of these categories became a chapter or section in the book. All Bible passages included were studied in their historical, grammatical, and scriptural contexts. Once my interpretations were complete, I compared these verses with commentators both past and present.

Finally, I compared my personal interpretation of the all the biblical passages to the historical interpretation of the evangelical church. Also, when I read, I attempted to let the Bible define and explain itself by itself. I studied the many words, ideas, and principles in the Bible and compared them to other scriptural passages to define, elucidate, describe, or explain a truth. At every moment, I labored at removing the cultural, language, and past biblical frameworks we so often impose upon the texts. I really opened my mind to look at the Scriptures from an objective point of view. This was especially important with the use of our English terminology which sometimes cannot provide a word that is precise enough to properly translate the Hebrew or Greek word in a passage.

I paid attention to analogies, metaphors, and similes used by both the inspired authors and the biblical characters that addressed the topic in some way for insight. Once the study was finished and the biblical framework was completed, I compared what I had discovered to books and articles on the subject to determine discrepancies, differences of opinion, and what might be missing. Once the further study was finished, this book was written.

Why must doctrinal study require such labor? I think the answer is found in the way God composed the Scriptures. The Lord did not write the Bible in consecutive narratives, a list of commands, or an organized outline of doctrines. Instead, it was written as men journeyed through life. To understand a subject fully, often we must pull out fragments of truth from many different places to discover the complete truth about a given topic. There are numerous treasures and gold nuggets buried within the pages of God's Word and the faithful must find it. This is how God wants His Word to be handled.

Only those willing to "labor in the Word and doctrine" will be able to discover its riches. Then, those who have found them are required to teach it to others. This is what I have done, and others like me. As a result, this book will be no small task to read. Since I cross reference so many verses, I have put the full texts in the book because it would be an impossible task to read even one paragraph without having to remember or even to look up every verse and passage referenced. I utilized the World English Translation because it is the only "no strings attached" English translation which can be quoted without limits except the few which are in the public domain. Though some of the translation is rough, I have pointed out the times when this has happened. I am so grateful for this copyright free translation.

Every aspect of this study touched on so many theological truths, that they could not possibly be incorporated into this book. As a result, I often left a particular truth with a few proof texts that could be filled in with a simple concordance

HOW CHRISTIANS MAY DEFEND THEMSELVES AGAINST ATTACK

study. Other truths were explained and left for the readers to research on their own. Also, I have repeated many passages over and over viewing them from many different angles. Though this might be tedious at times to read, it is crucial to discovering every truth concerning this topic.

In 1 Corinthians 14, the apostle commands all believers to be mature in their thinking.

1 Corinthians 14:20
Brothers, don't be children in thoughts, yet in malice be babies, but in thoughts be mature.

This book is for those who desire the deeper truths (the meat) of God's Word concerning this critical doctrine of self-defense. It is for those who desire to discover the depth and breadth of God's thinking on this topic or as Paul calls it "the mind of Christ" on this serious doctrine.

1 Corinthians 2:16
"For who has known the mind of the Lord, that he should instruct him?" But we have Christ's mind.

Therefore, the reading of this book will require much time, a real commitment, and thought. Passages might need to be referenced in their scriptural context and studied to confirm their truths. If you are capable, please do not skip this step in your growth as a Christian. It is critical to the understanding of these truths.

In 1 John 4, John discloses to his readers that they are to test the spirits.

1 John 4:4
You are of God, little children, and have overcome them; because greater is he who is in you than he who is in the world.

Here is my challenge to all my readers and a method by which God desires us to test truth. I want the readers to test the Spirit in me by the Spirit in them in order to verify the truths that I disclose based on my careful study.

In Acts 17, the Bereans are described as nobler because they closely examined the Holy Scriptures even though Paul was presenting the truth.

Acts 17:11
Now these were more noble than those in Thessalonica, in that they received the word with all readiness of mind, examining the Scriptures daily to see whether these things were so.

I encourage you to be "nobler" and examine the Scriptures I present to support my doctrinal statements.

Readers will notice that the book is written in a simple and straightforward style. This biblical framework on self-defense and the defense of others is not presented with a vast number of theological terms, complex philosophical concepts, obscure vocabulary, or my personal opinions. This design is intended to focus all of the reader's attention on the Bible and what it teaches concerning the subject. I am interested in allowing God to fully speak from His Holy Word. The words the Lord Almighty chooses to use through His inspired writers are the words that should teach us, as much as possible, before we add other terms for comprehension or clarification. It is my way of remaining true to God and His words to us.

Read the book, study the Scriptures contained within it, share the truths with others, because one day it may mean the difference between life and death for you or those you love.

Chapter 1

The Sinful Necessity

We must begin our study of self-defense and the defense of others by discussing the necessity of these actions due to the plan of redemption and the violence of sin. If mankind was not sinful and did not need redemption, there would not be a necessity for self-defense or the defense of others. How did this sinful condition originate, and must it necessitate a physical defense of oneself and others?

The Sacred Purpose

In eternity past, God, the Father, developed a plan to create a kingdom of people for His Son. These people would fall and need redemption. This would involve the incarnation of His only Son in human form to redeem man through His death on a cross. Once redeemed, those elected to eternal life would build His kingdom on earth until the end of all things. At this time, these saved ones will be outfitted with immortal bodies and spend eternity glorifying Him as all in the power of the Spirit glorify the Father. This would take much time and as a result, those involved would have to be protected from death until the end of the world as determined by the Father.

The Kingdom Gift

Therefore, the plan involved a kingdom of people given to the Son as a gift of love from the Father. In John 3, the disciples of John the Baptist came to him and inquired about Jesus who was baptizing in water as he also was. In his explanation, He discloses this truth about the kingdom.

John 3:35
The Father loves the Son, and has given all things into his hand.

In the high priestly prayer of Jesus, the Son repeats this truth over and over as He speaks to the Father. First, He addresses himself in the third person and then in the first. Notice, the word "given" which implies "given as a gift."

John 17:2
Even as you gave him authority over all flesh, he will give eternal life to all whom you have given him.

John 17:6
I revealed your name to the people whom you have given me [as a gift] out of the world. They were yours, and you have given them to me. They have kept your word.

John 17:7
Now they have known that all things whatever you have given me [as a gift] are from you [the Father].

John 17:9
I pray for them. I don't pray for the world, but for those whom you have given me [as a gift], for they are yours.

John 17:11
I am no more in the world, but these are in the world, and I am coming to you. Holy Father, keep them through your name which you have given me [as a gift], that they may be one, even as we are.

John 17:12
While I was with them in the world, I kept them in your name. Those

whom you have given me [as a gift] I have kept. None of them is lost, except the son of destruction, that the Scripture might be fulfilled.

In Colossians 1, the apostle Paul teaches this same truth while expanding our understanding that all of creation is a part of the gift of the kingdom.

Colossians 1:15-16
Who is the image of the invisible God, the firstborn of all creation. For by him all things were created, in the heavens and on the earth, things visible and things invisible, whether thrones or dominions or principalities or powers; all things have been created through him, and for him.

Notice, the two words "for Him." Everything in the universe was created "for Him." The Greek word translated "firstborn" means "to be the first among the born" or "preeminent one among others." God desired that His Son have a relationship with a kingdom of people who would glorify Him. They would enjoy a relationship of love with Him for all eternity as all glorified and loved the Father through the Spirit.

The Kingdom's Growth

So, as Adam and Eve walked in the garden, they were to be given as a gift to the God, the Son, by God, the Father. In Genesis 1:28, this is the reason they were given a powerful mandate by God when the Lord told them to "Be fruitful, multiply, fill the earth, and subdue it."

Genesis 1:28
God blessed them. God said to them, "Be fruitful, multiply, fill the earth, and subdue it. Have dominion over the fish of the sea, over the birds of the sky...over every living thing that moves on the earth."

They were to begin having children, with their children then having children until the earth was filled with human beings. As they and their offspring (us included) did this, they were to be in control of the entire earth and develop into many societies in one glorious kingdom on earth who honored the Son.

Who would rule man as man ruled the earth? The Son of God would, of course. Why? It was His kingdom, a gift from the Father. The Son and His kingdom of humans would then live their lives serving and glorifying the Father. All would be done in and through the Holy Spirit. All of this would be forever as men and woman continually ate of the tree of Life in the center of the garden. There would be no animosity, jealousy, envy, or hate, but only love and joy forever.

Genesis 2:9
Out of the ground Yahweh God made every tree to grow that is pleasant to the sight, and good for food, including the tree of life in the middle of the garden and the tree of the knowledge of good and evil.

The Sinful Fall

At some point, God told man that he could eat of any tree of the garden except one which was the Tree of Good and Evil.

Genesis 2:16-17
Yahweh God commanded the man, saying, "Of every tree of the garden you may freely eat: but of the tree of the knowledge of good and evil, you shall not eat of it: for in the day that you eat of it you will surely die."

God told them that in the day they disobeyed Him and ate the fruit, they would "die."

HOW CHRISTIANS MAY DEFEND THEMSELVES AGAINST ATTACK

A magnificent and powerful angel named Lucifer was placed in the garden. This angel saw all that God was doing for His Son and desired this for himself. He wanted the glory and power and kingdom that were being bestowed on the Son, so he devised a scheme to tempt these two humans into disobeying God.

Then, the angel turned himself into a serpent and deceived Eve into eating the fruit of the Tree of Good and Evil. She gave the fruit to Adam, and he ate also. As a result, they both died spiritually and would eventually die physically.

Genesis 3:4-7
The serpent said to the woman, "You won't surely die, for God knows that in the day you eat it, your eyes...opened, and you will be like God, knowing good and evil." When the woman saw that the tree was good for food, and that it was a delight to the eyes, and that the tree was to be desired to make one wise, she took of the fruit of it, and ate; and she gave some to her husband with her, and he ate. Both...eyes were opened, and they knew that they were naked. They sewed fig leaves together, and made themselves aprons.

The gift was now tainted and had to be redeemed. The plan was set into place in human history as evidenced by the curse of the serpent.

Genesis 3:14-15
Yahweh God said to the serpent, "Because you have done this, you are cursed above all livestock, and above every animal of the field. You shall go on your belly and you shall eat dust all the days of your life. I will put hostility between you and the woman, and between your offspring and her offspring. He will bruise your head, and you will bruise his heel."

Here God promised the woman would have a seed and the offspring from the seed would have conflict with the Devil's offspring. In essence, this was a very powerful prophecy of the coming Messiah and His redeemed people.

The Spiritual State of Man

As God worked out the great plan of redemption in human history, He would have to contend with man's sinful state which could lead to the murder of those involved in His plan before their time. The Bible describes this wicked condition.

First, man is lost and needs salvation. The Scriptures have much also to say about this condition.

Matthew 18:11
For the Son of Man came to save that which was lost.

Matthew 10:6
Rather, go to the lost sheep of the house of Israel.

John 10:16
I have other sheep, which are not of this fold.

Luke 15:8-9
Or what woman, if she had ten drachma coins, if she lost one drachma [unsaved], wouldn't light a lamp, sweep the house, and seek diligently until she found it? When she has found it, she calls...her friends and neighbors, saying, "Rejoice with me, for I have found the drachma which I had lost."

Second, man is wicked and deserves judgment. Though man is lost, he is also wicked, and this cannot be ignored.

Psalm 14:3
They (all humans) have all gone aside; they have together become corrupt. There is none who does good, no, not one.

Psalm 53:1
The fool has said in his heart, "There is no God." They are corrupt, and have done abominable iniquity. There is no one who does good.

As Christians, we must see man in the light of both these states. Viewing them as lost will help us to develop a desire to share the gospel with them and tolerate certain negative words and actions toward us. Seeing men as wicked helps us be cautious because violence can come from their condition. This will require defense against their violence. It would be foolish if a child of ours was physically attacked one on one by an unbeliever and we would respond not by defending him or her but by sharing the gospel as they hurt our child.

Their Spiritual Deadness

All unsaved people are spiritually dead. Spiritually dead people are more likely to become violent even to the point of murder. In Ephesians 2, Paul describes the spiritual state of believers before coming to Christ as Savior and Lord. People who have not received Christ are as lifeless and unresponsive spiritually as a dead person is physically.

Ephesians 2:1
You were made alive [spiritually] when you were dead through trespasses and sin.

David describes the spiritual deadness of human beings at birth.

Psalm 51:5
Behold, I was brought forth in iniquity. In sin...my mother conceive me.

Babies are born alive physically but are dead spiritually.

In Romans 5, Paul acknowledges that Christians became dead through Adam, and this was passed on to every human being. Then believers became fully alive through Christ. This refers to spiritual death and life.

Romans 5:15
But the free gift isn't like the trespass. For if by the trespass of the one the many died, much more did the grace of God, and the gift by the grace of...Christ, abound to the many.

All people are dead in their sins and wickedness. As dead people are completely oblivious to anything going on around them physically, the spiritually dead are oblivious to any spiritual truth, laws, or words and actions from God around them. It has no impact. They are spiritually lifeless. They are without any perception of the true spiritual things of the Lord God. The apostle Paul teaches this important truth in his letter to the Corinthians.

1 Corinthians 2:14
Now the natural man doesn't receive the things of the God's Spirit, for they are foolishness to him, and he can't know them, because they are spiritually discerned.

They cannot discern the things of God's Spirit because they are dead. The dead cannot perceive them.

Since all unsaved people are spiritually dead, they could become a threat to us, and we should be prepared to defend ourselves or those around us against their attack.

Their Satanic Slavery

All unsaved people are Satan's children. People who are the children of the Devil are more likely to become violent even to the point of murder. Those who do not know Christ can harm or kill because they are pawns and slaves of Satan and their master harms and kills.

In the second chapter of Ephesians, the apostle Paul asserts that the Devil reigns over the world of the unsaved.

Ephesians 2:1-2
You were made alive when you were dead in transgressions and sins, in which you once walked according to the course of this world, according to the prince of the power of the air, the spirit who now works in the children of disobedience.

Here, Paul makes several ominous statements concerning Satan. The Devil is "the prince of the air." This means that he hovers over the earth in control of its systems. He runs the "course of this world" which refers to the many peoples, societies, and cultures which inhabit the earth. He is the true spirit working in unbelieving people. Essentially, the plans, goals, and activities of the world can be traced to him.

When Satan offered Jesus the kingdoms of the world, it was a legitimate offer. Matthew records what happened.

Matthew 4:8-9
Again, the devil took him to an exceedingly high mountain, and showed him all the kingdoms of the world, and their glory. He said to him, "I will give you all of these things, if you will fall down and worship me."

He was offering Jesus the kingdoms he ruled. All Jesus had to do was submit to him. Jesus did not challenge his authority.

Matthew 4:10
Then Jesus said to him, "Ge behind me, Satan! For it is written, 'You shall worship the Lord your God...shall serve him only.'"

Instead, he refused to worship anyone but God, His Father.

After Lucifer enticed the first man to fall and he did, man's relationship with the Lord God virtually ended. Then Satan's relationship with man began. As a result, all fallen people are Satan's children.

1 John 3:10
In this the children of God are revealed, and the children of the devil. Whoever doesn't do righteousness is not of God, neither is he who doesn't love his brother.

As children of the Devil, they will speak and act like their father who is a murderer.

John 8:44
You are of your father, the devil, and you want to do the desires of your father. He was a murderer from the beginning, and doesn't stand in the truth, because there is no truth in him. When he speaks a lie, he speaks on his own; for he is a liar, and the father of lies.

The Devil is violent and so are his children. The unbeliever wants to do what their father desires and they, as he, will kill to get it.

Since all unsaved people are Satan's children, they can become a threat to us, and we should be prepared to defend ourselves or those around us against their attack.

Their Propensity Toward Sin

All unsaved people are compelled to sin. Those who are compelled to sin are more likely to become violent even to the point of murder. Paul refers to unbelievers as the "children of disobedience." All unsaved people have a natural propensity to disobey our God and rebel against His laws. This involves every kind of sin and wickedness which includes violence and murder.

Ephesians 2:1-2
You were made alive when you were dead in transgressions and sins, in which you once walked according to the course of this world, according to the prince of the power of the air, the spirit who now works in the children of disobedience.

All men are born as children of the Devil and one of their characteristics is to rebel and disobey.

First, they do these things because there is a spirit (Satan) that is working in them, and we know that he is rebellious. In his rebellion, Lucifer, their father stood against the Most High Himself and challenged Him.

Isaiah 14:13-14
But you said in your heart, "I will ascend to heaven; I will raise my throne above the stars of God, And I will sit on the mount of assembly in the recesses of the north. I will ascend above the heights of the clouds; I will make myself like the Most High."

Second, in physical bodies, there resides a "sin principle" or "flesh" which has appetites and desires which run counter to God's ways. Believers must fight against it, but unbelievers are its slaves. In Romans 7, Paul describes this sin principle or flesh that resides in the body.

Romans 7:17-20
So now it is no more I that do it, but sin which dwells in me. For I know that in me, that is, in my flesh, dwells no good thing. For desire is present with me, but I don't find it doing that which is good. For the good which I desire, I don't do; but the evil which I don't desire, that I practice. But if what I don't desire, that I do, it is no more I that do it, but sin which dwells in me.

He speaks of his difficult struggle with the sinful flesh but the unsaved have no struggle. They just follow their flesh and its many impulses. Some impulses can lead to violence.

Just a chapter before, Paul describes this "lack of struggle" as a bondage to sin. Mankind is in bondage to the flesh or "the body of sin."

Romans 6:6
Knowing this, that our old man was crucified with him, that the body of sin might be done away with, so that we would no longer be in bondage to sin.

Then in verse 7, he implies that people are chained to their sin and are slaves to it because Christians are freed from sin.

Romans 6:7
For he who has died has been freed from sin.

He continues in verse 12, to describe sin as reigning in their bodies as they obey its lusts.

Romans 6:12-14
Therefore don't let sin reign in your mortal body, that you should obey it in its lusts [passions]. Neither present your members to sin as instruments of unrighteousness, but present yourselves to God, as alive from the dead…members as instruments of righteousness to God. For sin will not have dominion over you. For you are not under law, but under grace.

Before receiving Christ, Christians presented their bodies as instruments of unrighteousness; sin had dominion over them.

Since all unsaved people are under compulsion to sin, they could become a threat to us, and we should be prepared to defend ourselves or those around us against their attack. If the unsaved are children of disobedience, why wouldn't they disobey God's command not to murder? If someone has what they want, why not take it violently, if necessary?

Their Continual Rejection

All unsaved people continually reject the Lord God and His blessings. People who reject God and His laws are more likely to become violent even to the point of murder.

In Romans 1, Paul indicates that those without Christ are in a continual state of rejection. They have knowledge of God and His blessings but reject it.

Romans 1:18
For the wrath of God is revealed from heaven against all ungodliness and unrighteousness of men who suppress the truth [about God] in unrighteousness.

Here, Paul explains that men suppress the truth about God in their sin. This means that as they learn about God, they reject it so they may sin. As they sin, the truth is suppressed. How does this occur?

The first way in which they continually reject God is by rejecting the knowledge of Him in His creation. They see so many things about Him but do not want Him.

Psalm 19:1-4
The heavens declare the glory [display of who He is] of God. The expanse shows his handiwork. Day after day they pour forth speech, and night after night they display knowledge. There is no speech nor language, where their voice is not heard. Their voice has gone out through all the earth, Their words to the end of the world. In them he has set a tent for the sun.

The psalmist declares that creation is speaking words about God's glory and His handiwork, and everyone hears His voice and understands what He is saying.

The words proceeding out of all creation to every part of the earth is the revelation of who God is.

Romans 1:19-20
Because that which is known of God is revealed in them, for God revealed it to them. For the invisible things of him since the creation of the world are clearly seen, being perceived through the things that are made, even his everlasting power and divinity, that they may be without excuse.

Creation is continually shouting out information about the nature, power, and attributes of the true God. These three aspects are "clearly seen." Because they can clearly see Him, when they continually reject Him, they are held responsible on judgment day.

Their rejection is described in Romans 1.

Romans 1:21
Because, knowing God, they didn't glorify him as God, neither gave thanks, but became vain in their reasoning, and their senseless heart was darkened.

They would not recognize Him as divine creator and thank Him for His blessings on this earth.

In Acts 14, Paul describes the blessings of the Lord God from creation upon all men which are a powerful witness of His existence and care for mankind.

Acts 14:17
Yet he didn't leave himself without witness, in that he did good and

gave you rains from the sky and fruitful seasons, filling our hearts with food and gladness."

Though blessed, they were rejectors of God.

As a result, these unbelievers begin to reason foolishly and vainly that something else must have happened instead. This leads to the deep darkening of their senseless (unwillingness to perceive the truth) hearts.

Now, they are living in darkness. In this blackness, they begin declaring their wisdom and their intellectual prowess. They think they are much wiser than the Supreme Being.

Romans 1:22
Professing themselves to be wise, they became fools.

Then, they will conjure up their own deities which come from the things on the earth or their own imaginations.

Romans 1:23
And traded the glory of the [true] incorruptible God for the likeness of an image of corruptible man, and of birds, and four-footed animals, and creeping things.

The demonic spirits come alongside and accommodate and deceive them with their own devious "close to the truth but not quite," "religions of works and deeds," or even deeper, darker, "Luciferian beliefs and practices." This is the reason that Paul calls these false religious systems the "doctrines of demons." They glorify and give thanks to demons.

1 Timothy 4:1
But the Spirit says expressly that in later times some will fall away from the faith, paying attention to seducing spirits and doctrines of demons.

As they are stumbling around in their pride, the demons seduce them into every kind of falsehood and error and moral wickedness and depravity.

Paul continues by describing God's reaction in His wrath which was to abandon man to every kind of perversion and evil. This was to allow man to experience the anger of a Holy God as he plunged deeper and deeper into darkness.

Romans 1:24-25
Therefore God also gave them up in the lusts of their hearts to uncleanness, that their bodies should be dishonored [or shamed] among themselves, who exchanged the truth [they saw] of God for a lie, and worshiped and served the creature rather than the Creator, who is blessed forever. Amen.

First, the apostle describes the abandonment of a man and woman to sexual perversion and impurity allowing them to follow their lusts unrestricted.

Romans 1:24-25
Therefore God also gave them up in the lusts of their hearts to uncleanness…their bodies should be dishonored among themselves, who exchanged the truth of God for a lie, and worshiped and served the creature rather than the Creator, who is blessed forever. Amen.

Second, God allowed women to abandon their natural function (which is childbearing) and pursue vile passions. Men were allowed to abandon their natural function (which is to marry, mate, provide) and seek and pursue after vile passions toward other men. These passions would control many and affect everyone else.

Romans 1:26-27
For this reason, God gave them up to vile passions. For their women changed the natural function into that which is against nature.

Likewise also the men, leaving the natural function of the woman, burned in their lust toward one another, men doing what is inappropriate with men, and receiving in themselves the due penalty of their error.

Third, God abandoned them to the natural results of their rejection of Him and His utter holiness which are immoral, unprincipled, shameless, degenerate minds. This leads to inappropriate, unnatural, outside God's blueprint, demonic, lawless, sinful, wicked, and the darkest of deeds that can be imagined in the human psyche and the demonic intellect. How do we know this?

The word translated "reprobate" is the opposite of a word that means "reliable, alert, watching." So, this refers to a mind that cannot be relied upon to make sensible decisions. It's all over the place. It cannot make sense of things. It has lost its capacity reason properly.

Romans 1:28
Even as they refused to have God in their knowledge, God gave them up to a reprobate mind, to do those things which are not fitting.

Then Paul lists some of the evil intentions that will now fill the hearts of men and women due to these nonsensical minds controlled by vile passions while following the doctrine of demons in their rejection of God and His blessings. Anything is possible from their polluted thoughts.

Romans 1:29-31
Being filled [immersed] with...unrighteousness, sexual immorality, wickedness, covetousness, maliciousness; full of envy, [add full of] murder, strife, deceit, evil habits, secret slanderers, backbiters, hateful to God, insolent, haughty, boastful, inventors of evil things, disobedient to parents, without understanding, covenant-breakers, without natural affection, unforgiving, unmerciful.

These sins pour forth into every kind of dark act including hideous and heinous violence which can be viewed in every society throughout history. These sins become the motives for murder.

Second, not only do they reject God and His blessings, but they also reject His ways and laws. They understand that they are in a state of continual wickedness and judgment through the condemnation of their consciences. In Romans 2, the apostle Paul is comparing the condemnation of the Jews to the judgment of the Gentiles. The Jews will be judged according to the Scriptures which God gave His people, but the Gentiles will be condemned according to the law that was put within them. This law comes is in the conscience.

Romans 2:13-16
For it isn't the hearers of the law who are righteous before God, but the doers of the law will be justified (for when Gentiles who don't have the law do by nature the things of the law, these, not having the law, are a law to themselves, in that they show the work of the law written in their hearts, their conscience testifying with them, and their thoughts among themselves accusing or else excusing them) in the day when God will judge the secrets of men, according to my gospel, by Jesus Christ.

The consciences within people are constantly accusing and condemning them for their sins. This battle within them is constantly raging and this is also rejected and suppressed by them. They must reject God and His truth concerning their evil thoughts, words, and ways.

Eventually, as each one opposes the righteous testimony of his or her conscience, it becomes evil, defiled, and seared. In Hebrews 10, the author describes the conscience of believers before they came to Christ as "evil." In this passage, the author uses a strong word meaning "evil or wicked."

HOW CHRISTIANS MAY DEFEND THEMSELVES AGAINST ATTACK

Hebrews 10:22
Let's draw near with a true heart in fullness of faith, having our hearts sprinkled from an evil conscience, and having our body washed with pure water.

This means that it begins to condemn righteous thoughts, words, and actions and condone unrighteous ones. It reverses the intent of God in giving man this critical feature.

As this condoning of wickedness grows, it produces an impure conscience.

Titus 1:15
To the pure, all things are pure; but to those who are defiled and unbelieving, nothing is pure; but both their mind and their conscience are defiled.

The word translated "defiled" means "to dye with another color, to stain, defile, pollute, sully, contaminate, or soil. This refers to the conscience changing in a way that it is now the same. The function or purpose (color) is different. It becomes stained and soiled from the world and contaminated and defiled by sin. Combined with a defiled mind, any kind of evil is possible including violence and murder.

Finally, these consciences become so calloused from sin, that they can no longer provide even an inkling of what a righteous thought, word, or deed is. This leads to propagating their unrighteousness to others. Those they target become seduced by their treachery.

1 Timothy 4:1-2
But the Spirit says expressly that in later times some will fall away from the faith, paying attention to seducing spirits and doctrines of demons, through the hypocrisy of men...speak lies, branded [seared, burned] in their own conscience as with a hot iron.

If we combine these truths with the ones in Romans 1, we find a powerful indictment of their evil. Then Paul lists some of the evil intentions that will now fill the hearts of men and women due to these nonsensical minds controlled by vile passions while following the doctrine of demons in their rejection of God and His blessings. Anything is possible from their polluted thoughts. Nothing inside of them can hinder their unrighteous thoughts, words, and actions because the condemning voice of righteousness has reversed itself and is now condoning their wickedness because it has become evil, stained, and calloused.

Therefore, since all the unsaved reject the knowledge of God and His blessings revealed from creation and oppose His righteous condemnation of their evil actions filling them with senseless, impure minds controlled by sinful passions, they can become a threat to us. As a result, we should be ready to defend ourselves or those around us against their attack.

Their Spiritual Darkness

All unsaved people live in constant spiritual darkness. Those who walk in this spiritual darkness are more likely to become violent even to the point of murder. This darkness is also referred to as blindness to spiritual things.

In Ephesians 4, Paul describes them as having a darkness in their understanding.

Ephesians 4:18
Being darkened in their understanding, alienated from the life of God, because of the ignorance...in them, because of the hardening of their hearts.

This darkness of understanding comes from their hardness of heart. The "hardness of heart" is another way of describing the last point. Their hearts (minds and consciences) have become calloused to the truth of God, His blessings, and laws. They want to sin and suppress the truth to the point that they can no longer understand it.

This can be seen as a blindness to light. Just as physically blind people cannot see the light, so spiritually blind people cannot see the spiritual light. The Devil preys upon them and in their hardness, he blinds them to truth.

2 Corinthians 4:3-4
Even if our gospel is veiled, it is veiled in those who perish; in whom the god of this world has blinded the minds of the unbelieving, that the light of the gospel of the glory of Christ, who is the image of God, should not dawn on them.

He does this by surrounding them with His deep darkness.

Colossians 1:13
Who delivered us out of the power [domain] of darkness...translated us into the kingdom of the Son of his love.

Unbelievers have not been delivered out of His domain. They live in darkness. The word translated "power or domain" carries the idea of "authority, rule, governing, jurisdiction, and managing the affairs of." They are in the control and rule of a darkness that blinds them.

As we just saw in his first letter to Timothy, Paul explains that the Serpent of Old has created a realm of falsehoods, lies, lusts, and wickedness for the unsaved to dwell in.

1 Timothy 4:1
But the Spirit says expressly that in later times some will fall away

from the faith, paying attention to seducing spirits and doctrines of demons.

In 1 John 2, the apostle John illustrates it with the picture of someone stumbling around.

1 John 2:11
"But he who hates his brother [a non-Christian] is in the darkness, and walks in the darkness, and doesn't know where he is going, because the darkness has blinded his eyes."

They are walking in the dark and it is not a straight path but a crooked one. Why? Everything is black and they cannot see where they are going.

In the Scriptures, light has two aspects to it. Morally it refers to living righteously. Doctrinally, it refers to knowing and following the truth. Therefore, darkness refers to lies and evil. Unbelievers are stumbling around in the darkness of lies and sin.

This is the world system that Satan has developed on this earth that is filled with his deep blackness. In 1 John 2, John characterizes this darkness morally.

1 John 2:15-16
Don't love the world, neither the things that are in the world. If anyone loves the world, the Father's love isn't in him. For all that is in the world, the lust of the flesh, the lust of the eyes, and the pride of life, isn't the Father's, but is the world's.

We already have seen the doctrinal falsehoods they follow. His world system is filled with demons that trick and seduce people into believing a wide variety of false ideas and lies in order to keep them blinded. The false doctrines will keep coming at them in a rapid-fire pace.

HOW CHRISTIANS MAY DEFEND THEMSELVES AGAINST ATTACK

In Romans 13, the apostle Paul depicts deeds of darkness as proceeding from their hearts.

Romans 12:13
Contributing to the needs of the saints; given to hospitality.

Also, "unfruitful deeds" are ultimately produced from this intense darkened state. These are the same sins that come from their futile minds. These are the wicked and worthless things done when no one is looking. These could also involve violent and murderous acts.

Ephesians 5:11
Have no fellowship with the unfruitful works of darkness, but rather even reprove them.

The problem is that they love the darkness and the evil that they do.

John 3:19
This is the judgment, that the light has come into the world, and men loved the darkness rather than the light...their works were evil.

If someone had been in darkness their whole lives and grew to love it, when some brings a light into that darkness, why would they not attempt to put the light out?

Finally, they take great pride in walking in the darkness of error and wickedness. They actually think their evil thoughts, words, and actions are wisdom.

Romans 1:21-22
Because knowing God, they didn't glorify him as God, and didn't give thanks, but became vain in their reasoning, and their senseless heart was darkened. Professing themselves to be wise, they became fools.

Since all unsaved people live in spiritual darkness, they could become a threat to us; therefore, we should be prepared to defend ourselves or those around us against their attack. Here are two final questions. In their pride, would man not kill? Would men not commit genocide and call it "collateral damage" for a higher good?

The Violent Results of the Fall

As Christians, we should not fall into the mistaken notion that mankind is good and noble. This is the lie of the world and the Devil. The world tells itself that it is good but simply does evil. They believe that in some way, those who desire to harm or kill are prevented from doing good by poverty, social injustice, mental illness, and a long list of reasons that are politically correct at any given time, but this is not so. Physical violence flows from the sinful desires of the flesh.

In Matthew 15:19, when Jesus describes the sinful deeds that come from the heart of people, He mentions murder.

Matthew 15:19
For out of the heart come evil thoughts, murders, adulteries, sexual sins, thefts, false testimony, and blasphemies.

When the apostle Paul describes the numerous sins men commit which become the motives that lead to violence and murder, the acts themselves are always described.

Romans 1:28-32
Even as they refused to have God in their knowledge, God gave them up to a reprobate mind, to do those things which are not fitting; being filled with…unrighteousness, sexual immorality, wickedness, covetousness, malice; full of envy, murder, strife, deceit, evil habits,

secret slanderers. backbiters, hateful to God, insolent, arrogant, boastful, inventors of evil things, disobedient to parents, without understanding, untrustworthy, no natural affection, unforgiving, unmerciful; who, knowing the ordinance of God, that those who practice such things are worthy of death, not only do the same, but also approve of those who practice them (DEJ).

Galatians 5:21
Envy, murders, drunkenness, orgies, and things like these; of which I forewarn you, even as I also forewarned you, that those who practice such things will not inherit God's Kingdom.

1 Timothy 1:9
As knowing this, that law is not made for a righteous person, but for the lawless and insubordinate, for the ungodly and sinners, for the unholy and profane, for murderers of fathers and murderers of mothers, for manslayers.

When listing sins, the other apostles list "murder" in the same fashion as well.

1 Peter 4:15
For let none of you suffer as a murderer, or a thief, or an evil doer, or a meddler in other men's matters.

Revelation 9:21
They didn't repent of their murders, their sorceries, their sexual immorality, or their thefts.

Revelation 21:8
But for the cowardly, unbelieving, sinners, abominable, murderers, sexually immoral, sorcerers, idolaters, and all liars, their part is in the lake that burns with fire and sulfur, which is the second death."

All unbelievers are potential murderers. The unsaved are in the same condition or state of sin. This leads some to murder. We see this throughout biblical history.

The human that was born first, Cain, became a murderer.

Genesis 4:8
Cain said to Abel, his brother, "Let's go into the field." While they were in the field, Cain rose up against Abel, his brother, and killed him.

By Genesis 6, the world had become completely evil which would have obviously included much murder as we can view among Paul's lists of sins.

Genesis 6:5
Yahweh saw that the wickedness of man was great in the earth, and that every imagination of the thoughts of man's heart was continually only evil.

After the flood, man began again to murder and so it goes to the end of Revelation.

As a result, those who become murderers must be stopped. God's structure to stop them is self-defense and the defense of others as we will be demonstrated throughout this book. No amount of talk, persuasion, therapy, or manipulation can stop the sin from acting violently inside mankind, defense is an absolute necessity.

Chapter 2

The Divine Demand

This sinful and wicked condition of man (which would lead some to murder) brought two important responses from God. First, He created the plan of redemption to save some. Second, He had to establish a way in which He could preserve and protect men from destroying themselves or the Lord God from continually judging them and sending catastrophe upon catastrophe to start over as he did the flood. God had to establish upon the earth restraints to deter men from killing each other and stop them if they do. These restraints center upon self-defense and the defense of others.

This preservation of all mankind through the fundamental structure of "defense" comes from the very person of God Himself. It flows out of the divine character. So, in the study of whether we can defend ourselves and others when violence comes, we must start with what the Lord God does when violence comes upon Him or others. In this chapter, we will discover that God physically defends Himself (His plans and purposes), those He loves, (His people) and the innocent (those who did not provoke the attack). In most discussions, these are usually referred to as "self-defense and the defense of others."

Once we learn that God defends Himself, those He loves, and the innocent, we will be reminded that we must imitate Him as He commands us. First, we will discuss God's actions and then it will lead to our actions as we imitate Him. After this, we will look at the various defense structures which God has established in the world to preserve mankind.

The Nature of God

The defense of ourselves, those we love, and the innocent is an expression of who God is and how He behaves in the world. We will view this through the divine framework of the apostle Paul. In Romans 1:20, Paul describes three aspects of God: His nature, attributes, and power.

Romans 1:20
For the invisible things of him since the creation of the world are clearly seen, being perceived through the things that are made, even his everlasting power and divinity, that they may be without excuse.

These defensive and protective actions flow from, express, and demonstrate these three aspects of God.

The Defense of God's Purposes and Plans

God is a God that defends His purposes and plans. Though God does not have to defend Himself because He cannot be hurt, He does defend Himself by defending His purposes and plans against those who desire to hinder or destroy them. This has occurred from the beginning.

The Defense Against Lucifer

Before the rebellion of mankind, there was a rebellion in heaven. One of the Lord God's greatest angels sought to take God's position in the universe and the Lord was compelled by His nature to defend Himself. In Isaiah 14, the prophet Isaiah presents a warning of the inevitable destruction of the King of Babylon, but the language goes beyond the King to the power behind him, the Devil.

HOW CHRISTIANS MAY DEFEND THEMSELVES AGAINST ATTACK

Isaiah 14:12-15
How you have fallen from heaven, morning star, son of the dawn! How you are cut down to the ground, who laid the nations low! You said in your heart, "I will ascend into heaven! I will exalt my throne above the stars of God! I will sit on the mountain of assembly, in the far north! I will ascend above the heights of the clouds! I will make myself like the Most High!" Yet you shall be brought down to Sheol, to the depths of the pit.

Lucifer rebels and God defends Himself and His Supreme authority by passing judgment on the Devil and the demons that followed him.

In Ezekiel 28, the prophet rails against the King of Tyre and once again proceeds beyond this evil king to the angelic presence behind him. In this passage, we are given additional details as to what happened.

Ezekiel 28:14
You were the anointed cherub who covers: and I set you, so that you were on the holy mountain of God; you have walked up and down in the middle of the stones of fire."

As we can see, Satan's dwelling place was right in the midst of God's presence.

Then Lucifer's desires became unholy.

Ezekiel 28:15-17
You were perfect in your ways from the day that you were created, until unrighteousness was found in you. By the abundance of your traffic they filled the midst of you with violence, and you have sinned: therefore I have cast you as profane out of the mountain of God; and I have destroyed you, covering cherub, from the midst of the stones of fire. Your heart was lifted up because of your beauty; you have corrupted your wisdom by reason of your brightness: I

have cast you to the ground; I have laid you before kings, that they may see you.

God responded by casting him out of heaven's abode and creating a place of ultimate punishment.

Matthew 25:41
Then he will say also to those on the left hand, 'Depart from me, you cursed, into the eternal fire which is prepared for the devil and his angels.

He will finally be punished in this lake of fire.

Revelation 20:10
The devil who deceived them was thrown into the lake of fire and sulfur, where are also the beast and the false prophet. They will be tormented day and night forever and ever.

God's purpose and plans will be eternally protected.

The Defense Against Man's Rebellion

Satan tempted Adam and Eve and they rebelled also. God had to defend His plans and purposes.

Genesis 3:22-24
Behold, the man has become like one of us, knowing good and evil. Now, lest he reach out his hand, and also take of the tree of life, and eat, and live forever'...God...drove out the man; and he [God] placed cherubim [angel] at the east of the garden of Eden, and a flaming sword which turned every way, to guard the way to the tree of life.

He could not have man in an unregenerate state for eternity. So, He threw them out of the garden and placed a warrior angel at its entrance to defend it from anyone entering it.

HOW CHRISTIANS MAY DEFEND THEMSELVES AGAINST ATTACK

The Defense Against God's Enemies

Also, God defends himself against His enemies. These are the ones who oppose Him, His ordinances, and His people.

When Deborah and Barak had defeated Jabin, king of Canaan, they sang this song of deliverance.

Judges 5:31
So let all your enemies perish, Yahweh, but let those who love him be as the sun when it rises in its strength. Then the land had rest forty years.

God's enemies will perish at His hand because they do not love Him and attempt to thwart His purposes and plans.

David declares that they speak against God and take His name in vain out of hate for Him. He begs God to judge them.

Psalm 139:19-24
If only you, God, would kill the wicked. Get away from me, you bloodthirsty men! For they speak against you [God] wickedly. Your enemies take your name in vain. Yahweh, don't I hate those who hate you? Am I not grieved with those who rise up against you? I hate them with perfect hatred. They have become my enemies.... See if there is any wicked way in me, and lead me in the everlasting way.

David so loved God that the Lord's enemies became his and God's purpose and plans became His purpose and plans.

The psalmist writes of the destruction that the Lord will bring upon His enemies both in this life and the life to come.

Psalm 92:9
For, behold, your enemies, Yahweh, for, behold, your enemies shall perish. All the evildoers will be scattered.

In Isaiah, God asserts that He will administer His justice upon His enemies. This would be in defense of Himself as He judged them and His purposes and plans as He protected His people from destruction.

Isaiah 1:24
Therefore the Lord, Yahweh of Armies, the Mighty One of Israel, says: "Ah, I will get relief from my adversaries, and avenge myself on my enemies."

The inspired prophet Nahum pronounces this same truth in His prophecy.

Nahum 1:2
Yahweh is a jealous God and avenges. Yahweh avenges and is full of wrath. Yahweh takes vengeance on his adversaries, and he maintains wrath against his enemies.

In 2 Samuel, Nathan indicts David for Uriah's murder which he had attempted to cover up.

2 Samuel 12:14
However, because by this deed you have given great occasion to Yahweh's enemies to blaspheme, the child also who is born to you will surely die."

The first child of his union with Bathsheba would die because he had shed innocent blood and shamed God's Name.

Finally, here is a short list of other passages that teach this truth that God defends Himself by defending His purposes and plans against His enemies.

Exodus 15:6
Your right hand, Yahweh, is glorious in power. Your right hand, Yahweh, dashes the enemy in pieces.

HOW CHRISTIANS MAY DEFEND THEMSELVES AGAINST ATTACK

Psalm 8:2
From the lips of babes and infants you have established strength, because of your adversaries, that you might silence the enemy and the avenger.

Psalm 68:1
Let God arise! Let his enemies be scattered! Let them who hate him also flee before him.

Psalm 68:21
But God will strike through the head of his enemies, the hairy scalp of such a one as still continues in his guiltiness.

God is a God who will defend Himself by defending His plans and purposes.

The Defense Against the Nation's Idols

The ancient world believed that the defeat of one's enemies was the defeat of the gods that protected them. This belief is critical in understanding the reason for God's defense.

When the Assyrians came up to battle King Hezekiah of Judah, they taunted the Lord God Almighty and encouraged the Hebrew people to surrender. The rationale was the fact that they had defeated all of the gods of the other nations and will defeat Judah's too.

2 Kings 18:29-35
The king says, "Don't let Hezekiah deceive you; for he will not be able to deliver you out of his hand. Don't let Hezekiah make you trust in Yahweh, saying, 'Yahweh will surely deliver us, and this city shall not be given into the hand of the king of Assyria.' Don't listen to Hezekiah." For the king of Assyria says, "Make your peace with me, and come out to me; and everyone of you eat from his own

vine, and everyone from his own fig tree, and everyone drink water from his own cistern; until I come and take you away to a land like your own land, a land of grain and new wine, a land of bread and vineyards, a land of olive trees and of honey, that you may live, and not die. Don't listen to Hezekiah, when he persuades you, saying, 'Yahweh will deliver us.' Has any of the gods of the nations ever delivered his land out of the hand of the king of Assyria? Where are the gods of Hamath, and of Arpad...of Sepharvaim, of Hena, and Ivvah? Have they delivered Samaria out of my hand? Who are they among all the gods of the countries, that have delivered their country out of my hand, that Yahweh...deliver Jerusalem out of my hand?"

When Goliath taunted Israel's army, David knew that He was taunting God Himself because the army was God's.

1 Samuel 17:9-10
If he is able to fight with me and kill me, then will we be your servants; but if I prevail against him and kill him, then you will be our servants and serve us." The Philistine said, "I defy the armies of Israel today! Give me a man, that we may fight together!"

1 Samuel 10:26
David spoke to the men who stood by him, saying, "What shall be done to the man who kills this Philistine and takes away the reproach from Israel? For who is this uncircumcised Philistine, that he should defy the armies of the living God?"

At times, because of their idolatry, God would taunt Israel to depend on their idols to defend them rather than Him.

Judges 10:13-14
Yet you have forsaken me and served other gods. Therefore I will save you no more. Go and cry to the gods which you have chosen, Let them save you in the time of your distress!"

So, the Lord God defends His plans and purposes.

HOW CHRISTIANS MAY DEFEND THEMSELVES AGAINST ATTACK

The Defense of God's People

In the Scriptures, God is continually defending His people both individually and as a nation. This is a truth that can be seen whenever the Old Testament is read. It is filled with battles between God's people and the nations around them.

The Appeal to His Love

Why does God defend His people? First, He loves them, and He protects those He loves from the evil of men. He enters into a relationship with some of mankind have been selected to be a love gift to His Son. In the Old Testament, it was the Jews who believed in Him in Israel and those Gentiles outside the Nation (Rahab and Ruth, for example).

Deuteronomy 33:3
Yes, he loves the people. All his saints are in your hand. They sat down at your feet. Each receives your words.

Deuteronomy 4:37
Because he loved your fathers, therefore he chose their offspring after them, and brought you out with his presence, with his great power, out of Egypt.

Deuteronomy 7:8
But because Yahweh loves you, and because he desires to keep the oath which he swore to your fathers, Yahweh has brought you out with a mighty hand and redeemed you out of the house of bondage, from the hand of Pharaoh king of Egypt.

1 Kings 10:9
Blessed is Yahweh your God, who delighted in you, to set you on the throne of Israel. Because Yahweh loved Israel forever, therefore he made you king, to do justice and righteousness."

God defended Israel and delivered them from Egypt because He loves His people.

In the New Testament, it was the saints who lived within the nations that God loved and defended through His Son. One example is the disciples at the arrest of Jesus who were defended by Jesus and protected from harm found in the High Priestly Prayer of Jesus.

John 17:23
I in them, and you in me, that they may be perfected into one; that the world may know that you sent me and loved them, even as you loved me.

John 17:12
While I was with them in the world, I kept them in your name. I have kept those whom you have given me. None of them is lost except the son of destruction, that the Scripture might be fulfilled.

John 18:7-9
Again therefore he asked them, "Who are you looking for?" They said, "Jesus of Nazareth." Jesus answered, "I told you that I am he. If therefore you seek me, let these go their way," that the word might be fulfilled which he spoke, "Of those whom you have given me, I have lost none."

God loves His saints and defends them as He did Israel.

The Appeal to His Own Divinity

Second, when God defends His people, it is expressed with words "for His sake." When the Lord is speaking, He will utter the words, "For my sake." This refers to who He is and what He desires. It is a declaration that God will defend His people because of who the Lord is and what He desires. When He demonstrates who He is and what He desires to the world for all to see, He uses the phrase "For my Name's sake." These are related because who God is and what He desires is always demonstrated through defending His people for all to see.

The Appeal to His Reputation

Throughout Israel's history, God was concerned about His reputation among the nations. Why? Israel was the light to the world and God's work in Israel was to draw people to Him.

When the spies from Joshua came to Jericho to view the fortifications, Rahab helps them because she believed in their God. Why? They had heard what He had done.

Joshua 2:9-11
She said to the men, "I know that Yahweh has given you the land, and that the fear of you has fallen upon us, and that all the inhabitants of the land melt away before you. For we have heard how Yahweh dried up the water of the Red Sea before you, when you came out of Egypt; and what you did to the two kings of the Amorites, who were beyond the Jordan, to Sihon and to Og, whom you utterly destroyed. As soon as we had heard it, our hearts melted, and there wasn't any more spirit in any man, because of you: for Yahweh your God, he is God in heaven above, and on earth beneath.

She knew that He was the true God because He had protected His people for His Name's sake.

The First Defense of Hezekiah

In 2 Kings 19, when the King of Assyria sent his armies to conquer Judah, King Hezekiah sent for Isaiah to beg God to defend them. This was His response.

2 Kings 19:32-35
Therefore, Yahweh says concerning the king of Assyria, "He will not come to this city, nor shoot an arrow there. He will not come before it with shield, nor cast up a mound against it. He will return the same way that he came, and he will not come to this city," says Yahweh. "For I will defend this city to save it, for my own sake, and for my servant David's sake." That night, Yahweh's angel went out, and struck one hundred eighty-five thousand in the camp of the Assyrians. When men arose early in the morning...all dead bodies.

God told the king He would defend them for "His own sake." His defense of His people grows out of His nature and love.

The Second Defense of Hezekiah

Sometime later, Hezekiah became sick unto death, and he begged the Lord to let him live longer. Isaiah was sent once again to speak to him on God's behalf.

2 Kings 20:6
I will add to your days fifteen years. I will deliver you and this city out of the hand of the king of Assyria. I will defend this city for my own sake, and for my servant David's sake.

The Lord was doing this for His own sake (and David's). Of course, He loved Israel and listened and agreed to fulfill the king's request. He was not about to let foreign factions come and destroy His people unless it was His will.

The Future Deliverance of Israel

In Isaiah 48, the prophet foretold the future defense of Israel from captivity. The Lord God delivers His people not because of who they are, but who He is.

HOW CHRISTIANS MAY DEFEND THEMSELVES AGAINST ATTACK

Isaiah 48:9-11
For my name's sake, I will defer my anger, and for my praise, I hold it back for you so that I don't cut you off. Behold, I have refined you, but not as silver. I have chosen you in the furnace of affliction. For my own sake, for my own sake, I will do it; for how would my name be profaned? I will not give my glory to another.

Notice, He will not allow His "Name" to be profaned among the nations and will not give His glory (reputation among the people) to another deity.

These deities would be the many false gods of the nation who imprisoned them. Though He was angry with them and threw them into affliction. He will defend them and pull them from that fire. Why? This is who He is and what He desires (for His own sake), and all must know this (for His name's sake). Why? He loved them.

The Past Deliverance from Egypt

In the book of Ezekiel, the prophet foretells the destruction and fall of Jerusalem to the Babylonians. As He indicts Israel, the Lord reminds them of His deliverance of the Hebrews from Egypt. This defense of His people was due to the display of who He is and what He desires.

Ezekiel 20:9-12
But I worked for my name's sake, that it should not be profaned in the sight of the nations, among which they were, in whose sight I made myself known to them, in bringing them out of the land of Egypt. So I caused them to go out of the land of Egypt, and brought them into the wilderness. I gave them my statutes, and showed them my ordinances, which if a man does, he will live in them. Moreover also I gave them my Sabbaths, to be a sign between me and them, that they might know that I am Yahweh who sanctifies them.

God continually appeals to who He is and what He desires as the primary motivation for His deliverance. God is a God of defense because it's in His nature to do so for those He loves.

The Assurance to the Fathers

When they rebelled against Him in the wilderness, God wanted to destroy them but refused.

Ezekiel 20:13-14
But the house of Israel rebelled against me in the wilderness. They didn't walk in my statutes, and they rejected my ordinances, which if a man keeps, he shall live in them. They greatly profaned my Sabbaths. Then I said I would pour out my wrath on them in the wilderness, to consume them. But I worked for my name's sake, that it should not be profaned in the sight of the nations, in whose sight I brought them out.

He would not have His Name profaned, so God defended His people whom He loved. All were to know this. It flows out of His nature.

The Reassurance to the Children

The Lord God Almighty disciplined those Hebrews by not bringing them into the promised land, but He did allow their children to survive for His Name's sake.

Ezekiel 20:16-20
Because they rejected my ordinances, and didn't walk in my statutes, and profaned my Sabbaths; for their heart went after their idols. Nevertheless my eye spared them, and I didn't destroy them. I didn't make a full end of them in the wilderness. I said to their children in the wilderness, 'Don't walk in the statutes of your

fathers. Don't observe their ordinances or defile yourselves with their idols. I am Yahweh your God. Walk in my statutes, keep my ordinances, and do them. Make my Sabbaths holy. They shall be a sign between me and you...I am Yahweh your God.

Again, for His name's sake, He allowed the children to live.

The Protection from Various Armies

All of this occurred while Israel had to defend themselves against the many nations they encountered in the wilderness. Yet, God protected them for His Name's sake.

First, they won the battle against Amalek.

Exodus 17:13
Joshua defeated Amalek and his people with the edge of the sword.

They fought and defeated the Canaanites.

Numbers 21:1-3
The Canaanite, the king of Arad, who lived in the South, heard that Israel came by the way of Atharim. He fought against Israel, and took some of them captive. Israel vowed a vow to Yahweh, and said, "If you will indeed deliver this people into my hand, then I will utterly destroy their cities." Yahweh listened to the voice of Israel, and delivered up the Canaanites; and they utterly destroyed them and their cities. The name of the place was called Hormah.

They found victory against the Amorites.

Numbers 21:21-25
Israel sent messengers to Sihon king of the Amorites, saying, "Let me pass through your land. We will not turn away into field or vineyard. We will not drink of the water of the wells. We will go by

the king's highway, until we have passed your border." Sihon would not allow Israel to pass through his border, but Sihon gathered all his people together, and went out against Israel into the wilderness, and came to Jahaz. He fought against Israel. Israel struck him with the edge of the sword, and possessed his land from the Arnon to the Jabbok, even to the children of Ammon; for the border of the children of Ammon was fortified. Israel took all these cities. Israel lived in all the cities of the Amorites, in Heshbon, and in all its villages.

They defeated the King of Bashan who warred against them.

Numbers 21:33-35
They turned and went up by the way of Bashan. Og the king of Bashan went out against them, he and all his people, to battle at Edrei. Yahweh said to Moses, "Don't fear him, for I have delivered him into your hand, with all his people, and his land. You shall do to him as you did to Sihon king of the Amorites…they struck him, with his sons and all his people, until there were no survivors….

No wonder as Moses brought to the edge of the Promised Land, He gave them a powerful exhortation.

Deuteronomy 20:1-4
When you go out to battle against your enemies, and see horses, chariots, and a people more numerous than you, you shall not be afraid of them; for Yahweh your God is with you, who brought you up out of the land of Egypt. It shall be, when you draw near to the battle, that the priest shall approach and speak to the people, and shall tell them, "Hear, Israel, you draw near today to battle against your enemies. Don't let your heart faint! Don't be afraid, nor tremble, neither be scared of them; for Yahweh your God is he who goes with you, to fight for you against your enemies, to save you."

God would always defend them. Why? It is who He is and what He desires. This must be demonstrated to all the world. There were several reasons for the numerous battles that the people of God had to fight, but by far the most important was the defense of His people to proclaim His Name.

The Future Protection of God's People

Ezekiel proclaims that God will come to rescue His people as He did in the past. It is who He is and what He desires.

Ezekiel 20:44
You will know that I am Yahweh, when I have dealt with you for my name's sake, not according to your evil ways, nor according to your corrupt doings, you house of Israel," says the Lord Yahweh.'"

Ezekiel 36:22
Therefore tell the house of Israel, "The Lord Yahweh says: 'I don't do this for your sake, house of Israel, but for my holy name, which you have profaned among the nations where you went. I will sanctify my great name, which has been profaned among the nations, which you have profaned among them. Then the nations will know that I am Yahweh, 'says the Lord Yahweh, 'when I am proven holy in you before their eyes.'"

God who defends those He loves wants all to know.

The Acknowledgement by David

Over and over God came to David's defense and the king responded with great praise and thanksgiving. David was grateful that a descendant would build God's house.

2 Samuel 7:17-25
Nathan spoke to David all these words, and according to all this vision. Then David the king went in, and sat before Yahweh; and he said, "Who am I, Lord Yahweh, and what is my house, that you have

brought me this far? This was yet a small thing in your eyes, Lord Yahweh; but you have spoken also of your servant's house for a great while to come; and this among men, Lord Yahweh! What more can David say to you? For you know your servant, Lord Yahweh. For your word's sake, and according to your own heart, you have worked all this greatness, to make your servant know it. Therefore you are great, Yahweh God. For there is no one like you, neither is there any God besides you, according to all that we have heard with our ears. What one nation in the earth is like your people, even like Israel, whom God went to redeem to himself for a people, and to make himself a name, and to do great things for you, and awesome things for your land, before your people, whom you redeemed to yourself out of Egypt, from the nations and their gods? You established for yourself your people Israel to be your people forever; and you, Yahweh, became their God. Now, Yahweh God, the word that you have spoken concerning your servant, and concerning his house, confirm it forever, and do as you have spoken.

What an incredible inspired assertion. Notice, this man after God's own heart understood that protecting His people came right out of the heart of the God that he had been seeking all His life.

The Recognition of Other Inspired Writers

Not only did David understand God's desire to protect and defend His people, but so did other inspired writers. We will consider a few of the many passages which teach this.

Psalm 31:1-3
In you, Yahweh, I take refuge. Let me never be disappointed. Deliver me in your righteousness. Bow down your ear to me. Deliver me speedily. Be to me a strong rock, a house of defense to save me. For you are my rock and my fortress, therefore for your name's sake lead me and guide me.

Asaph cries out to the Lord for deliverance by appealing to God's name among the peoples.

Psalm 79
God, the nations have come into your inheritance. They have defiled your holy temple. They have laid Jerusalem in heaps. They have given the dead bodies of your servants to be food for the birds of the sky, the flesh of your saints to the animals of the earth. They have shed their blood like water around Jerusalem. There was no one to bury them. We have become a reproach to our neighbors, a scoffing and derision to those who are around us. How long, Yahweh? Will you be angry forever? Will your jealousy burn like fire? Pour out your wrath on the nations that don't know you, on the kingdoms that don't call on your name; for they have devoured Jacob, and destroyed his homeland. Don't hold the iniquities of our forefathers against us. Let your tender mercies speedily meet us, for we are in desperate need. Help us, God of our salvation, for the glory of your name. Deliver us, and forgive our sins, for your name's sake. Why should the nations say, "Where is their God?" Let it be known among the nations, before our eyes...vengeance for your servants' blood is being poured out.

Here again, we have God's name (who He is and what He desires) appealed to in order to arouse Him to defend His people. God defends because of who He is.

The Defense of Innocent Blood

Not only does the Lord protect and defend those whom He loves but also the lives of the innocent. These are the ones (believing or unbelieving) who don't provoke the violent and murderous actions that come upon them. They are innocent regarding any behavior that would deserve being killed or physically harmed. When one is killed without provoking the murder, the Bible calls this "the shedding of innocent blood."

The Description of Innocent Blood

We are given a simple and clear definition of this type of innocence in the story of Saul's attempt to kill David. In 1 Samuel, the inspired writer describes the jealousy that King Saul felt when David began to win battle after battle. After a victory, the women would come out and sing and dance to a tune that sang David's praises.

1 Samuel 18:7
The women sang to one another as they played, and said, "Saul has slain his thousands, and David his ten thousands."

This angered Saul and caused him to seek David's death, even though David had done nothing to warrant it.

1 Samuel 18:8
Saul was very angry, and this saying displeased him. He said, "They have credited David with ten thousands, and they have only credited me with thousands. What can he have more but the kingdom?"

As a result of this song and the people's recognition of his greater feats, Saul sought to murder him.

After many unsuccessful attempts, the king approached his son Jonathon and asked for his help in killing David.

1 Samuel 19:1-4
Saul spoke to Jonathan his son, and to all his servants, that they should kill David. But Jonathan, Saul's son, greatly delighted in David. Jonathan told David, saying, "Saul my father seeks to kill you. Now therefore, please take care of yourself in the morning, and live in a secret place, and hide yourself. I will go out and stand beside my father in the field where you are, and I will talk with my father about you; and if I see anything, I will tell you." Jonathan spoke good of David to Saul his father, and said to him, "Don't let the king

sin against his servant, against David; because he has not sinned against you, and because his works have been very good toward you."

Jonathon refused because not only did he love him as a brother but knew that David was completely innocent of any wrong deserving of death.

1 Samuel 19:5
"For he put his life in his hand, and struck the Philistine, and Yahweh worked a great victory for all Israel. You saw it, and rejoiced. Why then will you sin against innocent blood, to kill David without a cause?"

In Jonathon's words we have "innocent blood" defined. It is killing without a righteous or legitimate cause. Then King Saul acknowledged that Jonathon was right, and David was innocent. Then, He turned from his plot.

1 Samuel 19:6
Saul listened to the voice of Jonathan: and Saul swore, "As Yahweh lives, he shall not be put to death."

Psalms and Proverbs speak of shedding innocent blood.

Psalm 10:8
He lies in wait near the villages. From ambushes, he murders the innocent. His eyes are secretly set against the helpless.

The innocent might involve those who are unaware that someone may desire to kill them because they did nothing wrong. They might be unable to defend themselves also.

Psalm 64:4
To shoot innocent men from ambushes. They shoot at him suddenly and fearlessly.

The innocent do not expect to be killed or harmed because they are not alert, and murder comes upon them suddenly.

Psalm 94:21
They gather themselves together against the soul of the righteous, and condemn the innocent blood.

The innocent are righteous and undeserving of death.

Proverbs 1:11
If they say, "Come with us. Let's lie in wait for blood. Let's lurk secretly for the innocent without cause.

Here again, the innocent are the ones who are killed for no legitimate reason. There is no cause to take their lives.

The Divine Condemnation

Due to God's righteous nature, He hates the shedding of innocent blood.

Proverbs 6:16-19
There are six things which Yahweh hates; yes, seven which are an abomination to him: arrogant eyes, a lying tongue, hands that shed innocent blood, a heart that devises wicked schemes, feet that are swift in running to mischief, a false witness who utters lies, and he who sows discord among brothers.

Notice, the Lord God hates "hands that shed innocent blood." This Almighty being despises those who murder the innocent without cause.

In Deuteronomy, Moses reminds the people of God's great works and His righteous commands that they must obey and the curses which will come if they refuse. When he mentions the shedding of innocent blood, he refers back to the Lord God's nature and desires.

Deuteronomy 21:9
So you shall put away the innocent blood from among you, when you shall do that which is right in Yahweh's eyes.

Deuteronomy 27:25
Cursed is he who takes a bribe to kill an innocent person. All the people shall say, "Amen."

The killing of the innocent was evil in God's eyes and would be cursed by Him.

The author of 2 Kings provides a summation of Manasseh's life and leadership. He presents the wicked rule of the king with extremely strong words.

2 Kings 21:1-2
Manasseh was twelve years old when he began to reign, and he reigned fifty-five years in Jerusalem. His mother's name was Hephzibah. He did that which was evil in Yahweh's sight, after the abominations of the nations whom Yahweh cast out before the children of Israel.

The worst of his wickedness was the continual shedding of innocent blood.

2 Kings 21:16
Moreover Manasseh shed innocent blood very much, until he had filled Jerusalem from one end to another; in addition to his sin with which he made Judah to sin, in doing that which was evil in Yahweh's sight.

This "shedding of Innocent blood" was an assault upon God's nature and person.

The Divine Command

God commands His people and demands from the world that innocent blood is never shed. Though this is seen in many places in the Scriptures, we will look at the experience of the prophet Jeremiah.

Jeremiah preached and prophesied in Judah during the time of the Babylonian's rise to power after Israel had fallen to the Assyrians. The prophet was sent to warn the people of coming judgment and to admonish them to turn back to the ways of righteousness.

In Jeremiah 7, Jeremiah stood by the temple and began to repeat the commandments of God that the people were to obey. He knew they would not like this.

Jeremiah 7:1-2
The word that came to Jeremiah from Yahweh, saying, "Stand in the gate of Yahweh's house, and proclaim this word there, and say, 'Hear Yahweh's word, all you of Judah, who enter in at these gates to worship Yahweh.'"

All were to be accountable to God for what was said.

One of those many declarations concerned the shedding of innocent blood.

Jeremiah 7:6
If you don't oppress the foreigner, the fatherless, and the widow, and don't shed innocent blood in this place, and don't walk after other gods to your own hurt.

They knew that they were not to shed innocent blood among themselves, but they were taking advantage of the those who could not defend themselves; the foreigner, those without fathers, and the ones without husbands. The Lord warns them to not commit this sin because He would judge them.

Later, Jeremiah travels to the king's palace and repeats the same commandments and warning.

Jeremiah 2:1-3
Yahweh said, "Go down to the house of the king of Judah, and speak this word, there: 'Hear Yahweh's word, king of Judah, who sits on David's throne, you, your servants, and your people who enter in by these gates. Yahweh says: "Execute justice and righteousness, and deliver him who is robbed out of the hand of the oppressor. Do no wrong. Do no violence to the foreigner, the fatherless, or the widow. Don't shed innocent blood in this place."

Once again, the Lord commands them not to shed innocent blood, which is just and right.

On one occasion, rather than respond in repentance, the prophets who were preaching prosperity sought to convince the princes that Jeremiah was worthy of death.

Jeremiah 26:10-11
When the princes of Judah heard these things, they came up from the king's house to Yahweh's house; and they sat in the entry of the new gate of Yahweh's house. Then the priests and the prophets spoke to the princes and to all the people, saying, "This man is worthy of death; for he has prophesied against this city, as you have heard with your ears."

Jeremiah verbally defends his innocence.

Jeremiah 26:12-13
Then Jeremiah spoke to all the princes and to all the people, saying, "Yahweh sent me to prophesy against this house and against this city all the words that you have heard. Now therefore amend your

ways and your doings, and obey Yahweh your God's voice; then Yahweh will relent from the evil that he has pronounced against you.

Then the prophet issues a warning.

Jeremiah 26:14-15
But as for me, behold, I am in your hand. Do with me what is good and right in your eyes. Only know for certain that, if you put me to death, you will bring innocent blood on yourselves, on this city, and on its inhabitants; for in truth Yahweh has sent me to you to speak all these words in your ears."

He proclaimed that they were not to shed innocent blood and, in their desire, to silence him, they would be breaking the very commandment he was proclaiming.

Jeremiah did not die that day because Ahikam came to his defense and protected him.

Jeremiah 26:24
But the hand of Ahikam the son of Shaphan was with Jeremiah, so that they didn't give him into the hand of the people to put him to death.

Yet, another innocent prophet had his blood shed in the place of Jeremiah because he took the prophet's mantel and proclaimed the same message.

Jeremiah 26:20-23
There was also a man who prophesied in Yahweh's name, Uriah the son of Shemaiah of Kiriath Jearim; and he prophesied against this city and against this land according to all the words of Jeremiah. When Jehoiakim the king, with all his mighty men and all the princes heard his words, the king sought to put him to death; but when Uriah heard it, he was afraid, and fled, and went into Egypt. Then Jehoiakim the king sent men into Egypt, Elnathan the son of

Achbor, and certain men with him, into Egypt; and they fetched Uriah out of Egypt, and brought him to Jehoiakim the king, who killed him with the sword, and cast his dead body into the graves of the common people.

Eventually, Judah was destroyed by Babylon for this and their many other sins.

The Lord God will not tolerate the shedding of innocent blood. This is who He is and what He desires.

The Divine Defense of the Innocent

Due to God's unwillingness to bear the shedding of blood that is innocent, God will judge the guilty and come to the defense of the innocent. The psalmist speaks of this truth.

Psalm 94:21-23
They gather themselves together against the soul of the righteous, and condemn the innocent blood. But Yahweh has been my high tower, my God, the rock of my refuge. He has brought on them their own iniquity, and will cut them off in their...wickedness. Yahweh, our God, will cut them off.

We can depend on the Lord God to judge the wicked who desire to shed our innocent blood and defend us from their evil intentions. God will not allow this to happen because He is a God who defends the innocent.

David knew this truth well because God was constantly protecting from the shedding of his innocent blood. In Psalm 63, David writes of this assurance.

Psalm 63:7-11
For you have been my help. I will rejoice in the shadow of your

wings. My soul stays close to you. Your right hand holds me up. But those who seek my soul to destroy it shall go into the lower parts of the earth. They shall be given over to the power of the sword. They shall be jackal food. But the king shall rejoice in God. Everyone who swears by him will praise him, for the mouth of those who speak lies shall be silenced.

David's son Absalom had gathered an army and run his father out of Jerusalem. David was hiding in the wilderness. He looked toward the day that God will deliver him. He knew that these enemies of his would be slain by the sword in battle and become food for wild animals. God had been his help and defender in the past and would do so again.

So, we can now understand that the defense of the innocent flows out of the nature of God. Our God watches over the innocent.

The Power of God

The next aspect that Paul refers to is God's power. God defends His purposes and plans, those He loves, and the innocent because He has the power to do so and desires to put that power on display.

In Psalm 106, the psalmist writes of this truth about God. In this song, he reviews what God had done as He defended His people and brought them out of Egypt.

Psalm 106:7-12
Our fathers didn't understand your wonders in Egypt. They didn't remember the multitude of your loving kindnesses, but [they] were rebellious at the sea, even at the Red Sea. Nevertheless he saved them for his name's sake, that he might make his mighty power known.

HOW CHRISTIANS MAY DEFEND THEMSELVES AGAINST ATTACK

He rebuked the Red Sea also, and it was dried up; so he led them through the depths, as through a desert. He saved them from the hand of him who hated them, and redeemed them from the hand of the enemy. The waters covered their adversaries. There was not one of them left. Then they believed his words. They sang his praise.

Then he makes a plea for His power in His defense once again. It was God's power displayed in His that brought His defense of those whom He loved for His name and reputation.

Psalm 106:47
Save us, Yahweh, our God, gather us from among the nations, to give thanks to your holy name, to triumph in your praise!

In Psalm 33, the author addresses the truth that God has the power to defend, protect, and deliver His people.

Psalm 33:12- 19
Blessed is the nation whose God is Yahweh, the people whom he has chosen for his own inheritance. Yahweh looks from heaven. He sees all the sons of men. From the place of his habitation he looks out on all the inhabitants of the earth, he who fashions all of their hearts; and he considers all of their works. There is no king saved by the multitude of an army. A mighty man is not delivered by great strength. A horse is a vain thing for safety, neither does he deliver any by his great power. Behold, Yahweh's eye is on those who fear him, on those who hope in his loving kindness, to deliver their soul from death, to keep them alive in famine.

The Lord demonstrates His supreme strength and power by continually delivering the people whom He loves.

We can clearly see this truth in many psalms.

Psalm 46:1
God is our refuge and strength, a very present help in trouble.

Psalm 59:16
But I will sing of your strength. Yes, I will sing aloud of your loving kindness in the morning. For you have been my high tower, a refuge in the day of my distress.

Psalm 62:7
My salvation and my honor is with God. The rock of my strength, and my refuge, is in God.

Psalm 66:3
Tell God, "How awesome are your deeds! Through the greatness of your power, your enemies submit themselves to you.

Psalm 68:35
You are awesome, God, in your sanctuaries. The God of Israel gives strength and power to his people. Praise be to God!

Psalm 150:1
Praise Yah! Praise God in his sanctuary! Praise him in his heavens for his acts of power!

The Lord defends His people because He has the power and desires to display that power for all to see.

In Exodus, we find a declaration of God's power to deliver and defend.

Exodus 32:11
Moses begged Yahweh his God, and said, "Yahweh, why does your wrath burn hot against your people, that you have brought out of the land of Egypt with great power and with a mighty hand?

The power of God is directed toward defending His people by rescuing them from Egypt. This declares who He is, and He reminds them of what He did. Why? They are His people, and He loves them.

HOW CHRISTIANS MAY DEFEND THEMSELVES AGAINST ATTACK

Deuteronomy 4:37
Because he loved your fathers, therefore he chose their offspring after them, and brought you out with his presence, with his great power, out of Egypt.

Deuteronomy 9:29
Yet they are your people and your inheritance, which you brought out by your great power and by your outstretched arm.

2 Kings 17:36
But you shall fear Yahweh, who brought you up out of the land of Egypt with great power and with an outstretched arm, and you shall bow yourselves to him, and you shall sacrifice to him.

In Isaiah 50, God questions Israel's lack of hope in their God to rescue them from the defeat of their enemies because of their sin. He has disciplined them but not abandoned them. They should not doubt His power to deliver them once again.

Isaiah 50:1-4
Yahweh says, "Where is the bill of your mother's divorce, with which I have put her away? Or to which of my creditors have I sold you? Behold, you were sold for your iniquities, and your mother was put away for your transgressions. Why, when I came, was there no one? When I called, why was there no one to answer? Is my hand shortened at all, that it can't redeem? Or have I no power to deliver? Behold, at my rebuke I dry up the sea. I make the rivers a wilderness. Their fish stink because there is no water, and die of thirst. I clothe the heavens with blackness. I make sackcloth their covering." I clothe the heavens with blackness. I make sackcloth their covering. The Lord Yahweh has given me the tongue of those who are taught, that I may know how to sustain with words him who is weary....

God's deliverance puts His power on display. He protects those He loves, His plans, purposes and the innocent. He does this for all to see to share His glory and bring others to Him.

The Attributes of God

The third aspect of God that Paul refers to in Romans 1:20 is God's qualities, attributes, or characteristics. He calls these His "invisibles." When God defends Himself, His plan and purposes, those He loves, and the innocent He expresses and displays His various attributes for all to see.

The Justice of God

When God defends Himself, His plans and purposes, the innocent, and those He loves, the Lord expresses and displays His justice for all to see.

The Just Character of God

Our God is a God who is just. He thinks, speaks, and acts justly.

Isaiah 61:8
For I, Yahweh, love justice. I hate robbery and iniquity. I will give them their reward in truth and I will make an everlasting covenant with them.

Jeremiah 9:24
"But let him who glories glory in this, that he has understanding, and knows me, that I am Yahweh who exercises loving kindness, justice, and righteousness in the earth, for I delight in these things," says Yahweh.

Isaiah 45:21
Declare and present it. Yes, let them take counsel together. Who has shown this from ancient time? Who has declared it of old? Haven't

HOW CHRISTIANS MAY DEFEND THEMSELVES AGAINST ATTACK

I, Yahweh? There is no…God besides me, a just God and a Savior. There is no one besides me.

Isaiah 51:4
Listen to me, my people; and hear me, my nation, for a law will go out from me, and I will establish my justice for a light to the peoples.

So, our Lord is a just God. He expresses and displays His justice for all to see.

His Expression and Display of Justice

The Scriptures indicate that God's defense comes from His justice.

In Jeremiah 11, God gave Jeremiah a message of judgment against the people of Jerusalem for pursuing after idols like an unfaithful spouse after a lover. Then the Lord disclosed to Jeremiah that the men of Anathoth were plotting against him, so Jeremiah called upon the Lord to judge them and vindicate him. The vindication would be the defense of Jeremiah and the destruction of the plotters.

Jeremiah 11:20
But, Yahweh of Armies, who judges righteously, who tests the heart and the mind, I will see your vengeance on them; for to you I have revealed my cause.

Then God answers Jeremiah out of His just nature and makes a judgment against these plotters and promises to defend the prophet by destroying them.

Jeremiah 11:21-23
Therefore Yahweh says concerning the men of Anathoth, who seek your life, saying, "You shall not prophesy in Yahweh's name, that

you not die by our hand;" therefore Yahweh of Armies says, "Behold, I will punish them. The young men will die by the sword. Their sons and their daughters will die by famine. There will be no remnant to them, for I will bring evil on the men of Anathoth, even the year of their visitation."

God defends out of His just character rendering just actions.

In 1 Samuel, David was fleeing from Saul and hid in a cave. Saul came into the cave to relieve himself and David spared his life. When Saul left the cave, David came out of hiding and called to the king from a distance. Notice that God judges and then defends.

1 Samuel 24:14-15
Against whom has the king of Israel come out? Whom do you pursue? A dead dog? A flea? May Yahweh therefore be judge, and give sentence between me and you, and see, and plead my cause, and deliver me out of your hand.

David calls on God's justice to act, judge him as the innocent one, and then deliver him from the attacker. Of course, this would mean either King Saul would change his mind or God would be with David as he defended himself if Saul attacked.

God decided to change his mind.

1 Samuel 24:16-17
It came to pass, when David had finished speaking these words to Saul, that Saul said, "Is that your voice, my son David?" Saul lifted up his voice, and wept. He said to David, "You are more righteous than I; for you have done good to me, whereas I have done evil to you.

The Lord God defended David in His justice that day. Justice, judgment, and defense go together.

HOW CHRISTIANS MAY DEFEND THEMSELVES AGAINST ATTACK

In 2 Kings 18, the Assyrians have come to conquer Judah. So, Hezekiah made a huge payment to appease them, and the Assyrians left Jerusalem. Sometime later, they decided to no longer honor the treaty and attack again. So, Isaiah declared God's deliverance would come from His just character.

Isaiah 33:22
For Yahweh is our judge...our lawgiver...our king. He will save us.

Here, Isaiah has confidence in God's justice which will pour forth into their defense from the treachery of the Assyrians. According to what we have learned thus far, Isaiah is saying that the Lord God will make a judgment and determine that His people are the ones He loved, they are an important part of His purposes and plan and are innocent in this situation. Then He will defend them.

Before this pronouncement, Isaiah has already prophesied what God would do to the King of Assyria and protect Hezekiah. In so doing, he also proceeds far into the future to exclaim the deliverance of His people from the nations round about in the millennium.

Isaiah 33:19-21
You will no longer see the fierce people, a people of a deep speech that you can't comprehend, with a strange language that you can't understand. Look at Zion, the city of our appointed festivals. Your eyes will see Jerusalem, a quiet habitation, a tent that won't be removed.... But there Yahweh will be with us in majesty, a place of wide rivers and streams....

Once again, we see the justice of God rendering a defense of His people. God defense flows out of His justice.

In Psalm 50, the psalmist Asaph declares that God is the righteous judge. This is the Hebrew way of speaking of God's just character. The Lord God judges in His righteousness due to His commandments on "right living."

Psalm 50:6
The heavens...declare his righteousness, for God himself is judge...

Then he makes a comparison between the Lord's judgment on righteous behavior and unrighteous behavior. Though this may have a future prophetic reference, it also has an earthly temporal context. We know this because this is how God has always dealt with His people and the nations around them.

First, the Lord explains that they were sacrificing as if He needed the sacrifice of animals, but He does not because He owns everything.

Psalm 50:8-10
I don't rebuke you for your sacrifices. Your burnt offerings are continually before me. I have no need for a bull from your stall, nor male goats from your pens. For every animal of the forest is mine, and the livestock on a thousand hills.

Instead, it is a certain kind of heart that He desired when coming before Him.

Psalm 50:14
Offer...the sacrifice of thanksgiving. Pay...vows to the Most High.

A thankful heart and obedient spirit will bring God's defense of them in time of trouble.

Psalm 50:15
Call on me in the day of trouble. I will deliver you...you will honor me.

They will continue this after their deliverance also.

HOW CHRISTIANS MAY DEFEND THEMSELVES AGAINST ATTACK

Now, to put it in our context God will defend those He loves (believers who are grateful and obedient), His plans and purposes (to be honored or glorified), and the innocent (ones who deserve protection because they do not attack others).

He continues with an indictment against both the false believers in Israel and the nation around them.

Psalm 50:16-21
But to the wicked God says, "What right do you have to declare my statutes, that you have taken my covenant on your lips, since you hate instruction, and throw my words behind you? When you saw a thief, you consented with him, and have participated with adulterers. "You give your mouth to evil. Your tongue frames deceit. You sit and speak against your brother. You slander your own mother's son. You have done these things, and I kept silent. You thought that I was just like you. I will rebuke you, and accuse you in front of your eyes.

According to God's just character, He judged the others as wicked (unbelieving), ungrateful, and disobedient. Though they brought their sacrifices, their hearts were cold.

God continues by describing the judgment that will come. Instead of defending them from trouble, He would bring it.

Psalm 50:22-23
Now consider this, you who forget God, lest I tear you into pieces… there be no one to deliver. Whoever offers…thanksgiving glorifies me, and prepares his way so that I will show God's salvation to him."

Notice, He says there will be "none to deliver." God will attack and no one will be able to defend them. In our context, though His laws and man's conscience prompt a deliverance, He will allow no man to stop His attack.

When Saul was searching for David, the Ziphites told Him his location and Saul surrounded him. In Psalm 54, David cries out for God's defense based on His just character.

Psalm 54:1-4
Save me, God, by your name. Vindicate me in your might. Hear my prayer, God. Listen to the words of my mouth. For strangers have risen up against me. Violent men have sought after my soul. They haven't set God before them…God…my helper. The Lord sustains…

David prays to be saved, delivered, and defended by His God. Then, He utters "vindicate me." The Hebrew word "vindicate" means "to execute judgment." He is asking God to judge Him and Saul and render a judgment which will be his deliverance because he is innocent in the situation. Saul is the attacker and God should defend David and He did.

Psalm 54:5-7
He will repay the evil to my enemies. Destroy them in your truth. With a free will offering, I will sacrifice to you. I will give thanks to your name, Yahweh, for it is good. For he has delivered me out of all trouble. My eye has seen triumph over my enemies.

He depends on God's deliverance because of His justice.

We can be assured that the Lord God will protect us in times of danger because He is just and defends Himself, His plan and purposes, those He loves, and the innocent. In His defense, He expresses and displays His justice for all to see.

The Righteousness of God

When God defends Himself, His plans and purposes, the innocent, and those He loves, the Lord expresses and displays His righteousness for all to see.

The Righteous Character of God

Our God is a God who is righteous. He thinks, speaks, and acts in righteousness.

Psalm 50:5-6
Gather my saints together to me, those who have made a covenant with me by sacrifice. The heavens shall declare his righteousness, for God himself is judge. Selah.

Psalm 71:19
God, your righteousness also reaches to the heavens. You have done great things. God, who is like you?

So, our Lord is a righteous God. He expresses and displays His righteousness for all to see.

His Expression and Display of Righteousness

The Scriptures indicate that God's defense comes from His righteousness.

In Psalm 145, the writer cries out for protection based on His righteousness.

Psalm 145:9-11
Deliver me, Yahweh, from my enemies. I flee to you to hide me. Teach me to do your will, for you are my God. Your Spirit is good. Lead me in the land of uprightness. Revive me, Yahweh, for your name's sake. In your righteousness, bring my soul out of trouble.

Here, the psalmist pleads with God to deliver him because it is the righteous thing to do.

We see the same plea in Psalm 31.

Psalm 31:1-2
In you, Yahweh, I take refuge. Let me never be disappointed. Deliver me in your righteousness. Bow down your ear to me. Deliver me speedily. Be to me a strong rock, a house of defense to save me.

Here, God is speaking and refers to His own righteousness to deliver them.

Isaiah 41:10
Don't you be afraid, for I am with you. Don't be dismayed, for I am your God. I will strengthen you. Yes, I will help you. Yes, I will uphold you with the right hand of my righteousness.

His right hand refers to God's power which is wielded for him.

We can be assured that the Lord God will protect us in times of danger because He is righteous and defends Himself, His plan and purposes, those He loves, and the innocent. In His defense, He expresses and displays His righteousness for all to see.

The Holiness of God

When God defends Himself, His plans and purposes, the innocent, and those He loves, the Lord expresses and displays His holiness for all to see.

The Holy Character of God

Our God is a God who is holy. He thinks, speaks, and acts in a holy way. Holiness refers to God being "sacred, set apart, and wholly different" from the world.

HOW CHRISTIANS MAY DEFEND THEMSELVES AGAINST ATTACK

1 Chronicles 16:10
Glory in his holy name. Let...heart of those who seek Yahweh rejoice.

Isaiah 6:2-3
Above him stood the seraphim. Each one had six wings. With two he covered his face. With two he covered his feet. With two he flew. One called to another, and said, "Holy, holy, holy, is Yahweh of Armies! The whole earth is full of his glory!"

So, our Lord God is a holy God. He expresses and displays His holiness for all to see.

His Expression and Display of Holiness

The Scriptures indicate that God's defense comes from His holiness.

In 1 Chronicles 16, David is celebrating the return of the Ark and sings a joyful song of praise, encouragement, and exhortation. He entreats the people to ask God for deliverance from the nations around them. Why? So, they can give thanks to His holy Name. It is His holiness that can be depended upon for their protection.

1 Chronicles 16:35
Say, "Save us...Gather us together and deliver us from the nations, to give thanks to your holy name, to triumph in your praise."

His deliverance and defense of their lives shows that He is sacred, separate, and "wholly different" from all other gods. The false gods of the nations were bitter and angry gods who often sought to harm those who were loyal to them.

In Psalm 89, the inspired writer speaks of the Lord God as their shield because He is God, king, and the Holy one.

Psalm 89:18
For our shield belongs to Yahweh, our king to the Holy One of Israel.

When the Ark was stolen by the Philistines, God destroyed their idol and devastated their population. They sent the Ark back and it was taken by the inhabitants of Beth Shemash. Over fifty thousand of their people were killed by God because they looked into the Ark. The people saw His power that day.

1 Samuel 6:19-20
He struck of the men of Beth Shemesh, because they had looked into Yahweh's ark.... The men of Beth Shemesh said, "Who is able to stand before Yahweh, this holy God? To whom shall he go up...?"

The standing before God refers to His opposition. He is too powerful to oppose. This deals with the defense of His people.

We can be assured that the Lord God will protect us in times of danger because He is holy and defends Himself, His plan and purposes, those He loves, and the innocent. In His defense, He expresses and displays His utter holiness for all to see.

The Mercy of God

When God defends Himself, His plans and purposes, the innocent, and those He loves, the Lord expresses and displays His mercy for all to see.

The Merciful Character of God

Our God is a God who is merciful. He thinks, speaks, and acts mercifully.

HOW CHRISTIANS MAY DEFEND THEMSELVES AGAINST ATTACK

Nehemiah 9:17
And refused to obey. They weren't mindful of your wonders that you did among them, but hardened their neck, and in their rebellion appointed a captain to return to their bondage. But you are a God ready to pardon, gracious and merciful, slow to anger, and abundant in loving kindness, and didn't forsake them.

Psalm 86:15
But you, Lord, are a merciful and gracious God, slow to anger, and abundant in loving kindness and truth.

So, our Lord is a merciful God. He expresses and displays His mercy for all to see.

His Expression and Display of Mercy

The Scriptures indicate that God's defense comes from His mercy.

In Psalm 59, the writer calls the Lord God his strength and high tower.

Psalm 59:17
To you, my strength, I will sing praises. For God is my high tower, the God of my mercy.

The word "strength" refers to His power and "high tower" was a tower above a city where many guards watched for danger to protect the people. Here, the psalmist depended on God's mercy which makes Him a powerful protector who watches for danger in order to defend and deliver him. Trouble cries out for mercy.

In Psalm 123, the psalmist cries out for that mercy of God to show itself in defense of him in his time of trouble.

Psalm 9:13
Have mercy on me, Yahweh. See my affliction by those who hate me, and lift me up from the gates of death.

The writer was in danger of being killed by his enemies and begged God for mercy. His mercy would pour forth in the Lord's defense of him.

We can be assured that the Lord God will protect us in times of danger because He is merciful and defends Himself, His plan and purposes, those He loves, and the innocent. In His defense, He expresses and displays His mercy for all to see.

The Loving Kindness of God

When God defends Himself, His plans and purposes, the innocent, and those He loves, the Lord expresses and displays His loving-kindness for all to see.

The Loving and Kind Character of God

Our God is a divine being who is loving and utterly kind. He thinks, speaks, and acts out of His loving-kindness and deep compassion.

Psalm 36:7
How precious is your loving kindness, God! The children of men take refuge under the shadow of your wings.

Psalm 59:16
But I will sing of your strength. Yes, I will sing aloud of your loving kindness in the morning. For you have been my high tower, a refuge in the day of my distress.

So, our Lord God is a loving and kind God. He expresses and displays His loving-kindness for all to see.

His Expression and Display of Loving-Kindness

The Scriptures indicate that God's defense comes from His loving-kindness.

In Psalm 145, the writer cries out for protection based on His Loving Kindness.

Psalm 145:10-12
All your works will give thanks to you, Yahweh. Your saints will extol you. They will speak of the glory of your kingdom, and talk about your power, to make known to the sons of men his mighty acts, the glory of the majesty of his kingdom. In your loving kindness, cut off my enemies, and destroy all those who afflict my soul, for I am your servant.

The inspired psalmist in Psalm 17, cries out for that same loving kindness to deliver him.

Psalm 17:7-8
Show your marvelous loving kindness, you who save those who take refuge by your right hand from their enemies. Keep me as the apple of your eye. Hide me under the shadow of your wings, from the wicked who oppress me, my deadly enemies, who surround me.

He pleads with God to deliver him because it is the loving and kind thing to do.

We can be assured that the Lord God will protect us in times of danger. Why? He expresses His lovingkindness for all to see as He defends Himself, His plan and purposes, those He loves, and the innocent.

The Goodness of God

When God defends Himself, His plans and purposes, the innocent, and those He loves, the Lord expresses and displays His goodness for all to see.

The Good Character of God

Our God is good. This means that He thinks, speaks, and acts in goodness.

Psalm 25:8
Good and upright is Yahweh, therefore he will instruct sinners in the way.

1 Chronicles 16:34
Oh give thanks to Yahweh, for he is good, for his loving kindness endures forever.

So, our Lord God is a good God. He expresses and displays His goodness for all to see.

His Expression and Display of Goodness

The Scriptures indicate that God's defense comes from His goodness.

In Psalm 31, the writer sings of his reliance upon God's protection (defense) because of His goodness.

Psalm 31:19
Oh how great is your goodness, which you have laid up for those who fear you, which you have worked for those who take refuge in you, before the sons of men!

In Psalm 34, the psalmist encourages all to taste of God's goodness when they take refuge in Him in time of danger. God will protect and defend those who rely on Him and His goodness.

Psalm 34:6-8
This poor man cried, and Yahweh heard him, and saved him out of all his troubles. Yahweh's angel encamps around those who fear him, and delivers them. Oh taste and see that Yahweh is good. Blessed is the man who takes refuge in him.

The prophet Nahum describes God as a stronghold in time of danger. We can take refuge in Him (rely on Him to defend us) because He knows us and is good.

Nahum 1:7-9
Yahweh is good, a stronghold in the day of trouble; and he knows those who take refuge in him. But with an overflowing flood, he will make a full end of her place, and will pursue his enemies into darkness. What do you plot against Yahweh? He will make a full end. Affliction won't rise up the second time.

The Lord God's help will come because He is good, and He will be our stronghold in times of trouble and danger.

We can be assured that the Lord God will protect us in times of danger because He is good and defends Himself, His plan and purposes, those He loves, and the innocent. In His defense He expresses and displays His goodness for all to see.

The Faithfulness of God

When God defends Himself, His plans and purposes, the innocent, and those He loves, the Lord expresses and displays His faithfulness for all to see.

The Faithful Character of God

Our God is a God who is faithful. He thinks, speaks, and acts faithfully.

Deuteronomy 7:9
Know therefore that Yahweh your God himself is God, the faithful God, who keeps covenant and loving kindness to a thousand generations with those who love him and keep his commandments,

Deuteronomy 32:4
The Rock: his work is perfect, for all his ways are just. A God of faithfulness who does no wrong, just and right is he.

Psalm 71:22
I will also praise you with the harp for your faithfulness, my God. I sing praises to you with the lyre, Holy One of Israel.

So, our Lord God is a faithful God. He expresses and displays His faithfulness for all to see.

His Expression and Display of Faithfulness

The Scriptures indicate that God's defense comes from His faithfulness.

In Psalm 91, the writer speaks of the confidence we can have in God's protection and defense because He is faithful in time of danger.

Psalm 91:1-5
He who dwells in the secret place of the Most High will rest in the shadow of the Almighty. I will say of Yahweh, "He is my refuge and my fortress; my God, in whom I trust." For he will deliver you from the snare of the fowler, and from the deadly pestilence. He will cover

you with his feathers. Under his wings you will take refuge. His faithfulness is your shield and rampart. You shall not be afraid of the terror by night, nor of the arrow that flies by day,

In Psalm 143, King David appeals to God's attributes of faithfulness and righteousness as he begs Him for deliverance from harm.

Psalm 143:1-3
Hear my prayer, Yahweh. Listen to my petitions [prayers]. In your faithfulness and righteousness, relieve [answer] me. Don't enter into judgment with your servant, for in your sight no man living is righteous. For the enemy pursues my soul. He has struck my life down to the ground. He has made me live in dark places, as those who have been long dead.

The Lord will come to deliver him because of His faithfulness.

We can be assured that the Lord God will protect us in times of danger because He is faithful and defends Himself, His plan and purposes, those He loves, and the innocent for all to see.

Since we have established that God is a divine being who defends Himself, those He loves, and the innocent, we can now move on to the various names, titles, and descriptions that demonstrate this.

The Father's Designations

The names, titles, and descriptions of God, the Father, speak of His defense of Himself (purposes and plan), those He loves, and the innocent. We will see that these titles are used of Him to give comfort in time of danger.

The numerous names, titles, and descriptions of the Father refer to His defense, deliverance, and protection.

The Almighty

The title of "Almighty" refers to God's power. His power is expressed and displayed to demonstrate He is stronger than all. We can trust in His power to save us not only eternally from damnation but also from danger on this earth.

Genesis 17:1
When Abram was ninety-nine years old, Yahweh appeared to Abram and said to him, "I am God Almighty. Walk before me and be blameless.

The Consuming Fire

The concept of a consuming fire deals with the fact that God has the power to consume anything He desires. No one can stand against Him. He has the power to defend us.

Exodus 15:7
In the greatness of your excellency, you overthrow those who rise up against you. You send out your wrath. It consumes them as stubble.

Hebrews 12:29
For our God is a consuming fire.

The Deliverer

The title of deliverer speaks directly to God's willingness to defend His people and the fact that we can trust in that. He will deliver us in times of trouble.

HOW CHRISTIANS MAY DEFEND THEMSELVES AGAINST ATTACK

Psalm 40:17
But I am poor and needy. May the Lord think about me. You are my help and my deliverer. Don't delay, my God.

The Dwelling Place

The truth that God is our dwelling place is always in the context of danger and protection. We live in His presence, and it is a place of great protection and calm because He is with us. He will defend us because we dwell with Him.
Psalm 90:1
Lord, you have been our dwelling place for all generations.

The Faithful God

The truth of God's faithfulness speaks to His promises. He promises to protect us, and He is faithful to do it.

Deuteronomy 7:9
Know therefore that Yahweh your God himself is…the faithful God, who keeps covenant and loving kindness to a thousand generations with those who love him and keep his commandments.

The Father

When Jesus gave His disciples an example of prayer, He began it with "Our Father." The Lord God is our Father. This truth means that God is our Father. As a result, He protects us.

Matthew 6:9
Pray like this: "Our Father in heaven, may your name be kept holy."

Luke 11:2
He said to them, "When you pray, say, 'Our Father in heaven, may your name be kept holy. May your Kingdom come. May your will be done on earth, as it is in heaven.

The Father of the Fatherless

For those who are fatherless, God will be with them if they place their faith in His Son. Now, the fatherless have someone to love and protect them.

Psalm 68:5
A father of the fatherless, and a defender of the widows, is God in his holy habitation.

The Fortress

A fortress is a shelter from danger. God is our shelter from danger because we can come to Him and trust in the walls of His power and love which surrounds us.

Jeremiah 16:19
Yahweh, my strength, and my stronghold, and my refuge in the day of affliction, the nations will come to you from the ends of the earth, and will say, "Our fathers have inherited nothing but lies, vanity and things in which there is no profit."

The God Full of Compassion

The Lord God's mercy, grace, loving kindness will express itself in His care and protection of us. This compassionate God will come to our help in time of trouble.

HOW CHRISTIANS MAY DEFEND THEMSELVES AGAINST ATTACK

Psalm 86:15-16
But you, Lord, are a merciful and gracious God, slow to anger, and abundant in loving kindness and truth. Turn to me, and have mercy on me! Give your strength to your servant. Save... your servant.

The God of the Whole Earth

Our God is the God of the whole earth. He is in control. No one can stand against Him if they put His people in danger no matter how powerful they are on the earth.

Isaiah 54:5
For your Maker is...Yahweh of Armies is his name...Holy One of Israel is your Redeemer. He will be called the God of the whole earth.

The God Who Works Wonders

God demonstrates His strength through His miracles. That strength will be expressed in our behalf when danger comes.

Psalm 77:14
You are the God who does wonders. You have made your strength known among the peoples.

The God Who Judges on Earth

Our God judges the inhabitants on the earth now and in eternity. The defense of His people is a part of that judgment.

Psalm 58:11
So that men shall say, "Most certainly there is a reward for the righteous. Most certainly there is a God who judges the earth."

The God Who Accomplishes All Things for Me

Our God answers our prayers, not only for spiritual issues but also when we cry for help in time of danger. The Lord will accomplish all things for us including our protection.

Psalm 57:2
I cry out to God Most High, to God who accomplishes my requests for me.

The God Who is Near, Not Far Off

God is a God who is near. We can depend upon Him to hear and come to our rescue. Wherever we go, He is right at our side.

Jeremiah 23:23
"Am I a God at hand," says Yahweh, "and not a God afar off?"

The God Most High

God is most high which means He is above all else. This is incredibly important for God's defense of His people. Who can come against us whom He cannot stop? Who can attempt evil or harm upon us with His superior power and supreme authority?

Genesis 14:18-20
Melchizedek king of Salem brought out bread and wine. He was priest of God Most High. He blessed him, and said, "Blessed be Abram of God Most High, possessor of heaven and earth. Blessed be

God Most High, who has delivered your enemies into your hand." Abram gave him a tenth of all.

The God Who Sees

Our God sees all upon the earth. he will see when danger comes and will provide protection for us.

Genesis 16:13-14
She called the name of Yahweh who spoke to her, "You are a God who sees," for she said, "Have I even stayed alive after seeing him?" Therefore the well was called Beer Lahai Roi. Behold, it is between Kadesh and Bered.

The Great and Dreadful God

Our God is great and can bring dread to those who may attempt to harm us as He comes to our defense.

Daniel 9:4
I prayed to Yahweh my God, and made confession, and said, "Oh, Lord, the great and dreadful God, who keeps covenant and loving kindness with those who love him and keep his commandments.

Psalm 68:35
You are awesome [dreadful], God, in your sanctuaries. The God of Israel gives strength and power to his people. Praise be to God!

The Great King Above All Gods

The nations will contend that their imaginary gods are real and will defend them. We know that demons are behind these false notions. Our God is real and is king above these false demonic empowered deities and can easily thwart any harm that they may want to do to us. He will come to our defense and bring victory.

Psalm 95:3
For Yahweh is a great God, a great King above all gods.

The Great King Over All the Earth

As the king over all the nations, whether they know it or not, God is in control and defends His people in His love and power.

Psalm 47:2
For Yahweh Most High…is a great King over all the earth.

The One Whom We Trust

Salvation is not the only truth in view here. God not only has the power to protect us from harm, but we can also trust in Him to do this. In fact, what believer does not depend upon God in their times of danger?

Psalm 144:2
My loving kindness, my fortress, my high tower, my deliverer, my shield, and he in whom I take refuge, who subdues my people under me.

The One Who Gives Strength and Power

As we defend ourselves and others from harm, God will provide the strength and power for victory.

HOW CHRISTIANS MAY DEFEND THEMSELVES AGAINST ATTACK

Psalm 68:34
Ascribe strength to God! His excellency is over Israel, his strength is in the skies.

Psalm 68:35
You are awesome, God, in your sanctuaries. The God of Israel gives strength and power to his people. Praise be to God!

The One Whom Conquered Great Kings

We see in Old Testament history, God smiting rulers and their nations for attempting harm upon His people. He will do the same for us.

Psalm 136:17
To him who struck great kings; for his loving kindness endures forever.

The Helper

What greater help can one need then protection from harm in this life and deliverance from eternal damnation in the life to come.

Hebrews 13:6-7
So that with good courage we say, "The Lord is my helper. I will not fear. What can man do to me?" Remember your leaders, men who spoke to you the word of God, and considering the results of...faith.

The Hiding Place

In His power and protection, the people whom God loves can hide themselves.

Psalm 32:7
You are my hiding place. You will preserve me from trouble. You will surround me with songs of deliverance. Selah.

The High Tower

As towers were used to watch for danger, so God watches for danger against His people and will come to their aid whenever they need Him.

Psalm 18:2
Yahweh is my rock, my fortress, and my deliverer; my God, my rock, in whom I take refuge; my shield, and the horn of my salvation, my high tower.

The Hope in the Day of Evil

When evil comes, we can hope in God's deliverance from that intended harm.

Jeremiah 17:17-18
Don't be a terror to me. You are my hope in the day of evil. Let them be disappointed who persecute me, but let not me be disappointed....

The Husband of Israel

As a husband protects his wife, God protects His people. He will be our protection also.

Isaiah 54:5
For your Maker is your husband; Yahweh of Armies is his name. The Holy One of Israel is your Redeemer. He will be called the God of the whole earth.

HOW CHRISTIANS MAY DEFEND THEMSELVES AGAINST ATTACK

The Lord God of gods

God is sovereign and ruler over all the demonic forces who pretend to be gods themselves and fool the nations. There is nothing that they can do if God decides to stop them. They cannot hurt His people.

Joshua 22:22
The Mighty One, God, Yahweh, the Mighty One, God, Yahweh, he knows; and Israel shall know: if it was in rebellion, or if in trespass against Yahweh (don't save us today).

The Lord Mighty in Battle

Our God is a God who is mighty and powerful in battle. He has won victory after victory against the enemies of Israel and will do battle for us when we are in trouble.

Psalm 24:8
Who is the King of glory? Yahweh...mighty in battle.

The Man of War

Our God is so identified with defending His people from harm that He is known as a person of war.

Exodus 15:3
Yahweh is a man of war. Yahweh is his name.

The Mighty

Our God is incredibly powerful and will come to our aid in times of danger as He did with Israel.

Isaiah 1:24-25
Therefore the Lord, Yahweh of Armies, the Mighty One of Israel, says: "Ah, I will get relief from my adversaries, and avenge myself on my enemies." I will turn my hand on you, thoroughly purge away your dross, and will take away all your tin.

The Refuge

God as our refuge. This speaks volumes about His care and concern for us. God provides safety and shelter in times of trouble and great distress.

Psalm 91:1-2
He who dwells in the secret place of the Most High will rest in the shadow of the Almighty. I will say of Yahweh, "He is my refuge and my fortress; my God, in whom I trust."

The Shield

The shield is a weapon that repels the blows of a sword and the pummeling of arrows. It protects warriors from harm. Our Almighty God is like this. He will come and shield us from harm.

Psalm 3:3
But you, Yahweh, are a shield around me, my glory, and the one who lifts up my head.

The Savior

The word "savior" means "deliverer." God not only saves us eternally from condemnation, but He also deliverers us from evil temporally.

HOW CHRISTIANS MAY DEFEND THEMSELVES AGAINST ATTACK

2 Samuel 22:3
God is my rock in whom I take refuge; my shield, and the horn of my salvation, my high tower, and my refuge. My savior, you save me from violence.

The Strength

God is our strength when trouble comes. This means He will miraculously defend us or will empower us to defend ourselves. He has more strength than all that exist in His universe and no one can stop Him.

1 Samuel 15:29
Also the Strength of Israel will not lie nor repent; for he is not a man, that he should repent.

The Strength of My Heart

God will strengthen the hearts of His people when danger comes. This means He will give us confidence in trouble.

Psalm 73:26
My flesh and my heart fails, but God is the strength of my heart and my portion forever.

Zechariah 12:5
The chieftains of Judah will say in their heart, "The inhabitants of Jerusalem are my strength in Yahweh of Armies their God."

The Sun and Shield

As a sun, the Lord God warms and gives light in the midst of trouble. As a shield, He protects from harm. The shield was large enough to hide behind and could not be pierced. In the same way, we can stand behind our God.

Psalm 84:11
For Yahweh God is a sun and a shield. Yahweh will give grace and glory. He withholds no good thing from those who walk blamelessly.

The Sword of Thy Excellency

God has the most powerful sword of all in that He can do anything. Who can stand against His defense of us?

Deuteronomy 33:29
You are happy, Israel! Who is like you, a people saved by Yahweh, the shield of your help, the sword of your excellency? Your enemies will submit themselves to you. You will tread on their high places.

The Strength and Song

God is such a powerful supernatural presence in times of danger that he will put a confident song upon our lips as He provides strength to defend. To be able to sing demonstrates joy and peace in the midst of trouble.

Exodus 15:2
Yah is my strength and song. He has become my salvation. This is my God, and I will praise him; my father's God, and I will exalt him.

Isaiah 12:1-2
In that day you will say, "I will give thanks to you, Yahweh; for though you were angry with me, your anger has turned away and you comfort me. Behold, God is my salvation. I will trust, and will not be afraid; for Yah, Yahweh, is my strength and song; and he has become my salvation.

The Lord of Hosts (Armies)

This title is seen all over the Bible. It is a military title that indicates that our God is a commander over a multitude of angels. God uses them to protect His people both physically and spiritually. I am placing all of them in this book to drive him the point that we have a warring God who defends His people if needed.

Psalm 69:6
Don't let those who wait for you be shamed through me, Lord Yahweh of Armies. Don't let those who seek you be brought to dishonor through me, God of Israel.

Isaiah 1:24
Therefore the Lord, Yahweh of Armies, the Mighty One of Israel, says: "Ah, I will get relief from my adversaries, and avenge myself on my enemies.

Isaiah 3:1
For, behold, the Lord, Yahweh of Armies, takes away from Jerusalem and from Judah supply and support, the whole supply of bread, and the whole supply of water.

Isaiah 3:15
What do you mean that you crush my people, and grind the face of the poor?" says the Lord, Yahweh of Armies.

Isaiah 10:16
Therefore the Lord, Yahweh of Armies, will send among his fat ones leanness; and under his glory a burning will be kindled like the burning of fire.

Isaiah 10:23
For the Lord, Yahweh of Armies, will make a full end, and that determined, throughout all the earth.

Isaiah 10:24
Therefore the Lord, Yahweh of Armies, says "My people who dwell in Zion, don't be afraid of the Assyrian, though he strike you with the rod, and lift up his staff against you, as Egypt did.

Isaiah 10:33
Behold, the Lord, Yahweh of Armies, will lop the boughs with terror. The tall will be cut down, and the lofty will be brought low.

Isaiah 19:4-5
I will give over the Egyptians into the hand of a cruel lord. A fierce king will rule over them," says the Lord, Yahweh of Armies. The waters will fail from the sea, and the river will be wasted and become dry.
Isaiah 22:5
For it is a day of confusion, and of treading down, and of perplexity, from the Lord, Yahweh of Armies, in the valley of vision, a breaking down of the walls, and a crying to the mountains.

Isaiah 22:12
In that day, the Lord, Yahweh of Armies, called to weeping, to mourning, to baldness, and to dressing in sackcloth.

Isaiah 22:14-15
Yahweh of Armies revealed himself in my ears, "Surely this iniquity will not be forgiven you until you die," says the Lord, Yahweh of Armies. The Lord, Yahweh of Armies says, "Go, get yourself to this treasurer, even to Shebna, who is over the house, and say,

Isaiah 28:22
Now therefore don't be scoffers, lest your bonds be made strong; for I have heard a decree of destruction from the Lord, Yahweh of Armies, on the whole earth.

Jeremiah 2:19-20
"Your own wickedness will correct you, and your backsliding will rebuke you. Know therefore and see that it is an evil and bitter thing,

HOW CHRISTIANS MAY DEFEND THEMSELVES AGAINST ATTACK

that you have forsaken Yahweh your God, and that my fear is not in you," says the Lord, Yahweh of Armies. For long ago I broke off your yoke, and burst your bonds....

Jeremiah 46:10
For that day is of the Lord, Yahweh of Armies, a day of vengeance, that he may avenge himself of his adversaries. The sword will devour and be satiated, and will drink its fill of their blood; for the Lord, Yahweh of Armies, has a sacrifice in the north country by the river Euphrates.

Jeremiah 49:5
Behold, I will bring a terror on you," says the Lord, Yahweh of Armies, "from all who are around you. All of you will be driven completely out, and there will be no one to gather together the fugitives.

Jeremiah 50:25
Yahweh has opened his armory, and has brought out the weapons of his indignation; for the Lord, Yahweh of Armies, has a work to do in the land of the Chaldeans.

Jeremiah 50:31
"Behold, I am against you, you proud one," says the Lord, Yahweh of Armies; "for your day has come, the time that I will visit you."

Amos 3:13-14
"Listen...testify against the house of Jacob," says the Lord Yahweh, the God of Armies. For in the day that I visit the transgressions of Israel on him, I will also visit the altars of Bethel; and the horns of the altar will be cut off, and fall to the ground.

Amos 5:16
Therefore Yahweh, the God of Armies, the Lord, says: "Wailing will be in all the wide ways; and they will say in all the streets, 'Alas! Alas!' and they will call the farmer to mourning, and those who are skillful in lamentation to wailing."

Amos 6:8
"The Lord Yahweh has sworn by himself," says Yahweh, the God of Armies: "I abhor the pride of Jacob...detest his fortresses. Therefore I will deliver up the city with all that is in it.

Amos 9:5
For the Lord, Yahweh of Armies, is he who touches the land and it melts, and all who dwell in it will mourn; and it will rise up wholly like the River, and will sink again, like the River of Egypt.

Malachi 1:14
"But the deceiver is cursed...for I am a great King," says Yahweh of Armies, "and my name is awesome among the nations."

Malachi 3:1
"Behold, I send my messenger, and he will prepare the way before me; and the Lord, whom you seek, will suddenly come to his temple; and the messenger of the covenant, whom you desire, behold, he comes!" says Yahweh of Armies.

Now that we have established that God is a divine being who defends Himself, those He loves, and the innocent, we will conclude this discussion with the truth that God desires His children to behave as He Himself behaves. It includes defending ourselves, those we love, and the innocent.

The Saint's Divine Imitation

One of the major themes in the Scriptures is that the Lord God desires His children to behave as He behaves. We see this principle both in the Old and New Testaments.

We are commanded to be holy like God is holy. Holiness speaks of being wholly separate and different from the world. The world thinks one way and the saints think another. The world speaks one way, and we speak another. The world acts one way, and we act another.

Leviticus 11:44-45
For I am Yahweh your God. Sanctify yourselves therefore, and be holy; for I am holy. You shall not defile yourselves with any kind of creeping thing that moves on the earth. For I am Yahweh who brought you up out of the land of Egypt, to be your God. You shall therefore be holy, for I am holy.

1 Peter 1:15-16
But just as he who called you is holy, you yourselves also be holy in all of your behavior. Because it is written, "You shall be holy; for I am holy."

In Matthew 5, the Lord Jesus commands that we be perfect as our Father is. This is our earthly goal and purpose. It is to be perfect in our thinking, speaking, and behaving as He is.

Matthew 5:48
Therefore you shall be perfect...as your Father in heaven is perfect.

Though this cannot be fully achieved in this life without the redemption of our bodies, it is our pursuit. Therefore, what God thinks, speaks, and does concerning self-defense and the defense of others is the way in which we are to think, speak, and act. We know this because we are instructed to defend ourselves and others as we will see. This truth is a theme woven throughout this book.

In summary, the Lord God defends Himself (His purposes and plans), those He loves, and the innocent and He expects us to do the same.

Chapter 3

The World's Preservation

In the first chapter, we considered mankind's spiritually desperate condition which involved his spiritual deadness, his Satanic slavery, propensity toward sin, continual rejection, and spiritual darkness. This unholy condition leads mankind to commit every kind of sin including murder. As Christians, we know God's first response to this condition coming from His nature, power. and attributes is the plan of redemption.

As we saw in the last chapter, pouring forth from that same nature, power, and attributes is His second response which is self-defense and the defense of others. In general, the Lord God desires to preserve man from his own annihilation or from God's continual judgement of man as in the flood so He might save some, judge others, and bless all upon the earth. In this chapter, we will discuss the numerous specifics of this preservation of mankind and in the next chapter the specifics of His defense structures to accomplish it.

Let us begin with an overview. The redemption of man is not simply the Son coming to die on the cross for our sins, but it includes so much more. This redemptive plan involves all of human history upon the earth, mankind's final judgment, a new heaven and earth, and the entrance to an eternity of glory. It begins with the gift of the kingdom to the Son and then ends with the Son turning it over to the Father.

In 1 Corinthians 15:28, Paul explains that human history will culminate in all things being brought in subjection to Christ and then to the Father.

1 Corinthians 15:28
When all things have been subjected to him, then the Son will also himself be subjected to him who subjected all things to him, that God may be all in all.

For this to occur, God must place His Son in the flesh into human history among the sinful men who murder. He must also call out from among these wicked sinners those who are to be saved. Afterward, He must have them live among these unsaved, sometimes violent, people to share the gospel with them and bring others into the kingdom. Finally, those saved must grow into the image of His Son. As they do this, they must be preserved from the violence of wicked men.

First, this is accomplished by the Lord God tempering His wrath through His patience so as not to bring a constant and continual judgment upon man as He did with the flood.

In 2 Peter 3, the apostle explains this truth. Here, Peter is speaking of the unsaved mockers in his day who criticized believers because God had not come to judge the world as they said He would. So, Peter provides the reason.

2 Peter 3:5-6
For this they willfully forget that there were heavens from of old, and an earth formed out of water and amid water by the word of God, by which means the world that existed then, being overflowed with water, perished.

Here, Peter asserts that God poured out His judgment on mankind in the flood upon earth but would not do it again. He stopped Himself from a continual cycle of judgment for mankind.

Now, He is choosing this time to store up His wrath until a day of great judgment.

HOW CHRISTIANS MAY DEFEND THEMSELVES AGAINST ATTACK

2 Peter 3:7
But the heavens that exist now and the earth, by the same word have been stored up for fire, being reserved against the day of judgment and destruction of ungodly men.

The reason God is not judging evil is due to His patience. The Lord God is patient with unbelievers so He can bring those chosen into the kingdom.

2 Peter 3:8-9
But don't forget this one thing, beloved, that one day is with the Lord as a thousand years, and a thousand years as one day. The Lord is not slow concerning his promise, as some count slowness; but he is patient with us, not wishing that anyone should perish, but that all should come to repentance.

Then the time will come, and His judgment will pour forth upon the earth. We will see that this judgment will be God's final defense of Himself and His people. This is an important truth we must understand.

Second, as God waits patiently to judge and condemn the unsaved so He might bring some into the kingdom, He must allow evil to express itself as He works out His redemptive plan in human history. Because He is a loving, merciful, and gracious God, He allows unsaved man to experience the constant witness to His existence through His extraordinary creation, conscience, and His blessings upon the earth as man lives out his earthly life. Also, the unsaved must be allowed to live their predetermined time to accomplish the purposes God has for them. For the saved, it means that God must protect the unsaved from being killed before they could be saved. Once saved, they must be protected to share the gospel with the unsaved and to build each other up in the faith. Of course, He must preserve the Messiah and His Messianic line. The plan of redemption involves the preservation of life.

The Protection of the Messianic Line

For His anticipated Messiah to be identified by the world, God provided prophecies which foretold the ancestral line of this Savior. Each of the men and women in that line had to be protected from the lusts of sinful men who might kill them before the birth of the next descendent. When Matthew and Luke presented the Messianic credentials of Jesus Christ, they traced His lineage back to David for the legal and blood line of Jesus and then all the way to Adam, the first man. All were protected.

From Adam to Noah

Jesus came from a line of believers. Luke traces Jesus from Adam through Seth to Noah's son Shem before the flood.

Luke 3:36-38
The son of Cainan, the son of Arphaxad, the son of Shem, the son of Noah, the son of Lamech, the son of Methuselah, the son of Enoch, the son of Jared, the son of Mahalaleel, the son of Cainan, the son of Enos, the son of Seth, the son of Adam, the son of God.

The line from Adam to Shem had to be preserved.

From Noah to Abraham

His description of the Messiah's line from God's people continues until Abraham.

Luke 3:34-36
The son of Jacob, the son of Isaac, the son of Abraham, the son of Terah, the son of Nahor, the son of Serug, the son of Reu, the son of

Peleg, the son of Eber, the son of Shelah, the son of Cainan, the son of Arphaxad, the son of Shem, the son of Noah, the son of Lamech.

The line from Noah to Abraham had to be protected.

From Abraham to David

Luke portrays Jesus as a descendent of Abraham.

Luke 3:31-34
The son of Melea, the son of Menan, the son of Mattatha, the son of Nathan, the son of David, the son of Jesse, the son of Obed, the son of Boaz...son of Salmon, the son of Nahshon, the son of Amminadab, the son of Aram, the son of Hezron, the son of Perez, the son of Judah, the son of Jacob, the son of Isaac, the son of Abra-ham, the son of Terah, the son of Nahor.

The Messiah was to be from the line of Abraham.

Genesis 12:2-3
I will make of you a great nation. I will bless you and make your name great. You will be a blessing. I will bless those who bless you, and.... All the families of the earth will be blessed through you.

Genesis 22:18
All the nations of the earth will be blessed by your offspring, because you have obeyed my voice.

The Messiah would come through the line of Isaac.

Genesis 21:12
God said to Abraham, "Don't let it be grievous in your sight because of the boy, and because of your servant. In all that Sarah says to you, listen to her voice. For your offspring will be named through Isaac.

He would also come through Isaac's Son Jacob.

Numbers 24:17
I see him.... A star will come out of Jacob. A scepter will rise out of Israel, and shall strike through...Moab...crush all the sons of Sheth.

Then He would descend from Jacob's son, Judah.

Genesis 49:10
The scepter will not depart from Judah, nor the ruler's staff from between his feet, until he comes to whom it belongs. The obedience of the peoples will be to him.

The Savior would come from the line of Jesse.

Isaiah 11:1
A shoot will come out of the stock of Jesse, and a branch out of his roots will bear fruit.

Abraham and his descendants to Jesse had to be preserved.

From David to Jesus

Luke explains that Jesus was in the blood line of David through Mary. Matthew asserts that He was in the legal line of David from Solomon.

Luke 3:31
The son of Melea, the son of Menan, the son of Mattatha, the son of Nathan, the son of David.

Matthew 1:6-7
Jesse became the father of King David. David became the father of Solomon by her who had been Uriah's wife. Solomon became the father of Rehoboam.

The line from David to Jesus had to be preserved.

Many prophecies identifying the ancestors of the Messiah had to be fulfilled which meant those in His line had to be protected. They could not be killed by evil men.

The Safeguarding of the Messiah

The parents of Jesus would also have to be protected from being killed before Mary had Jesus. Then Jesus would have to be protected while still a baby.

The Deliverance at His Birth

The Messiah was to be God in human form. This meant He was to be born of a human woman from the seed of God.

Luke 1:35
The angel answered her, "The Holy Spirit will come on you, and the power of the Most High will overshadow you. Therefore also the holy one who is born from you will be called the Son of God.

Matthew 1:18
Now the birth of Jesus Christ was like this: After his mother, Mary, was engaged to Joseph, before they came together, she was found pregnant by the Holy Spirit.

Matthew 1:20
But when he thought about these things, behold, an angel of the Lord appeared to him in a dream, saying, "Joseph, son of David, don't be afraid to take to yourself Mary as your wife, for that which is conceived in her is of the Holy Spirit.

For this to be accomplished, the parents of Jesus had to be protected from evil men who might harm or kill them.

Once born, the Messiah Himself must be delivered from any threat to His life as an innocent infant. This was directly accomplished by Lord God through His angelic army who appeared to the shepherds. They were not only there to speak of the birth of the Savior. Warriors protect first and foremost.

Luke 2:13-14
Suddenly, there was with the angel a multitude of the heavenly army praising God, and saying, "Glory to God in the highest, on earth peace, good will toward men."

Next, His angel appeared to the wisemen and told them not to inform Herod as to the newborn King's location.

Matthew 2:12
Being warned in a dream not to return to Herod, they went back to their own country another way.

Finally, an angel appeared to Joseph commanding him to travel to Egypt to protect the child.

Matthew 2:13
Now when they had departed, behold, an angel of the Lord appeared to Joseph in a dream, saying, "Arise and take the young child and his mother, and flee into Egypt, and stay there until I tell you, for Herod will seek the young child to destroy him."

Jesus had to be protected from being murdered during his infancy.

The Preservation During His Childhood

As He grew, Jesus had to be protected from death in order for Him to begin His ministry of the proclamation of the gospel. This was accomplished through the death of Herod.

HOW CHRISTIANS MAY DEFEND THEMSELVES AGAINST ATTACK

Matthew 2:19-20
But when Herod was dead, behold, an angel of the Lord appeared in a dream to Joseph in Egypt, saying, "Arise and take the young child and his mother, and go into the land of Israel, for those who sought the young child's life are dead."

Then the parents moved to Nazareth from Egypt to protect the child from Herod's son.

Matthew 2:21-23
He arose and took the young child and his mother, and came into the land of Israel. But when he heard that Archelaus was reigning over Judea in the place of his father, Herod, he was afraid to go there. Being warned in a dream, he withdrew into the region of Galilee, and came and lived in a city called Nazareth; that it might be fulfilled which was spoken through the prophets that he will be called a Nazarene.

Like other parents, Mary and Joseph kept a close eye on the Son of God as He was growing up to protect Him from any physical harm that could come His way.

Luke 2:42-45
When he was twelve years old, they went up to Jerusalem according to the custom of the feast, and when they had fulfilled the days, as they were returning, the boy Jesus stayed behind in Jerusalem. Joseph and his mother didn't know it, but supposing him to be in the company, they went a day's journey, and they looked for him among their relatives and acquaintances. When they didn't find him, they returned to Jerusalem, looking for him.

Luke 2:48-52
When they saw him, they were astonished, and his mother said to him, "Son, why have you treated us this way? Behold, your father and I were anxiously looking for you." He said to them, "Why were you looking for me? Didn't you know that I must be in my Father's house?" They didn't understand the saying which he spoke to them.

And he went down with them, and came to Nazareth. He was subject to them, and his mother kept all these sayings in her heart. And Jesus increased in wisdom and stature, and in favor with God and men.

They feared that harm would come to Him without them.

The Protection During His Ministry

Once His ministry began, the Anointed One would have to have been safeguarded from death until the time of the cross. For three long years, the Lord Jesus Christ would have to be protected from being murdered by evil men.

John 8:20
Jesus spoke these words in the treasury, as he taught in the temple. Yet no one arrested him, because his hour had not yet come.

Jesus had the power to defend Himself through the Spirit as seen by the falling down of all who had come to cease and arrest Him.

John 18:6
When therefore he said to them, "I am he," they went backward, and fell to the ground.

Jesus also had an army of angels at His disposal.

Matthew 26:53
Or do you think that I couldn't ask my Father, and he would even now send me more than twelve legions of angels?

John 18:11
Jesus therefore said to Peter, "Put the sword into its sheath. The cup which the Father has given me, shall I not surely drink it?"

The Lord Jesus could not be killed before the time had come. During every moment of His ministry, the Father would have to safeguard His only Son's life. Nothing could change the Father's redemptive plan.

The Deliverance on the Cross

Once He was on the cross, He would be protected until the exact time the Father had determined for Him to die. This would include the very moment of death.

John 19:30
When Jesus therefore had received the vinegar, he said, "It is finished." Then he bowed his head, and gave up his spirit.

As can be clearly seen, the Anointed one (Messiah) had to be protected from assassination while he ministered upon the earth in order to be the sacrifice on the cross under the exact circumstances dictated by God the Father. This seems quite obvious but is important to this understanding.

The Perpetuation of the Saved

If those who will be saved are chosen before the foundation of the world, then they must be preserved from death in their unsaved state until they come to Christ. Then, they must be protected to serve the Lord until their earthly time ends.

The Election Before Birth

Before birth, God chose us to be a part of His kingdom. He determined who would come to His Son.

Ephesians 1:4
Just as He chose us in Him before the foundation of the world, that we would be holy and blameless before Him. In love.

2 Thessalonians 2:13
But we should always give thanks to God for you, brethren beloved by the Lord, because God has chosen you from the beginning for salvation through sanctification by the Spirit and faith in the truth.

The Sending of a Preacher

This requires someone to preach the gospel to us. The Lord God's simple method is to bring the gospel from one person to another.

Romans 10:14
How then will they call on him in whom they have not believed? How will they believe in him whom they have not heard? How will they hear without a preacher? And how will they preach unless they are sent? As it is written: "How beautiful are the feet of those who preach the Good News of peace, who bring glad tiding..."

The Provision of Faith

Then He gave us the faith through grace to believe.

Ephesians 2:8-9
For by grace you have been saved through faith, and that not of yourselves; it is the gift of God, not of works, that no one would boast.

As the Lord works out the circumstances to bring us to Him, He must protect us from death at the hands of evil men. This may mean protection through many years of life.

The Responsibility to Serve

Once saved, we must render the service that He has for us. This will involve building the kingdom numerically through evangelism and spiritually through ministering to the saints.

Ephesians 4:11-16
He gave some to be apostles...some, prophets; and some, evangelists; and some, shepherds and teachers; for the perfecting of the saints, to the work of serving to the building up of the body of Christ, until we all attain to the unity of the faith and of the knowledge of the Son of God, to a full grown man, to the measure of the stature of the fullness of Christ, that we may no longer be children, tossed back and forth and carried about with every wind of doctrine, by the trickery of men, in craftiness, after the wiles of error; but speaking truth in love, we may grow up in all things into him who is the head, Christ, from whom all the body, being fitted and knit together through that which every joint supplies, according to the working in measure of each individual part, makes the body increase to the building up of itself in love.

Throughout human history, God has put His people and His Messiah into a world of violence. They must be protected from the whims, lusts, and desires of evil men.

The Safekeeping of the Human Race

Throughout human history, the Lord God had to prevent the human race from destroying itself. His desire was for all mankind to be safe so they could experience their blessings from Him on the earth. Those who saw God's grace entered the Kingdom and would be protected until their purpose had been served. Those who rejected God's blessings would be preserved for judgment and condemnation at the world's end.

The Protection from Full Annihilation

God made a covenant with Noah not to destroy it by flood. Until the time, the earth will have its days and seasons.

Genesis 8:20-22
Noah built an altar to Yahweh, and took of every clean animal, and of every clean bird, and offered burnt offerings on the altar. Yahweh smelled the pleasant aroma. Yahweh said in his heart, "I will not again curse the ground...for man's sake because the imagination of man's heart is evil from his youth. I will never again strike every living thing, as I have done." While the earth remains, seed time and harvest, and cold and heat, and summer and winter, and day and night will not cease.

Within this promise are two powerful implications. First, God bound Himself not to destroy all mankind again in His wrath and start over. The second, is the promise that He will not allow men to destroy themselves. The earth will remain, the harvest will continue to come, the seasons go on, and day and night will not cease.

The Constant Witness of God in Safety

God allows unsaved man to experience the witness to His existence through His creation, conscience, and His blessings upon the earth as man lives out his earthly life.

The Lord God declares His existence in creation. It declares who He is day and night.

Romans 1:20
For the invisible things of him since the creation of the world are clearly seen, being perceived through the things that are made, even his everlasting power and divinity, that they may be without excuse.

HOW CHRISTIANS MAY DEFEND THEMSELVES AGAINST ATTACK

Psalm 19:1-6
The heavens declare [display] the glory of God. The expanse shows his handiwork. Day after day they pour out speech, and night after night they display knowledge. There is no speech nor language, where their voice is not heard. Their voice has gone out through all the earth, their words to the end of the world. In them he has set a tent for the sun, which is as a bridegroom coming out of his room, like a strong man rejoicing to run his course. His going out is from the end of the heavens, his circuit to its ends. There is nothing hidden from its heat.

The Lord God demonstrates His existence in the human conscience which will direct men and women to follow His laws and prosper.

Romans 2:15
In that they show the work of the law written in their hearts, their conscience testifying with them...their thoughts among themselves accusing or else excusing them.

The Lord continually blesses mankind putting on display His love, grace, and mercy.

Matthew 5:45
That you may be children of your Father who is in heaven. For he makes his sun to rise on the evil and the good, and sends rain on the just and the unjust.

Acts 14:17
Yet he didn't leave himself without witness, in that he did good and gave you rains from the sky and fruitful seasons, filling our hearts with food and gladness.

Here, the Lord God is constantly revealing His existence so men can enjoy their lives. Some will see Him and believe in His only Son. Others will be without excuse on judgment day because God is continually telling them He exists.

The Preservation of the Unsaved for Service

The majority of the earth's population at any given time will be primarily the unsaved. n Matthew 7, Jesus confirms this truth.

Matthew 7:13-14
Enter in by the narrow gate; for the gate is wide and the way is broad that leads to destruction, and there are many who enter in by it. How the gate is narrow and the way is restricted that leads to life! There are few who find it (DEJ).

A narrow road implies that a minority of people will be saved, and the majority will not. Though He continually shows His love, grace, and mercy to them through His creation, most people will reject God.

Then why would God preserve them from murder? Why would God care? He desires to continually witness to them concerning His presence. Paul presents this truth in Acts 14.

Acts 14:17
Yet he didn't leave himself without witness, in that he did good and gave you rains from the sky and fruitful seasons, filling our hearts with food and gladness.

Also, God is so loving that He desires even those who rebel against Him to experience His blessings upon the earth. In Matthew 5, Jesus speaks of this truth.

Matthew 5: 44-45
But I tell you, love your enemies, bless those who curse you, do good to those who hate you, and pray for those who mistreat you and persecute you, that you may be children of your Father who is in heaven. For he makes his sun to rise on the evil and the good, and sends rain on the just and the unjust

HOW CHRISTIANS MAY DEFEND THEMSELVES AGAINST ATTACK

Here, Jesus desires believers to love and serve the unsaved, but God desires the unsaved to serve believers. Though not emphasized in Christianity today, this is the truth.

God preserves the unsaved because He wants the unsaved to serve His children. Since they make up the majority of the population, believers need their service in their daily lives. King Solomon spoke of this truth.

Ecclesiastes 2:26
For to the man who pleases him, God gives wisdom, knowledge, and joy; but to the sinner he gives travail, to gather and to heap up, that he may give to him who pleases God....

Finally, He utilizes the services of unsaved men to keep order upon the earth and administer His justice. It is not possible to use only believers.

Romans 13: 4
For he is a servant of God to you for good. But if you do that which is evil, be afraid, for he doesn't bear the sword in vain; for he is a servant of God, an avenger for wrath to him who does evil.

Most of these authorities are not saved but they serve Him anyway.

The Safeguarding of Mankind for Judgment

Those who do not believe in Jesus Christ live as long as God desires. In Psalm 139, David speaks of God determining the days of one's life before birth.

Psalm 139:16
Your eyes saw my body. In your book they were all written, the days that were ordained for me, when as yet there were none of them.

So, God determines how long people live and no one can bring another's death until God's timetable. Once unbelievers die, they are readied for judgment.

Hebrews 9:27
Inasmuch as it is appointed for men [people] to die once, and after this, judgment.

This also God's determination.

God also determines the timetables of His judgments. In the book of Revelation, John describes the process that Christ will use to take back the earth by a series of judgments. For this to occur, men must be alive on the earth. He cannot allow them to destroy themselves before their predetermined times.

Revelation 5:6
Then I saw a Lamb, looking as if it had been slain, standing at the center of the throne...

Revelation 5:7
He went and took the scroll from the right hand of him who sat on the throne.

The lamb removes each of the seven seals with the last being the seven trumpet judgments. The seventh trumpet judgment becomes the seven bowl judgments. When these are fulfilled, the Lord returns to the earth for the battle of Armageddon.

After this, believers who survived the tribulation will enter the Lord Christ's kingdom on earth in human bodies. During His thousand-year reign, some of these saved people will have unsaved children who will be gathered together by the Devil for a final battle on the earth. Then the judgment of unbelievers will occur at the great white throne. Man will be preserved to fully experience these judgments.

HOW CHRISTIANS MAY DEFEND THEMSELVES AGAINST ATTACK

In Summary, God responded to man's sinful condition by creating the plan of redemption which would save some and condemn others. For the plan to be accomplished, he had to preserve from death the Messiah and His ancestors, other participants in His plan, the unsaved before they believed in Him, and the saved so they could serve Him. He also desired to preserve the unsaved from death because He wanted them to continually witness the proclamation of His existence and experience the blessings of His grace and service of His people. The Lord wanted to utilize the unsaved in service to His people and o prepare them for judgment according to His timetable. He even had to preserve them from His own wrath and their complete annihilation of each other. In the next chapter, we will see that God established defense structures to accomplish this preservation.

DEFENDING YOUR LIFE

Chapter 4

The Defensive Structure

To accomplish the purposes discussed in the last chapter, God built into mankind a series of structures centered on the defense of ourselves, those we love, and the innocent based on His nature, power, and attributes.

The World-Wide Judgments

At first, in order demonstrate to man and the angels, His manifold grace, God allowed man to function according to His fallen nature without a world-wide judgment until the flood. As a result, man proved that he would continually do evil and was in desperate need of a Savior.

Genesis 6:5-6
Yahweh saw that the wickedness of man was great in the earth, and that every [single] imagination of the thoughts of man's heart was continually only evil. Yahweh was sorry that he had made man on the earth, and it grieved him in his heart.

Of course, this included murder. As a result, murder had to be dealt with.

The Earth's World-Wide Flood

Due to wrath, God orchestrated a world-wide judgment through the flood. Due to His constant wrath, God bound Himself with Noah to never destroy man by flood again.

Genesis 9:8-11
Then God said to Noah and to his sons with him: "I now establish my covenant with you and with your descendants after you and with every living creature that was with you — the birds, the livestock and all the wild animals, all those that came out of the ark with you — every living creature on earth. I establish my covenant with you: Never again will all life be destroyed by the waters of a flood; never again will there be a flood to destroy the earth."

The flood upon the earth wiped out a multitude of evil men. At first, all was well, but it was not long before man's evil reared its ugly head again.

The Race's World-Wide Dispersion

As soon as man began to multiply on the earth again, his evil nature reared its ugly head and disobeyed God. Rather than spread out through the earth and multiply, man desired to remain together. They attempted to create one nation, one capital, and one false religion out of their wicked hearts.

Genesis 11:1-4
Now the whole world had one language and a common speech. As people moved eastward, they found a plain in Shinar and settled there. They said to each other, "Come, let's make bricks and bake them thoroughly." They used brick instead of stone, and tar for mortar. Then they said, "Come, let us build ourselves a city, with a tower that reaches to the heavens, so that we may make a name for ourselves; otherwise we will be scattered over the face of the whole earth."

When God saw that man was once again rebelling against Him, the Lord God scattered mankind across the earth into different language groups. This divided man significantly so he would not unite for thousands of years.

HOW CHRISTIANS MAY DEFEND THEMSELVES AGAINST ATTACK

Genesis 11:5-9
But the Lord came down to see the city and the tower the people were building. The Lord said, "If...one people speaking the same language they have begun to do this, then nothing they plan to do will be impossible for them. Come, let us go...and confuse their language so they will not understand each other." So, the Lord scattered them from there over all the earth, and they stopped building the city. That is why it was called Babel-because there the Lord confused the language of the whole world. From there the Lord scattered them over the face of the whole earth.

These groups would create families, clans, tribes, cities, regions, and even nations who would live in constant tension with each other. The world would not be able to unite for thousands of years. Since God would not flood the earth again in world-wide judgment, evil men would keep other men in check. Then, regions and nations would do the same.

The Hinderance of Evil in Society

In order for God to preserve the plan of redemption's many participants from being killed by the rest of mankind, the Lord God established various laws and structures within human life and among the members of mankind to prevent the continual murder by evil men or to stop it if it came.

The Safeguard of Individual Self-Defense

The fundamental safeguard of continual violence is self-defense and the defense of others. First, for an attacker, the probability that his victims will defend themselves or others will come to their defense will force them to truly reconsider attacking people at all. In fact, most violent urges will subside when faced with defense by people that they want to harm. Second, the defense victims will often stop the violence once it has begun. Why was this important? After the flood, the Lord changed the basic framework of nature. The harmonious relationship that mankind had with the animals as he named them and had dominion over them had ceased. Now, animals would be afraid of men because they would provide the food for them. This meant that they (man and animals) would each be defending themselves against the other which would cause a tremendous amount of bloodshed.

Genesis 9:2-3
The fear of you and the dread of you will be on every animal of the earth, and on every bird of the sky. Everything that moves along the ground and all the fish of the sea are delivered into your hand. Every moving thing that lives will be food for you. As I gave you the green herb, I have given everything to you.

Self-defense would become the standard as men protected themselves from animals while those animals were protecting themselves from men. Solomon mentions this natural order in Proverbs chapter nine. In this passage, the Lord God gives only one stipulation.

Genesis 9:4
But flesh with the life of it, the blood of it, you shall not eat.

So, the Lord God identified blood as containing the life-giving principle of all flesh (animals and man). Therefore, no one was to eat the blood of animals.

Then the Lord continues with a general principle to guide men's interactions with one another once the killing began. God knew that men would murder and kill. They had done it before the flood and would do it again. Why? As mentioned previously, murder was rampant before the flood.

HOW CHRISTIANS MAY DEFEND THEMSELVES AGAINST ATTACK

The first child ever born killed his brother.

Genesis 4:8
Cain said to Abel, his brother, "Let's go into the field." While they were in the field, Cain rose up against Abel.

We learn from John that Cain was instigated by Satan to kill Abel because his brother's deeds were righteous.

1 John 3:12
Unlike Cain, who was of the evil one, and killed his brother. Why did he kill him? Because his deeds were evil, and his brother's righteous.

When God confronted Him, the Lord alluded to this powerful truth about the blood.

Genesis 4:10
Yahweh said, "What have you done? The voice of your brother's blood cries to me from the ground.

Abel's life-giving principle was crying out that it had been taken from Abel.

As punishment, Cain was cast out to become a wanderer, and he knew that he would be killed. So, he begged the Lord God for mercy.

Genesis 4:13-14
Cain said to Yahweh, "My punishment is greater than I can bear. Behold, you have driven me out today from the surface of the ground. I will be hidden from your face...I will be a fugitive and a wanderer in the earth. Whoever finds me will kill me."

So, the Lord God Almighty gave Cain a specific sign which would not allow anyone to kill him.

Genesis 4:15
Yahweh said to him, "Therefore whoever slays Cain, vengeance will be taken on him sevenfold." Yahweh appointed a sign for Cain, so that anyone finding him would not strike him.

Later, one of his descendants, Lamech killed a man. His action became a proverb and a jingle among the people.

Genesis 4:23-24
Lamech said to his wives, "Adah and Zillah, hear my voice. You wives of Lamech, listen to my speech, for I have slain a man for wounding me, a young man for bruising me. If Cain will be avenged seven times, truly Lamech seventy-seven times."

As one can see, if it happened before the flood, it would happen much more after the flood. Why? Now, mankind will be hunting animals for food. This will require weapons. More weapons will be carried. Sin will take its toll. Men will again kill each other.

Then, in verses 5-6, the Lord sets His retribution for killing.

Genesis 9:5-6
I will surely require accounting for your life's blood. At the hand of every animal I will require it. At the hand of man, even at the hand of every man's brother, I will require the life of man. Whoever sheds man's blood, his blood will be shed by man, for God made man in his own image.

Though this passage is used for capital punishment by a government, it is much broader than that.

A government was not created yet and would not be created until many years later. When this command was given, there was only Noah and his family. This command would need to be applied at that time and the days following as they multiplied and filled the earth as multiple societies developed. They were not to become "blood thirsty."

But with the command to eat animals, the shedding of blood would become routine and must not carry over into human life. Men taking the lives of other men would never be acceptable to God. As the Lord God would hold accountable animals for their shedding of human blood, so will mankind be held accountable. This accounting would prevent violence as a deterrent and end the violence once it began.

How will God accomplish this accounting? Notice, God says, "At the hand of man, even at the hand of every man's brother, I will require the life of man. Whoever sheds man's blood, his blood will be shed by man." If a man takes another man's life, then a man will take his. This will be done by the man himself in self-defense or by his brother or relative in defense of him or in dispensing justice for what the man did. This can be the only way to properly interpret this passage.

After this, God summarizes what he means. This is the principle of "blood for blood." If man sheds man's blood, then another man will shed his blood. This would become the most basic deterrent to killing someone. You kill, you will be killed. If you attempt to kill, you may be killed. The man who would attempt to murder another man would defend himself and take that man's life.

We see exactly the same thing in the animal kingdom when the prey attempts to defend itself. If a predator attacks its prey, then the prey, of possible, will attack the predator. Then God reiterates His initial command to man.

Genesis 9:7
As for you, be fruitful and multiply. Increase abundantly in the earth, and multiply in it (DEJ).

At this point, God makes His covenant with Noah that He would never destroy the earth as they multiplied.

God's initial structure had been put into place. Even the animal kingdom also found themselves hunting and killing each other. In Psalm 104, the psalmist speaks of this truth.

Psalm 104:21
The young lions roar after their prey, and seek their food from God.

Here the inspired writer is attributing the lion seeking food to kill as from to the Lord God. It is His order in nature. This is so obvious, but this new order presupposes predators and their preys constantly defending themselves.

When David faced Goliath his confidence in God came from his self-defense against lions and bears. When David told King Saul that he would stand up against Goliath, Saul questioned his judgment being just a youth.

1 Samuel 17:34-36
David said to Saul, "Your servant was keeping his father's sheep; and when a lion or a bear came, and took a lamb out of the flock, I went out after him, and struck him, and rescued it out of his mouth. When he arose against me, I caught him by his beard, and struck him, and killed him. Your servant struck both the lion and the bear. This uncircumcised Philistine shall be as one of them, since he has defied the armies of the living God."

Next, David attributes his victory in killing them in self-defense as God's work.

1 Samuel 17:37
David said, "Yahweh who delivered me out of the paw of the lion, and out of the paw of the bear, he will deliver me out of the hand of this Philistine." Saul said to David, "Go! Yahweh will be with you."

After attributing the victory in his self-defense to God against the animals, he now attributes his victory against Goliath, the Philistine, to God. They knew self-defense was God's natural order after the flood.

To summarize, God will take man's life through another man. God expects man to defend himself and then He will work His will through it. This defense will deter men from violence and if it doesn't, the brother will come to justly avenge him. Later, the government took over many of those duties. This is how God will hold men accountable. The Lord God is always watching to see whether men will value life as he values it. It may not be indiscriminately taken by others. Though individual defense is the fundamental safeguard, it is not the only one. These other structures grow out of this.

The Safeguard of a Conscience

Next, God placed a conscience in man which would direct him in his defense of himself and others. First, it would prevent him from committing a violent act. Second, defense would prompt the victim into defending himself or others into defending him if violent came. Since we have studied the second chapter of Romans 2 concerning our conscience, we will look at only one verse as a reminder. Here is Paul's appeal to follow our consciences. The apostle did not want his readers to numb their righteous consciences through their disobedience to authorities.

Romans 13:5
Therefore you need to be in subjection, not only because of the wrath, but also for conscience' sake.

He explains that Christians need to subject themselves to their consciences by obeying the law as it tells us to do so we will not have it accusing us (if its righteous) and excusing us (if it calloused or seared). The Lord God's law commands men not to commit murder or to defend themselves if murder comes upon them or others. Our consciences testify of this.

In Acts 24, Paul describes how he kept his conscience clean by following it and not battling against it.

Acts 24:16
In this I also practice always having a conscience void of offense toward God and men.

We discussed in the first chapter that men suppress the truth of creation and their consciences in their sin. This means that they will ignore, deny, or replace the truth with lies in order to do whatever they want. As men continually ignore, deny, or replace their consciences with their own lies or the lies of others, their consciences become weak and defiled. This means it becomes increasingly unable to discern the truth and misguides men. It also become defiled and impure leading men in the wrong direction.

Through much experience, we do see that rejecting one's conscience in the area of violence and murder is one the last bastions to fall regarding the conscience. Most men do not kill for harm. Also, we see, that men defending themselves and others is the first inclination from the conscience.

In the book of Judges, there was a judge who ruled Israel named Samson. When attacked, God would give him great strength. The book describes an incident where he faced a roaring lion. What did he do? What did his conscience tell him to do? What was he inclined to do?

Judges 14:5-6
Then Samson went down to Timnah with his father and his mother

and came to the vineyards of Timnah; and behold, a young lion roared at him. Yahweh's Spirit came mightily on him, and he tore him as he would have torn a young goat with his bare hands, but he didn't tell his father or his mother what he had done.*

We see that Samson defended himself. He didn't question if he was allowed to defend himself, he knew he was. It was only a case of needing his supernatural strength which God gave him at that moment. This was another confirmation that he could defend himself.

Later, he was enamored with and deceived by a prostitute named Delilah. She was a Philistine woman. His enemies and the enemies of his people were the Philistines. They wanted Delilah to discover what made Samson strong so they could defeat him. So, Delilah asked Samson to tell her what made him strong and then she would pretend that Philistines were at his door and see if he would lose his strength.

Judges 16:4-5
It came to pass afterward that he loved a woman in the valley of Sorek, whose name was Delilah. The lords of the Philistines came up to her and said to her, "Entice him, and see in which his great strength lies, and by what means we may prevail against him, that we may bind him to afflict him; and we will each give you eleven hundred pieces of silver."

So, Samson told Delilah that she should bind him with seven cords.

Judges 16:8-9
Then the lords of the Philistines brought up to her seven green cords which had not been dried, and she bound him with them. Now she had an ambush waiting in the inner room. She said to him, "The Philistines are on you, Samson!" He broke the cords as a flax thread is broken when it touches the fire. So his strength was not known.

So, Samson jumped up to defend himself. He had absolutely no hesitation. He knew that he could defend himself because harm was coming upon him. It was not provoked in this event though he had retaliated before.

The second time, Samson told Delilah if he was bound with new ropes, he would lose his strength.

Judges 16:12
So Delilah took new ropes and bound him with them, then said to him, "The Philistines...on you, Samson!" The ambush was waiting in the inner room. He broke them off his arms like a thread.

When Delilah told him the Philistines had come, he jumped up again to defend himself.

When asked again, he told Delilah to weave seven locks of his head with fabric and he would lose his strength.

Judges 16:14
She fastened it with the pin, and said to him, "The Philistines are on you, Samson!" He awakened out of his sleep, and plucked away the pin of the beam and the fabric.

Here, he wakes up again and attempts to defend himself with no concern whatsoever.

She kept urging him until he told her the truth.

Judges 16:16-18
When she pressed him daily with her words and urged him, his soul was troubled to death. He told her all his heart and said to her, "No razor has ever come on my head; for I have been a Nazirite to God from my mother's womb. If I am shaved, then my strength will go from me and I will become weak, and be like any other man." When Delilah saw that he had told her all his heart, she sent and called for

HOW CHRISTIANS MAY DEFEND THEMSELVES AGAINST ATTACK

the lords of the Philistines, saying, "Come up this once, for he has told me all his heart." Then the lords of the Philistines came up to her and brought the money in their hand.

Now, she cut his hair and his strength left him.

Judges 16:19-21
She made him sleep on her knees; and she called for a man and shaved off the seven locks of his head; and she began to afflict him, and his strength went from him. She said, "The Philistines are upon you, Samson!" He awoke out of his sleep, and said, "I will go out as at other times, and shake myself free." But he didn't know that Yahweh had departed from him. The Philistines laid hold on him and put out his eyes; and they brought him down to Gaza and bound him with fetters of bronze; and he ground at the mill in the prison.

This time when he jumped up to defend himself, he did not have his supernatural strength because the Lord God had taken it away. Why? It was obviously not because the strength was in his hair or that he should not have been following his conscience by defending himself. He lost it because he chose his Philistine wife over God. He chose to submit to Delilah rather than God. He most likely had taken the Nazarite vow and had defiled himself by allowing her to cut his long hair. Notice, he slept on his knees.

These both were violations of the vow.

Numbers 6:5
All the days of his vow of separation no razor shall come on his head, until the days are fulfilled in which he separates himself to Yahweh. He shall be holy. He shall le...locks of the hair of his head grow long.

Lastly, God wanted to use him to destroy the Philistines the rule that the Philistines had over His people Israel. So, he let his parents disobey Him and find a Philistines wife him.

Judges 14:4
But his father and his mother didn't know that it was of Yahweh; for he sought an occasion against the Philistines. Now at that time the Philistines ruled over Israel.

And this is how the entire series on incidences started.

This is mentioned because Samson's defense against the lion and the Philistines was from following his conscience. It is the first thing we would do.

In summary, God has placed within man a conscience to accuse him if he decides to be violent and stop him by it prompting his victim to defend himself or others. Even if many consciences are seared, many will still follow these two dictates. This will hinder violence from erupting.

The Protection of Parents

The protection of parents involves three responsibilities. The first is to protect, defend, and deliver children from any harm that may come upon them.

We can see this demonstrated when the parents of Jesus could not find him in their caravan at the age of twelve. They went to find Him. This is parental protection.

Luke 2:42-45
When he was twelve years old, they went up to Jerusalem according to the custom of the feast, and when they had fulfilled the days, as they were returning, the boy Jesus stayed behind in Jerusalem. Joseph and his mother didn't know it, but supposing him to be in the company, they went a day's journey, and they looked for him among their relatives and acquaintances. When they didn't find him, they returned to Jerusalem, looking for him.

HOW CHRISTIANS MAY DEFEND THEMSELVES AGAINST ATTACK

They did exactly what parents should do which was to search for their child and make sure He was safe.

The second involves teaching them to protect, defend, and deliver themselves from harm.

Proverbs 1:8
My son, listen to your father's instruction, and don't forsake your mother's teaching.

Proverbs 4:17
For they eat the bread of wickedness and drink the wine of violence.

Proverbs 10:11
The mouth of the righteous is a spring of life, but violence covers the mouth of the wicked.

Proverbs 21:7
The violence of the wicked will drive them away, because they refuse to do what is right.

Proverbs 24:2
For their hearts plot violence and their lips talk about mischief.

These are just a few principles concerning violence, killing, and murder found in the Scriptures.

The third involves teaching them ways to resolve conflicts and calm anger in themselves and others to prevent violence and ultimately murder.

Proverbs 4:10-12
Listen, my son, and receive my sayings. The years of your life will be many. I have taught you in the way of wisdom. I have led you in straight paths. When you go, your steps will not be hampered. When you run, you will not stumble.

Proverbs 3:31
Don't envy the man of violence. Choose none of his ways.

Proverbs 10:6
Blessings are on the head of the righteous, but violence covers the mouth of the wicked.

Proverbs 13:2
By the fruit of his lips, a man enjoys good things, but the unfaithful crave violence.

Proverbs 16:29
A man of violence entices his neighbor, and leads him in a way that is not good.

Proverbs 26:6
One who sends a message by the hand of a fool is cutting off feet and drinking violence.

Proverbs 11:12
One who despises his neighbor is void of wisdom, but a man of understanding holds his peace.

Proverbs 12:20
Deceit is in the heart of those who plot evil, but joy comes to the promoters of peace.

Proverbs 16:7
When a man's ways please Yahweh, he makes even his enemies to be at peace with him.

Proverbs 29:9
If a wise man goes to court with a foolish man, the fool rages or scoffs, and there is no peace.

Here again, parents are to teach their children how to prevent violence, handle conflict, and seek peace.

HOW CHRISTIANS MAY DEFEND THEMSELVES AGAINST ATTACK

Parents know that this instruction will not be easy for the child to obey so they must be disciplined and trained.

Proverbs 13:24
One who spares the rod hates his son, but one who loves him is careful to discipline him.

Proverbs 22:6
Train up a child in the way he should go, and when he is old he will not depart from it.

Proverbs 22:15
Folly is bound up in the heart of a child: the rod of discipline drives it far from him.

Proverbs 29:15
The rod of correction gives wisdom, but a child left to himself causes shame to his mother.

Proverbs 29:17
Correct your son, and he will give you peace; yes, he will bring delight to your soul.

So, the training of parents becomes an important process in the prevention of bloodshed. It is also critical in the protection against violence.

As we look at the lives of David and his sons, we see David being unwilling to discipline his children and they rebelled against him. When Amnon tricked his half-sister Tamar into serving him while he pretended to be very ill, he raped her. David had allowed Tamar to serve Amnon alone when that was inappropriate for a maiden to do for any man. When her brother Absalom found out what his half-brother had done, he told Tamar he would handle it. When David discovered what happened, he did nothing.

2 Samuel 13:21-23
But when king David heard of all these things, he was very angry. Absalom spoke to Amnon neither good nor bad; for Absalom hated Amnon, because he had forced his sister Tamar. After two full years, Absalom had sheep shearers in Baal Hazor, which is beside Ephraim: and Absalom invited all the king's sons.

So, Absalom took revenge on Amnon two years later and had him killed. When David found out he banned Absalom from his palace for three years. This incited his son to overthrow him, and David had to run for his life. Absalom was killed and David mourned over his son's death.

Since David did not protect his daughter, punish Amnon for his sin, protect him from Absalom, or discipline Absalom properly, he found himself hiding in the wilderness without a kingdom. He was not following the parental paradigm God had developed to prevent that violence.

What a terrible situation everyone was in. The ultimate result was the division of David's family, David losing his kingdom to Absalom, and then Amnon and Absalom losing their lives in death. David did not take his responsibility to protect his children from harm or defend them when harm came. At the same time, Absalom should have confronted his father and asked him to take action. When David did nothing, it allowed Absalom's rage to intensify. It seems that David did not consider how Absalom or Tamar felt.

In summary, parents must first protect, defend, and deliver children from harm. The second involves teaching them to protect, defend, and deliver themselves from harm. The third involves teaching them ways to resolve conflicts and calm anger in themselves and others to prevent violence. This is an important structure put into place by God to preserve the saved and unsaved from harm.

The Oversight of Family

As families grew, they protected one another from murder and other violence. This also becomes a deterrent to attacking because people know they must contend with their families. Those families grow into clans and tribes who stuck together. These relatives provided protection from within and without.

First, we see a powerful example in the life of Abraham and his nephew Lot. In Genesis 13, God commanded Abraham to go into the land of Canaan. The Lord was giving him and his descendants this land as an inheritance. So, Abraham left Haran, sojourned through Egypt, and landed at the Negev.

By this time, he was travelling with his nephew Lot. Both were wealthy and possessed much livestock, tents, silver, gold, family, servants, and hired men. The number of animals was so large that the men tending them had already begun arguing and fighting over the land to feed them.

When Abraham considered this conflict, he realized that they could no longer stay together. He recognized that they were brothers and that was far more important than arguing and fighting over land, water, and food for their animals. In addition, it would be too dangerous to quarrel and become divided. The Canaanites and Perizzites dwelt in the land and posed a real threat to their safety. They would need protection from them. They could not afford to be battling each other.

He confronted Lot and explained these key concepts and gave him a choice of where he would want to live. If Lot went to the right, Abraham would go to the left. If Lot went to the left, he would go to the right. When Lot saw the valley of the Jordan, he chose that area. Water was everywhere, and it looked like the Garden of Eden. Abraham settled in Canaan and his nephew settled in the valley near Sodom. His uncle Abraham had taught Lot a peaceful way to resolve conflict.

Next, he would teach his nephew how relatives defend one another. When Lot, his family, and all his possessions were captured by a coalition of kings, his uncle came to the rescue.

Genesis 14:1-16
In the days of Amraphel, king of Shinar; Arioch, king of Ellasar; Chedorlaomer, king of Elam; and Tidal, king of Goiim, they made war with Bera, king of Sodom; Birsha, king of Gomorrah; Shinab, king of Admah; Shemeber, king of Zeboiim; and the king of Bela (also called Zoar)....They took all the goods of Sodom and Gomorrah, and all their food, and went their way. They took Lot, Abram's brother's son, who lived in Sodom, and his goods, and departed. One who had escaped came and told Abram, the Hebrew. At that time, he lived by the oaks of Mamre, the Amorite, brother of Eshcol and brother of Aner. They were allies of Abram. When Abram heard that his relative was taken captive, he led out his three hundred eighteen trained men, born in his house, and pursued as far as Dan. He divided himself against them by night, he and his servants, and struck them, and pursued them to Hobah, which is on the left hand of Damascus. He brought back all the goods, and also brought back his relative Lot and his goods, and the women also, and the other people.

Abraham also intervened on his behalf to rescue him from the judgment of the Lord God on Sodom and Gomorrah. When God visited him, the Lord spoke of His intentions to destroy Sodom and Gomorrah.

Genesis 18:20-22
Yahweh said, "Because the cry of Sodom and Gomorrah is great, and because their sin is very grievous, I will go down now, and see whether their deeds are as bad as the reports which have come to me. If not, I will know." The men turned from there, and went toward Sodom, but Abraham stood yet before Yahweh.

HOW CHRISTIANS MAY DEFEND THEMSELVES AGAINST ATTACK

Since Abraham knew that his nephew lived there and was righteous, he began to question God as to how many would have to live in those cities to be spared. So, Abraham begins his questioning about fifty righteous people.

Genesis 18:24
What if there are fifty righteous within the city? Will you consume and not spare the place for the fifty righteous who are in it?

He continues with the questioning until he gets to only ten righteous. As with the others, the Lord God responds with a positive answer. Of course, the Lord would not destroy the city, if there were ten righteous. This was the most important question he could ask God to protect his nephew because he had less than ten in his immediate family.

Genesis 18:32
He said, "Oh don't let the Lord be angry, and I will speak just once more. What if ten are found there?" He said, "I will not destroy it for the ten's sake."

Even though his wife was consumed for looking back, Lot and his family were spared.

Genesis 19:17
It came to pass, when they had taken them out, that he said, "Escape for your life! Don't look behind you, and don't stay anywhere in the plain. Escape to the mountains, lest you be consumed!"

Lot asked if he could go to Zoar, and it was granted for him to go there instead.

Genesis 19:21-22
He said to him, "Behold, I have granted your request concerning this thing also, that I will not overthrow the city of which you have spoken. Hurry, escape there, for I can't do anything until you get there." Therefore the name of the city was called Zoar.

Though family members would support the parents in their responsibility, in this section, we considered the most likely scenario which was family protecting, defending, and delivering family members from any harm. We have already learned that the brothers of a victim are usually the ones to defend them both from the words of God in Genesis chapter nine and His laws given to Israel concerning the manslayer.

The Protection of Governments

These families grew into clans and then towns and cities who protected one another and kept each other in check. Though Jericho was captured by Israel through a miraculous event from God, they were example of a city who protected and defended their citizens. This was common as it is today.

After Israel entered the promised land, they sent spies to search out the fortifications and protections of the first city that had to be conquered. The name of this city which would go down in history was Jericho.

Joshua 2:1-3
Joshua the son of Nun secretly sent two men out of Shittim as spies, saying, "Go, view the land, including Jericho." They went and came into the house of a prostitute whose name was Rahab, and slept there. The king of Jericho was told, "Behold, men of the children of Israel came in here tonight to spy out the land." Jericho's king sent to Rahab, saying, "Bring out the men who have come to you, who have entered into your house; for they have come to spy out all the land."

Notice, the city government took immediate action to protect its citizens. It did not leave them to face the enemy alone. It also had laws and the king thought Rahab may have broken them. Though this is obvious, it is incredibly important.

HOW CHRISTIANS MAY DEFEND THEMSELVES AGAINST ATTACK

The spies went to Rahab who had a house on the wall that surrounded the city.

Joshua 2:15
Then she let them down by a cord through the window; for her house was on the side of the wall, and she lived on the wall.

Every evening the guards of the city would shut the gate to protect the people.

Joshua 2:5
About the time of the shutting of the gate, when it was dark, the men went out. Where the men went, I don't know. Pursue them quickly. You may catch up with them.

Finally, for Joshua to take the city, he had to destroy the wall that protected it and was its greatest defense.

Joshua 6:20
So the people shouted and the priests blew the trumpets. When the people heard the sound of the trumpet, the people shouted with a great shout, and the wall fell down flat, so that the people went up into the city, every man straight in front of him, and they took the city.

The next town the Hebrews encountered was Ai.

Joshua 8:3
So Joshua arose, with all the warriors, to go up to Ai. Joshua chose thirty thousand men, the mighty men of valor, and sent them out....

Israel was defeated by them the first time because of the sin of Achan, but the second time they won the battle.

Joshua 8:14-17
When the king of Ai saw it, they hurried and rose up early, and the men of the city went out against Israel to battle, he and all his people,

at the time appointed, before the Arabah; but he didn't know that there was an ambush against him behind the city. Joshua and all Israel made as if they were beaten before them, and fled by the way of the wilderness. All the people who were in the city were called together to pursue after them. They pursued Joshua, and were drawn away from the city. There was not a man left in Ai or Bethel who didn't go out after Israel. They left the city open, and pursued Israel. The ambush arose quickly out of their place, and they ran as soon as he had stretched out his hand and entered into the city and took it. They hurried and set the city on fire.

Though Ai lost to the Israelites, the city government defended its people. The city had an army to protect and defend it.

As cities grew into region and regions into nations, laws were developed, and local police were created to enforce those laws and protect and defend citizens from each other. A national army was established in order to defend the country from others. The citizens were to submit to their laws.

In Romans 13, Paul explains that the government and its structure is God's structure for protecting its citizens.

Romans 13:3-5
For rulers are not a terror to the good work, but to the evil. Do you desire to have no fear of the authority? Do that which is good, and you will have praise from the authority, for he is a servant of God to you for good. But if you do that which is evil, be afraid, for he doesn't bear the sword in vain; for he is a servant of God, an avenger for wrath to him who does evil.... conscience' sake.

Though there are other structures God has put into place to prevent or stop violence, these are the most important. They are sufficient to establish the validity of self-defense and the defense of others.

Chapter 5

The Scriptural Understanding

We have just discussed the defense structures God has put into place to protect those who are in the direct line of the Messiah and the participants in the kingdom before and after they are saved. These structures will allow the unsaved to enjoy His blessings and preserve mankind alive for the Day of Judgment. The primary structure and the unifying factor weaved throughout the rest of these structures is self-defense and the defense of others by individuals, parents, immediate and extended families, cities, regions, and nations as they follow their consciences. These structures maintain God's principle of "blood for blood" in Genesis chapter nine. This does not teach capital punishment of the government only Why? No actual governments were established at the time. Instead, individuals, family, then clans, and larger units were to administer this principle from that day forward.

In this chapter, we will distinguish between the different kinds of killing and then define self-defense and the defense of others. We will consider the attitudes and motives that separate the two and then discuss how self-defense and the defense of others fits with other familiar passages which may on the surface appear contradictory but are consistent.

The Scriptural Distinctions in Killing

To understand this important truth, we will begin with the Ten Commandments. In Exodus 20:13, the Lord God gave Moses this commandment, "You shalt not murder." This is a general statement without any qualification. Does this mean that all killing for whatever reason and circumstances is a sin and never should be done? Or is it a general statement that is a summary truth which could be written on two stone slates?

The Nature of the Ten Commandments

The Ten Commandments are a set of statements that are meant to be a summation of God's laws. These were simple, basic statements capable of being written down on stone tablets and not black and white declarations which have no exceptions or qualifying descriptions. When we consider this, the words of Jesus in Matthew 5 come to mind. It is in this passage that the Lord Jesus expands the understanding of the sixth commandment concerning murder. Why? The Jews had taken the commandment as only physical (a black and white concept) and Jesus explained that the heart intent was an intricate part of the commandment. They were told not to commit "murder of the heart." This was not a new teaching but a qualifying description of the commandment itself. Why? As was just pointed out, the Ten Commandments aren't black and white statements but summaries or general principles.

In the same sermon, we see Jesus dealing with another of the ten commandments which is clarified by an additional description.

Matthew 5:27-28
You have heard that it was said, "You shall not commit adultery;" but I tell you that everyone who gazes at a woman to lust after her has committed adultery with her already in his heart.

Jesus explains that it has a heart component and not just a physical one. This is to point out that these were summary statements and not meant to be taken without qualification.

After the Ten Commandments were delivered, God gave additional ordinances which explained in more detail His intended meaning. This occurred on four separate occasions. These were delivered to the Jews at Mount Sinai (Exodus, Leviticus), at the completion of the Tabernacle (Numbers), at the border of Land of Promise (Deuteronomy), and after the land was conquered and divided among the twelve tribes (Joshua). These laws were repeated at critical times in their history to remind the people of God's laws with some detailed descriptions.

The Killing with Intent

So, what does the sixth commandment refer to? It refers to the killing of a human being for evil and harm. This is the key distinction that separates it from the other types of killing. Murder involves an evil intent. How was this presented?

In one passage, it is clearly stated, and, in the others, it is assumed. We know this by comparing them to the other kinds of killing in the same passages. The Lord God made a clear distinction among them. This will become obvious as our study proceeds. As a result, I have added "with evil intent" in brackets in the original text.

The first set of laws involved the murder of man for evil and harmful purposes. Here it is stated directly.

Exodus 21:14
If a man schemes and comes presumptuously on his neighbor to kill him, you shall take him from my altar, that he may die.

We can see that this law focuses on people who kill according to an evil motive and plan they have in their minds. Of course, the motive and plan could be conceived in the moment.

Here are the same laws but the motive and plan or evil intent is assumed which is important to the interpretation. I have put this assumption in brackets.

Exodus 21:12
One who strikes a man [with evil intent] so that he dies shall surely be put to death.

Leviticus 24:17
He who strikes any man [with evil intent] mortally shall surely be put to death.

Leviticus 24:21
He who kills an animal shall make it good; and he who kills a man [with evil intent] shall be put to death.

Even today, when we speak of murder, we almost always assume that we are referring to killing by a person who intended to do it. We put other kinds of killing in a different category as God does in His law.

In the next set of passages, we see instruments being used to strike someone that would obviously kill him. These would not make sense unless it was assumed that another did not have a comparable weapon. The man without the weapon would be defenseless. The man with the weapon obviously intended to kill him.

Numbers 35:16-19
But if he struck him with an instrument of iron, so that he died, he is a murderer. The murderer shall surely be put to death. If he struck him with a stone in the hand, by which a man may die, and he died, he is a murderer. The murderer shall surely be put to death. Or if he struck him with a weapon of wood in the hand, by which a man may die, and he died, he is a murderer. The murderer shall surely be put to death. The avenger of blood shall himself put the murderer to death. When he meets him, he shall put him to death.

These weapons had to be capable of killing a man. Then the evil intent is explained.

Numbers 35:20-21
If he shoved him out of hatred, or hurled something at him while lying in wait, so that he died, Or in hostility struck him with his hand, so that he died, he who struck him shall surely be put to death. He is a murderer. The avenger of blood shall put the murderer to death when he meets him.

Notice, the laws provide different motives of the murderer for evil or harm. They are because of hatred, lying in wait (a planned attack), or hostility.

Numbers 35:30-31
Whoever kills any person, the murderer shall be slain based on the testimony of witnesses; but one witness shall not testify alone against any person so that he dies. Moreover you shall take no ransom for the life of a murderer who is guilty of death. He shall surely be put to death.

The testimony of the witnesses would encompass not only the actual killing but the facts that would indicate an evil intent behind it.

We see the same indication of an evil intent described in the ordinances given in Deuteronomy by Moses again. Notice the description of the evil motive or intent that is indicated in this law.

Deuteronomy 19:11-13
But if any man hates his neighbor, lies in wait for him, rises up against him, strikes him mortally so that he dies, and he flees into one of these cities; then the elders of his city shall send and bring him there, and deliver him into the hand of the avenger of blood, that he may die. Your eye shall not pity him, but you shall purge the innocent blood from Israel that it may go well with you.

Here, Moses makes clear the intent that defines the killing of a man as murder. The murderer lied in wait and when the opportunity came, he killed the man. This shows he intended to do the man harm. This is in direct contrast to the manslayer who kills someone accidentally which will now be defined.

The Killing Without Intent

The second kind of killing of human beings was the killing of a person by mistake. This is usually referred to by the term "manslayer" to distinguish it from "murderer" in the various English Bible translations. In Israel, when one accidentally killed another, they could find sanctuary in the cities of refuge designated by the Lord to protect themselves until they could be tried, and their innocence determined by a city's elders.

The first description of the manslayer was someone who did not lie in wait to kill another.

Exodus 21:13
But if he did not lie in wait for him, but God allows it to happen; then I will appoint you a place where he shall flee (DEJ).

The manslayer did not plan the killing as a murderer would, but it just happened. This would be the killing of a human being by accident which God allowed in His sovereignty.

These next set of passages describe the act of murder using a Hebrew word that means "ignorant, unaware, in error, or unwittingly" which is translated here by "unintentionally."

Numbers 35:11
Then you shall appoint for yourselves cities to be cities of refuge for you, that the man slayer who kills any person unintentionally may flee there (DEJ).

HOW CHRISTIANS MAY DEFEND THEMSELVES AGAINST ATTACK

Joshua 20:3
That the man slayer who kills any person unintentionally or accidentally may flee there. They shall be to you for a refuge from the avenger of blood (DEJ).

Notice, the manslayer did not desire to kill the person. It was unintentional.

Joshua 20:9
These were the appointed cities for all the children of Israel, and for the alien who lives among them, that whoever kills any person unintentionally might flee there, and not die by the hand of the avenger of blood, until he stands trial before the congregation.

In the Joshua 20:3 passage, the author couples the word "unintentional" with the word translated "accidentally." This word means "without knowledge, cunning, perception, or discernment." Again, the contrast is with the murderer who is intentional in his desire to harm and the one who is not.

Numbers 35:23
Or with any stone, by which a man may die, not seeing him, and cast it on him so that he died, and he was not his enemy and not seeking his harm.

The last Hebrew term used for the "manslayer" translated "ignorantly" in the passages below is a word literally meaning "without, no, or negative." The idea would be killing "without intent, or no negative intent."

Deuteronomy 19:4
This is the...the man slayer who shall flee there...Whoever kills his neighbor ignorantly, and didn't hate him in time past (DEJ).

Joshua 20:5
If the avenger of blood pursues him, then they shall not deliver up

the man slayer into his hand; because he struck his neighbor ignorantly, and didn't hate him before (DEJ).

The manslayer did not previously hate the person he killed. There was no intention or motive for the killing as a murderer would have had.

In Numbers 35, there is a description of the killing without intent of evil or harm.

Numbers 35:22-24
But if he shoved him suddenly without hostility, or hurled on him anything without lying in wait, or with any stone, by which a man may die, not seeing him, and cast it on him so that he died, and he was not his enemy and not seeking his harm, then the congregation shall judge between the striker and the avenger of blood according to these ordinances.

Notice, there is no evil or harmful intent of the manslayer. He has no hostility, did not plan it (lying in wait), could not see him, and did it suddenly.

In the last passage, Moses provides an illustration.

Deuteronomy 19:5
As when a man goes into the forest with his neighbor to chop wood and his hand swings the ax to cut down the tree, and the head slips from the handle and hits his neighbor so that he dies — he shall flee to one of these cities and live.

It truly was accidental, and this is the distinction.

So far, we have seen two different kinds of killing. First, the killing with an evil intent which we would refer to as "murder." The second kind of killing is accidental. The person did not desire or intend to kill. It happened by accident. The third kind of killing is discussed next. When finished, we will come to discover that killing in self-defense or the defense of others are not found in these laws.

The Killing for Justice

The third kind of killing is to render justice. This would also refer to capital punishment today. In ancient times, a family would send a "blood avenger" (usually a brother) to kill the murderer. Again, this is the "brother" referred to in Genesis chapter nine.

Numbers 35:19
The avenger of blood shall himself put the murderer to death. When he meets him, he shall put him to death.

Numbers 35:21
Or in hostility struck him with his hand, so that he died, he who struck him shall surely be put to death. He is a murderer. The avenger of blood shall put the murderer to death when he meets him.

Numbers 35:24
Then the congregation shall judge between the striker and...avenger of blood according to these ordinances.

Numbers 35:25
The congregation shall deliver the man slayer out of the hand of the avenger of blood, and the congregation shall restore him to his city of refuge, where he had fled. He shall dwell therein until the death of the high priest, who was anointed with the holy oil.

Numbers 35:27
And the avenger of blood finds him outside of the border of his city of refuge, and the avenger of blood kills the man slayer, he shall not be guilty of blood.

Deuteronomy 19:6
Otherwise, the avenger of blood might pursue the man slayer while hot anger is in his heart and overtake him, because the way is long, and strike him mortally, even though he was not worthy of death, because he didn't hate him in time past.

Deuteronomy 19:12
Then the elders of his city shall send and bring him there and deliver him into the hand of the avenger of blood, that he may die.

Joshua 20:3
That the manslayer...kills...person accidentally or unintentionally may flee there. They shall be to you for a refuge from the avenger of blood.

Joshua 20:5
If the avenger of blood pursues him, then they shall not deliver up the manslayer into his hand...he struck... neighbor unintentionally, and didn't hate him before.

Joshua 20:9
These were the appointed cities for all the children of Israel, and for the alien who lives among them, that whoever kills any person unintentionally might flee there, and not die by the hand of the avenger of blood, until he stands trial before the congregation.

So, the brother of the murdered person would be designated by the family to administer justice by killing the murderer. This would satisfy God's ordinance of "an eye for an eye, and a tooth for a tooth, and a life for a life" and "blood for blood."

The determination of the guilt or innocence of a person that killed, if that were necessary, would be made in the cities of refuge.

Numbers 35:6
The cities which you shall give to the Levites, they shall be the six

cities of refuge, which you shall give for the man slayer to flee to. Besides them you shall give forty-two cities.

Numbers 35:13
The cities which you shall give shall be for you six cities of refuge. You shall give three cities beyond the Jordan...cities of refuge.

Joshua 20:2
Speak to the children of Israel, saying, "Assign the cities of refuge, of which I spoke to you by Moses."

Joshua 21:27
They gave to the children of Gershon, of the families of the Levites, out of the half-tribe of Manasseh Golan in Bashan with its pasture lands, the city of refuge for the man slayer, and Be Eshterah with its pasture lands: two cities.

Joshua 21:32
Out of the tribe of Naphtali, Kedesh in Galilee with its pasture lands, the city of refuge for the man slayer, Hammothdor with its pasture lands, and Kartan with its pasture lands: three cities.

These cities would protect the manslayer from the avenger of blood, but they had to remain in one of the cities until the death of the high priest. If they did not, they could be killed by the manslayer.

Numbers 35:11
Then you shall appoint for yourselves cities to be cities of refuge for you...man slayer who kills any person unwittingly may flee there.

Numbers 35:12
The cities shall be for your refuge from the avenger, that the man slayer not die until he stands before the congregation for judgment.

Numbers 35:15
These six cities shall be refuge for the children of Israel, for the

stranger, and for the foreigner living among them, that everyone who kills any person unwittingly may flee there.

If it were not clear whether the killer was a murderer or a manslayer, the elders of the city of refuge would put him on trial. If he was found guilty of murder, he was to be cast out of the city and into the hands of the blood avenger. If he was innocent, he was to be protected.

Finally, it is important to note self-defense and the defense of others is not mentioned or referred to in these passages. Why? It was not murder or manslaying. In fact, immediately after the divine laws were given in Deuteronomy 19, the Lord provides His rules for battle and war which encompasses self-defense and the defense of others.

Deuteronomy 20:1-6
When you go out to battle against your enemies, and see horses, chariots, and a people more numerous than you, you shall not be afraid of them; for Yahweh your God is with you, who brought you up out of the land of Egypt. It shall be, when you draw near to the battle, that the priest shall approach and speak to the people, and shall tell them, "Hear, Israel, you draw near today to battle against your enemies. Don't let your heart faint! Don't be afraid, nor tremble, neither be scared of them; for Yahweh your God is he who goes with you, to fight for you against your enemies, to save you." The officers shall speak to the people, saying, "What man is there who has built a new house, and has not dedicated it? Let him go and return to his house, lest he die in the battle, and another man dedicate it. What man is there who has planted a vineyard, and has not used its fruit? Let him go and return to his house, lest he die in the battle, and another man use its fruit.

Here self-defense and the defense of others is in view and not listed directly in the laws. As we can so clearly see that as they defended themselves and the nation from enemies, God Himself would protect and defend them also.

The Killing to Protect

The fourth kind of killing is to protect the innocent (the victim or the ones protecting the victim). This is called "self-defense" when it is to be done for oneself and the defense of others when it refers to more than oneself. Rather than define self-defense and the defense of others, the Holy Scriptures simply assume it.

The Scriptural Description of Defense

So, what exactly is self-defense and the defense of others? What distinguishes self-defense from a fight, an assault, or even war? The answer once again is assumed. It is never defined but constantly described. As we study the many actions of defense by God and his people, we will discover that it is the act of stopping violence upon us and ending the future threat of it, if necessary.

The Defense Defined

In man-to-man combat, if someone is attempting to take our lives and will not stop unless he is killed then we must take his. This happened with David facing Goliath. When Goliath made his challenge, it involved a battle to the death.

1 Samuel 17:8-10
He stood and cried to the armies of Israel, and said to them, "Why have you come out to set your battle in array? Am I not a Philistine, and you servants to Saul? Choose a man for yourselves, and let him come down to me. If he is able to fight with me and kill me, then will we be your servants; but if I prevail against him and kill him, then you will be our servants and serve us." The Philistine said, "I defy

the armies of Israel today! Give me a man, that we may fight together!" Goliath would not have stopped, he had to be killed.

When Goliath saw that David would be his adversary, he threatened his life.

1 Samuel 17:43-44
The Philistine said to David, "Am I a dog, that you come to me with sticks?" The Philistine cursed David by his gods. The Philistine said to David, "Come to me, and I will give your flesh to the birds of the sky and to the animals of the field."

When God gave Moses His law concerning theft, it was clear that unwarranted murder was unacceptable. The law has three parts. The first, deals with a theft breaking into a home in the dark.

Exodus 22:2
If the thief is found breaking in, and is struck so that he dies, there shall be no guilt of bloodshed for him.

The idea conveyed here is the inability of the homeowner to identify the thief and the weapons he may be using because it is dark. if there is a struggle and most likely there will be, the homeowner is not guilty of breaking God's law if he kills him. Obviously, it does not mean anytime anyone breaks in, we have a free pass to kill the person. It refers to the possibility occurring by a reasonable person where one cannot see.

The second part addresses theft during the day. Because it is light out, the person sees the burglar and kills him anyway. He is guilty.

Exodus 22:3
If the sun has risen on him, he is guilty of bloodshed. He shall make restitution. If he has nothing, then he shall be sold for his theft.

HOW CHRISTIANS MAY DEFEND THEMSELVES AGAINST ATTACK

It cannot be self-defense because that is already dealt with. It must refer to killing the robber without the necessity.

Exodus 22:4
If the stolen property is found in his hand alive, whether it is ox, donkey, or sheep, he shall pay double.

Instead, it is assumed, he will be caught and have to pay a double payment in restitution.

The action of self-defense and the defense of others has the main purpose of stopping violence and then ending a threat.

The Defense Illustrated

In the Old Testament, we are given many illustrations and examples of self-defense and the defense of others. These are always seen as a normal part of life without explanation.

When Nehemiah went back to the promised land from his captivity in Babylon, he encountered many adversaries. As he and his people built the city wall, they prepared to defend themselves. First, he put families into groups. Each family carried weapons and defended a particular area where their family members were working.

Nehemiah 4:13
Therefore I set guards in the lowest parts of the space behind the wall, in the open places. I set the people by family groups with their swords, their spears, and their bows.

They expected the Lord's help in this endeavor.

Nehemiah 4:14
I looked, and rose up, and said to the nobles, to the rulers, and to the

rest of the people, "Don't be afraid of them! Remember the Lord, who is great and awesome, and fight for your brothers, your sons, your daughters, your wives, and your houses."

Those who were able to carry a weapon in one hand and work in the other did so. If they could not do this, they carried weapons at the side.

Nehemiah 14:15-18
When our enemies heard that it was known to us, and God had brought their counsel to nothing, all of us returned to the wall, everyone to his work. From that time forth, half of my servants did the work, and half of them held the spears, the shields, the bows, and the coats of mail; and the rulers were behind all the house of Judah. Those who built the wall, and those who bore burdens loaded themselves; everyone with one of his hands did the work, and with the other held his weapon. Among the builders, everyone wore his sword at his side, and so built. He who sounded the trumpet was by me.

These were not soldiers in Israel's army but regular people who were attempting to rebuild their nation and were being opposed.

Notice, there is no discussion or resistance to the idea that they should defend themselves.

Nehemiah 4:19-20
I said to the nobles, and to the rulers and to the rest of the people, "The work is great and large, and we are separated on the wall, far from one another. Wherever you hear the sound of the trumpet, rally there to us. Our God will fight for us."

Once again, as they defended themselves, they trusted that God would be with them and protect them. They expected for God to guide them to fight well.

HOW CHRISTIANS MAY DEFEND THEMSELVES AGAINST ATTACK

They carried their weapons everywhere and were always ready for to make a physical defense.

Nehemiah 4:21-23
So we did the work. Half of the people held the spears from the rising of the morning until the stars appeared. Likewise at the same time I said to the people, "Let everyone with his servant lodge within Jerusalem, that in the night they may be a guard to us, and may labor in the day." So neither I, nor my brothers, nor my servants, nor the men of the guard who followed me, none of us took off our clothes. Everyone took his weapon to the water.

This was much like the "Old West" when men carried guns everywhere they went. In many places, people still do (if the law allows it).

When David's son Absalom had taken the throne from him illegally, David had to run for his life. In the wilderness of Judea, he contemplated the demise of his enemies.

Psalm 63:9-11
But those who seek my soul, to destroy it, Shall go into the lower parts of the earth. They shall be given over to the power of the sword. They shall be jackal food. But the king shall rejoice in God. Everyone who swears by him will praise him, For the mouth of those who speak lies shall be silenced.

David and his men were innocent and would have to defend themselves from Absalom and his army.

David expected that those who sought to kill him would end up dead and in the chambers of hell. There would be a battle and many swords would be drawn. His enemies would be left in the open field dead and become food for jackals. His enemies would be silenced and those who were loyal to him, the king, would rejoice in their victory in God.

David always saw God as His defender even though he defended himself. He knew that this was acceptable to His God. In Psalm 18, he sings of God's protection after he had vanquished all his enemies, especially Saul.

Psalm 18:1-5
I love you, Yahweh, my strength. Yahweh is my rock, my fortress, and my deliverer; my God, my rock, in whom I take refuge; my shield, and the horn of my salvation, my high tower. I call on Yahweh, who is worthy to be praised;...I am saved from my enemies. The cords of death surrounded me. The floods of ungodliness made me afraid. The cords of Sheol were around me. The snares of death came on me. In my distress I called on Yahweh, and cried to my God. He heard my voice out of his temple. My cry before him came into his ears.

David saw the Lord as His physical protector when he had to defend himself. These were enemies who desired nothing less than to kill him.

Psalm 18:17-19
He delivered me from my strong enemy, from those who hated me; for they were too mighty for me. They came on me in the day of my calamity, but Yahweh was my support. He brought me out also into a large place. He delivered me, because he delighted in me.

The King was overwhelmed but God worked in mighty ways. How? He did not continuously work miracles, instead, He worked as David fought.

King David felt that God had taught him how to bear arms, use them, and defend himself.

Psalm 18:34-40
He teaches my hands to war, so that my arms bend a bow of bronze. You have also given me the shield of your salvation. Your right hand sustains me. Your gentleness has made me great. You have enlarged

HOW CHRISTIANS MAY DEFEND THEMSELVES AGAINST ATTACK

my steps...My feet have not slipped. I will pursue my enemies, and overtake them. I won't turn away until they are consumed. I will strike them through, so that they will not be able to rise. They shall fall under my feet. For you have armed me with strength to the battle. You have subdued under me those who rose up against me. You have also made my enemies turn their backs to me, that I might cut off those who hate me.

Now, he would be relentless in his pursuit to kill all of them. Why? He knew God would protect him.

As a result, Lord God deserved to be praised for His great and powerful deliverance.

Psalm 18:46-50
Yahweh lives! Blessed be my rock. Exalted be the God of my salvation, even the God who executes vengeance for me, and subdues peoples under me. He rescues me from my enemies. Yes, you lift me up above those who rise up against me. You deliver me from the violent man. Therefore I will give thanks to you, Yahweh, among the nations, and will sing praises to your name. He gives...deliverance to his king, and shows loving kindness to his anointed, to David and to his offspring, forever more.

The Lord's protection as David protected himself was to be exalted.

David would be referring to the enemies that wanted to kill him. This included Saul before David became king as well as his many battles as king. Notice, he felt that the Lord God had protected him as he defended himself both as a commoner and as the king of Israel. The enemies that David is referring to are the ones who sought to kill him not those he disliked.

When his nephew Lot was captured by a coalition of kings who desired to conquer Sodom and Gomorrah, Abraham, his uncle, went, fought them, and rescued him. Afterward, he plundered the kings. When this was over, he gave an offering to Melchizedek.

Genesis 14:13-16
One who had escaped came and told Abram, the Hebrew. At that time, he lived by the oaks of Mamre, the Amorite, brother of Eshcol and brother of Aner. They were allies of Abram. When Abram heard that his relative was taken captive, he led out his three hundred eighteen trained men, born in his house, and pursued as far as Dan. He divided himself against them by night, he and his servants, and struck them, and pursued them to Hobah, which is on the left hand of Damascus. He brought back all the goods, and also brought back his relative Lot and his goods, and the women also, and the other people.

Then, Melchizedek came out to bless Abraham for what he had done. This is critical because this king is a type of Christ and His actions are God's verification.

Genesis 14:17-19
The king of Sodom went out to meet him after his return from the slaughter of Chedorlaomer and the kings who were with him, at the valley of Shaveh (that is, the King's Valley). Melchizedek king of Salem brought out bread and wine. He was priest of God Most High. He blessed him, and said, "Blessed be Abram of God Most High, possessor of heaven and earth.

Notice, the comments of the author of Hebrews concerning this same event.

Hebrews 7:1-2
For this Melchizedek, king of Salem, priest of God Most High, who met Abraham returning from the slaughter of the kings and blessed him, to whom also Abraham divided a tenth part of all (being first, by interpretation, "king of righteousness", and then also "king of Salem", which means "king of peace."

HOW CHRISTIANS MAY DEFEND THEMSELVES AGAINST ATTACK

Here, Abraham is mentioned as slaughtering the kings. Why would he speak this way of what Abraham had done if his defense of his nephew was wrong? Why would he come out to bless him in the name of God? The reason is that his defense was righteous and just.

This so important. We must understand that people of the Bible, God's people, assumed that self-defense or even the defense of others (especially family members) was a holy act (Genesis 9) and still is.

The Defense Explained

Here is another critical consideration in our understanding of defense. The defense of ourselves and others entails using enough force as necessary to stop the harm to us or others. It does not mean only to kill or be killed. This defense does not include the fact that every single time a person is threatened with being killed, he has the right and obligation to kill the other person. He does not. Here are some of the reasons for this statement.

The Implication of God's Accountability

This first reason takes us back to Genesis chapter nine. As God laid out his new rule that men could hunt animals for food, He speaks of holding both accountable for the killing. Though we have looked at this passage before, let's view it from the perspective of accountability to God.

Genesis 9:5
I will surely require accounting for your life's blood. At the hand of every animal I will require it. At the hand of man, even at the hand of every man's brother, I will require the life of man.

Here, God states that life is in the blood. If blood is shed by taking a life (killing) then God will hold us accountable. For what will He hold us accountable? Obviously, it is whether killing was necessary in the situation. If killing occurs, God will hold accountable both parties and will discern who is responsible and whether it was necessary to do it. If a wicked man attacks a person and the person defends himself by killing the attacker. God will hold accountable the killer for attempting to kill the person and the victim for killing him.

If the brother or other family member comes to intervene in the victim's behalf and kills the one attempting to murder the victim, God will hold the brother accountable. If the brother of the one killed comes to administer justice as a manslayer, he will be held accountable for the shedding of the blood of the victim. The accountability will involve the answers to the questions, "Was it necessary to kill the person and was it just?

Then in verse 6, God explains how he will administer his justice when he decides who is guilty.

Genesis 6:6
Whoever sheds man's blood, his blood will be shed by man, for God made man in his own image.

Man will administer God's justice. If blood is shed by man, then another man will shed his blood. It will be done by the man himself who is the victim in self-defense or the brother of the man who will recompense the killing of his innocent brother by killing the man (now replaced by the government if one is in place).

If the victim could have stopped the man in a different way that was at his disposal and skill level and turn him over to authorities, he should do this instead. What if he killed the attacker out of an evil motive like anger or revenge, then God will hold him accountable. How did He do this?

In ancient times when no government was established or it was the law, the manslayer brother or other family member would come to kill him. When there is a government in place, the officials would do it. Even with the manslayer in Israel, the elders would decide to shelter him from the brother if he were innocent. If guilty, then he would be sent out of the city to face his punishment. This is how the Lord God holds men accountable and administers His justice by other men. So, the necessity of killing a man is implicit in Genesis chapter nine.

We will discover in our study of Peter and the sword that the apostle swung it at the Lord's arrest and Jesus stopped him. It was not because they were wrong in their desire and actions to defend Jesus, but instead they would have shed innocent blood which was their own because they were outnumbered and were already released to leave. Also, no angels had been sent to defend Him because it was His time to die. We will discover in another chapter that these truths just discussed fit perfectly with the words and actions of the disciples and the Lord at His arrest.

The Inclination of the Conscience

Second, our consciences demand it. If we see someone kill another in self-defense, the first question that it always asked is "Did he have to kill him to stop him?" We do this because we know intuitively that killing is a last resort. How do we know this? We just do because our consciences tell us this is just and right. It also tells us that if we could stop him without killing him that would be better. Why would we even have to argue this point, it is obvious to any reasonable person. In war, why do we take captives? We do it to preserve life.

The Investigation of the Government

Though the role of the governmental authorities in self-defense will be discussed at length in its own chapter, we will merely touch on it here. In 1 Peter 2, Peter explains our role and theirs.

1 Peter 2:13-15
Therefore subject yourselves to every ordinance of man for the Lord's sake: whether to the king, as supreme; or to governors, as sent by him for vengeance on evildoers and for praise to those who do well. For this is the will of God, that by well-doing you should put to silence the ignorance of foolish men.

Paul says that we are to submit to governments. Government officials, police, and others, whether they be of republics or monarchies, will still ask the same questions as stated above, "Did he have to kill him to stop him?" Judgment is usually rendered in the same form based on whether the person had to kill him or not. If he did, it would be self-defense. If he could have kept him alive, it would be considered self-defense once he had stopped the attacker and then murder when he continued to harm him unto death. It is obvious that governments made of men with consciences follow them.

The Indication of the Law

A careful examination of God's laws also brings us to this same conclusion. In the Old Testament, God's laws were given with a critical standard. Justice was to be administered with an equivalent or equal retribution. This was called "an eye for an eye and a tooth for a tooth."

Exodus 21:22-25
If men fight and hurt a pregnant woman so that she gives birth

HOW CHRISTIANS MAY DEFEND THEMSELVES AGAINST ATTACK

prematurely, and yet no harm...fined as much as the...husband demands and the judges allow. But if any harm...you must take life for life, eye for eye, tooth for tooth, hand for hand, foot for foot, burning for burning, wound for wound, and bruise for bruise.

Leviticus 24:17-20
He who strikes any man mortally shall surely be put to death. He who strikes an animal mortally shall make it good, life for life. If anyone injures his neighbor, it shall be done to him as he has done: fracture for fracture, eye for eye, tooth for tooth. It shall be done to him as he has injured someone.

Deuteronomy 19:20-21
Those who remain shall hear, and fear, and will never again commit any such evil among you. Your eyes shall not pity: life for life, eye for eye, tooth for tooth, hand for hand, foot for foot.

Sometimes, the consequences did not have to be exactly the same but of equal significance. Here the servant was freed rather than the master being maimed equally.

Exodus 21:26-27
If a man strikes his servant's eye, or his maid's eye, and destroys it, he shall let him go free for his eye's sake. If he strikes out his male servant's tooth, or his female servant's tooth, he shall let the servant go free for his tooth's sake.

God's justice demands equal retribution. Someone who attempts to kill us deserves the equal force in return. We stop them and, if necessary, kill them to do it. This is also an "eye for an eye and a tooth for a tooth" as God's law states.

These points indicate that one should only defend himself with the equal force that one brings upon them in order to stop them. If one is attempting to kill someone that person should use the force equal to stopping him. If he can only stop him by killing him then this is just. If he attempts to stop him and out of hatred, anger, or revenge decides to kill him, then this would be murder. Of course, these motives would only come into play if he could have stopped short of killing him.

One would expect that in the heat of the moment, some of these feelings will emerge. Yet, we would expect someone to have enough self-control to use just enough to stop them if possible. Sometimes, the skill level might not allow this to happen. Someone who has skill with guns may be able to shoot the person in the leg or shoulder, but an unskilled person may not. The skilled person may be more accountable for a killing than the unskilled. This is one of the reasons for governments. They must determine guilt.

This is what happened with David and Goliath. David had to kill Goliath because the giant told him that he would kill him and there would no other way of stopping him. In the case of Nehemiah, we would expect Nehemiah to have told the people to fight for their lives. if they were attacked. If some remained alive, then they would be taken captive, and their fates would have to be decided. Most likely, Nehemiah would have consulted with Cyrus, the King of Persia by letter who had sent him back to his land.

In the case of David's loss of his throne to his son Absalom, he would have to fight in battle, take captives, and decide their fate, according to Israel's law. Often, the rulers would be killed either in battle or taken in captivity to be killed. This was done because they instigated the war and would need to be permanently stopped because they would rise again to battle them. This would prevent other armies from attacking.

After Joshua issued warnings to the cities he was going to attack, the people of Gibeon surrendered and made a treaty with Israel. When other kings in the area heard what Gibeon had done, five of them came up against Gibeon. In Joshua 10, he records what happened.

Joshua 10:5-8
Therefore the five kings of the Amorites, the king of Jerusalem, the king of Hebron, the king of Jarmuth, the king of Lachish, and the king of Eglon, gathered themselves together and went up, they and all their armies, and encamped against Gibeon, and made war against it. The men of Gibeon sent to Joshua at the camp at Gilgal, saying, "Don't abandon your servants! Come up to us quickly and save us! Help us; for all the kings of the Amorites that dwell in the hill country have gathered together against us." So Joshua went up from Gilgal, he, and the whole army with him, including all the mighty men of valor. Yahweh said to Joshua, "Don't fear them, for I have delivered them into your hands. Not a man of them will stand before you."

Joshua won the battle and captured the five kings.

Joshua 10:26-27
Afterward Joshua struck them, put them to death, and hanged them on five trees. They were hanging on the trees until the evening. At the time of the going down of the sun, Joshua commanded, and they took them down off the trees, and threw them into the cave in which they had hidden themselves, and laid great stones on the mouth of the cave, which remain to this very day.

Why did Joshua have to kill all five of the kings? First, to stop them from attacking again. Losing the ruler stops the people who are following him. Second, he wanted to prevent other nations from attacking them once they saw what happened.

These are the two reasons that Abraham had to slay the kings who took Lot, his family, and possessions. They had come against the nations without provocation and would do it again and again. So, they had to pay the price of retribution. The only other way to stop them would be to annihilate the entire army and slaughter all the people. It would be against God's laws and impossible to do.

This is the reason that God gave specific commands to His people as they conquered the promised land. Remember, in Deuteronomy 20, God told His people to send a message before battle to allow the people to surrender so innocent blood would not be shed. We saw that Jericho and others were given a chance to surrender for this very reason.

Deuteronomy 20:10-15
When you draw near to a city to fight against it, then proclaim peace to it. It shall be, if it gives you answer of peace and opens to you, then it shall be that all the people who are found therein shall become forced laborers to you, and shall serve you. If it will make no peace with you, but will make war against you, then you shall besiege it. When Yahweh your God delivers it into your hand, you shall strike every male of it with the edge of the sword; but the women, the little ones, the livestock, and all that is in the city, even all its plunder, you shall take for plunder for yourself. You may use the plunder of your enemies, which Yahweh your God has given you. Thus you shall do to all the cities which are very far off from you, which are not of the cities of these nations.

Notice, the truth of retribution we just studied primarily demands that a murderer be killed. This is "eye for an eye" and "blood for blood." The concept of a murderer (who kills a man for evil motives) being placed in a prison to be fed, clothed, and housed for the rest of his life supported by the people and the victims themselves is unbiblical.

So, self-defense or the defense of others primarily deals with responding to violence with the same force to stop the violence as used against us. If killing is not necessary to stop the violence, then it should not be done. There are exceptions when it comes to this truth. It is important to remind us that we have already discovered that putting murderers to death, will stop their violence and may deter others doing the same. Though some may disagree, this is God's law.

The Scriptural Parameters of Defense

Many people conceive of self-defense based on its possible abuses rather than what it is. They mix up the thoughts and intents of the heart with the actions that need to be taken to defend oneself from harm. The reasoning goes like this: if you defend yourself, then you are taking revenge, retaliating, hating, and lashing out in anger. Therefore, all self-defense of any kind is wrong. Yet, self-defense in the Bible has nothing to do with these motives. Self-defense has everything to do with actions which are preventing and stopping people from harming us or others. Defense come from love and concern.

One of the issues that arises when people speak of self-defense is the idea that this is retaliation or revenge. It is not, rather it is the administration of justice to those who want to harm us of others. It should not be done out of anger, rage, retaliation, or revenge but the preservation of life. Again, in the heat of the moment those feelings may come but must be resisted in order to administer the appropriate justice.

The Defense Without Revenge

Our English word "revenge" has several meanings. The one that immediately comes to mind is retaliating for an evil act out of anger and bitterness in order to get even. This is what usually comes to mind when this English word is read, but the terms in both Hebrew and Greek do not mean this. They only portray the sense of justice and a just act.

In Romans 12, Paul speaks of God's desire to administer justice.

Romans 12:19
Don't seek revenge yourselves, beloved, but give place to God's wrath. For it is written, "Vengeance belongs to me; I will repay, says the Lord."

The Greek terms translated "revenge" and "vengeance" come from the same word which refers to administering justice. Therefore, the translation should be, "Do not seek justice for yourselves but allow God to administer the justice.

This makes us think that God will do this directly, but this is not what Paul means because he immediately moves into one of God's structures for administering His justice which are governing authorities.

Romans 13:1
Let every soul be in subjection to the higher authorities, for there is no authority except from God, and those who exist are ordained by God.

So, Paul is explaining that we are not to administer what we would consider "vigilante Justice" but allow the Lord God to administer His justice through His structures.

He is not saying "Do not seek getting even with people because God will get even with people." Nor is He saying, "Do not get even with people because God will administer justice." What is in view here is the wrong that is done to us that the authorities should handle or are not serious enough to even notify them.

We know this perspective is correct because of the words in the passage just before it.

HOW CHRISTIANS MAY DEFEND THEMSELVES AGAINST ATTACK

Romans 12:17-18
Repay no one evil for evil. Respect what is honorable in the sight of all men. If it is possible, as much as it is up to you, be at peace with all men.

Paul is stating that Christians should seek peace with all men as much as possible. One of those ways is to not repay evil for evil. We should not become "mini-authorities" going after every person who annoys or transgresses us. We should let the higher authorities take care of it more important issues and let the others go. Every transgression against us does not need to be met with a similar transgression against them.

Also, we should show respect to what is respected among all people. Since we are believers and citizens of heaven, it is easy for us to reject things unbelievers honor such as certain celebrations or customs and practices, but instead we should honor them. This causes peace not disharmony.

After his admonition to not run around administering vigilante justice to everyone that transgresses us, he provides a different reaction. This response is for those transgressions that are too small to demand self-defense.

Romans 12:20-21
Therefore "If your enemy is hungry, feed him. If he is thirsty, give him a drink; for in doing so, you will heap coals of fire on his head." Don't be overcome by evil, but overcome evil with good.

So, we cannot allow the transgressions of others toward us, however small or large, overcome us so that we begin to do evil to them and destroy the peace we have.

How does this relate to self-defense? Protecting ourselves or others from physical harm is not in view here. If it were, then it would be a part of God's "vengeance is mine" because it is one of structures that is set into place for administering His justice. Also, the governing authorities would allow the defense of oneself and others. The idea that we should not stop anyone from harming ourselves or others, whether for our faith or not, is not in view in this passage. In fact, it is not taught anywhere in the Scriptures. What is in view would be that moment self-defense stops the person and rather than turn him over to the authorities, we kill him instead. We stopped which was all that was necessary, but we took the unneeded final step which was a vigilante justice which did not allow the authorities to do their God-given role also. This is wrong.

In his letter to the Thessalonians, Paul again asserts that Christians should not return evil for evil.

1 Thessalonians 5:15
See that no one returns evil for evil to anyone, but always follow after that which is good, for one another, and for all.

Then he states that we should seek their good instead. As we will soon see, seeking the good of others not only means protecting others from harm but stopping those who are attempting to harm them. This is for their good also.

In Peter's first letter, the apostle discusses this same critical truth.

1 Peter 3:8-9
Finally, all of you be like-minded, compassionate, loving as brothers, tenderhearted, courteous, not rendering evil for evil, or insult for insult; but instead blessing, knowing that you were called to this, that you may inherit a blessing. For, "He who would love life and see good days, let him keep his tongue from evil and his lips from speaking deceit. Let him turn away from evil and do good. Let him seek peace and pursue it."

HOW CHRISTIANS MAY DEFEND THEMSELVES AGAINST ATTACK

As Christians we are not to be retaliating and seeking revenge for every single word or deed against us. What better way to show compassionate, love, and tenderheartedness, than to protect others from harm?

The Defense Without Anger

Some will say that self-defense is wrong because anger is involved but it should not be. If one has taken martial arts, he learns very quickly that anger gets in the way of making clear decisions as to what actions must be taken when defending oneself. This is true in self-defense and defending others also. Of course, anger will arise as we are defending ourselves or others because we care ourselves and others, but we must at all times get control of it and remain focused and calm.

Therefore, if we defend ourselves or others from physical violence, it should not be done out of anger. It is anger which will push us beyond the stopping of violence (defense) to the next level whatever that may be. Certainly, it could push us to murder the person when the force we used subdued him.

In Psalm 37, the writer explains what happens when anger is allowed to take control of one's mind and heart.

Psalm 37:8-9
Refrain from anger and turn from wrath; do not fret — it leads only to evil. For those who are evil will be destroyed, but those who hope in the Lord will inherit the land.

As we defend ourselves, we cannot allow anger to get control of us, because it will drive us beyond defense to murder.

Anger is one of the only emotions that God's children are not allowed to express. Paul commands this.

Ephesians 4:31
Let all bitterness, wrath, anger, outcry, and slander, be put away from you, with all malice.

Colossians 3:8
But now you also put them all away: anger, wrath, malice, slander, and shameful speaking out of your mouth.

We must remove our anger and wrath. The first word refers to a general anger, and the second to quick-tempered wrath.

Of course, the question arises, "What about feelings of anger, are they sinful?"

In Ephesians 4:26-27, Paul answers the question.

Ephesians 4:26-27
Be angry, and don't sin. Don't let the sun go down on your wrath, and don't give place to the devil.

The Greek word translated "be angry" is the standard word for general anger. Let's take a moment for a short Greek grammar lesson. The verb "be angry" is in the present passive imperative tense.

It conveys three crucial meanings. First, the verb "be angry" is in the "imperative." This means that Paul is giving all a command. Second, this verb is in the present tense which indicates continuous action in present time. This means that the anger does not just arise and leave as fast as it came, it could stay awhile. Third, it is in the passive voice which indicates that it has been instigated by an outside source. Something from outside the person is prompting the inward feeling. This anger is inside of us, but someone or something is provoking or stirring it up whether that is the intention or not. It comes upon us without our volition.

HOW CHRISTIANS MAY DEFEND THEMSELVES AGAINST ATTACK

Of course, if someone is attempting to harm us or those we love, anger may arise and burn inside us. We must put it away or keep it at bay as we respond in self-defense. Otherwise, we may go beyond "stopping the person" to the evil that may come by allowing our anger to reign inside us.

If the feelings of anger are aroused, this is not the sin. The sin is the manifestation of the feeling of anger in thoughts, words, and deeds that is sin. This is why Paul says, "And do not sin." In the second half of the verse, Paul adds, "Don't let the sun go down on your wrath." This word "wrath" is a different word than the first one. The Greek word translated "wrath" here emphasizes the provoking of the anger. The provocation itself is in view. So, Paul is essentially saying this, "Do not let the sun go down on the provocation of that anger."

Whatever instigated the anger must be dealt with, if at all possible, by sunset. Can we find a peaceful means to resolving a conflict rather than violence? This might entail a warning to someone who wants to bring harm, "I do not want this to become violent, but if it does, I will defend myself and _____." Or "Why don't we take a moment and talk about the situation, rather than becoming violent?"

At the very least, some action must be taken to resolve the issue by sunset. This is the intent of Paul's words. It may take longer than a day, but we should get started. This cannot always happen because we may be unable to let the anger go long enough to really discuss it. So, the next best approach is to set up a time to resolve the issue.

In Psalm 4:4, David provides the answer. In this dramatic psalm, David is angry. Many opponents have risen against him, and he cries out to the Lord in prayer. As he describes his anguish, he turns his attention to his future readers and explains what to do when one of God's people is angry.

Psalm 4:4
Tremble, and do not sin; meditate upon your bed, and be still. Selah

Here David speaks of trembling in anger because his enemies are spreading lies about him. He is so angry that his whole body is trembling. When this feeling begins to build, what do we do with it?

First, we go to our bed. Though this may sound strange with careful consideration, it makes perfect sense. They lived in a Bedouin world of tents. Like our bedrooms of today, the room with the "bed" would be separate from the other rooms by a covering. This would be the only place someone could be alone. He does not mean to literally go to our beds but to remove ourselves from the situation which is provoking the anger. We might call it today taking a "time out." We must leave the scene of the crime, so to speak. Our bed is a quiet spot away from the provocation.

It fits perfectly with Paul's injunction to "put it or take it away." We literally take the ball of fiery anger away from the situation to a restful place. The Hebrew word translated "bed" can also mean "lying down." This word conveys the idea of resting and relaxing. So, while this talking is going on, we are resting. Now, in the midst of a confrontation, we should leave. If we cannot, then we must take a moment to go within and compose ourselves.

Second, we must "meditate." This is not the concept of meditation we have today. The Hebrew word literally means "speak or talk." Who are we speaking to? We are talking the situation over with God through prayer and the Word. We are dealing with our anger, battling it within, and recognizing that to express our anger is wrong and will not glorify God.

During this critical time, we may pray for wisdom.

HOW CHRISTIANS MAY DEFEND THEMSELVES AGAINST ATTACK

James 1:5
But if any of you lacks wisdom, let him ask of God, who gives to all liberally and without reproach, and it will be given to him.

We should search for solutions to the issue making us angry. It is through these that we are able to subdue our anger and renew a biblical perspective. If this anger is due to a potential violent confrontation, we should review the principles of self-defense we are currently discussing.

Psalm 119:50
This is my comfort in my affliction, for your word has revived me.

During this time, we should be confessing our sins, forgiving the person who made us angry, and figuring out the best way to respond when we leave the time out.

While we are involved in this process, David explains the final step, "be still." Stop everything else. All our thoughts, words, and actions come to a halt. Our body stops. We stop and take the necessary time to process the situation in our minds. He is essentially saying, "Calm down." Anger must never be allowed to run rampant in our conflicts. This may not be possible before self-defense except for a deep breath.

In summary, we have now discovered that self-defense, the defense of those we love, and the innocent are clearly distinguishable from killing intentionally, accidentally, and for justice.

DEFENDING YOUR LIFE

Chapter 6

The Divine Expression

Now, we must return to the subject of self-defense and the defense of others being an expression of God's nature, power, and attributes. Throughout biblical history, we see God either defending His people from harm or lifting His protection due to sin. He defended His people by promising His protection and then delivering it miraculously, angelically, or through Israel's army. When Israel departed from His ways, He sent armies against them and lifted His protection.

As we discovered in a previous chapter, if God is a God of self-defense and defending others, then we should be people who defend ourselves and others from harm by acting like Him. This is His way of preserving mankind from murder and we must do the same as His instruments.

The Divine Promise

In the Old Testament, the Lord God promised to defend His people and give them victory over all nations. Then, he fulfilled that promise by defending them. After Israel was set free by the Lord from their captivity, Moses led the people from Egypt, through the wilderness, and to the edge of the promised land.

All during this time God promised to defend His people and then He did this very thing. Here are some examples of those promises and fulfillments.

The Defeat of The Canaanites Promised

When the Hebrew people encountered the Canaanites, God promised to defend them.

Numbers 21:1-3
The Canaanite, the king of Arad, who lived in the South, heard that Israel came by the way of Atharim. He fought against Israel, and took some of them captive. Israel vowed a vow to Yahweh, and said, "If you will indeed deliver this people into my hand, then I will utterly destroy their cities." Yahweh listened to the voice of Israel, and delivered up the Canaanites; and they utterly destroyed them and their cities. The name of the place was called Hormah.

God kept His promise.

The Defeat of The Amorites Promised

When the Israelites went into the territory of Bashan, God promised to defend His people from King Og as he and his army met Israel in battle.

Deuteronomy 3:1-3
Then we turned, and went up the way to Bashan. Og the king of Bashan came out against us, he and all his people, to battle at Edrei. Yahweh said to me, "Don't fear him; for I have delivered him, with all his people, and his land, into your hand. You shall do to him as you did to Sihon king of the Amorites, who lived at Heshbon." So Yahweh our God delivered into our hand Og also, the king of Bashan, and all his people. We struck...no one was left to him remaining.

Once again, God expressed His divine desire to defend His people. He promised to deliver them from Og, the king of Bashan, and He did.

HOW CHRISTIANS MAY DEFEND THEMSELVES AGAINST ATTACK

As the twelve tribes of Israel entered the promised land, the Lord God commanded them to conquer it. God promised to defend His people as they did this.

The Defeat of The AI Promised

Though they were defeated the first time by the people of AI because Achan and his family violated God's law. The Lord promised to defend them a second time since their sins were dealt with properly by Joshua.

Joshua 8:7-8
And you shall rise up from the ambush, and take possession of the city; for Yahweh your God will deliver it into your hand.... when you have seized the city, that you shall set the city on fire. You shall do this according to Yahweh's word. Behold, I have commanded you.

After this, Ai was defeated according to God's promise.

Joshua 8:24
When Israel had finished killing all the inhabitants of Ai in the field, in the wilderness in which they pursued them, and they had all fallen by the edge of the sword, until they were consumed, all Israel returned to Ai, and struck it with the edge of the sword.

Here is the divine expression of God's character and His desire to defend His people.

The Defeat of Many Cities Promised

God Continually promised Israel that they would have their own land, He promised to defend them as they battled a variety of nations to conquer it.

Genesis 17:8
I will give to you, and to your offspring after you, the land where you are traveling...land of Canaan, for an everlasting possession. I will be their God.

Leviticus 25:38
I am Yahweh your God, who brought you out of the land of Egypt, to give you the land of Canaan, and to be your God.

Deuteronomy 32:49
Go up into this mountain of Abarim, to Mount Nebo, which is in the land of Moab, that is across from Jericho; and see the land of Canaan, which I give to the children of Israel for a possession.

Joshua 3:10
Joshua said, "By this you shall know that the living God is among you...he will without fail drive the Canaanite, the Hittite, the Hivite, the Perizzite, the Girgashite, the Amorite, and the Jebusite out from before you."

Joshua 10:42-43
Joshua took all these kings and their land at one time, because Yahweh, the God of Israel, fought for Israel. Joshua returned, and all Israel with him, to the camp to Gilgal.

God did just as He had promised from one battle to the next. This God defends His people.

The Defeat of a Coalition of Kings Promised

Sometimes, the armies of Israel had to fight the armies of different nations. At other times, the people of Canaan heard of their impending arrival and joined their armies together to defeat them. At those times, the Lord God promised to defend His people.

Joshua 11:1-5
When Jabin king of Hazor heard of it, he sent to Jobab king of Madon, to the king of Shimron, to the king of Achshaph, and to the kings who were on the north, in the hill country, in the Arabah south of Chinneroth, in the lowland, and in the heights of Dor on the west, to the Canaanite on the east and on the west, the Amorite, the Hittite, the Perizzite, the Jebusite in the hill country, and the Hivite under Hermon in the land of Mizpah. They went out, they and all their armies with them, many people, even as the sand that is on the seashore in multitude, with very many horses and chariots. All these kings met together; and they came and encamped together at the waters of Merom...Yahweh said to Joshua, "Don't be afraid because of them; for tomorrow at this time, I will deliver them up all slain before Israel....

So, Joshua did as God had commanded and attacked the massive army.

Joshua 11:7-8
So Joshua came suddenly, with...the warriors, against them by the waters of Merom....Yahweh delivered them into the hand of Israel, and they struck them...chased them to...Sidon, and to Misrephoth Maim...to...valley of Mizpah eastward. They struck...until they left...no one remaining.

Once again, God promised to defend His people and He fulfilled that promise with a great victory.

The Defeat of The Canaanites Promised

After Joshua had passed away, God's people had trouble with some of the people groups who were still in the land. As a result, they sought God's will. They desired to seek God's help against these difficult enemies. When the Canaanites came against them, they sought God's help.

Judges 1:1
After the death of Joshua, the children of Israel asked of Yahweh, saying, "Who should go up for us first against the Canaanites, to fight against them?"

God answered them by promising a powerful victory. Judah enlisted the help of the tribe of Simeon and both their armies and God defended them.

Judges 1:2-4
Yahweh said, "Judah shall go up. Behold, I have delivered the land into his hand." Judah said to Simeon his brother, "Come up with me into my lot, that we may fight against the Canaanites; and I likewise will go with you into your lot." So Simeon went with him. Judah went up...Yahweh delivered the Canaanites...the Perizzites into their hand. They struck ten thousand men in Bezek.

The Lord defended them just as He had promised.

During the time of the Judges, Israel often disobeyed the Lord, and He would allow their enemies to conquer them. When His people repented, the Lord would promise to fight for them, defend them, and defeat their enemies. Here are some examples.

The Defeat of Mesopotamia Promised

In the time Othniel was judging Israel, God promised to deliver the people of Israel from the threat of the king of Mesopotamia.

Judges 3:9-10
When the children of Israel cried to Yahweh, Yahweh raised up a savior to the children of Israel, who saved them, even Othniel the son of Kenaz, Caleb's...brother. The Yahweh's Spirit came on him,

and he judged Israel; and he went out to war, and Yahweh [God] delivered Cushan Rishathaim king of Mesopotamia into his hand. His hand prevailed against Cushan Rishathaim.

The Lord God did as He promised and defended Israel from harm.

The Defeat of The Benjaminites Promised

The eleven tribes of Israel set their minds to go up against their twelfth tribe, Benjamin, because they were protecting the men who lived in the city of Gibeah who had committed a terrible atrocity. They inquired of God and He promised that He would defend them against Benjamin for disobeying His laws as they went in battle.

Judges 20:18
The children of Israel arose, went up to Bethel, and asked counsel of God. They asked, "Who shall go up for us first to battle against the children of Benjamin?" Yahweh said, "Judah first."

Judges 20:23
The children of Israel went up and wept before Yahweh until evening; and they asked of Yahweh, saying, "Shall I again draw near to battle against the children of Benjamin my brother?" Yahweh said, "Go up against him."

Judges 20:28
And Phinehas, the son of Eleazar, the son of Aaron, stood before it in those days, saying, "Shall I yet again go out to battle against the children of Benjamin my brother, or shall I cease?" Yahweh said, "Go up; for tomorrow I [Yahweh] will deliver him into your hand."

God promised victory to His people and the Lord fulfilled it by defending them.

In the time of the kings from Saul to the final destruction of the nation by the Babylonians, God promised to defend His people and He did.

The Defeat of The Philistines Promised (1)

During the time of King Saul, David was on the run from him with a band of six hundred men. Saul was jealous of his many victories and thought he would take his kingdom from him. As he traveled, David discovered that the Philistines were plundering a city of his own people, the tribe of Judah. So, David sought God's will and God promised a victory.

1 Samuel 23:1-6
David was told, "Behold, the Philistines are fighting against Keilah, and are robbing the threshing floors." Therefore David inquired of Yahweh, saying, "Shall I go and strike these Philistines?" Yahweh said to David, "Go strike the Philistines...save Keilah." David's men said to him, "Behold, we are afraid here in Judah. How much more then if we go to Keilah against the armies of the Philistines?" Then [King] David inquired of Yahweh...again. Yahweh answered him, and said, "Arise, go down to Keilah...I will deliver the Philistines into your hand." [King] David and his men went to Keilah, and fought with the Philistines, and brought away their livestock, and killed them with a great slaughter. So David saved the inhabitants of Keilah. When Abiathar the son of Ahimelech fled to David to Keilah, he came down with an ephod in his hand.

Again, we see the Lord protecting His people.

The Defeat of The Jebusites Promised

When David became king, he went against the Jebusites to take Jerusalem for Israel. God promised to defend him.

HOW CHRISTIANS MAY DEFEND THEMSELVES AGAINST ATTACK

2 Samuel 5:1-10
Then all the tribes of Israel came to David at Hebron, and spoke, saying, "Behold, we are your bone and your flesh. In times past, when Saul was king over us, it was you who led Israel out and in. Yahweh said to you, 'You will be shepherd of my people Israel, and you will be prince over Israel.'" So all the elders of Israel came to the king to Hebron, and king David made a covenant with them in Hebron...Yahweh; and they anointed David king over Israel. David was thirty years old when he began to reign, and he reigned forty years. In Hebron he reigned over Judah seven years and six months; and in Jerusalem he reigned thirty-three years over all Israel and Judah. The king and his men went to Jerusalem against the Jebusites...Nevertheless David took the stronghold of Zion. This is David's city.... David lived in the stronghold, and called it the city of David. David built round about from Millo and inward. David grew greater...for Yahweh, the God of hosts, was with him.

Here, God defended them just as He had promised.

The Defeat of The Philistines Promised (2)

Once the Philistines heard that David had become king, they thought this was a good opportunity to attack Israel.

2 Samuel 5:17-20
When the Philistines heard that they had anointed David king over Israel, all the Philistines went up to seek David, but David heard about it and went down to the stronghold. Now the Philistines had come and spread themselves in the valley of Rephaim. David inquired of Yahweh, saying, "Shall I go up against the Philistines? Will you deliver them into my hand?" Yahweh said to [King] David, "Go up; for I will certainly deliver the Philistines into your hand." David came to Baal Perazim, and David struck them there. Then he said, "Yahweh has broken my enemies before me, like the breach of waters." Therefore he called the name of that place Baal Perazim.

Over and over, the Lord God promised to protect and defend His people and He did.

The Defeat of The Philistines Promised (3)

The Philistines lost their battle with King David but were persistent in their desires to conquer Israel. So, they came up against him again. Here, God not only promised victory but also provided a tactical strategy to accomplish this.

2 Samuel 5:22-25
The Philistines came up yet again, and spread themselves in the valley of Rephaim. When David inquired of Yahweh, he said, "You shall not go up. Circle around behind them, and attack them in front of the mulberry trees. When you hear the sound of marching in the tops of the mulberry trees, then stir yourself up; for then Yahweh has gone out before you to strike the army of the Philistines." David did so, as Yahweh commanded him, and struck the Philistines all the way from Geba to Gezer.

As always, God continued to promise His defense of His people and then came through with His deliverance. This is a powerful God who defends His people.

The Defeat of The Syrians Promised

After Solomon died, Israel was divided into two nations. Ten of the tribes kept the name Israel. The tribe of Judah with Benjamin became Judah. During the reign of Ahab in Israel, the Syrians joined forces with other kings and demanded that Israel turn over anything that he wanted from the king and the people. Though Ahab was willing to give him all he had, the people were not. When the citizenry refused, a massive army arose and came to defeat God's people. Since the Syrians were steeped in idolatry, God promised to defend Israel.

1 Kings 20:11-21
The king of Israel answered, "Tell him, 'Don't let him who puts on his armor brag....'" When [King] Ben Hadad heard this message, as he was drinking, he and the kings...said to his servants, "Prepare to attack!" So they prepared to attack the city. Behold, a prophet came...to Ahab king of Israel, and said, Thus says Yahweh, "Have you seen all this great multitude? behold, I will deliver it into your hand this day; and you shall know that I am Yahweh." Ahab said, "By whom?" He said, "Thus says Yahweh, By the young men of the princes of the provinces." Then he said, "Who shall begin the battle?" He answered, "You." Then he mustered the young men of the princes of the provinces, and they were two hundred and thirty-two: and after them he mustered all the people...of Israel, being seven thousand. They went out...But Ben-hadad was drinking himself drunk in the pavilions, he and the kings, the thirty-two kings who helped him.... So these went out of the city, the young men of the princes of the provinces, and the army which followed them. They killed everyone...and the Syrians fled, and Israel pursued them: and Ben-hadad the king of Syria escaped on a horse.... The king of Israel went out...struck the horses and chariots...killed the Syrians with a great slaughter.

This powerful enemy was defeated by God just as the Lord had promised. Again, we see the Lord God coming to defend His people from their enemies. He is the great protector.

The Defeat of The Syrians Promised (2)

Since Ben-Hadad had escaped, he would return again. So, God sent His prophet to predict their return and prepare His people. Again, the Lord God promised that he would bring them victory.

DEFENDING YOUR LIFE

1 Kings 20:22--27
The prophet came near to the king of Israel, and said to him, Go, strengthen yourself, and mark, and see what you do; for at the return of the year the king of Syria will come up against you. The servants of the king of Syria said to him, Their god is a god of the hills; therefore they were stronger than we: but let us fight against them in the plain, and surely we shall be stronger than they. Do this thing: take the kings away, every man out of his place, and put captains in their room; and number you an army, like the army that you have lost, horse for horse, and chariot for chariot; and we will fight against them in the plain, and surely we shall be stronger than they. He listened to their voice, and did so. It happened at the return of the year, that Ben-hadad mustered the Syrians, and went up to Aphek, to fight against Israel. The children of Israel were mustered, and were provisioned, and went against them: and the children of Israel encamped before them like two little flocks of kids; but the Syrians filled the country.

Then the Lord God Almighty sent His prophet to assure Ahab of God's defense even though the army was so much larger.

1 Kings 20:28-30
A man of God came near and spoke to the king of Israel, and said, Thus says Yahweh, Because the Syrians have said, Yahweh is a god of the hills...he is not a god of the valleys; therefore will I deliver...this great multitude into your hand, and you shall know that I am Yahweh. They encamped one over against the other seven days. So it was, that in the seventh day the battle was joined; and the children of Israel killed of the Syrians one hundred thousand footmen in one day. But the rest fled to Aphek, into the city; and the wall fell on twenty-seven thousand men who were left...."

So, the Lord God fulfilled His promise of deliverance with a mighty win for His people. God defends those He loves. he will come to their aid when they call on Him and will protect them.

The Defeat of Edom Promised

King Jehoram of Judah was an evil man. He married the daughter of the wicked King Ahab of Israel and behaved like Him also. When the Edommites surrounded Judah, God gave them victory because He had promised David that he would never let his descendants (the line of Judah) perish.

2 Chronicles 21:3-10
Their father gave them great gifts of silver, of gold, and of precious things, with fortified cities in Judah; but he gave the kingdom to Jehoram, because he was...firstborn. Now when Jehoram had risen up over the kingdom of his father, and had strengthened himself, he killed all his brothers with the sword, and also some of the princes of Israel. Jehoram was thirty-two years old when he began to reign, and he reigned eight years in Jerusalem. He walked in the way of the kings of Israel, as did Ahab's house; for he had Ahab's daughter as his wife. He did that which was evil in Yahweh's sight. However Yahweh [God] would not destroy David's house, because of the covenant that he had made with David, and as he promised to give a lamp to him and to his children always. In his days Edom revolted from...Judah, and made a king over themselves. Then Jehoram went there with his captains and all his chariots with him. He rose up by night and struck the Edomites who surrounded him, along with the captains of the chariots. So Edom revolted from under the hand of Judah to this day. Then Libnah revolted at the same time from under his hand, because he had forsaken Yahweh, the God of his fathers.

Though God was dissatisfied with Jehoram's wickedness, he defended His people to fulfill a promise to David.

The Defeat of The Syrians Promised (3)

Here, the author of 2 Kings describes the defeat of Israel by the Syrians because of the disobedience of the kings. Once the people repented God would promise to help them defeat the enemy. Then, this cycle would continue.

2 Kings 13:1-5
In the twenty-third year of Joash the son of Ahaziah, king of Judah, Jehoahaz the son of Jehu began to reign over Israel in Samaria for seventeen years. He did that which was evil in Yahweh's sight, and followed the sins of Jeroboam...which he made Israel to sin. He didn't depart from it. Yahweh's anger burned against Israel, and he delivered them into the hand of Hazael king of Syria, and into the hand of Benhadad the son of Hazael, continually. Jehoahaz begged Yahweh, and Yahweh listened to him; for he saw the oppression of Israel, how the king of Syria oppressed them. (Yahweh gave Israel a savior, so that they went out from under the hand of the Syrians; and the children of Israel lived in their tents as before.

Here, the Lord promised to defend Israel and our great God fulfilled it.

If defending those He loves is a part of His own nature and we are to think, speak, and act like Him, **then we d**o the same.

God's Miraculous Protection

As we continue our discussion of the Lord God Almighty's defense of His people, we come to the second aspect of this important characteristic. God not only promised to defend His people through their own efforts but also defended His people in direct and miraculous ways.

The Miraculous Deliverance from Egypt

After seventy years of captivity in the land of Egypt, the Lord God determined that it was time to defend His people.

HOW CHRISTIANS MAY DEFEND THEMSELVES AGAINST ATTACK

When He sent Moses to secure their release and was refused, God sent ten vicious plagues upon the Egyptians. Finally, Pharaoh released His people.

Exodus 12:29-35
At midnight, Yahweh struck all the firstborn in the land of Egypt, from the firstborn of Pharaoh who sat on his throne to the firstborn of the captive who was in the dungeon, and all the firstborn of livestock. Pharaoh rose up in the night, he, and all his servants, and all the Egyptians; and there was a cry in Egypt, for there was not a house where there was not one dead. He called for Moses and Aaron by night, and said, "Rise up, get out from among my people...you and the children of Israel...go, serve Yahweh, as you have said! Take both your flocks and your herds, as you have said, and be gone; and bless me also!" The Egyptians were urgent with the people, to send them out of the land in haste...The children of Israel did according to...Moses; and they asked of the Egyptians jewels...and...clothing.

Here, God Almighty defends Israel by performing powerful and awesome miracles.

The Miraculous Deliverance from Pharaoh

After releasing God's people, Pharaoh had a major change of heart. So, he gathered his chariots, horses, and army to pursue the Hebrews in the wilderness. As he was about to catch up with them, the Lord God's glory stood between them. It was a light by night to His people, but darkness to the Egyptians. Then, the Almighty parted the Red Sea and the nation walked on dry land through the water.

Exodus 14:5-9
The king of Egypt was told that the people had fled; and the heart of Pharaoh and of his servants was changed towards the people, and they said, "What is this we have done, that we have let Israel go from

serving us?" He prepared his chariot, and took his army with him; and he took six hundred chosen chariots, and all the chariots of Egypt, and captains over all them. Yahweh hardened the heart of Pharaoh king of Egypt, and he pursued the children of Israel; for the children of Israel went out with a high hand. The Egyptians pursued them. All the horses and chariots of Pharaoh, his horsemen, and his army overtook them encamping by the sea...before Baal Zephon.

Exodus 14:19-22
The angel of God, who went before...Israel, moved and went behind them; and the pillar of cloud moved from before them, and stood behind them. It came between the camp of Egypt and the camp of Israel; and there was the cloud and...darkness, yet gave it light by night: and one didn't come near the other all night. Moses stretched out his hand over the sea, and Yahweh caused the sea to go back by a strong east wind all night, and made the sea dry land, and the waters were divided. The children of Israel went into the middle of the sea on the dry ground, and the waters were a wall to them on their right hand, and on their left.

Then, the cloud was lifted, and the Egyptian army entered into the dry land and the sea overcame them.

Exodus 14:23-28
The Egyptians pursued, and went in after them into the middle of the sea: all of Pharaoh's horses, his chariots, and his horsemen. In the morning watch, Yahweh looked out on the Egyptian army through the pillar of fire and of cloud, and confused the Egyptian army. He took off their chariot wheels, and they drove them heavily; so that the Egyptians said, "Let's flee from the face of Israel, for Yahweh fights for them against the Egyptians!" Yahweh said to Moses, "Stretch out your hand over the sea, that the waters may come...on the Egyptians, on their chariots, and on their horsemen." Moses stretched out his hand over the sea...the sea returned to its strength when the morning appeared...the Egyptians fled against it. Yahweh [God] overthrew the Egyptians in the middle of the sea. The waters returned, and covered the chariots and the horsemen, even

all Pharaoh's army that went in after them into the sea. There remained not so much as one of them.

We see miracle after miracle that God performs to defend and deliver His people. God is a God of protection, defense, and deliverance.

The Miraculous Defeat of Jericho

The story of Jericho involved truly a miraculous victory for Israel. God, both asked them to attack Jericho as a judgment upon the sin of those people and protected them when He did. It was at Jericho that God miraculously destroyed the walls and brought a great defeat upon those people.

Joshua 6:1-5
Now [city of] Jericho was tightly shut up because of the children of Israel...Yahweh said to Joshua, "Behold, I have given into your hand Jericho, and the king of it, and the mighty men of valor. You shall compass the city, all the men of war, going about the city once. Thus shall you do six days. Seven priests shall bear seven trumpets of rams' horns before the ark: and the seventh day you shall compass the city seven times, and the priests shall blow the trumpets. It shall be that when they make a long blast with the ram's horn, and when you hear the sound of the trumpet, all the people shall shout with a great shout; and the wall of the city shall fall down... the people shall go up every man straight before him."

Joshua 6:20-21
So the people shouted, and [the priests] blew the trumpets; and it happened, when the people heard the sound of the trumpet, that the people shouted with a great shout, and the wall fell down flat, so that the people went up into the city, every man straight before him, and they took the city. They utterly destroyed all that was in the city, both man and woman...with the edge of the sword.

Again, God provided a miraculous victory for His people as the walls came down. This is what the great and powerful Lord God does. He defends His people. These deliverances are actions proceeding from His character.

The Miraculous Deliverance of Gideon

After this, Gideon was asked to trust the Lord God and battle according to His ways which were miraculous.

Judges 7:19-22
So Gideon and the hundred men...with him came to the outermost part of the camp in the beginning of the middle watch, when they had but newly set the watch. Then they blew the trumpets and broke in pieces the pitchers that were in their hands. The three companies blew the trumpets, broke the pitchers, and held the torches in their left hands and the trumpets in their right hands with which to blow; and they shouted, "The sword of Yahweh and of Gideon!" They each stood in his place around the camp, and all the army ran; and they shouted, and put them to flight. They blew the three hundred trumpets, and Yahweh set every man's sword against his fellow and against all the army; and the army fled...

Rather than depending on his own brute strength, the Lord God wanted Gideon to depend on Him. So, God defended His people in a miraculous way.

The Miraculous Defeat of the Amorites

When the kings of Amorites went to war against the allies of Israel, the Gibeonites, Joshua sent his army to battle them. As the battle began, God supernaturally confused their minds and gave the battle to Israel. Then as they retreated, God miraculously threw hailstones as big as boulders on them.

HOW CHRISTIANS MAY DEFEND THEMSELVES AGAINST ATTACK

Joshua 10:5
Therefore he...kings of the Amorites, the king of Jerusalem, the king of Hebron, the king of Jarmuth, the king of Lachish, the king of Eglon, gathered themselves together, and went up, they and all their hosts, and encamped against Gibeon, and made war against it. 6 The men of Gibeon sent to Joshua at the camp at Gilgal, saying, "Don't abandon your servants! Come up to us quickly and save us! Help us; for all the kings of the Amorites that dwell in the hill country have gathered together against us."

Joshua 10:8-11
Yahweh said to Joshua, Don't fear them: for I have delivered them into your hands; there shall not a man of them stand before you. Joshua therefore came on them suddenly; [for] he went up from Gilgal all the night. Yahweh confused them before Israel, and he killed them with a great slaughter at Gibeon, and chased them by the way of the ascent of Beth-horon, and struck them to Azekah, and to Makkedah. It happened, as they fled from before Israel, while they were at the descent of Beth-horon, that Yahweh cast down great stones from the sky on them to Azekah, and they died: they were more who died with the hailstones than they whom the children of Israel killed with the sword.

More were killed by the hailstones than by the sword. God miraculously protected and defended His people.

The Miraculous Defeat of the Amalekites

While God's people were wondering in the wilderness, the Amalekites attacked them, and the Lord God miraculously defended them.

Exodus 17:8-15
Then Amalek came...fought with Israel in Rephidim. Moses said to Joshua, "Choose men for us...go out, fight with Amalek. Tomorrow

I will stand on the top of the hill with God's rod in my hand. So Joshua did as Moses had told him, and fought with Amalek; and Moses, Aaron, and Hur went up to the top of the hill. It happened, when Moses held up his hand, that Israel prevailed; and when he let down his hand, Amalek prevailed. But Moses' hands were heavy; and they took a stone, and put it under him, and he sat on it. Aaron and Hur held up his hands, the one on the one side, and the other on the other side. His hands were steady until sunset. Joshua defeated Amalek and his people with the edge of the sword. Yahweh said to Moses, "Write this for a memorial in a book, and rehearse it in the ears of Joshua: that I will utterly blot out the memory of Amalek...."

Here, God works miraculously to defend His people.

The Miraculous Defeat of the Canaanites

During the time of the judges, the people of Israel sinned, and God allowed them to be defeated. When they repented the Lord told them to go up against their conquerors and He would give them a great victory.

Judges 4:12-17
They told Sisera that Barak the son of Abinoam was gone up to Mount Tabor. Sisera gathered together all his chariots, even nine hundred chariots of iron, and all the people who were with him, from Harosheth of the Gentiles, to the river Kishon. Deborah said to Barak, "Go; for this is the day in which Yahweh has delivered Sisera into your hand. Hasn't Yahweh gone out before you?" So Barak went down from Mount Tabor, and ten thousand men after him. Yahweh confused Sisera, all his chariots, and all his army, with the edge of the sword before Barak. Sisera abandoned his chariot and fled away on his feet. But Barak pursued the chariots and the army to Harosheth of the Gentiles; and all the army of Sisera fell by the edge of the sword. There was not a man left. However Sisera fled away on his feet to the tent of Jael the wife of Heber the Kenite....

Here, the Lord God miraculously confused the vast army of Sisera and gave the victory to Barak. God defends His own people.

The Miraculous Defeat of the Philistines

When the hated and feared Philistines drew near to Israel for battle, the nation inquired of God. The Lord God Almighty proclaimed a miraculous victory if the nation of Israel would repent of their idolatry. So, Saul, the king, and Samuel, the high priest, offered a sacrifice to the Lord Almighty and the children of Israel repented of their sins. It pleased the Lord, and He performed an awesome miracle.

1 Samuel 7:7-12
When the Philistines heard that the children of Israel were gathered together at Mizpah, the lords of the Philistines went up against Israel. When the children of Israel heard it, they were afraid of the Philistines. The children of Israel said to Samuel, "Don't stop crying to Yahweh our God for us, that he will save us out of the hand of the Philistines." Samuel took a suckling lamb, and offered it for a whole burnt offering to Yahweh. Samuel cried to Yahweh for Israel; and Yahweh answered him. As Samuel was offering up the burnt offering, the Philistines came near to battle against Israel; but Yahweh thundered...on that day on the Philistines...confused them; and they were struck down before Israel. The men of Israel...pursued the Philistines, and struck them, until they came under Beth Kar. Then Samuel took a stone and set it between Mizpah and Shen, and called its...saying, "Yahweh helped us until now."

Here again, God creates thunder and confuses the Philistines, and they were struck down before Israel. Direct powerful miracles demonstrate the Lord God's willingness to defend His people. This God that defends His people. The victories confirm this over and over again.

The Miraculous Defeat of the Philistines (2)

As the Philistines prepared to fight Israel, Jonathon, the king's son, took his armor bearer and went to battle alone.

1 Samuel 14:11-17
Both of them revealed themselves to the garrison of the Philistines: and the Philistines said, "Behold, the Hebrews are coming out of the holes...they had hidden themselves!" The men of the garrison answered Jonathan and his armor bearer, and said, "Come up to us...we will show you some-thing!" Jonathan said to his armor bearer, "Come up after me; for Yahweh has delivered them into the hand of Israel." Jonathan climbed up on his hands and on his feet, and his armor bearer after him...they fell before...them...That first slaughter, which Jonathan and his armor bearer made, was about twenty men, within as it were half a furrow's length in an acre of land. There was a trembling in the camp, in the field, and among all the people; the garrison, and the raiders also trembled; and the earth quaked, so there was an exceedingly great trembling. The watchmen of Saul in Gibeah of Benjamin looked; and behold, the multitude melted away and scattered. When they had counted...Jonathan and his armor bearer were not there.

1 Samuel 14:23
So Yahweh saved Israel that day; and the battle passed over....

In the second battle, God caused a great trembling of the earth and handed a miraculous victory to them. God defends His people through miracles.

The Miraculous Defeat of the Moabites

After the nation of God's people was divided into Israel and Judah, the two kings went up together in battle against the Moabites. The prophet Elisha asked God to defend them.

HOW CHRISTIANS MAY DEFEND THEMSELVES AGAINST ATTACK

2 Kings 3:16-20
He said, "Yahweh says, 'Make this valley full of trenches.' For Yahweh says, 'You will not see wind, neither will you see rain, yet that valley will be filled with water, and you will drink...your livestock and your other animals. This is an easy thing in Yahweh's sight. He will...deliver the Moabites into your hand. You shall strike every fortified city...and shall fell every good tree, and stop all springs of water, and mar [destroy] every good piece of land with stones.'" In the morning...water came by the way of Edom, and the country was filled with water.

Though the Hebrews saw the water and drank from it to revive themselves, the Moabites saw it as blood and thought Israel had been slaughtered. As a result, the Hebrew army defeated them.

2 Kings 3:21-26
Now when all the Moabites heard that the kings had come up to fight against them, they gathered themselves together, all who were able to put on armor, young and old, and stood on the border. They rose up early in the morning, and the sun shone on the water, and the Moabites saw the water opposite them as red as blood. They said, "This is blood. The kings are surely destroyed, and they have struck each other. Now therefore, Moab, to the plunder!" When they came to the camp of Israel, the Israelites rose up and struck the Moabites, so that they fled before them; and...went forward into the land attacking the Moabites. They beat down the cities; and on every good piece of land each man cast his stone, and filled it. They also stopped all the springs of water, and felled all the good trees, until in Kir Haresheth all they left was its stones; however the men armed with slings went around it, and attacked it. When the king of Moab saw that the battle was too severe for him, he took with him seven hundred men who drew a sword, to break through to the king of Edom; but they could not.

God miraculously delivered His people from harm. This is His way and has always been His way.

The Miraculous Defeat of the Ethiopians

When Asa became king over Judah, he attempted to reign righteously as his father Abijah had. When the Ethiopians came up against him, he called on God for His help and the Lord miraculously answered him in a great victory.

2 Chronicles 14:9-14
Zerah the Ethiopian came out against them with an army of a million troops and three hundred chariots, and he came to Mareshah. Then Asa went out to meet him, and they set the battle in array in the valley of Zephathah at Mareshah. Asa cried to Yahweh his God, and said, Yahweh, there is none besides you to help, between the mighty and him who has no strength: help us, Yahweh our God; for we rely on you, and in your name are we come against this multitude. Yahweh, you are our God; don't let man prevail against you. So Yahweh struck the Ethiopians before Asa, and before Judah; and the Ethiopians fled. Asa and the people who were with him pursued them to Gerar: and there fell of the Ethiopians so many that they could not recover themselves; for they were destroyed before Yahweh, and before his host; and they carried away very much booty. They struck all the cities round about Gerar; for the fear of Yahweh came on them: and they despoiled all the cities; for there was much spoil in them.

Here, the Lord defended His people.

The Miraculous Defeat of the Three Nations

Three nations came up to war against Judah. The king prayed to the Lord for deliverance. When God assured him of the victory over the armies of the Moabites, Ammonites, and Meunites, he marched into battle with a procession of priests singing and shouting many praises to God. He was rejoicing ahead of time for the defense God would bring.

HOW CHRISTIANS MAY DEFEND THEMSELVES AGAINST ATTACK

2 Chronicles 20::21-25
When he had taken counsel with the people, he appointed those who should sing to Yahweh, and give praise in holy array, as they went out before the army, and say, Give thanks to Yahweh; for his loving kindness endures forever. When they began to sing and to praise, Yahweh [the Lord] set ambushers against the children of Ammon, Moab...Mount Seir, who had come against Judah; and they were struck. For the children of Ammon and Moab stood up against the inhabitants of Mount Seir, utterly to kill and destroy them: and when they had finished the inhabitants of Seir, everyone helped to destroy another. When Judah came to the place overlooking the wilderness, they looked at the multitude; and behold, they were dead bodies fallen to the earth...no one...escaped. When Jehoshaphat and his people came to take their plunder, they found among them in abundance both riches and dead bodies, and precious jewels, which they stripped off...themselves, more than...could carry away...they were three days in taking the plunder....

Once again, God provides a miraculous defense.

The Miraculous Defeat of The Syrian Army

When the Syrian army attempted to defeat Israel, Elisha the prophet supernaturally provided their location to Israel's king in order to protect him. As a result, every time the king tried to capture Israel's king escaped. This enraged the ruler of Syria.

When he discovered that Elisha was disrupting his plans, he took immediate action against the prophet.

2 Kings 6:12-17
One of his servants said, "No, my lord, O king; but Elisha, the prophet who is in Israel, tells the king of Israel the words that you speak in your bedroom." He said, "Go and see where he is, that I

may send and get him." He was told, "Behold, he is in Dothan." Therefore he sent horses, chariots, and a great army there. They came by night, and surrounded the city. When the servant of the man of God had risen early, and gone out, behold, an army with horses and chariots was around the city. His servant said to him, "Alas, my master! What shall we do?" He answered, "Don't be afraid; for those who are with us are more than those who are with them." Elisha prayed, and said, "Yahweh, please open his eyes, that he may see." Yahweh opened the young man's eyes; and he saw: and behold, the mountain was full of horses and chariots of fire around Elisha.*

After God blinded the army, Elisha recommended that the people feed them and send them home. The army returned to their homeland. God had defended His people again.

The Miraculous Defeat of The Syrians

Sometime later, the Syrian army returned to, once again, defeat Israel. This time, the army surrounded the land so the Hebrews could not get food. Rather than blame himself, the king of Israel blamed Elisha. When he came to seize Elisha, the prophet predicted a great victory against the Syrians. Then the siege by them would be lifted. Four leprous men went to give themselves up to the Syrian army and found that they had been scattered due to a great miracle.

2 Kings 7:5-8
They rose up in the twilight, to go to the camp of the Syrians. When they had come to the outermost part of the camp of the Syrians, behold, no man was there. For the Lord had made the army of the Syrians to hear the sound of chariots, and the sound of horses, even the noise of a great army; and they said to one another, "Behold, the king of Israel has hired against us the kings of the Hittites and the kings of the Egyptians to attack us." Therefore they arose and fled in the twilight, and left their tents, and their horses, and their

HOW CHRISTIANS MAY DEFEND THEMSELVES AGAINST ATTACK

donkeys, even the camp...and fled for their life. When these lepers came to the outermost part of the camp, they went into one tent, and ate and drank, and carried away silver, gold, and clothing, and went and hid it....

Finally, they went and reported to the king what God had done and he sent his messengers to view it for themselves.

2 Kings 7:13-17
One of his servants answered, "Please let some people take five of the horses that remain, which are left in the city. Behold, they are like all the multitude of Israel who are left in it. Behold, they are like all the multitude of Israel who are consumed. Let's send and see." Therefore they took two chariots with horses; and the king sent them out to the Syrian army, saying, "Go and see." They went after them to the Jordan; and behold, all the path was full of garments and equipment which the Syrians had cast away in their haste. The messengers returned, and told the king. The people went out and plundered the camp of the Syrians. So a seah of fine flour was sold for a shekel, and two measures of barley for a shekel, according to Yahweh's word. The king appointed the captain on whose hand he leaned to be in charge of the gate; and the people trampled over him....

God defended His people in a direct and miraculous way.

The Miraculous Defeat of The Assyrians

After the Assyrians had taken Israel into captivity, the two tribes of the nation of Judah were left behind. The king of the Assyrians sent messengers to Hezekiah, King of Judah, to surrender because their one God would not and could save them. After Hezekiah, the king, inquired of Isaiah, God said that He would destroy the army Himself. God would not allow such arrogance against Him and His people.

2 Kings 19:32-35
Therefore Yahweh says concerning the king of Assyria, "He will not come to this city, nor shoot an arrow there. He will not come before it with shield, nor cast up a mound against it. By the way that he came, by the same he will return, and he will not come to this city," says Yahweh. "For I will defend this city to save it, for my own sake, and for my servant David's sake." That night, Yahweh's angel went out, and struck one hundred eighty-five thousand in the camp of the Assyrians. When men arose early in the morning, behold, these were all dead bodies. So Sennacherib king of Assyria departed, and went and returned, and lived at Nineveh. As he was worshiping in the house of...his god, Adrammelech and Sharezer struck him with the sword; and they escaped into...Ararat. Esar Haddon his son reigned in his place.

Once again, the Lord God defended His people with a great miracle.

God's Angelic Intervention

Not only do we see our God defending His people but the angels also. These powerful, righteous beings can be seen coming to the defense of individuals and nations. Righteous angels can only behave righteously. Therefore, as we may follow their examples in coming to the aid of others who are in the path of harm. Throughout the Old Testament, God has used his angels to accomplish His will both in the heavenlies and on earth. Though we may see them delivering messages through physical appearances, dreams, and visions, they are primarily seen in defense mode on behalf of God's people.

In the book of Psalms, over and over the Lord is lauded for His angelic protection and defense. When He delivered David from death at the hands of the Philistine king, David praised God for His protection in Psalm 34.

HOW CHRISTIANS MAY DEFEND THEMSELVES AGAINST ATTACK

Psalm 34:7
Yahweh's angel encamps around those who fear him, and delivers them.

In Psalm 91, the psalmist is writing a song about taking refuge in the Lord.

Psalm 91:11
For he will put his angels in charge of you, to guard you in all your ways.

Here, the psalmist describes how God is like a mother bird taking us under his powerful wings. We do not have to be frightened of terrors at night, danger in the day, disease in the darkness, or the destruction at noon. Why? Believers are protected by angels. Notice the word "guard."

This continual danger that this psalmist is writing about is not only spiritual danger, but it also involves physical danger that may require a strong defense. Notice also, God has put them "in charge" of protecting us. So, we see this powerful defense of angels. Since these angels move within the spirit realm, much of their protection will be unseen.

Jesus speaks of this angelic protection of believers when the disciples argue over who is the greatest.

Matthew 18:10
See that you don't despise one of these little ones, for I tell you that in heaven their angels always see the face of my Father...in heaven.

The "little ones" in this passage does not refer to children as many assume. The context reveals that Jesus is addressing the argument among his disciples as to who was the greatest. Jesus explains to them that you must come into the kingdom as a child, humble and trusting, not as a prideful adult.

Then He describes how God cares so much for all of His little ones (Christians) so much that if someone causes them to stumble, they would be better off attaching themselves to a stone and throwing themselves in the ocean. In fact, God is so concerned about all His children that they have angels in heaven who are assigned to protect them and must report back to God face to face. They are in charge of keeping us out of danger. These are one of the many duties that they perform for our God.

The Angelic Defense in the Wilderness

Angels will protect man from other evil men. After their escape from Egypt, Israel stopped at Mount Sinai. Moses had to receive instructions as to how this nation would exist under God's new theocratic structure. God promised Moses He would protect and defend them as they proceeded into the Promised Land. This protection would involve angels.

In Exodus 23, Moses presents the angelic presence that would go before them to protect and defend them when it became necessary.

Exodus 23:20-23
Behold, I send an angel before you, to keep you by the way, and to bring you into the place which I have prepared. Pay attention to him, and listen to his voice. Don't provoke him, for he will not pardon your disobedience, for my name is in him But if you indeed listen to his voice, and do all that I speak, then I will be an enemy to your enemies, and an adversary to your adversaries. For my angel shall go before you...bring you...to the Amorite, the Hittite, the Perizzite, the Canaanite, the Hivite, and the Jebusite; and I will cut them off.

Here, the Lord God promises to send His angels to protect His people from wicked, evil nations who would attack.

HOW CHRISTIANS MAY DEFEND THEMSELVES AGAINST ATTACK

The Angelic Defense Despite Idolatry

Even though the people of God were sinning by creating an image of God as a golden calf, the Lord promised Moses that his angel would still defend his people. At the same time, God would punish those who turned against Him.

Exodus 32:30-36
On the next day, Moses said to the people, "You have sinned a great sin. Now I will go...to Yahweh. Perhaps I shall make atonement for your sin." Moses returned to Yahweh, and said, "Oh, this people have sinned a great sin, and have made themselves gods of gold. Yet now, if you will, forgive their sin – and if not, please blot me out of your book which you have written." Yahweh said to Moses, "Whoever has sinned against me, I will blot him out of my book. Now go, lead the people to the place of which I have spoken to you. Behold, my angel shall go before you. Nevertheless, in the day when I punish, I will punish them for their sin." Yahweh struck the people, because of what they did with the calf, which Aaron made.

Over and over, God is promising angelic protection and defense against these mighty warring nations.

The Angelic Defense of Elisha

The well-known story of Elisha and the chariots of fire is a story of angelic defense. The angels had surrounded Elisha to protect Him. You might remember that the Syrian army were attempting to surprise Israel and defeat them. Time and time again, somebody revealed their location. This allowed the Israelites to escape. When the King of Syria discovered that it was the prophet Elisha prophesying of his plans, he sent a great mass of warriors to seize him. The morning this vast array of soldiers arrived, Elisha's servant went out and saw that they had surrounded the city,

When he asked Elisha the reason for his calm in the face of impending death and their destruction, Elisha begged the Lord to open his eyes to see who was protecting them. When He did, the servant saw angels riding on chariots of fire which created a wall of protection around the two.

2 Kings 6:14-18
Therefore sent he there horses, and chariots, and a great host: and they came by night, and surrounded the city. When the servant of the man of God was risen early, and gone forth, behold, a host [literally "army"] with horses and chariots was round about the city. His servant said to him, Alas, my master! how shall we do? He answered, Don't be afraid; for those who are with us are more than those who are with them. Elisha prayed, and said, Yahweh, Please open his eyes, that he may see. Yahweh opened the eyes of the young man; and he saw: and, behold, the mountain was full of horses and chariots of fire round about Elisha. When they [the Syrians] came down to him, Elisha prayed to Yahweh, and said, Please smite this people with blindness. He struck them with blindness according to the word of Elisha.

Once again, we see the angels in defense mode.

The Angelic Defense Against the Assyrians

In the last section, we also discovered that the Lord God had miraculously defended His people against the Assyrians when Hezekiah was king. The Lord God struck one hundred and eighty-thousand soldiers through only one angel.

2 Kings 19:35-36
That night, Yahweh's angel went out, and struck one hundred eighty-five thousand in the camp of the Assyrians. When men arose early in the morning, behold, these were all dead.... So Sennacherib king of Assyria departed...and returned, and lived at Nineveh.

HOW CHRISTIANS MAY DEFEND THEMSELVES AGAINST ATTACK

Here is the angelic defense of God's people.

The Angelic Defense Against Babylon

After the Babylonians conquered Assyria, they went after Judah and conquered them. It was their custom to take some of the leaders of the conquered land back to their palace and train them to become leaders in Babylon. Three of them were Shadrach, Meshach, and Abednego. When the three men were asked to bow down to worship the image of the king, they refused. As a result, the king was outraged and threw them into the fiery furnace.

Daniel 3:19-23
Then Nebuchadnezzar was full of fury...the form of his appearance was changed against Shadrach, Meshach, and Abednego. He spoke, and commanded that they should heat the furnace seven times more than it was usually heated. He commanded certain mighty men who were in his army to bind Shadrach, Meshach, and Abednego, and to cast them into the burning fiery furnace. Then these men were bound in their pants, their tunics, and their mantles, and their other clothes, and were cast into the middle of the burning fiery furnace. Therefore because the king's commandment was urgent, and the furnace exceedingly hot, the flame of the fire killed those men who took up Shadrach, Meshach, and Abednego. These...men...fell down bound into the middle of the burning fiery furnace.

Daniel 3:24-26
Then Nebuchadnezzar the king was astonished and rose up in haste. He spoke and said to his counselors, "Didn't we cast three men bound into the middle of the fire?" They answered the king, "True, O king." He answered, "Look, I see four men loose, walking in the middle of the fire, and they are unharmed. The appearance of the fourth is like a son of the gods." Then Nebuchadnezzar came near to the mouth of the...fiery furnace. He spoke and said, "Shadrach,

Meshach, and Abednego, you servants of the Most High God, come out, and come here!"

When the king looked into the enclosure, he saw four figures, not three. This fourth was an angelic presence. These were not angels sent to encourage and comfort them but to deliver. Angels defend.

The Angelic Defense Against Darius

When the officials of the court became insanely jealous of Daniel and his wisdom, understanding, and favor with the king, they convinced Darius to pass an edict. It stated that no one could pray to anyone but Darius for thirty days because they knew Daniel went to pray to his God three times a day. When Daniel heard this, he went home, stood before his window for all to see, and prayed to God.

Daniel 6:10
When Daniel knew that the writing was signed, he went into his house (now his windows were open in his room toward Jerusalem) and he kneeled on his knees three times a day, and prayed, and gave thanks before his God, as he did before.

Immediately, these evil men informed the king of Daniel's flagrant violation of his edict.

Daniel 6:13
Then they answered and said before the king, "That Daniel, who is of the children of the captivity of Judah, doesn't respect you, O king, nor the decree that you have signed, but makes his petition three times a day."

The king was compelled to follow his own law, even though he loved and respected Daniel.

HOW CHRISTIANS MAY DEFEND THEMSELVES AGAINST ATTACK

Daniel 6:11
Then the king, when he heard these words, was very displeased, and set his heart on Daniel to deliver him; and he labored until the going down of the sun to rescue him.... Then the king commanded, and they brought Daniel, and cast him into the den of lions.

As he threw Daniel into the lion's den, King Darius begged Daniel to please pray to his God for deliverance.

Daniel 6:16-17
Then the king commanded, and they brought Daniel, and cast him into the den of lions. The king spoke and said to Daniel, "Your God whom you serve continually, he will deliver you." The king spoke and said to Daniel, "Your God whom you serve continually, he will deliver you." A stone was brought, and laid on the mouth of the den; and the king sealed it with his own signet, and with the signet of his lords; that nothing might be changed concerning Daniel.

That night the king put away all his entertainment and just fasted.

Daniel 6:18
Then the king went to his palace, and passed the night fasting. No musical instruments were brought before him; and his sleep fled from him.

The next morning the king rushed to the den to see if Daniel was still alive.

Daniel 6:20-22
When he came near to the den to Daniel, he cried with a troubled voice. The king spoke and said to Daniel, "Daniel, servant of the living God, is your God, whom you serve continually, able to deliver you from the lions?" Then Daniel said to the king, "O king, live forever! My God has sent his angel, and has shut the lions' mouths, and they have not hurt me; because as before him innocence was found in me; and also before you, O king, I have done no harm."

To the joy of both Daniel and the king, an angel had delivered David defending him against the lions and the evil plot of his jealous enemies.

The Angelic Defense of Lot

Abraham had an angelic visitation days before the cities of Sodom and Gomorrah were destroyed by the Lord God. As they described what would occur, Abraham reasoned with them in order to protect his nephew Lot and his family. He loved Lot and wanted to protect him.

Genesis 18:22-32
The men turned from there, and went toward Sodom, but Abraham stood yet before Yahweh. Abraham came near, and said, "Will you consume the righteous with the wicked? What if there are fifty righteous within the city? Will you consume and not spare the place for the fifty righteous who are in it? May it be far from you to do things like that, to kill the righteous with the wicked, so that the righteous should be like the wicked. May that be far from you. Shouldn't the Judge of all the earth do right?" Yahweh said, "If I find in Sodom fifty righteous within the city, then I will spare the whole place for their sake." Abraham answered, "See now, I have taken it on myself to speak to the Lord, although I am dust and ashes. What if there will lack five of the fifty righteous? Will you destroy all the city for lack of five?" He said, "I will not destroy it if I find forty-five there." He spoke to him yet again..."

Abraham continued his question until the Lord said that He would spare Lot.

Genesis 18:32-33
He said, "I will not destroy it for...ten's sake." Yahweh went his way...as he had finished communing with Abraham, and Abraham returned to his place.

HOW CHRISTIANS MAY DEFEND THEMSELVES AGAINST ATTACK

Here, the Lord God indicates that Lot would be saved. He would not let the righteous die with the unrighteous.

So, the angels entered the city to rescue Lot. While there, the men of the city came and wanted to have relations with them. Lot brought them into his house. When the men were going to storm the house, the angels protected all inside by striking the men blind.

Genesis 19:9-11
They said, "Stand back!" Then they said, "This...fellow came in to live as a foreigner, and he appoints himself a judge. Now we will deal worse with you than with them!" They pressed hard on the man Lot, and came near to break the door. But the men reached out their hand, and brought Lot into the house to them, and shut the door. They struck the men who were at the door of the house with blindness, both small and great, so that they wearied themselves to find the door.

Then the angels protected them by warning those inside that judgment was coming and they needed to leave. So, all of them left the city. They made sure that Lot and his family made it as far as Zoar.

Genesis 19:15-22
When the morning came, then the angels hurried Lot, saying, "Get up! Take your wife and your two daughters who are here, lest you be consumed in the iniquity of the city." But he lingered; and the men grabbed his hand, his wife's hand, and his two daughters' hands, Yahweh being merciful to him; and they took him out, and set him outside of the city. It came to pass, when they had taken them out, that he said, "Escape for your life! Don't look behind you... don't stay anywhere in the plain. Escape to the mountains, lest you be consumed!" Lot said to them, "Oh, not so, my lord. See now, your servant has found favor in your sight, and you have magnified your loving kindness, which you have shown to me in saving my life. I

can't escape to the mountain, lest evil overtake me, and I die. See now, this city [Zoar] is near to flee to, and it is a little one. Oh let me escape there...and my soul will live." He said to him, "Behold, I have granted your request concerning this thing also, that I will not overthrow the city of which you have spoken. Hurry, escape there, for I can't do anything until you get there." Therefore.... Zoar.

The angels protected them from any harm.

The Angelic Defense of The Apostles

After Pentecost, the apostles of the Lord were imprisoned for their preaching of the gospel and performing miracles. The leaders were not only jealous of their influence but were disturbed by their message. They also did not like the apostles blaming them for killing their Messiah, even though their accusations were true.

Acts 5:16-18
The multitude...came together from the cities...bringing sick people and those who were tormented by unclean spirits: and they were all healed. But the high priest rose up, and all those who were with him...they were filled with jealousy and laid hands on the apostles, then put them in public custody.

Did God Almighty come to their defense? Yes, as He did in the Old Testament, He sent his angel to release them.

Acts 5:19
But an angel of the Lord opened the prison doors by night, and brought them out and said, "Go stand and speak in the temple to the people all the words of this life."

Once again, we see angels protecting God's people. God and His angels can and will defend those God loves!

The Angelic Defense of Peter

Later, Herod bound Peter in chains and threw him into prison with the desire to execute him the next day.

Acts 12:6-10
The same night...Herod was about to bring him out, Peter was sleeping between two soldiers, bound with two chains. Guards in front of the door kept the prison. Behold, an angel of the Lord stood by him, and a light shone in the cell. He struck Peter on the side, and woke him up, saying, "Stand up quickly!" His chains fell off from his hands. The angel said to him, "Put on...clothes, and tie on your sandals." He did so. He said to him, "Wrap your cloak around you, and follow me." He went out, and followed him. He didn't know that what was done by the angel was real, but thought he saw a vision. When they were past the first and the second guard, they came to the iron gate that leads into the city, which opened to them by itself. They went out...passed on through one street...the angel departed from him.

Here, we learn that an angel was dispatched to rescue Peter and this angel did. This was a supernatural angelic defense.

The Divine Chastisement (No Defense)

Another way in which we know that God demonstrates that He defends His people is by withholding His defense when His people Israel sinned against Him. We can see over and over their defeat because of the Lord's refusal. Though this may seem like an odd argument, it is nevertheless very powerful. Much discussion is being provided to demonstrate that God continually defends His people. The fact that at times, God did not defend those He loved is the other side of the two-sided coin. God normally defends, but not always.

The Defeat of Hebrews by the Amalekites

In Deuteronomy, Moses reviewed the rebellion of Israel in the wilderness when they were commanded by God to enter the land of the Amorites. Before they did this, they sent spies to seek out information on the situation.

Deuteronomy 1:23-28
The thing pleased me well. I took twelve of your men, one man for every tribe. They turned and went up into the hill country, and came to the valley of Eshcol, and spied it out. They took some of the fruit of the land in their hands and brought it down to us, and brought us word again, and said, "It is a good land which Yahweh our God gives to us." Yet you wouldn't go up, but rebelled against the commandment of Yahweh your God. You murmured in your tents, and said, "Because Yahweh hated us, he has brought us out of the land of Egypt, to deliver us into the hand of the Amorites to destroy us. Where are we going up? Our brothers have made our heart melt, saying, 'The people are greater and taller than we. The cities are great and fortified up to the sky....'"

Their leader, Moses, focused on the report of the goodness of the land. He strongly proclaimed that he knew God would protect them.

The Hebrew people viewed the situation through human eyes and became fearful and doubted God's protection. As a result of this, they murmured against God and His servant.

Deuteronomy 1:29-31
Then I said to you, "Don't be terrified. Don't be afraid of them. Yahweh your God, who goes before you, he will fight for you, according to all that he did for you in Egypt before your eyes, and in the wilderness where you have seen how that Yahweh your God carried you, as a man carries his son, in all the way that you went, until you came to this place."

HOW CHRISTIANS MAY DEFEND THEMSELVES AGAINST ATTACK

Moses attempted to assure the people that God would defend them. They were encouraged to remember what God had done in delivering them from the Egyptians and trust the Lord to protect them from this enemy.

Unfortunately, they were a stubborn people and rejected the Lord's promises for deliverance.

Deuteronomy 1:32-33
Yet in this thing you didn't believe Yahweh your God, who went before you on the way, to seek out a place for you to pitch your tents in: in fire by night, to show you by what way you should go, and in the cloud by day.

They had a visible sign of His defense day and night and still refused to believe. They were a rebellious and hard-hearted people.

The Lord became angry and pronounced His judgement: they would not enter the Promised Land. Suddenly, they repented and decided to stubbornly follow God's direction. They would go to battle against the Amorites. Moses warned them not to engage the Amorites in battle because God would not come to their defense.

Deuteronomy 1:43-44
So I spoke to you...you didn't listen; but you rebelled against the commandment of Yahweh, and were presumptuous, and went up into the hill country. The Amorites, who lived in that hill country, came out against you and chased you as bees do, and beat you down in Seir, even to Hormah.

Once again, the Lord God refused to defend His people and Israel experienced a horrible defeat. They were to remember this when they wanted to rebel again. God will not tolerate their sin and idolatry.

The Defeat of Israel by the Residents of AI

The armies of Israel were to fight against the citizens of the city of AI and take nothing as plunder. When one of them stole some of their gold, the Lord God refused to protect them.

Joshua 7:1-5
But the children of Israel committed a trespass...Achan, the son of Carmi...took of the devoted thing: and the anger of Yahweh was kindled against the children of Israel. Joshua sent men from Jericho to Ai, which is beside Beth-aven, on the east side of Bethel, and spoke to them, saying, Go up and spy out the land. The men went up and spied out Ai. They returned to Joshua, and said to him, Don't let all the people go up; but let about two or three thousand men go up and strike Ai; don't make all the people to toil there; for they are but few. So there went up there of the people about three thousand men: and they fled before the men of Ai. The men of Ai struck of them about thirty-six men; and they chased them [from] before the gate even to Shebarim, and struck them at the descent; and the hearts of the people melted, and became as water.

Here, the Lord God lifted His protection and did not defend Israel which caused a stunning defeat. Afterward, Achan was judged, and AI was defeated by the Israelites.

The Defeats of Israel in Judges

In the opening chapters of the book of Judges, the author provides a description of the Lord's unwillingness to defend them against their enemies because they had rebelled against Him and followed the ways of the nations around them.

When Joshua ruled the people, they were commanded to drive out the people from the land. Because they refused, the Lord allowed Israel to be constantly tormented by them.

HOW CHRISTIANS MAY DEFEND THEMSELVES AGAINST ATTACK

Judges 2:1-3
Yahweh's angel came up from Gilgal to Bochim. He said, "I brought you out of Egypt, and have brought you to the land which I swore to give your fathers. I said, 'I will never break my covenant with you. You shall make no covenant with the inhabitants of this land. You shall break down their altars.' But you have not listened to my voice. Why have you done this? Therefore I also said, 'I will not drive them out from before you; but they shall be in your sides, and their gods will be a snare to you.'"

After the death of Joshua, the next generation did not have a relationship with the Lord God and so committed idolatry against Him.

Judges 2:10-12
After...that generation were gathered to their fathers [died], another generation arose after them who didn't know [God] Yahweh, nor the work which he had done for Israel. The children of Israel did that which was evil in Yahweh's sight, and served the Baals. They abandoned Yahweh, the God of their fathers, who brought them out of the land of Egypt, and followed other gods...bowed themselves down to them; and they provoked Yahweh to anger.

When they sinned, the Lord God handed them over to their enemies.

Judges 2:13-15
They abandoned Yahweh, and served Baal [idol] and the Ashtaroth. Yahweh's anger burned against Israel, and he delivered them into the hands of raiders who plundered them. He sold them into the hands of their enemies all around, so that they could no longer stand...Wherever they went out, Yahweh's hand was against them for evil, as Yahweh had spoken, and...had sworn to them; and they were very distressed.

After this, the people would repent, and God would raise up a judge to rule and deliver them.

Judges 2:16-17
Yahweh raised up judges, who saved them out of the hand of those who plundered them. Yet they didn't listen to their judges; for they prostituted themselves to other gods, and bowed themselves down to them. They quickly turned away from the way in which their fathers walked, obeying Yahweh's commandments. They didn't do so.

So, through the righteous judge, the Lord would deliver them. Then, they would fall back again.

Unfortunately, this happened over and over again. They took advantage of the Lord's compassion and forgiveness. Often, it would be worse than the generation before them.

Judges 2:18-19
When Yahweh raised up judges for them, then Yahweh was with the judge, and saved them out of the hand of their enemies all the days of the judge; for it grieved Yahweh because of their groaning by reason of those who oppressed them and troubled them. But when the judge was dead, they turned back, and dealt more corruptly than their fathers in following other gods to serve them and to bow down to them. They didn't cease what they were doing, or give up their stubborn ways.

We also discover that God had left the enemies of Israel in the land to see if they would turn to Him for help and cling to Him in trust, but they failed miserably.

Judges 2:21-23
I also will no longer drive out any of the nations that Joshua left when he died from before them; that by them I may test Israel, to see if they will keep Yahweh's way to walk therein, as their fathers kept it, or not." So Yahweh left those nations, without driving them out hastily. He didn't deliver them into Joshua's hand.

God will withhold His deliverance because of sin.

The Defeat of King Saul by the Philistines

After Samuel's death, the Philistines came up against Israel. King Saul wanted to know if God would help them defeat this wretched enemy. When the king inquired of God in the usual ways, the Lord did not respond. So, Saul went to a spirit medium in defiance of God's law to determine God's will in the situation.

1 Samuel 28:3-7
When Saul saw the army of the Philistines, he was afraid, and his heart trembled greatly. When Saul inquired of Yahweh, Yahweh didn't answer him....

When King Saul met with the witch of Endor, the Lord God made the Prophet Samuel appear and he rebuked Saul and predicted his defeat and death by the Philistines.

1 Samuel 28:16-19
Samuel said, "Why then do you ask me, since Yahweh has departed from you...has become your adversary? Yahweh has done to you as he spoke by me. Yahweh has torn the kingdom out of your hand, and given it to your neighbor, even to David. Because you didn't obey Yahweh's voice, and didn't execute his fierce wrath on Amalek, therefore Yahweh has done this.... Moreover Yahweh will deliver Israel also with you into the hand of the Philistines; and tomorrow you and your sons will be with me. Yahweh will deliver the army of Israel also into the hand of the Philistines."

This is exactly what happened. The Philistines went after the Israelite army with a vengeance. They wanted the death of the king and his sons.

1 Chronicles 10:1-7
Now the Philistines fought against Israel...Israel fled from...the Philistines, and fell...slain on...Gilboa. The Philistines followed

hard after Saul and after his sons; and the Philistines killed...sons of Saul. The battle went hard against Saul, and the archers overtook him.... So Saul died with his three sons; and all his house died together. When all the men of Israel who were in the valley saw that they fled, and that Saul and his sons were dead, they abandoned their cities, and fled; and the Philistines came and lived in them.*

God withdrew His help and Israel was defeated. Because of sin, God refused to defend His people.

The Defeat of Rehoboam by the Egyptians

During the reign of Rehoboam, the people of Israel fell into Idolatry.

1 Kings 14:21-24
Rehoboam the son of Solomon reigned in Judah....Judah did that which was evil in the sight of Yahweh...they provoked him to jealousy with their sins which they committed, above all that their fathers had done....they also built...high places, and pillars, and Asherim, on every high hill, and under every green tree; and there were...sodomites in the land: they did according to...abominations of the nations which Yahweh drove out before the children of Israel.

This greatly displeased God and He allowed the king of Egypt to come up against them.

2 Chronicles 12:2-3
It happened in the fifth year of king Rehoboam, that Shishak king of Egypt came up against Jerusalem, because they had trespassed against Yahweh, with twelve hundred chariots... sixty thousand horsemen. The people were without number....

God sent the prophet Shemaiah to rebuke them and explain that God had sent the Egyptians against them.

HOW CHRISTIANS MAY DEFEND THEMSELVES AGAINST ATTACK

2 Chronicles 12:5-6
Now Shemaiah the prophet came to Rehoboam, and to the princes of Judah, who were gathered together to Jerusalem because of Shishak, and said to them, "Thus says Yahweh, You have forsaken me, therefore have I also left you in the hand of Shishak." Then the princes of Israel and the king humbled themselves; and they said, "Yahweh is righteous."

When they heard this, they repented of their wickedness and recognized God's righteousness.

As a result, the Lord God promised some defense.

2 Chronicles 12:6-8
Then the princes of Israel and the king humbled themselves; and they said, "Yahweh is righteous." When Yahweh saw that they humbled themselves, Yahweh's word came to Shemaiah, saying, "They have humbled themselves. I will not destroy them; but I will grant them some deliverance, and my wrath won't be poured out on Jerusalem by the hand of Shishak. Nevertheless they will be his servants, that they may know my service, and the service of the kingdoms of the countries."

Once again, the Lord demonstrates that He is a God who will defend His people, but He will refuse if they fall into sin. Yet, with repentance He may relent.

The Defeat of King Joash by the Syrians

Here, the author of Second Kings describes the defeat of Israel by the Syrians because of their disobedience.

2 Kings 13:1-3
In the twenty-third year of Joash the son of Ahaziah, king of Judah, Jehoahaz the son of Jehu began to reign over Israel in Samaria for

seventeen years. He did that which was evil in Yahweh's sight, and followed the sins of Jeroboam the son of Nebat, with which he made Israel to sin. He didn't depart from it. Yahweh's anger burned against Israel....he delivered them into the hand of Hazael king of Syria, and into the hand of Benhadad the son of Hazael, continually.

They were utterly defeated because of their sin. This was to provoke Israel to repent of their wickedness. Finally, when the king repented, the Lord resumed His protection and Israel defeated the Syrians.

2 Kings 13:4-5
Jehoahaz begged Yahweh...for he {God} saw the oppression of Israel, how the king of Syria oppressed them. (Yahweh gave Israel a savior, so that they went out from under the hand of the Syrians; and the children of Israel lived in their tents as before.

Here, we see the Lord God Almighty withhold His defense due to sin. The people knew this and sinned anyway over and over again.

The Defeat of Manasseh by the Assyrians

When Manasseh was the king of Israel, he led his people into idolatry. He was a man with a hardened heart toward the Lord God.

2 Chronicles 33:9
Manasseh seduced Judah and the inhabitants of Jerusalem, so that they did evil more than did the nations whom Yahweh destroyed before the children of Israel.

When the Lord God spoke to the king and his subjects, no one would listen. The people had become utterly hardened to any spiritual truth, holiness, and righteousness.

2 Chronicles 33:10
Yahweh spoke to Manasseh [the king], and to his people; but they gave no heed.

This angered God and He decided to destroy with a defeat by the Egyptian army.

2 Chronicles 33:11
Therefore Yahweh brought on them the captains of the host of the king of Assyria, who took Manasseh in chains, and bound him with fetters, and carried him to Babylon.

Manasseh was taken into slavery, and He cried out to God for help and the Lord delivered him.

2 Chronicles 33:11-13
When he was in distress, he begged Yahweh his God, and humbled himself greatly before the God of his fathers. He prayed to him; and he was entreated of him, and heard his supplication, and brought him again to Jerusalem into his kingdom. Then Manasseh knew that Yahweh he was God.

The Lord consistently defends His people unless His wrath is kindled.

The Final Defeat of Judah by Babylonians

After the Assyrians defeated Israel, Judah had provoked the Lord also with their idolatry and sin. Jeremiah was sent to them to remind them of the Lord's continual warning to repent over the years.

Jeremiah 25:1-3
The word that came to Jeremiah concerning all the people of Judah, in the fourth year of Jehoiakim the son of Josiah, king of Judah (this

was the first year of Nebuchadnezzar king of Babylon), which Jeremiah...spoke to all the people of Judah, and to all the inhabitants of Jerusalem: From the thirteenth year of Josiah...king of Judah, even to this day, these twenty-three years, Yahweh's word...I have spoken to you, rising up early and speaking; but you have not listened.

Since they would not listen, the prophet Jeremiah issues God's final warning.

Jeremiah 25:4-6
Yahweh has sent to you all his servants the prophets, rising up early and sending them (but you have not listened or inclined your ear to hear), saying, "Return now everyone from his evil way, and from the evil of your doings, and dwell in the land that Yahweh has given to you and to your fathers, from of old and even forever more. Don't go after other gods to serve them or worship them...don't provoke me to anger with the work of your hands; then I will do you no harm."

Again, they would not listen.

Jeremiah 25:7
"Yet you have not listened to me," says Yahweh; "that you may provoke me to anger with the work of your hands to your own hurt."

So, Jeremiah predicts they will be destroyed and taken into captivity by Babylon.

Jeremiah 25:8-11
Therefore Yahweh of Armies says: "Because you have not heard my words, behold, I will send and take all the families of the north...and I will send to Nebuchadnezzar the king of Babylon, my servant, and will bring them against this land, and against its inhabitants, and against all...nations around. I will utterly destroy them, and make them an astonishment, and a hissing, and perpetual desolations. Moreover I will take from them the voice of mirth and the voice of gladness, the voice of the bridegroom and the voice of the bride, the

HOW CHRISTIANS MAY DEFEND THEMSELVES AGAINST ATTACK

sound of the millstones [turning], and the light of the lamp. This whole land will be a desolation.

This is exactly what happened.

The land had been besieged twice already and now the king of Babylon would take the city of Jerusalem.

2 Kings 24:11-14
Nebuchadnezzar king of Babylon came to the city while his servants were besieging it, and Jehoiachin the king of Judah went out to the king of Babylon, he, and his mother, and his servants, and his princes, and his officers; and the king of Babylon captured him in the eighth year of his reign. He carried out from there all the treasures of Yahweh's house, and the treasures of the king's house, and cut in pieces all the vessels of gold, which Solomon king of Israel had made in Yahweh's temple, as Yahweh had said. He carried away all Jerusalem, and all the princes, and all the mighty men of valor, even ten thousand captives, and all the craftsmen and the smiths. No one remained....

Their constant sin led to God withholding His defense.

In summary, the Lord expresses Himself by defending His people. It was promised over and over, and God gave them great victories again and again. The exceptions came when God refused to defend them due to idolatry and sin. As was discovered in a previous chapter, since we are to act just like our God, then we too may defend ourselves and others.

Chapter 7

The Human Expectation

We are currently studying the character of God and our imitation of Him. We have learned that our God is a just God who defends His purposes and plans, those He loves, and the innocent. As a result, four things occur: first, God's people expected God to protect them, Second, His people assumed God would answer their prayers in times of trouble. Third, they trusted God to deliver them because they had seen Him do it time and time again and God desired that they have this confidence. Fourth, when God did not deliver them, they were shocked and complained because that is who He is.

The Relational Presumption

First, there are numerous examples of Israel's presumption that God would defend them because He defends those He loves. He protects ones who have a relationship with Him. As a result, when victory came, it was attributed directly to His power and might.

The Defeat of Five Kings Attributed to God

When Abraham and his nephew Lot had come into the land of Canaan, Abraham gave Lot the choice as to which region of the land he could settle in. Lot chose the area of Sodom and Gomorrah. So, Lot and his family began living in the area of Sodom and Gomorrah. Sometime after, it was attacked by five kings. Of course, since Lot and his family lived there, they were taken captive.

Genesis 14:1-3
In the days of Amraphel, king of Shinar, Arioch, king of Ellasar, Chedorlaomer, king of Elam, and Tidal, king of Goiim, they made war with Bera, king of Sodom, and with Birsha, king of Gomorrah, Shinab, king of Admah, and Shemeber, king of Zeboiim, and the king of Bela (also called Zoar). All these joined together in the valley of Siddim (also called the Salt Sea). They served Chedorlaomer for twelve years, and in the thirteenth year they rebelled.

The Kings, who ruled over the land where Lot lived, went up against them and lost the war.

Genesis 14:8
The king of Sodom, and the king of Gomorrah, and the king of Admah, and the king of Zeboiim, and the king of Bela (also called Zoar) went out; and they set the battle in array against them in the valley of Siddim.

Genesis 14:10
Now the valley of Siddim was full of tar pits; and the kings of Sodom and Gomorrah fled, and some fell there, and those who remained fled to the hills.

Then, the kings plundered the cities and captured Lot and his family.

Genesis 14:11-12
They took all the goods of Sodom and Gomorrah, and all their food, and went their way. They took Lot, Abram's brother's son, who lived in Sodom, and his goods, and departed.

As soon as Abraham heard what had happened, he took decisive action to deliver his nephew.

HOW CHRISTIANS MAY DEFEND THEMSELVES AGAINST ATTACK

Genesis 14:14-15
When Abram heard that his relative was taken captive, he led out his three hundred eighteen trained men, born in his house, and pursued as far as Dan. He divided himself against them by night, he and his servants, and struck them, and pursued them to Hobah, which is on the left hand of Damascus. 16 He brought back all the goods, and also brought back his relative Lot and his goods, and the women also, and the other people.

There is no indication that he asked God first since it was a form of self-defense. Abraham expected His God to protect Him.

After Abraham rescued his nephew with the nephew's family and goods, he returned and was greeted by a man who was both a king and a priest.

Genesis 14:18
Melchizedek king of Salem brought out bread and wine. He was priest of God Most High.

The king and priest attributed the victory to God's defense of Abram not to Abram alone.

Genesis 14:19-20
He blessed him, and said, "Blessed be Abram of God Most High, possessor of heaven and earth. Blessed be God Most High, who has delivered your enemies into your hand."

The author of Hebrews mentions Melchizedek as a true priest of God.

Hebrews 7:1
For this Melchizedek, king of Salem, priest of God Most High, who met Abraham returning from the slaughter of the kings and blessed him.

This authenticates these words concerning God's protection of Abraham. We can expect God to protect us.

The Defeat of Goliath Attributed to God

When Israel went out to battle against the Philistines, they were met by the challenge of a giant Philistine warrior. This mighty man had a powerful challenge.

1 Samuel 17:8-10
He stood and cried to the armies of Israel, and said to them, "Why have you come out to set your battle in array? Am I not a Philistine, and you servants to Saul? Choose a man for yourselves, and let him come down to me. If he is able to fight with me and kill me, then will we be your servants; but if I prevail against him and kill him, then you will be our servants and serve us." The Philistine said, "I defy the armies of Israel today! Give me a man, that we may fight together!"

This frightened the entire army of Israel and King Saul. They were not sure what to do.

1 Samuel 17:11
When Saul and all Israel heard those words of the Philistine, they were dismayed and greatly afraid.

Many days went by, and then young David brought food to his brothers on the field. While David was there, he heard the daily challenge.

1 Samuel 17:23-24
As he talked with them, behold, the champion, the Philistine of Gath, Goliath by name, came up out of the ranks of the Philistines, and said the same words; and David heard them. All the men of Israel, when they saw the man, fled from him and were terrified.

HOW CHRISTIANS MAY DEFEND THEMSELVES AGAINST ATTACK

David could not believe the arrogant words of this soldier.

1 Samuel 17:26
David spoke to the men who stood by him, saying, "What shall be done to the man who kills this Philistine and takes away the reproach from Israel? For who is this uncircumcised Philistine, that he should defy the armies of the living God?"

David believed that the army of Israel was actually the army of the Living God.

When Saul heard the words of David, he called the young man to him.

1 Samuel 17:31-33
When the words were heard which David spoke, they rehearsed them before Saul; and he sent for him. David said to Saul, "Let no man's heart fail because of him. Your servant will go and fight with this Philistine." Saul said to David, "You are not able to go against this Philistine to fight with him; for you are but a youth, and he a man of war from his youth."

When he met him, he was disappointed because David was young and inexperienced compared to Goliath.

David was not afraid. Why? God had delivered him from lions and bears and would do the same against this Philistine. David expected God to defend him as he defended himself.

1 Samuel 17:34-37
David said to Saul, "Your servant was keeping his father's sheep; and when a lion or a bear came and took a lamb out of the flock, I went out after him, struck him, and rescued it out of his mouth. When he arose against me, I caught him by his beard, struck him, and killed him. Your servant struck both the lion and the bear. This uncircumcised Philistine shall be as one of them, since he has defied

the armies of the living God." David said, "Yahweh, who delivered me out of the paw of the lion and out of the paw of the bear, will deliver me out of the hand of this Philistine." Saul said to David, "Go! Yahweh will be with you."

When David stood before the warrior, Goliath mocked him because he did not expect their God to deliver this young man from his grasp.

1 Samuel 17:43-44
The Philistine said to David, "Am I a dog, that you come to me with sticks?" The Philistine cursed David by his gods. The Philistine said to David, "Come to me, and I will give your flesh to the birds of the sky and to the animals of the field."

David proclaimed that he came in God's name and that God would stand with him. Their God would deliver him this day, and all would know that He defends His people.

1 Samuel 17:45-49
Then David said to the Philistine, "You come to me with a sword, with a spear, and with a javelin; but I come to you in the name of Yahweh of Armies, the God of the armies of Israel, whom you have defied. Today, Yahweh will deliver you into my hand. I will strike you and take your head from off you. I will give the dead bodies of the army of the Philistines today to the birds of the sky and to the wild animals of the earth, that all the earth may know that there is a God in Israel, and that all this assembly may know that Yahweh doesn't save with sword and spear; for the battle is Yahweh's, and he will give you into our hand." When the Philistine arose, and walked and came near to meet David...David put his hand in his bag, took a stone and slung it, and struck the Philistine in his forehead. The stone sank into his forehead, and he fell on his face to the earth.

The battle was quickly over as David felled Goliath with a slingshot and a few smooth stones.

HOW CHRISTIANS MAY DEFEND THEMSELVES AGAINST ATTACK

1 Samuel 17:50
So David prevailed over the Philistine with a sling and with a stone, and struck the Philistine and killed him; but there was no sword David's hand.

God had delivered David just as David had said. Though God never spoke to David, he attributed his victory to God.

God had aided him in the past against many wild animals and would do so again against a giant such as Goliath. Even though King Saul and his army were afraid, young David was not. He knew his God would protect him from harm. This was his expectation. No one questioned David's declaration that God had been with him as he felled the giant. God defends his people both individually and corporately.

The Defeat of Enemies Attributed to God

Many of David's victories in battle as king were attributed to God even though the Lord had not spoken directly to David about His involvement in many of them. King David expected God's defense and then attributed it to Him when victory came. One example of this was the return of Jerusalem to Israel.

After David became king, he attacked Jerusalem to take it back from their enemies. This victory and others also were attributed by the author of 1 Chronicles to God.

1 Chronicles 11:3-6
So all the elders of Israel came to the king to Hebron; and David made a covenant...in Hebron before Yahweh; and they anointed David king over Israel, according to Yahweh's word by Samuel. David and all Israel went to Jerusalem (also called Jebus); and the Jebusites, the inhabitants of the land, were there. The inhabitants of

Jebus said to David, "You will not come in here." Nevertheless David took the stronghold of Zion....David said, "Whoever strikes the Jebusites first shall be chief and captain." Joab the son of Zeruiah went up first, and was made chief.

After this victory, the chronicler attributes that victory and the ones to come to God's power.

1 Chronicles 11:9
David grew greater and greater; for Yahweh of Hosts [armies] was with him.

Notice, the Lord is called the "God of Armies." The growing "greater and greater" implies his many victories in battle and the "was with him" denotes God's defense of him though God did not speak to him directly.

The author of 2 Samuel ascribes the warrior's numerous victories in battle to the Lord God's defense of David and his men. First, the inspired writer describes some of the victories.

2 Samuel 8:1
After this it happened...David struck the Philistines, and subdued them: and David took the bridle of the mother city out of the hand of the Philistines.

2 Samuel 8:2
He struck Moab, and measured them with the line, making them to lie down on the ground; and he measured two lines to put to death, and one full line to keep alive. The Moabites became servants....

2 Samuel 8:3-4
David struck also Hadadezer...king of Zobah, as he went to recover his dominion at the River. David took from him one thousand seven hundred horsemen, and twenty thousand footmen: and David hamstrung all the chariot horses....

HOW CHRISTIANS MAY DEFEND THEMSELVES AGAINST ATTACK

2 Samuel 8:5-6
When the Syrians of Damascus came to help Hadadezer king of Zobah, David struck of the Syrians two and twenty thousand men.... David put garrisons in Syria of Damascus; and the Syrians became servants to David, and brought tribute. Yahweh gave victory to David wherever he went.

2 Samuel 8:13
David got him a name when he returned from smiting the Syrians in the Valley of Salt, even eighteen thousand men.

Then, the author of the book concludes his description with a declaration that attributed all to God's help and deliverance.

2 Samuel 8:14
He put garrisons...throughout all Edom...and...the Edomites became servants to David. Yahweh gave victory to David wherever he went.

The exact same battles were mentioned by the author of 1 Chronicles with the victories being attributed to God's power.

1 Chronicles 18:13
He [David] put garrisons in Edom; and...Edomites became servants to David. Yahweh gave victory to David wherever he went.

The people expected the Lord to come to their aid and when He did, they attributed their victories to Him.

The Defeat of Israel Attributed to God

When Rehoboam, the son of Solomon, was crowned King of Israel, ten of the tribes rebelled. They set up the northern kingdom of Israel and Rehoboam reigned over the southern kingdom of Judah. Sometime later, Abijah was crowned king of Judah, and Jeroboam became king of Israel.

When the two kings were to go to war against each other, Abijah appealed to the northern nation to return and become the one country that God had promised to King David. Then he accused the people of Israel of falling into idolatry while Judah was worshiping the true God. As a result, King Abijah warned them that God would be with Judah and Israel would be defeated.

2 Chronicles 13:12
Behold, God is with us at our head, and his priests with the trumpets of alarm to sound an alarm against you. Children of Israel, don't you fight against Yahweh, the God of your fathers; for you shall not prosper.

The people would not listen to Abijah's warning and sent their army to ambush them from behind, but the Lord God was with Judah, and they defeated the Israelites. The King of Judah prayed for God to defend them, and He answered.

2 Chronicles 13:13-17
But Jeroboam caused an ambush to come...behind them: so they were before Judah, and the ambush was behind them. When Judah looked back, behold, the battle was before and behind them; and they cried to Yahweh, and the priests sounded with the trumpets. Then the men of Judah gave a shout: and as the men of Judah shouted, it happened, that God struck Jeroboam and all Israel before Abijah and Judah. The children of Israel fled before Judah; and God delivered them into their hand. Abijah and his people killed them with a great slaughter...there fell...slain of Israel five hundred thousand...

Though this "striking of Jeroboam's forces may have been supernatural, it appears more likely the author is describing their terror. The trumpets sounded and this loud, furious war cry came from the mouths of Judah's confident army. This war howl frightened the armies of the north and they fled. As Israel fled, Judah slaughtered them.

Whether it was natural or supernatural, God was at work. Notice, the author's comment after his historical record.

2 Chronicles 13:18
Thus the children of Israel were brought under at that time, and the children of Judah prevailed, because they relied on Yahweh, the God of their fathers.

Here the author attributes the victory to God in whom they had trusted to be their head and go before them in battle. The people expected God to defend them, and He did.

The Defeat of Ammon Attributed to God

During the reign of Jotham, king of Judah, he attempted to follow the ways of the Lord God.

2 Chronicles 27:1-4
Jotham was twenty-five years old when he began to reign, and he reigned sixteen years in Jerusalem....He did that which was right in Yahweh's eyes, according to all that his father Uzziah had done....he didn't enter into Yahweh's temple. The people still acted corruptly. He built the upper gate of Yahweh's house, and he built much on the wall of Ophel. Moreover he built cities in the hill country of Judah, and in the forests he built fortresses and towers.

During his reign, he fought with the Ammonites and won the battle.

2 Chronicles 27:5
He also fought with the king of the children of Ammon, and prevailed against them. The children of Ammon gave him the same year one hundred talents of silver, ten thousand cors of wheat, and ten thousand cors of barley. The children of Ammon also gave that much to him in the second year, and in the third.

Then the chronicler asserts that God made Jotham mighty because he obeyed Him.

2 Chronicles 27:6
So Jotham became mighty, because he ordered his ways before Yahweh his God.

There is no indication that God had spoken directly to Jotham. Instead, because he followed God, God was there to defend him. Once again, it is important to see that Jotham expected God's help and God came to His defense.

The Assumption of Answered Prayer

Second, when God's people were in trouble, they prayed for His protection. They assumed that God would answer their prayers and deliver them, and He did. They knew that most of the time, it would be a violent end to the ones who were attempting to hurt them. In the Psalms, there are many prayers for God's deliverance. Some of David's psalms have ascriptions describing the situation in which David needed help. He prayed for God's protection and the Lord came through for Him. We will consider the prayers of David in the order of the time of their occurrences in David's life, rather than the order of the Psalms.

The Prayer for Protection from Saul's Men

The ascription of Psalm 59, states "A poem by David, when Saul sent, and they watched the house to kill him."

After David had defeated Goliath through God's help, the people sang his praises.

HOW CHRISTIANS MAY DEFEND THEMSELVES AGAINST ATTACK

1 Samuel 18:6-9
As they came, when David returned from the slaughter of the Philistine, the women came out of all the cities of Israel, singing and dancing, to meet king Saul with tambourines, with joy, and with instruments of music. The women sang to one another as they played, and said, "Saul has slain his thousands, and David his ten thousands." Saul was very angry, and this saying displeased him. He said, "They have credited David with ten thousands, and they have only credited me with thousands. What can he have more but the kingdom?" Saul watched David from that day and forward.

As a result, the king designed a series of schemes to get David killed, but none of them were effective. Finally, Saul went after David directly.

David had married Saul's daughter Michal. After one of Saul's rages, he sought to arrest David.

1 Samuel 19:9-10
An evil spirit from Yahweh was on Saul, as he sat in his house with his spear in his hand; and David was playing with his hand. 10 Saul sought to pin David to the wall with the spear; but he slipped away out of Saul's presence, and he stuck the spear into the wall. David fled, and escaped that night.

After David fled, Saul sent soldiers to David and Michal's house to capture David so he could put him to death. Though not mentioned in this narrative, David prayed for the Lord God's protection as we will see from the psalm. As a result, Michal came up with a plan to give David time to make quick escape.

1 Samuel 19:10-12
Saul sent messengers to David's house, to watch him, and to kill him [David] in the morning. Michal, David's wife, told him, saying, "If you don't save your life tonight, tomorrow you will be killed."

So Michal let David down through the window. He went away, fled, and escaped.

After David had fled, his wife took the household idols and placed them on his bed and covered them over to resemble a sick David. She was sure that this would fool them and if it didn't, he would at least have time to escape.

1 Samuel 19:13
Michal took the teraphim, and laid it in the bed, and put a pillow of goats' hair at its head, and covered it with clothes.

When Michal was asked, she told the men that David was sick in bed.

1 Samuel 19:14
When Saul sent messengers to take David, she said, "He is sick."

Though this did not fool Saul, David was able to escape their grasp for the time being.

1 Samuel 19:15-16
Saul sent the messengers to see David, saying, "Bring him up to me in the bed, that I may kill him." When the messengers came in, behold, the teraphim was in the bed, with...pillow of goats' hair...

When confronted, Michal claimed that David threatened her, so she had no choice but to mislead them.

1 Samuel 19:17
Saul said to Michal, "Why have you deceived me like this and let my enemy go, so...he has escaped?" Michal answered Saul, "He said to me, 'Let me go! Why should I kill you?'"

In the psalm, David recounts his prayer for deliverance. It was a cry for God to defend him.

HOW CHRISTIANS MAY DEFEND THEMSELVES AGAINST ATTACK

Psalm 59:1-4
Deliver me from my enemies, my God. Set me on high from those who rise up against me. Deliver me from the workers of iniquity. Save me from the bloodthirsty men. For, behold, they lie in wait for my soul. The mighty gather themselves together against me, not for my disobedience, nor for my sin, Yahweh. I have done no wrong, yet they are ready to attack me. Rise up, behold, and help me!

Through his wife Michal's plan, God came to his defense and protected him.

Psalm 59:10-13
My God will go before me with his loving kindness. God will let me look at my enemies in triumph. Don't kill them, or my people may forget. Scatter them by your power, and bring them down, Lord our shield. For the sin of their mouth, and the words of their lips, let them be caught in their pride, for the curses and lies which they utter. Consume them in wrath. Consume them, and they will be no more. Let them know that God rules in Jacob, to the ends of the earth. Selah.

In the psalm, as he writes also of God's protection of his people from the nations, he appeals to God using two titles.

Psalm 59:5-6
You, Yahweh God of Armies, the God of Israel, rouse yourself to punish the nations. Show no mercy to the wicked traitors. Selah. They return at evening, howling like dogs...prowl around the city.

Psalm 59
Don't kill them, or my people may forget. Scatter them by your power, and bring them down, Lord our shield.

He uses military terms to speak of God's defense of his life and eventually the life of God's people. The Lord Almighty is a God of defense.

The Prayer against Doeg's Betrayal

As David was running from Saul, he arrived in the land of Nob. He immediately went to the tabernacle and asked the high priest, Ahimelech, to provide him with some food and weapons. One of Saul's men, Doeg, was there. He was not considered a Jew, but an Edomite.

1 Samuel 21:7
Now a certain man of the servants of Saul was there that day, detained before Yahweh; and his name was Doeg the Edomite, the best of the herdsmen who belonged to Saul.

Later, Doeg, the Edomite, the overseer of Saul's shepherds, disclosed to the king that he saw Ahimelech helping David. Though King Saul's enemy was long gone, the High Priest Ahimelech had helped him, nevertheless.

1 Samuel 22:9
Then Doeg the Edomite, who stood by the servants of Saul, answered and said, "I saw the son of Jesse coming to Nob, to Ahimelech the son of Ahitub.

As a result, Saul ordered the high priest and eighty-five other priests to be killed almost eliminating the entire lineage of Eli. Since his men would not do such a treacherous deed as take their swords against God's priests, he ordered Doeg to do it. Not only did Doeg kill them but went to Nob and killed their families and their animals.

1 Samuel 22:18-19
The king said to Doeg, "Turn and attack the priests!" Doeg the Edomite turned, and he attacked the priests, and he killed on that day eighty-five people who wore a linen ephod. He struck Nob, the city of the priests, with the edge of the sword, both men and women, children and nursing babies, and cattle...with the edge of the sword.

HOW CHRISTIANS MAY DEFEND THEMSELVES AGAINST ATTACK

At the beginning of Psalm 52, the description speaks of this incident.

Psalm 52
For the Chief Musician. A contemplation by David, when Doeg the Edomite…told Saul, "David has come to Ahimelech's house."

Here, Doeg had already killed the priests and many of the inhabitants of Nob.

So, David's prayer of deliverance to God spoke of his trust that God would administer His justice to such an evil man as Doeg.

Psalm 52:1-3
Why do you boast of mischief, mighty man? God's loving kindness endures continually. Your tongue plots destruction, like a sharp razor, working deceitfully. You love evil more than good, lying rather than speaking the truth. Selah.

Psalm 52:5
God will likewise destroy you forever. He will take you up, and pluck you out of your tent, and root you out of the land of the living. Selah.

Then, David expressed his trust in God's continual defense of him.

Psalm 52:8-9
But as for me, I am like a green olive tree in God's house. I trust in God's loving kindness forever and ever. I will give you thanks forever, because you have done it. I will hope in your name, for it is good, in the presence of your saints.

God is a God who defends His people, and we can trust in Him. Of course, this is most often done through the actions of His people as God guides them.

The Prayer for Defense from King of Gath

There are two psalms written after David left Ahimelech and landed in the realm of the King of Gath.

Psalm 56:1
A poem by David, when the Philistines seized him in Gath.

Psalm 34:1
By David; when he pretended to be insane before Abimelech, who drove him away, and he departed.

In the record of 1 Samuel 21, the inspired writer identifies the ruler of Gath as King Achish. The one who inserted the description used the more generic term for a ruler at that time which was Abimelech. This is much like the use of "pharaoh" in Egypt. Both describe the event recorded in 1 Samuel 21.

Gath was in the land of the Philistines, the archenemy of Israel. Though David thought they might protect him because he was running from their enemy, they did not. Instead, they feared him because he was a mighty warrior. So, he debated over what they should do with him.

1 Samuel 21:10-11
David arose, and fled that day for fear of Saul, and went to Achish the king of Gath. The servants of Achish said to him, "Isn't this David the king of the land? Didn't they sing to one another about him in dances, saying, 'Saul has slain his thousands, David his ten thousands?'"

David prayed to God and then came up with a plan to avoid arrest. This would involve him feigning madness.

1 Samuel 21:12-15
David laid up these words in his heart, and was very afraid of Achish

HOW CHRISTIANS MAY DEFEND THEMSELVES AGAINST ATTACK

the king of Gath. He changed his behavior before them...pretended to be insane in their hands, and scribbled on the doors of the gate, and let his spittle fall down on his beard. Then Achish said to his servants, "Look, you see the man is insane. Why then have you brought him to me? Do I lack madmen, that you have brought this fellow to play the madman in my presence? Should this fellow come into my house?"

This misleading of the Philistines was effective, and David was spared. Immediately, he fled for his life.

1 Samuel 22:1
David therefore departed from there, and escaped [fled] to the cave of Adullam.

In Psalm 56, David recounts his prayer for deliverance.

Psalm 56:1-3
Be merciful to me, God, for man wants to swallow me up. All day long, he attacks and oppresses me. My enemies want to swallow me up all day long, for they are many who fight proudly against me. When I am afraid, I will put my trust in you.

David's cry for mercy is a pleading for deliverance. He was overwhelmed by his enemies.

In Psalm 34, David expressed his plea for God's defense as a crying out in desperation.

Psalm 34:6
This poor man cried, and Yahweh heard him, and saved him out of all his troubles.

In these psalms, David speaks of the Lord God's protection and deliverance in times of trouble. He expected God would answer his prayers when he needed God to defend him.

Psalm 56:14
For you have delivered my soul from death, and prevented my feet from falling, that I may walk before God in the light of the living.

Psalm 34:4
I sought Yahweh, and he answered me, and delivered me from all my fears.

This protection and deliverance provoked David to make a powerful declaration concerning God's defense of His people as He answers their prayers for help.

Psalm 34:17-22
The righteous cry, and Yahweh hears, and delivers them out of all their troubles. Yahweh is near to those who have a broken heart, and saves those who have a crushed spirit. Many are the afflictions of the righteous, but Yahweh delivers him out of them all. He protects all of his bones. Not one of them is broken. Evil shall kill the wicked. Those who hate the righteous shall be condemned. Yahweh redeems the soul of his servants. None of those who take refuge in him shall be condemned.

So, God will defend His people as they pray to Him.

The Prayer for Help in the Cave

The descriptions before two of David's songs and prayers portray David as crying for help from a cave.

Psalm 57
For the Chief Musician. To the tune of "Do Not Destroy." A poem by David, when he fled from Saul, in the cave.

Psalm 142:1
A contemplation by David, when he was in the cave. A Prayer.

HOW CHRISTIANS MAY DEFEND THEMSELVES AGAINST ATTACK

On two occasions, David hid in a cave. One was the cave of Adullum, and the other was the cave in Engedi. Since the two psalms do not provide a clue as to the exact incident, we will consider both events because they are amazing stories which describe the powerful defense God can provide for His people when they pray to Him for help.

The first incident occurred in the cave in the territory of Adullum. In Joshua 12, Joshua describes the kings they had defeated.

Joshua 12:7
These are the kings of the land whom Joshua and the children of Israel struck beyond the Jordan westward, from Baal Gad in the valley of Lebanon even to Mount Halak, that goes up to Seir. Joshua gave it to the tribes of Israel for a possession according to their divisions.

One of the kings was the King of Adullum.

Joshua 12:15
The king of Libnah, one; the king of Adullam, one.

Later, Joshua lays out the portions of the land of Canaan that went to each tribe.

Joshua 15:20
This is the inheritance of the tribe of the children of Judah according to their families.

The land of Adullum is mentioned.

Joshua 15:35
Jarmuth, Adullam, Socoh, Azekah.

So, the "cave of Adullum" was in the land of Adullum.

David fled to this cave when he ran from the King of Gath. He was accompanied by some men. In 1 Samuel 21, David mentions them in response to the priest's question about the purity of the ones who would eat the showbread. He claimed that the men with him had been chaste.

1 Samuel 21:5
David answered the priest, and said to him, "Truly, women have been kept from us as usual these three days. When I came out, the vessels of the young men were holy, though it was only a common journey. How much more then today shall their vessels be holy?"

There would not have been enough men to protect him from Saul and his army.

While he was there or immediately after, he might have written this one or both psalms entreating God for help.

Psalm 57:1
Be merciful to me, God, be merciful to me, for my soul takes refuge in you. Yes, in the shadow of your wings, I will take refuge, until disaster has passed.

Psalm 142:1-3
I cry with my voice to Yahweh. With my voice, I ask Yahweh for mercy. I pour out my complaint before him. I tell him my troubles. When my spirit was overwhelmed within me, you knew my route. On the path in which I walk, they have hidden a snare for me.

This cry brought a powerful response from God because men from the surrounding area came to support and defend him.

1 Samuel 22:1-2
David therefore departed from there, and escaped to Adullam's cave. When his brothers and all his father's house heard it, they went

down there to him. Everyone who was in distress, everyone who was in debt, and everyone who was discontented, gathered themselves to him; and he became captain over them. There were with him about four hundred men.*

After this, he was able to gain the help of the king of Moab.

1 Samuel 22:3-4
David went from there to Mizpeh of Moab, and he said to the king of Moab, "Please let my father and my mother come out with you, until I know what God will do for me." He brought them before the king of Moab; and they lived with him all the time that David was in the stronghold.

In the second incident, David hid in a cave at En Gedi from Saul and his forces.

1 Samuel 24:1-2
When Saul had returned from following the Philistines, he was told, "Behold, David is in the wilderness of En Gedi." Then Saul took three thousand chosen men out of all Israel, and went to seek David and his men on the rocks of the wild goats.

David prayed for deliverance. Here are some additional words of prayer from the two psalms.

Psalm 57:2-3
I cry out to God Most High, to God who accomplishes my requests for me. You love evil more than good, lying rather than speaking the truth. Selah.

Psalm 142:5-7
I cried to you, Yahweh. I said, "You are my refuge, my portion in the land of the living." Listen to my cry, for I am in desperate need. Deliver me from my persecutors, for they are too strong for me. Bring my soul out of prison, that I may give thanks to your name....

God delivered David in a very special way. Saul went into the cave to relieve himself not knowing that David was there.

1 Samuel 24:3-4
He came to the sheep pens by the way, where there was a cave; and Saul went in to relieve himself. Now David and his men were staying in the innermost parts of the cave. David's men said to him, "Behold, the day of which Yahweh said to you, 'Behold, I will deliver your enemy into your hand, and you shall do to him as it shall seem good to you.'" Then David arose, and cut off the skirt of Saul's robe secretly.

Rather than kill the king, David cut off a portion of his robe without his knowledge.

After he had left, this man of God identified himself to Saul with respect.

1 Samuel 24:7-8
So David checked his men with these words, and didn't allow them to rise against Saul. Saul rose up out of the cave, and went on his way. David also arose afterward, and went out of the cave, and cried after Saul, saying, "My lord the king!" When Saul looked behind him, David bowed with his face to the earth, and showed respect.

David cried out to Saul explaining that he could have killed him but did not.

1 Samuel 24:9-10
David said to Saul, "Why do you listen to men's words, saying, 'Behold, David seeks to harm you?' Behold, today your eyes have seen how Yahweh had delivered you today into my hand in the cave. Some urged me to kill you; but I spared you; and I said, I will not stretch out my hand against my lord; for he is Yahweh's anointed.

Because of this, Saul stopped pursuing him for a time.

1 Samuel 24:16-17
It came to pass, when David had finished speaking these words to Saul, that Saul said, "Is that your voice, my son David?" Saul lifted up his voice, and wept. He said to David, "You are more righteous than I; for you have done good to me, whereas I have done evil to you.

God had delivered David just as he had asked.

David's response was praise and thanksgiving.

Psalm 57:7-11
My heart is steadfast, God. My heart is steadfast. I will sing, yes, I will sing praises. Wake up, my glory! Wake up, lute and harp! I will wake up the dawn. I will give thanks to you, Lord, among the peoples. I will sing praises to you among the nations. For your great loving kindness reaches to the heavens, and your truth to the skies. Be exalted, God, above the heavens.

Psalm 142:7
Bring my soul out of prison, that I may give thanks to your name. The righteous will surround me, for you will be good to me.

Again, we see God defending His people who ask for help.

The Prayer of Deliverance from the Ziphites

The description before Psalm 54 sets the stage for another assault by Saul upon David. This event occurred between the hiding of David in the two caves.

Psalm 54
For the Chief Musician. On stringed instruments. A contemplation by David, when the Ziphites came and said to Saul, "Isn't David hiding himself among us?"

As David continued his escape from the clutches of Saul, he fled into the land of Ziph and hid among the people.

1 Samuel 23:14-15
David stayed in the wilderness in the strongholds, and remained in the hill country in the wilderness of Ziph. Saul sought him every day, but God didn't deliver him into his hand. David saw that Saul had come out to seek his life. David was in the wilderness of Ziph in the woods.

By this time, Saul had lost track of David. This only created in him a stronger desire to find David and end his life and the threat against his kingdom once and for all.

Then the Ziphites came to Saul and told him that David was hiding among them.

1 Samuel 23:19-20
Then the Ziphites came up to Saul to Gibeah, saying, "Doesn't David hide himself with us in the strongholds in the woods, in the hill of Hachilah, which is on the south of the desert? Now therefore, O king, come down. According to all the desire of your soul to come down; and our part will be to deliver him up into the king's hand."

Saul asked the Ziphites, who came to him, to find David. When David discovered their plot, he fled to the wilderness of Moan and Saul pursued after him.

1 Samuel 23:24-25
They arose, and went to Ziph before Saul: but David and his men were in the wilderness of Maon, in the Arabah on the south of the desert. Saul and his men went to seek him. When David was told, he went down to the rock, and stayed in the wilderness of Maon.

Eventually Saul surrounded David and began to close in on him.

HOW CHRISTIANS MAY DEFEND THEMSELVES AGAINST ATTACK

1 Samuel 23:25-26
When Saul heard that, he pursued David in the wilderness of Maon. Saul went on this side of the mountain, and David and his men on that side of the mountain; and David hurried to get away for fear of Saul; for Saul and his men surrounded David and his men to take them.

Then God answered David's prayer and defended him in a divine providential way.

1 Samuel 23:27-28
But a messenger came to Saul, saying, "Hurry and come; for the Philistines have made a raid on the land!" So Saul returned from pursuing David, and went against the Philistines. Therefore they called that place Sela Hammahlekoth.

In Psalm 54, David speaks of his prayer for help.

Psalm 54:1-3
Save me, God, by your name. Vindicate me in your might. Hear my prayer, God. Listen to the words of my mouth. For strangers have risen up against me. Violent men have sought after my soul. They haven't set God before them. Selah.

Here, David declares his trust in God to come to his aid as he prays for deliverance.

Psalm 54:4-5
Behold, God is my helper. The Lord is the one who sustains my soul. He will repay the evil to my enemies. Destroy them in your truth.

Then, the Lord God delivered him by having Saul attacked by the Philistines.

Psalm 54:6-7
With a free will offering, I will sacrifice to you. I will give thanks to

your name, Yahweh, for it is good. For he has delivered me out of all trouble. My eye has seen triumph over my enemies.

Once again, the Lord God defends His people who pray to Him for their deliverance.

The Prayer against Absalom's Takeover

The description before Psalm 63 indicates that David was in the wilderness of Judah when he wrote this powerful and encouraging psalm.

Psalm 63
A Psalm by David, when he was in the desert of Judah.

There were two different times that David found himself in this desert. The first one was when David was fleeing Saul (1 Samuel 23:13-14). But the second incident is most likely the event that triggered this great psalm. It is found in 2 Samuel 15:23-28 when he was being pursued by Absalom his son.

In verse 11, David refers to himself when he says, "But the king will rejoice in God." He could not have been referring to Saul, who was intending to kill him in the first incident. Saul was not rejoicing in God. Instead, it refers to the takeover of his kingdom from Absalom, David's son.

In 2 Samuel 15, Absalom conspired to overthrow his father and so each day he would stand at the gate where justice was dispensed and convince the people that his father did not care about their legal matters or conflicts.

2 Samuel 15:2-4
Absalom rose up early, and stood beside the way of the gate. When any man had a suit which should come to the king for judgment,

HOW CHRISTIANS MAY DEFEND THEMSELVES AGAINST ATTACK

then Absalom called to him, and said, "What city are you from?" He said, "Your servant is of one of the tribes of Israel." Absalom said to him, "Behold, your matters are good and right; but there is no man deputized by the king to hear you." Absalom said moreover, "Oh that I were made judge in the land, that every man who has any suit or cause might come to me, and I would do him justice!"

Day after day, Absalom questioned his father's integrity and then he suggested that he himself would be a much better choice.

2 Samuel 15:6
Absalom did this sort of thing to all Israel who came to the king for judgment. So Absalom stole the hearts of the men of Israel.

Eventually, he won the hearts of much of the populace and readied himself for the takeover.

When the time came, he acted swiftly.

2 Samuel 15:10-11
But Absalom sent spies throughout all the tribes of Israel, saying, "As soon as you hear the sound of the trumpet, then you shall say, 'Absalom is king in Hebron!'" Two hundred men went with Absalom out of Jerusalem, who were invited, and went in their simplicity; and they didn't know anything.

When David found out, he fled with his loyal subjects into the wilderness of Judah.

2 Samuel 15:13-14
A messenger came to David, saying, "The hearts of the men of Israel are after Absalom." David said to all his servants who were with him at Jerusalem, "Arise! Let's flee; or else none of us will escape from Absalom. Hurry to depart, lest he overtake us quickly, and bring down evil on us, and strike the city with the edge of the sword.... Behold, your servants are ready to do whatever..."

It was in this desert that he called upon the Lord for help.

First, he cries out to God for deliverance.

Psalm 63:1- 4
God, you are my God. I will earnestly seek you. My soul thirsts for you. My flesh longs for you, in a dry and weary land, where there is no water. So I have seen you in the sanctuary, watching your power and your glory. Because your loving kindness is better than life, my lips shall praise you. So I will bless you while I live. I will lift up my hands in your name.

He puts all his trust in God's character and power.

Psalm 63:5-8
My soul shall be satisfied as with the richest food. My mouth shall praise you with joyful lips, when I remember you on my bed, and think about you in the night watches. For you have been my help. I will rejoice in the shadow of your wings. My soul stays close to you. Your right hand holds me up.

He knows that the Lord God will come to his defense, and he will completely defeat the forces who have taken over his kingdom.

Psalm 63:9-10
But those who seek my soul to destroy it shall go into the lower parts of the earth. They shall be given over to the power of the sword. They shall be jackal food.

Finally, he anticipates the time when those who remained loyal to him as king will praise God for His great victory.

Psalm 63:11
But the king shall rejoice in God. Everyone who swears by him will praise him, for the mouth of those who speak lies shall be silenced.

HOW CHRISTIANS MAY DEFEND THEMSELVES AGAINST ATTACK

This is exactly what happened. The two armies met on the battlefield and God delivered David.

2 Samuel 18:6-8
So the people [David's army] went out into the field against Israel [Absalom's army]; and the battle was in the forest of Ephraim. The people of Israel were struck there before David's servants, and there was a great slaughter there that day of twenty thousand men. For the battle was there spread over the surface of all the country, and the forest devoured more people that day than the sword devoured.

Here, David expected his prayers to be answered.

God loves His people and will defend them. His people can expect that He will go before them and defend them when trouble comes. We can pray and then we should anticipate God's deliverance.

The Prayers of Others for Deliverance

In this section, a list of prayers will be provided without their contexts which demonstrate an expectation and trust that God will defend the author.

Psalm 5:3
Yahweh, in the morning you will hear my voice. In the morning I will lay my requests before you, and will watch expectantly.

Psalm 6:4
Return, Yahweh. Deliver my soul, and save me for your loving kindness' sake.

Psalm 7:1
Yahweh, my God, I take refuge in you. Save me from all those who pursue me, and deliver me.

Psalm 7:10
My shield is with God, who saves the upright in heart.

Psalm 12:1
Help, Yahweh; for the godly man ceases. For the faithful fail from among the children of men.

Psalm 17:7
Show your marvelous loving kindness, you who save those who take refuge by your right hand from their enemies.

Psalm 18:3
I call on Yahweh, who is worthy to be praised; and I am saved from my enemies.

Psalm 20:9
Save, Yahweh! Let the King answer us when we call!

Psalm 22:21
Save me from the lion's mouth! Yes, you have rescued me from the horns of the wild oxen.

Psalm 22:20
Deliver my soul from the sword, my precious life from the power of the dog.

Psalm 25:20
Oh keep my soul, and deliver me. Let me not be disappointed, for I take refuge in you.

Psalm 28:9
Save your people, and bless your inheritance. Be their shepherd also, and bear them up forever.

Psalm 31:2
Bow down your ear to me. Deliver me speedily. Be to me a strong rock, a house of defense to save me.

HOW CHRISTIANS MAY DEFEND THEMSELVES AGAINST ATTACK

Psalm 31:2
Bow down your ear to me. Deliver me speedily. Be to me a strong rock, a house of defense to save me.

Psalm 31:4
Pluck me out of the net that they have laid secretly for me, for you are my stronghold.

Psalm 31:15
My times are in your hand. Deliver me from the hand of my enemies, and from those who persecute me.

Psalm 31:16
Make your face to shine on your servant. Save me in your loving kindness.

Psalm 40:13
Be pleased, Yahweh, to deliver me. Hurry to help me, Yahweh.

Psalm 44:7
But you have saved us from our adversaries, and have shamed those who hate us.

Psalm 55:16-17
As for me, I…call on God. Yahweh will save me. Evening, morning, and at noon, I will cry out in distress. He will hear my voice.

Psalm 59:2
Deliver me from the workers of iniquity. Save me from the bloodthirsty men.

Psalm 60:5
So that your beloved may be delivered, save with your right hand, and answer us.

Psalm 69:1
Save me, God, for the waters have come up to my neck!

Psalm 70:1
Hurry, God, to deliver me. Come quickly to help me, Yahweh.

Psalm 71:2
Deliver me in your righteousness, and rescue me. Turn your ear to me, and save me.

Psalm 80:3
Turn us again, God. Cause your face to shine, and we will be saved.

Psalm 80:7
Turn us again, God of Armies. Cause your face to shine, and we will be saved.

Psalm 80:19
Turn us again, Yahweh God of Armies. Cause your face to shine, and we will be saved.

Psalm 82:4
Rescue the weak and needy. Deliver them out of the hand of the wicked."

Psalm 86:2
Preserve my soul, for I am godly. You, my God, save your servant who trusts in you.

Psalm 86:16
Turn to me, and have mercy on me! Give your strength to your servant. Save the son of your servant.

Psalm 106:47
Save us, Yahweh, our God, gather us from among the nations, to give thanks to your holy name, to triumph in your praise!

Psalm 107:13
Then they cried to Yahweh in their trouble, and he saved them out of their distresses.

HOW CHRISTIANS MAY DEFEND THEMSELVES AGAINST ATTACK

Psalm 107:19
Then they cry to Yahweh in their trouble, he saves them out of their distresses.

Psalm 108:6
That your beloved may be delivered, save with your right hand, and answer us.

Psalm 109:21
But deal with me, Yahweh the Lord, for your name's sake, because your loving kindness is good, deliver me.

Psalm 109:26
Help me...my God. Save me according to your loving kindness.

Psalm 116:6
Yahweh preserves the simple. I was brought low, and he saved me.

Psalm 118:25
Save us now, we beg you, Yahweh...send prosperity now.

Psalm 119:94
I am yours. Save me, for I have sought your precepts.

Psalm 119:117
Hold me up, and I will be safe, and will have respect for your statutes continually.

Psalm 119:146
I have called to you. Save me! I will obey your statutes.

Psalm 119:170
Let my supplication come before you. Deliver me according to your word.

Psalm 120:2
Deliver my soul, Yahweh, from lying lips, from a deceitful tongue.

Psalm 143:9
Deliver me, Yahweh, from my enemies. I flee to you to hide me.

Psalm 144:7
Stretch out your hand from above, rescue me, and deliver me out of great waters, out of the hands of foreigners.

Psalm 144:11
Rescue me, and deliver me out of the hands of foreigners, whose mouths speak deceit, whose right hand is a right hand of falsehood.

Genesis 32:11
Please deliver me from the hand of my brother, from the hand of Esau; for I fear him, lest he come and strike me and the mothers with the children.

1 Samuel 7:8
The children of Israel said to Samuel, "Don't stop crying to Yahweh our God for us...he will save us out of the hand of the Philistines."

1 Samuel 26:24
Behold, as your life was respected today in my eyes, so let my life be respected in Yahweh's eyes...let him deliver me out of... oppression.

2 Samuel 22:4
I call on Yahweh, who is worthy to be praised; So, shall I be saved from my enemies.

2 Kings 19:19
Now therefore, Yahweh our God, save us, I beg you, out of his hand, that all the kingdoms of the earth may know that you, Yahweh, are God alone.

1 Chronicles 16:35
Say, "Save us, God of our salvation! Gather us together and deliver us from the nations, to give thanks to your holy name, to triumph in your praise."

HOW CHRISTIANS MAY DEFEND THEMSELVES AGAINST ATTACK

2 Chronicles 20:9
If evil comes on us – the sword, judgment, pestilence, or famine – we will stand before this house, and before you (for your name is in this house), and cry to you in our affliction, and you will hear and save.

Isaiah 37:20
Now therefore, Yahweh our God, save us from his hand, that all the kingdoms of the earth may know that you are Yahweh, even you only.

Jeremiah 17:14
Heal me, O Yahweh, and I will be healed. Save me, and I will be saved; for you are my praise.

In these prayers, there is a powerful expectation that God will answer their prayers and come to their defense.

The Confidence of Trust in Him

There was a confidence that if they trusted the Lord in their lives, he would defend and protect them. It was what they believed because God said He would, and they saw Him do it time and time again.

The Trust God Desires

First, the Lord God said He would. Moses explained God's defense of His people.

Deuteronomy 20:1-4
When you go out to battle against your enemies, and see horses, chariots, and a people more numerous than you, you shall not be

afraid of them; for Yahweh your God is with you, who brought you up out of the land of Egypt. It shall be, when you draw near to the battle, that the priest shall approach and speak to the people, and shall tell them, "Hear, Israel, you draw near today to battle against your enemies. Don't let your heart faint! Don't be afraid, nor tremble, neither be scared of them; for Yahweh your God is he who goes with you, to fight for you against your enemies, to save you."

God claims He will defend them and wants His people to trust in this truth.

The Trust God Demonstrated

Second, they had experienced God's protection as they trusted Him. As we just saw, David trusted God to protect him against the army of Absalom.

Psalm 63:5-7
My soul shall be satisfied as with the richest food. My mouth shall praise you with joyful lips, when I remember you on my bed, and think about you in the night watches. For you have been my help. I will rejoice in the shadow of your wings.

Here, David is praising God for always defending him. His thoughts go this in the day and in the night as guard.

The Trust We Should Have

Now, he speaks of his soul clinging to God in trust. He knows God will fight with him and destroy his enemies.

Psalm 63:8-11
My soul stays close to you. Your right hand holds me up. But those who seek my soul to destroy it shall go into the lower parts of the

earth. They shall be given over to the power of the sword. They shall be jackal food. But the king shall rejoice in God. Everyone who swears by him will praise him, for the mouth of those who speak lies shall be silenced.

He looks forward to the time that he will be rejoicing in God because of the great victory, his loyal follows will praise God, and his enemies will be silenced.

As can be seen God protects His people and we can trust in Him for this. Here are several passages that speaks of this real confidence in the Lord's protection. The context is not even necessary to see this truth.

1 Samuel 17:47
And that all this assembly may know that Yahweh doesn't save with sword and spear; for the battle is Yahweh's, and he will give you into our hand.

Jeremiah 16:19
Yahweh, my strength, and my stronghold, and my refuge in the day of affliction, the nations will come to you from the ends of the earth, and will say, "Our fathers have inherited nothing but lies, vanity and things in which there is no profit."

Psalm 27:1
Yahweh is my light and my salvation. Whom shall I fear? Yahweh is the strength of my life. Of whom shall I be afraid?

Psalm 28:8-9
Yahweh is their strength. He is a stronghold of salvation to his anointed. Save your people, and bless your inheritance. Be their shepherd also, and bear them up forever.

Psalm 31:4
Pluck me out of the net that they have laid secretly for me, for you are my stronghold.

Psalm 37:39
But the salvation of the righteous is from Yahweh. He is their stronghold in the time of trouble.

Psalm 37:40
Yahweh helps them and rescues them. He rescues them from the wicked and saves them, because they have taken refuge in him.

Psalm 86:1-2
Hear, Yahweh, and answer me, for I am poor and needy. Preserve my soul, for I am godly. You, my God, save your servant who trusts in you.

Proverbs 20:22
Don't say, "I will pay back evil." Wait for Yahweh, and he will save you.

Here again, we see God's people trusting Him and exhorting others to do the same. God's people are inclined to expect God to defend them.

The People's Complaints of Disbelief

Though God promised to defend His people, at times He refused or even brought armies against them because of their sin and idolatry. When this occurred, the people cried out in complaint because they could not believe God would not defend them. They expected Him to deliver them because they were His people. They expected Him to defend them because that is who He is and what He does.

Since this truth is so evident, as we did in the last section, we will simply list some passages which demonstrate this. It is left up to the readers to consider the context if they feel it necessary.

The Complaint in Historical Narratives

Here are two examples of complaints in the history books.

Judges 6:12-14
Yahweh's angel appeared to him, and said to him, "Yahweh is with you, you mighty man of valor!" Gideon said to him, "Oh, my lord, if Yahweh is with us, why then has all this happened to us? Where are all his wondrous works which our fathers told us of, saying, 'Didn't Yahweh bring us up from Egypt?' But now Yahweh has cast us off, and delivered us into the hand of Midian." Yahweh looked at him, and said, "Go in this your might, and save Israel from the hand of Midian. Haven't I sent you?"

1 Samuel 4:2-3
The Philistines put themselves in array against Israel. When they joined battle, Israel was defeated by the Philistines, who killed about four thousand men of the army in the field. When the people had come into the camp, the elders of Israel said, "Why has Yahweh defeated us today before the Philistines? Let's get the ark of Yahweh's covenant out of Shiloh and bring it to us, that it may come among us and save us out of the hand of our enemies."

They could not understand why God did not defend them, they expected Him to.

The Complaints in the Prophetic Literature

There are many complaints in the prophets, but a few will suffice.

Jeremiah 8:20
The harvest is past. The summer has ended, and we are not saved. For the hurt of the daughter of my people am I hurt: I mourn; dismay has taken hold on me.

Jeremiah 14:8 For the hurt of the daughter
You hope of Israel, its Savior in the time of trouble, why should you be as a foreigner in the land, and as a wayfaring man who turns aside to stay for a night?

Jeremiah 14:9
Why should you be like a scared man, as a mighty man who can't save? Yet you, Yahweh, are in the middle of us, and we are called by your name. Don't leave us.

Lamentations 4:17
Our eyes still fail, looking in vain for our help. In our watching we have watched for a nation that could not save.

Habakkuk 1:2
Yahweh, how long will I cry, and you will not hear? I cry out to you "Violence!" and will you not save? Here again, God not delivering them was unimaginable.

The Complaints in the Songs and Prayers

Of course, the Psalms are filled with the complaints of no deliverance.

Psalm 10:1
Why do you stand far off, Yahweh? Why do you hide yourself in times of trouble?

Psalm 22:1
My God, my God, why have you forsaken me? Why are you so far from helping me, and from the words of my groaning?

Psalm 42:5
Why are you in despair, my soul? Why are you disturbed…Hope in God! For I shall still praise him for the saving help of his presence.

HOW CHRISTIANS MAY DEFEND THEMSELVES AGAINST ATTACK

Psalm 42:9
I will ask God, my rock, "Why have you forgotten me? Why do I go mourning because of the oppression of the enemy?"

Psalm 42:11
Why are you in despair, my soul? Why are you disturbed within me? Hope in God...the saving help of my countenance, and my God.

Psalm 43:2
For you are the God of my strength. Why have you rejected me? Why do I go mourning because of the oppression of the enemy?

Psalm 43:5
Why are you in despair, my soul? Why are you disturbed within me? Hope in God! For I shall still praise him: my Savior, my helper, and my God.

Psalm 44:23-24
Wake up! Why do you sleep, Lord? Arise! Don't reject us forever. Why do you hide your face...forget our affliction...our oppression?

Psalm 49:5
Why should I fear in the days of evil, when iniquity at my heels surrounds me?

Psalm 74:1
God, why have you rejected us forever? Why does your anger smolder against the sheep of your pasture?

Psalm 74:10-11
How long, God, shall the adversary reproach? Shall the enemy blaspheme your name forever? Why do you draw back your hand, even your right hand? Take it from your chest and consume them!

Psalm 79:10
Why should the nations say, "Where is their God?" Let it be known among the nations, before our eyes...vengeance for your servants....

Psalm 88:14
Yahweh, why do you reject my soul? Why do you hide your face from me?

Defense from their God was so expected that they even sang their complaints.

Here we have discovered that disbelief and utter confusion came when God did not protect His people. They expected God to come to their defense. Why? The Lord is a God of protection and defense.

The Lord's Complaint of Distrust

There were times when God chastised His people for not trusting and relying on Him and rather pursuing the help of other nations. He wanted them to expect His deliverance.

The Lord promised to protect His people and demanded they rely upon Him.

Jeremiah 39:18
"For I will surely save you, and you won't fall by the sword, but you will escape with your life; because you have put your trust in me," says Yahweh.

His people sometimes refused.

Isaiah 30:15
For thus said the Lord Yahweh, the Holy One of Israel, "You will be saved in returning and rest. Your strength will be in quietness and in confidence." You refused.

This caused the Lord God to chastise them. Again, we will just present several passages because the point is clear.

HOW CHRISTIANS MAY DEFEND THEMSELVES AGAINST ATTACK

Isaiah 30:2-3
Who set out to go down into Egypt, and have not asked my advice, to strengthen themselves in the strength of Pharaoh, and to take refuge in the shadow of Egypt! Therefore the strength of Pharaoh will be your shame, and the refuge in the shadow of Egypt your confusion.

Isaiah 31:1
Woe to those who go down to Egypt for help, and rely on horses, and trust in chariots because they are many, and in horsemen because they are very strong, but they don't look to the Holy One of Israel, and they don't seek Yahweh!

Psalm 52:7
Behold, this is the man who didn't make God his strength, but trusted in the abundance of his riches, and strengthened himself in his wickedness.

Isaiah 57:13
When you cry, let those whom you have gathered deliver you; but the wind will take them. A breath will carry them all away: but he who takes refuge in me will possess the land and will inherit my holy mountain."

As can be seen, God desired men to trust in Him and expect Him to defend them. The Lord held them accountable when they do not.

In summary, God is a God who defends His Name and reputation, His purposes and plan, the people He loves, and the Innocent. As a result, His people expected Him to protect them. We studied examples of their presumptions that He would protect the ones with whom He had a relationship. We discovered that His people prayed for deliverance assuming God would answer through His protection. Over and over, we see God's people confident in His deliverance. When God did not deliver His people, they found themselves in utter disbelief. Then, they complained to Him. Even God expected His people to trust in Him and held them accountable when they did not trust Him. The Lord chastised His people when they sought help from the nations around because they refuse to trust in Him.

As God defends His people, we ought to defend others also. Won't people that we love expect us to defend them in time of danger? If they asked, wouldn't they assume we will come? Would they not trust in us to defend them if we had done this in the past? Would we not desire them to trust us? Lastly, they would be shocked if we refused to help. Why? It is the human expectation for God to defend and for us to defend! When we do this, we are imitating Him.

Chapter 8

The Natural Inclination

Defending oneself and others is a natural inclination. It is something we simply do naturally when threatened. God has put within our hearts a deep desire to defend ourselves, those we love, and the innocent. In this chapter, we will study some of the areas of life where this natural inclination is seen with the purpose of demonstrating that defense is put into our hearts by God.

The Familial Response

The natural desire to defend ourselves, those we love, and the innocent begins in the family. Family members protect each other. This can be observed throughout the Scriptures.

A Mother's Protection

When Pharaoh commanded the Hebrew mid-wives to kill every male baby born, the parents of Moses hid him for as long as they could. Then, the mother and father of Moses protected him as an infant by orchestrating his adoption by Pharaoh's daughter.

Exodus 2:1-10
A man of the house of Levi went and took a daughter of Levi as his wife. The woman conceived and bore a son. When she saw that he was a fine child, she hid him three months. When she could no longer hide him, she took a papyrus basket for him, and coated it with tar

and with pitch. She put the child in it, and laid it in the reeds by the river's bank. His sister stood far off, to see what would be done to him. Pharaoh's daughter came down to bathe at the river. Her maidens walked along by the riverside. She saw the basket among the reeds, and sent her servant to get it. She opened it, and saw the child, and behold, the baby cried. She had compassion on him, and said, "This is one of the Hebrews' children." Then his sister said to Pharaoh's daughter, "Should I go and call a nurse for you from the Hebrew women, that she may nurse the child for you?" Pharaoh's daughter said to her, "Go." The young woman went and called the child's mother. Pharaoh's daughter said to her, "Take this child away, and nurse him for me, and I will give you your wages." The woman took the child, and nursed it. The child grew, and she brought him to Pharaoh's daughter, and he became her son. She named him Moses, and said, "Because I drew him out of the water."

His parent's natural inclination was to protect their son and their plan succeeded.

A Father's Prayer

When David committed adultery with Bathsheba and murdered her husband to cover it up, the Lord's judgment was to take his infant son. David response would be typical of any father in that situation. He begged God to let him live. He attempted to protect his son through his prayers which were his only defense in this incident.

2 Samuel 12:13-18
David said to Nathan, "I have sinned against Yahweh." Nathan said to David, "Yahweh also has put away your sin. You will not die. However, because by this deed you have given great occasion to Yahweh's enemies to blaspheme, the child also who is born to you will surely die." Nathan departed to his house. Yahweh struck the child that Uriah's wife bore to David, and it was very sick. David therefore begged God for the child; and David fasted, and went in,

and lay all night on the ground. The elders of his house arose beside him, to raise him up from the earth: but he would not, and he didn't eat bread with them. On the seventh day, the child died. David's servants were afraid to tell him that the child was dead, for they said, "Behold, while the child was yet alive, we spoke to him, and he didn't listen to our voice. How will he then harm himself, if we tell him that the child is dead?" But when David saw that his servants were whispering together, David perceived that the child was dead; and David said to his servants, "Is the child dead?"*

Though David's natural inclination was to protect his son, he failed.

An Uncle's Defense

Abraham's natural inclination was to rescue his nephew Lot when he was captured.

Genesis 14:8-16
The king of Sodom, and the king of Gomorrah, the king of Admah, the king of Zeboiim, and the king of Bela (also called Zoar) went out; and they set the battle in array against them in the valley of Siddim against Chedorlaomer king of Elam, Tidal king of Goiim, Amraphel king of Shinar, and Arioch king of Ellasar; four kings against the five. Now the valley of Siddim was full of tar pits; and the kings of Sodom and Gomorrah fled, and some fell there. Those who remained fled to the hills. They took all the goods of Sodom and Gomorrah, and all their food, and went their way. They took Lot, Abram's brother's son, who lived in Sodom, and his goods, and departed. One who had escaped came and told Abram, the Hebrew. At that time, he lived by the oaks of Mamre, the Amorite, brother of Eshcol and brother of Aner. They were allies of Abram. When Abram heard that his relative was taken captive, he led out his three hundred eighteen trained men, born in his house, and pursued as far as Dan. He divided himself against them by night, he and his servants, and

struck them, and pursued them to Hobah, which is on the left hand of Damascus. He brought back all the goods, and also brought back his relative Lot and his goods, and the women also, and the other people.

Abram responded in the most natural way - defend Lot.

A Family's Flight

When Mary and Joseph were informed of Herod's desire to murder their infant, they did not hesitate to flee to Egypt.

Matthew 2:13-14
Now when they had departed, behold, an angel of the Lord appeared to Joseph in a dream, saying, "Arise and take the young child and his mother, and flee into Egypt, and stay there until I tell you, for Herod will seek the young child to destroy him." He arose and took the young child and his mother by night and departed into Egypt.

Mary and Joseph's natural inclination was to follow the Lord and flee in order to defend their child's life.

A Father's Alarm

After Mary and Joseph were told to return to Israel by an angel, they chose to live in Nazareth to protect his Son.

Matthew 2:19-23
But when Herod was dead, behold, an angel of the Lord appeared in a dream to Joseph in Egypt, saying, "Arise and take the young child and his mother, and go into the land of Israel, for those who sought the young child's life are dead." He arose and took the young child and his mother, and came into the land of Israel. But when he heard that Archelaus was reigning over Judea in the place of his father,

HOW CHRISTIANS MAY DEFEND THEMSELVES AGAINST ATTACK

Herod, he was afraid to go there. Being warned in a dream, he withdrew into the region of Galilee, and came and lived in a city called Nazareth; that it might be fulfilled which was spoken through the prophets that he will be called a Nazarene.

Joseph's natural inclination was to live in an area far from the son of Herod to protect his Son.

A Parent's Concern

When the parents of Jesus discovered that he was not with the caravan, they panicked and began to search for him.

Luke 2:42-52
When he was twelve years old, they went up to Jerusalem according to the custom of the feast, and when they had fulfilled the days, as they were returning, the boy Jesus stayed behind in Jerusalem. Joseph and his mother didn't know it, but supposing him to be in the company, they went a day's journey, and they looked for him among their relatives and acquaintances. When they didn't find him, they returned to Jerusalem, looking for him. After three days they found him in the temple, sitting in the middle of the teachers, both listening to them, and asking them questions. All who heard him were amazed at his understanding and his answers. When they saw him, they were astonished, and his mother said to him, "Son, why have you treated us this way? Behold, your father and I were anxiously looking for you." He said to them, "Why were you looking for me? Didn't you know that I must be in my Father's house?" They didn't understand the saying which he spoke to them. And he went down with them, and came to Nazareth. He was subject to them, and his mother kept all these sayings in her heart. And Jesus increased in wisdom and stature, and in favor with God and men.

Mary and Joseph's hurried response to find Jesus was the natural inclination that parents have inside them.

These are just a few examples of a family's inclination to defend other family members from harm. Protecting family members is completely natural as the Bible demonstrates.

A Brother's Protection

When Reuben, the brother of Joseph, realized that his brothers were going to kill Joseph, he defended his brother by providing an alternate plan so he could secretly rescue him at another time.

Genesis 37:21-22
Reuben heard it, and delivered him out of their hand, and said, "Let's not take his life." Reuben said to them, "Shed no blood. Throw him into this pit that is in the wilderness, but lay no hand on him" that he might deliver him out of their hand, to restore him to his father. When Joseph came to his brothers, they stripped Joseph of his coat, the coat of many colors that was on him, and they took him, and threw him into the pit. The pit was empty. There was no water in it.

Though Reuben's natural desire was to defend and save his brother, he could not succeed.

A Spouse's Defense

As Moses is presenting the various laws of God, one of the laws assumes the natural impulse a wife will have to defend her husband in a fight.

Deuteronomy 25:11-12
When men strive against each other, and the wife of one draws near to deliver her husband out of the hand of him who strikes him, and puts out her hand, and grabs him by his private parts, then you shall cut off her hand. Your eye shall have no pity.

HOW CHRISTIANS MAY DEFEND THEMSELVES AGAINST ATTACK

The defense of the wife was a natural inclination and expected by the Lord God, He simply did not want her to take a certain unacceptable action in that defense.

The Disposition to Watch

Another illustration of the human inclination to defend oneself and others is the natural disposition for people to watch for danger. People understand that danger could come suddenly, and they must be prepared by watching for it. Why would someone watch for danger? It is because they want to defend themselves and those they care about.

In ancient times, cities would have walls around them to protect its citizens from attack. A clear example of this is the city of Jericho which was the first city attacked by Israel when they entered the promised land. The city was surrounded by a high wall that had to be scaled or pummeled with stones to destroy it so an enemy could attack. This was something that could not be done easily.

Joshua 6:1-5
Now Jericho was tightly shut up because of the children of Israel. No one went out, and no one came in. Yahweh said to Joshua, "Behold, I have given Jericho into your hand, with its king and the mighty men of valor. All of your men of war shall march around the city, going around the city once. You shall do this six days. Seven priests shall bear seven trumpets of rams' horns before the ark. On the seventh day, you shall march around the city seven times, and the priests shall blow the trumpets. It shall be that when they make a long blast with the ram's horn, and when you hear the sound of the trumpet, all the people shall shout with a great shout; then the city wall will fall down flat, and the people shall go up...."

The wall had to be demolished so an army could invade.

On the wall, there would be guards who would watch for danger from an invader to protect the people. Sometimes, towers were built to lift the guards high enough to watch a large area. When Asa became king, he sought the Lord and God gave him peace throughout the land. So, the king took the opportunity to fortify his cities against attack. Notice, he built towers.

2 Chronicles 14:7-8
For he said to Judah, "Let's build these cities, and make walls around them, with towers, gates, and bars. The land is yet before us, because we have sought Yahweh our God. We have sought him, and he has given us rest on every side." So they built and prospered.

High towers allowed them to watch for danger to see enemies coming from miles away to allow time to prepare for defense.

The Watching in Real Life

As before, the passages that mention the watchmen will only be listed. The context can be looked up if needed.

1 Samuel 14:16
The watchmen of Saul in Gibeah of Benjamin looked; and behold, the multitude melted away and scattered.

2 Samuel 13:34
But Absalom fled. The young man who kept the watch lifted up his eyes, and looked, and behold, many people were coming by way of the hillside behind him.

2 Samuel 18:24
Now David was sitting between the two gates; and the watchman went up to the roof of the gate to the wall, and lifted up his eyes, and looked, and, behold, a man running alone.

HOW CHRISTIANS MAY DEFEND THEMSELVES AGAINST ATTACK

2 Kings 9:17
Now the watchman was standing on the tower in Jezreel, and he spied the company of Jehu as he came, and said, "I see a company." Joram said, "Take a horseman, and send to meet them...."

Isaiah 21:6
For the Lord said to me, "Go, set a watchman. Let him declare what he sees.

Here, we see watchmen keep an eye out for enemies or some other danger. This is a natural inclination.

The Watching in Prophecy

The idea of "watching for danger" is used in prophecy to warn of coming judgment among other things. In Nahum 2, the city of Nineveh would be judged for their wickedness, they could watch for their conquerors to come and even prepare for their defense, but it would be of useless.

Nahum 2:1
He who dashes in pieces has come up against you. Keep the fortress! Watch the way! Strengthen your waist! Fortify...power mightily!

In Habakkuk 2, the prophet asked God why He would allow the Chaldeans to conquer them when they were more wicked than Israel. He would watch and wait for the answer.

Habakkuk 2:1
I will stand at my watch, and set myself on the ramparts, and will look out to see what he will say to me, and what I will answer concerning my complaint.

The best of God's people was like useless thorn branches and judgment was coming. The people should watch for the visitation of God's wrath (the conquering nation) and the day they will wonder in confusion as they are being destroyed.

Micah 7:4
The best of them is like a brier. The most upright is worse than a thorn hedge. The day of your watchmen, even your visitation, has come; now is the time of their confusion.

All readers of these prophecies understood exactly what this "watching for danger" involved. "Watching for danger" is a natural inclination.

The Watching in Analogies

The Holy Scriptures often take everyday events, common practices, and ordinary customs and use them as analogies for spiritual truth. In the following passages, we see watching for physical danger used as an analogy of watching for spiritual danger. This is important because if something from life is used as an analogy, it means that what is referred to is a common practice. It is utilized in the analogy because people would understand what it meant.

Proverbs 8:34
Blessed is the man who hears me, watching daily at...gates, waiting at my door posts.

Ezekiel 3:17
Son of man, I have made you a watchman to the house of Israel. Therefore hear the word from my mouth, and warn them from me.

Ezekiel 33:2
Son of man, speak to the children of your people, and tell them, "When I bring the sword on a land, and the people of the land take a man from among them, and set him for their watchman."

HOW CHRISTIANS MAY DEFEND THEMSELVES AGAINST ATTACK

Ezekiel 33:6-7
But if the watchman sees the sword come, and doesn't blow the trumpet, and the people aren't warned, and the sword comes, and takes any person from among them; he is taken away in his iniquity, but his blood I will require at the watchman's hand. So you, son of man: I have set you a watchman to the house of Israel. Therefore hear the word from my mouth, and give them warnings from me.

Hosea 9:8
A prophet watches over Ephraim with my God. A fowler's snare is on all of his paths, and hostility in the house of his God.

So, the watching for danger was a natural way people would respond to the possibility of violent men attempting harm upon them. They had watchmen on the walls, towers, and at their gates. Why? The next natural response was to defend themselves and others.

The Propensity to Guard

As was mentioned earlier, cities would be guarded also. These guards would be the first line of defense against an attack. They would provide enough time to allow for the army or even the populace to arm themselves to do battle. Again, we will only list some of the passages which mention them since there has been much discussion already. The point is that guarding others has always been a common practice and still is.

The Guards of the King

Due to the importance of a king, he would have his own team of guards protecting him from danger and being ready to defend him from harm.

Genesis 40:4
The captain of the guard assigned them to Joseph, and he took care of them. They stayed in prison many days.

Genesis 41:10
Pharaoh was angry with his servants, and put me in custody in the house of the captain of the guard, with the chief baker.

1 Samuel 22:14
Then Ahimelech answered the king, and said, "Who among all your servants is so faithful as David, who is the king's son-in-law, captain of your body guard, and honored in your house?

2 Samuel 23:23
He was more honorable than the thirty, but he didn't attain to the three. David set him over his guard.

These are just a few of the examples of guards who were prepared to keep the king from danger.

The Guards of the City

As the cities were built, guards were created to protect the people. Without this common practice, no one would feel safe in the city.

1 Chronicles 26:16
To Shuppim and Hosah westward, by the gate of Shallecheth, at the causeway that goes up, watchman opposite watchman.

Jeremiah 51:12
Set up a standard against the walls of Babylon! Make the watch strong! Set the body guard prepare the ambushes; for Yahweh has both purposed and done that which he spoke concerning the inhabitants of Babylon.

HOW CHRISTIANS MAY DEFEND THEMSELVES AGAINST ATTACK

These are two illustrations of the natural inclination to recruit guards to protect the citizenry from harm.

The Guards of the People

There are times in which people must guard themselves and others. When there are no official guards, there will be occasions where people will naturally arm themselves when danger is perceived. This occurred when Nehemiah and many Hebrews came back from their captivity to rebuild their land. There were those who had been living in the land for a long time who did not welcome them. Because they felt threatened, the people armed themselves.

Nehemiah 4:9
But we made our prayer to our God, and set a watch against them day and night because of them.

Nehemiah 4:22-23
Likewise at the same time I said to the people, "Let everyone with his servant lodge within Jerusalem, that in the night they may be a guard to us, and may labor in the day." So neither I, nor my brothers, nor my servants, nor the men of the guard who followed me, none of us took off our clothes. Everyone took his weapon to the water.

Nehemiah 7:3
I said to them, "Don't let the gates of Jerusalem be opened until the sun is hot; and while they stand guard, let them shut the doors, and you bar them: and appoint watches of the inhabitants of Jerusalem, everyone in his watch, with everyone near his house."

Nehemiah 12:25
Mattaniah, and Bakbukiah, Obadiah, Meshullam, Talmon, Akkub, were gatekeepers keeping the watch at the storehouses of the gates.

It does not require that much thought to comprehend the importance of having people around who are guarding others from danger. They are in plain sight to deter evil and to respond if evil occurs. These are obvious truths, but it is important to state them to confirm that defense of ourselves, those we love, and the innocent are natural inclinations from God.

The Penchant for Carrying Weapons

The many weapons mentioned in the Bible were discussed in another chapter. In this section, it must be pointed out that the weapons were built, possessed, and then often carried by the general populace rather than exclusively by the military or police. It is a natural desire within people to have weapons to protect themselves and those they love. Those who do not carry weapons are assuming they will never be in danger or those with weapons will quickly come to their aid. We see neither of these notions in the Scriptures.

The Building of Weapons

Ancient man always built himself weapons for protection. Of course, they would also use them offensively, but it stands to reason the first purpose would be defensive.

When the Assyrians came to raid God's people, Hezekiah immediately began to build up his armory.

2 Chronicles 32:1-8
After these things and this faithfulness, Sennacherib king of Assyria came, entered into Judah, and encamped against the fortified cities, and intended to win them for himself. When Hezekiah saw that

HOW CHRISTIANS MAY DEFEND THEMSELVES AGAINST ATTACK

Sennacherib had come, and that he was planning to fight against Jerusalem, he took counsel with his princes and his mighty men to stop the waters of the springs which were outside of the city, and they helped him. So, many people gathered together and they stopped all the springs....He took courage, built up all the wall that was broken down, and raised it up to the towers, with the other wall outside, and strengthened Millo in David's city, and made weapons and shields in abundance. He set captains of war over the people, and gathered them together to him in the wide place at the gate of the city, and spoke encouragingly to them, saying, "Be strong and courageous. Don't be afraid or dismayed because of the king of Assyria, nor for all the multitude who is with him; for there is a greater one with us than with him. An arm of flesh is with him, but Yahweh our God is with us to help us and to fight our battles." The people rested themselves on the words of Hezekiah king of Judah.

The ones who would receive the weapons would have been any man who could still wield them.

We see this clearly when the Moabites were about to do battle with the Israelites.

2 Kings 3:21
Now when all the Moabites heard that the kings had come up to fight against them, they gathered themselves together, all who were able to put on armor, young and old, and stood on the border.

All, who were able, came out to defend themselves.

The Carrying of Weapons by the Priests

Sometime after Israel split into two kingdoms, Judah was ruled by Ahaziah, the son of Jehoshaphat. He was treacherous toward the people because he followed the advice of his evil mother. When he passed away, the mother took control of the kingdom. She killed the potential heirs to the throne and ruled herself. The youngest son of Ahaziah was rescued and kept in hiding until he was seven. Then, several leaders gathered the heads of the households and the Levites (the priestly line) and prepared to stand against the queen (mother of Ahaziah) and declare Joash (only surviving son) King of Judah.

2 Chronicles 23:3-7
They went around in Judah, and gathered the Levites out of all the cities of Judah, and the heads of fathers' households of Israel, and they came to Jerusalem. All the assembly made a covenant with the king in God's house. He said to them, "Behold, the king's son must reign, as Yahweh has spoken concerning the sons of David. This is the thing that you must do. A third part of you, who come in on the Sabbath, of the priests and of the Levites, shall be gatekeepers of the thresholds. A third part shall be at the king's house; and a third part at the gate of the foundation. All the people will be in the courts of Yahweh's house. But let no one come into Yahweh's house, except the priests and those who minister of the Levites. They shall come in, for they are holy, but all the people shall follow Yahweh's instructions. The Levites shall surround the king, every man with his weapons in his hand. Whoever comes into the house, let him be slain. Be with the king when he comes in, and when he goes out."

Here, the priests are seen protecting Joash, the new king, with weapons in their hands.

The Carrying of Weapons by the People

Once again, we have come to the story of Nehemiah which demonstrates self-defense by the average person.

Nehemiah 4:17
Those who built the wall...those who bore burdens...everyone with one of his hands did the work, and with the other held his weapon.

Nehemiah 4:23
So neither I, nor my brothers, nor my servants, nor the men of the guard who followed me, none of us took off our clothes. Everyone took his weapon to the water.

As we will see, a person usually had a staff to protect himself and also could acquire a sword if the perceived danger would be greater than a staff could defend against.

The Declaration of None to Defend

Another way in which we can understand the importance of self-defense and the defense of others is by studying reactions when someone does not come to our defense. If the defense of others is a natural inclination among humans, then they would verbalize the fact that no one came to rescue them. If deliverance is critical, then no deliverance will be equally important. Here are several examples from the Scriptures expressing this fact.

The Declaration in the Historical Narratives

Here are several illustrations of declarations in the inspired history of Israel. As with other sections, we will cite the passages alone without the context because this is another obvious truth.

Deuteronomy 22:27
For he found her in the field, the pledged to be married lady cried, and there was no one to save her.

Deuteronomy 28:29
You will grope at noonday, as the blind gropes in darkness, and you

shall not prosper in your ways. You will only be oppressed and robbed always, and there will be no one to save you.

Deuteronomy 28:31
Your ox will be slain before your eyes…. Your donkey will be violently taken away from before your face…. Your sheep will be given to your enemies, and you will have no one to save you.

Judges 12:2-3
Jephthah said to them, "I and my people were at great strife with the children of Ammon; and when I called you, you didn't save me out of their hand. When I saw that you didn't save me, I put my life in your hand, and passed over against the children of Ammon, and Yahweh delivered them into my hand. Why then have you come up to me today, to fight against me? Then Jephthah gathered together all the men of Gilead, and fought…Manasseh."

Judges 18:28
There was no deliverer, because it was far from Sidon, and they had no dealings with anyone else; and it was in the valley that lies by Beth Rehob. They built the city and lived in it.

1 Samuel 10:27
But certain worthless fellows said, "How could this man save us?" They despised him, and brought him no tribute. But he held his peace.

1 Samuel 11:3
The elders of Jabesh said to him, "Give us seven days, that we may send messengers to all the borders of Israel; and then, if there is no one to save us, we will come out to you."

2 Samuel 22:41-43
You have also made my enemies turn their backs on me, that I might cut off those who hate me. They looked, but there was no one to save; even to Yahweh, but he didn't answer them. Then I beat them as small as the dust of the earth. I crushed them…spread them abroad.

They could not understand why no one came to defend them. They knew it was a natural inclination for others to come to their aid. We know this intuitively because it comes from inside us and we know we ought to defend and deliver others.

The Declarations in the Prophetic Literature

There are many declarations in the prophets concerning the fact that no one came to deliver them.

Isaiah 5:29
Their roaring will be like a lioness. They will roar like young lions. Yes, they shall roar, and seize their prey and carry it off, and there will be no one to deliver.

Isaiah 42:22
But this is a robbed and plundered people. All of them are snared in holes, and they are hidden in prisons. They have become captives, and no one delivers, and a plunder, and no one says, 'Restore them!'

Daniel 8:4
I saw the ram pushing westward, northward, and southward. No animals could stand before him. There wasn't any who could deliver out of his hand; but he did according to his will, and magnified himself.

Here again, no one delivering them was unimaginable. It is assumed that this is a natural urge.

The Declarations in the Songs and Prayers

Of course, the Psalms are filled with declarations of no deliverance. Defense from someone was so expected that they even sang of their declarations. Here are just two examples.

Psalm 7:2
Lest they tear apart my soul like a lion, ripping it in pieces, while there is no one to deliver.

Psalm 71:11
Saying, "God has forsaken him. Pursue and take him, for no one will rescue him."

Here we have discovered that disbelief and utter confusion came when others did not protect them. Why? They knew it was natural within man to defend others.

As can be seen, the expectation is that a defender will come when one is in trouble because it is deep within our hearts to come to the aid of those we love or for whom we care.

The Impulse to Defend Others

When trouble comes for people in the Scriptures, we see the human inclination by others to come to their defense and rescue displayed. We intuitively know this. Someone screams for help; others will come to their defense. When no one does, people react in horror because of the apathy or fear. Again, just two examples should suffice.

The Rescue by David and His Men

In 1 Samuel 22, we are told the story of David's escape from the clutches of Saul. While a fugitive, he hid in a cave in the land of Adullum.

1 Samuel 22:1-2
David therefore departed from there, and escaped to Adullam's cave.

HOW CHRISTIANS MAY DEFEND THEMSELVES AGAINST ATTACK

When his brothers and all his father's house heard it, they went down there to him. Everyone who was in distress, everyone who was in debt, and everyone who was discontented, gathered themselves to him; and he became captain over them. There were with him about four hundred men.

David had gathered a band of malcontents who were drawn to him, and they became his army.

When news came that the inhabitants of Keilah, his fellow Hebrews, had been attacked by the dreaded Philistines, he acted quickly.

1 Samuel 23:1-4
David was told, "Behold, the Philistines are fighting against Keilah, and are robbing the threshing floors." Therefore David inquired of Yahweh, saying, "Shall I go and strike these Philistines?" Yahweh said to David, "Go strike the Philistines, and save Keilah." David's men said to him, "Behold, we are afraid here in Judah. How much more then if we go to Keilah against the armies of the Philistines?" Then David inquired of Yahweh yet again. Yahweh answered him, and said, "Arise, go down to Keilah; for I will deliver the Philistines into your hand."

As a man of God, David asked the Lord if he should go rescue his countrymen, and the Lord God Almighty answered in the affirmative.

As a result, David took his men and went to defend his people from their enemies.

1 Samuel 23:5-6
David and his men went to Keilah, and fought with the Philistines, and brought away their livestock, and killed them with a great slaughter. So David saved the inhabitants of Keilah. When Abiathar the son of Ahimelech fled to David to Keilah, he came down with an ephod in his hand.

Notice, David heard the news of harm coming to his people and immediately wanted to act. It is a human inclination to desire to defend the helpless.

The Treaties to Protect Nations

We see both sides of this impulse to defend or be defended constantly among rulers. They make treaties to protect each other against the attacks of other nations.

One example comes from the enemies of David and Israel which is found in 2 Samuel 10. In this story, the Ammonites have just set a new king upon their throne. David desires to honor him because of the kindness the new king's father had shown him.

2 Samuel 10:1-2
After this, the king of the children of Ammon died, and Hanun his son reigned in his place. David said, "I will show kindness to Hanun the son of Nahash, as his father showed kindness to me." So David sent by his servants to comfort him concerning his father. David's servants came into the land of the children of Ammon.

Unfortunately, they thought David was being insincere, so they abused the delegation that David had sent to honor the new king.

2 Samuel 10:3-5
But the princes of the children of Ammon said to Hanun their lord, "Do you think that David honors your father, in that he has sent comforters to you? Hasn't David sent his servants to you to search the city, to spy it out, and to overthrow it?" So Hanun took David's servants, shaved off one half of their beards...cut off their garments in the middle, even to their buttocks, and sent them away. When they told David this, he sent to meet them, for the men were greatly ashamed. The king said, "Wait...and then return."

HOW CHRISTIANS MAY DEFEND THEMSELVES AGAINST ATTACK

Of course, this angered King David, and the Ammonites immediately sought the help of the Syrians.

2 Samuel 10:6
When the children of Ammon saw that they had become odious to David, the children of Ammon sent and hired the Syrians of Beth Rehob, and the Syrians of Zobah, twenty thousand footmen, and the king of Maacah with one thousand men, and the men of Tob twelve thousand men.

When he heard that the Syrians would defend them, King David gathered his army.

2 Samuel 10:7
When David heard of it, he sent Joab, and all the army of the mighty men. 8 The children of Ammon came out, and put the battle in array at the entrance of the gate. The Syrians of Zobah and of Rehob, and the men of Tob and Maacah, were by themselves in the field.

As Joab contemplated the size of the armies of his enemies, he divided the warriors of Israel into two groups with each taking on one of the armies.

2 Samuel 10:9-12
Now when Joab saw that the battle was set against him before and behind, he chose of all the choice men of Israel, and put them in array against the Syrians. The rest of the people he committed into the hand of Abishai his brother; and he put them in array against the children of Ammon. He said, "If the Syrians are too strong for me, then you shall help me; but if the children of Ammon are too strong for you, then I will come and help you. Be courageous, and let's be strong for our people, and for the cities of our God...may Yahweh do what seems good to him."

Notice, that Joab divided his army into two, so each could defend the other, if necessary. David's kingdom defeated the armies. Seeking help in defense is natural impulse.

At times, even Israel and Judah would stop fighting each other to help defend each other as one army. One example is found in the battle of Ahab and Jehoshaphat against the Syrians. The Syrians had taken Ramoth Gilead from Israel and King Ahab wanted to defend them and take the city back. When the king of Judah met with him, he immediately asked him if they could join forces to return Ramoth Gilead to Israel's domain. Jehoshaphat agreed.

1 Kings 22:1-4
They continued three years without war between Syria and Israel. In the third year, Jehoshaphat the king of Judah came down to the king of Israel. The king of Israel said to his servants, "You know that Ramoth Gilead is ours, and we do nothing, and don't take it out of the hand of the king of Syria?" He said to Jehoshaphat, "Will you go with me to battle to Ramoth Gilead?" Jehoshaphat said to the king of Israel, "I am as you are, my people as your people, my horses as your horses." Jehoshaphat said to the king of Israel, "Please inquire first for Yahweh's word."

Here again, we have rulers desiring to make treaties to protect themselves and to defend their people.

In this chapter, we discovered that the Scripture provides many illustrations that the defense of others or seeking our own defense is a truly natural phenomenon, that proceeds from our humanness. This can be clearly seen through the many familial responses of protection, the dispositions to watch for danger, the propensities to guard against evil, the building of weapons and then carrying them when needed by both priests and the people, the declarations that there was no one to defend people, and the examples of David defending his countrymen and rulers creating treaties to deliver one another in times of trouble. Defending ourselves, those we love, and the innocent is perfectly natural.

Chapter 9

Start 6-12-21

The Protective Judgments

The judgments of the Lord God are a defense of Himself and His people either in this life, the life to come, or both. In essence, they protect. The death of the unrighteous and its resultant judgment delivers God's people from evil and harm now and eternally. They will be kept from harming the people God loves again and again. Death and redemption eternally save the righteous from evil and harm because believers are outfitted with supernatural bodies and an eternal state in the presence and safety of God. The judgment of Satan, demons, and the wicked keep them forever locked up in torment which protects believers from harm.

We must understand that judgment is God's ultimate defense of Himself, His many purposes and plan, and His people. It is the triumph of many wars and battles both in the human and divine realm. The Lord God gains the victory and vanquishes His enemies forever. They can never again hurt His people. This is similar to judges administering justice to murderers by either locking them up for life or taking their lives. They will never harm another again. It's not just justice but a protection. It is a final defense. Once again, as our God defends Himself (His purposes and plan), those He loves, and the innocent, he expects us to do the same.

The Judgment in the Garden

Man was ultimately in a vulnerable state. As long as He existed in his human form with the potential of disobeying God, he posed a real threat to his fellow man. The angels had already fallen and the potential of Satan's influence on them would have taken a toll on the gift of a kingdom of people that God was giving His Son. With the offspring of all mankind in the couple's loins, their potential rebellion had to be realized immediately. God had to push man to make a choice to obey or disobey.

Now, sin entered the human race through one man.

Romans 5:12
Therefore as sin entered into the world through one man, and death through sin; so death passed to all men, because all sinned.

Whether man sinned in Adam or was left to sin on his own, every human being would have rebelled at some time in their lives. As a result, spiritual and physical death would have come. This is easy to understand because all sin.

Romans 3:23
For all have sinned, and fall short of the glory of God.

As a result, the human race was redeemed by one man.

Romans 5:15
But the free gift isn't like the trespass. For if by the trespass of the one the many died, much more did the grace of God, and the gift by the grace of the one man, Jesus Christ, abound to the many.

In His redemption, man would be forever safe from sin and evil because He would be changed on the inside which would keep Him from harming himself and others.

Romans 7:24-25
What a wretched man I am! Who will deliver me out of the body of this death? I thank God through Jesus Christ, our Lord! So then with the mind, I myself serve God's law, but with the flesh, sin's....

Also, he would see change on the outside being outfitted with immortal, glorified, invulnerable bodies which could never be harmed by others.

1 Corinthians 15:42-44
So also is the resurrection of the dead. The body is sown perishable; it is raised imperishable. It is sown in dishonor; it is raised in glory. It is sown in weakness; it is raised in power. It is sown a natural body; it is raised a spiritual body. There is a natural body and there is also a spiritual body.

As a result of these two changes, one final part of God's defense would be complete, and He would have victory over the forces of evil both human and angelic.

1 Corinthians 15:54-56
But when this perishable body will have become imperishable, and this mortal will have put on immortality, then what is written will happen: "Death is swallowed up in victory. Death, where is your sting? Hades, where is your victory?" The sting of death is sin, and the power of sin is the law. But thanks be to God, who gives us the victory through our Lord Jesus Christ.

In the second passage, Paul quotes Isaiah and Hosea. In Isaiah, the prophet is predicting the future kingdom of God which will reign forever.

Isaiah 25:8
He has swallowed up death forever! The Lord Yahweh will wipe away tears from off all faces. He will take the reproach of his people away from off all the earth, for Yahweh has spoken it.

This future reign is seen as a great victory against the forces of evil (both demonic and human) by the Lord God of Hosts (angelic armies). Though we may not have thought of it from this viewpoint, this is nevertheless true.

Isaiah 25:6
In this mountain, Yahweh of Armies will make all peoples a feast of choice meat, a feast of choice wines, of choice meat full of marrow, of well refined choice wines.

Then in Hosea, the inspired prophet is speaking of the coming destruction of Israel by the Assyrians. In the midst of this horrific indictment, God provides a glimpse into the final victory His people will have over death. Here, he refers to spiritual death, not physical death because many will die. Though many will die, the true Israel will ultimately be saved.

Hosea 13:14
I will ransom them from the power of Sheol. I will redeem them from death! Death, where are your plagues? Sheol, where is your destruction? "Compassion will be hidden from my eyes."

It must be noted that redemption is found in the midst of war in these passages. It is discussed as victory in battle.

As a result, in God's first judgment, He did not allow man to remain in his sinful state by eating continually from the tree of life. Instead, the Lord defended man from himself and all others because they would sin like him. So, in his sinful state, God threw man out of the garden. At the end of each man's life, physical death would come as promised. Then in the Day of Judgment, their final death and condemnation or faith in Christ and salvation.

The Judgment of the Flood

When left to their own urges and desires, the new world of men became completely corrupt. The intent of every man's heart was evil. He constantly dreamed of committing sin.

HOW CHRISTIANS MAY DEFEND THEMSELVES AGAINST ATTACK

Genesis 6:5-7
Yahweh saw that the wickedness of man was great in the earth... every imagination of the thoughts of man's heart was continually only evil. Yahweh was sorry that he had made man on the earth, and it grieved him in his heart. Yahweh said, "I will destroy man whom I have created from the surface of the ground – man, along with animals, creeping things, and birds of the sky – for I am sorry that I have made them."

Man was at a crossroads and about to destroy himself since it had only eight people who were still righteous.

As a result, God decided another judgment was in order. This judgment would defend the eight righteous people who were left on the earth and end the men who had murderous and evil intentions continually in their hearts. They would never threaten His people again.

So, God decided to begin again by flooding the earth and starting over with Noah and his family.

Genesis 6:8-13
But Noah found favor in Yahweh's eyes. This is the history of the generations of Noah: Noah was a righteous man, blameless among the people of his time. Noah walked with God. Noah became the father of three sons: Shem, Ham, and Japheth. The earth was corrupt before God, and the earth was filled with violence. God swathe earth, and saw that it was corrupt, for all flesh had corrupted their way on the earth. 13 God said to Noah, "I will bring an end to all flesh, for the earth is filled with violence through them. Behold, I will destroy them and the earth.

The protection of Noah and his family was the deliverance of all mankind. These unrighteous people would experience the judgment of the flood and would never harm any person again. Then, the final judgment would seal their fate.

The Judgment of the Dispersion

As mankind began to multiply on the earth after the flood, mankind rebelled again against God's commands, rather than spreading through the earth and multiplying, they decided to create their own society apart from God.

Genesis 11:1-4
The whole earth was of one language and of one speech. As they traveled east, they found a plain in the land of Shinar, and they lived there. They said to one another, "Come, let's make bricks, and burn them thoroughly." They had brick for stone, and they used tar for mortar. They said, "Come, let's build ourselves a city, and a tower whose top reaches to the sky, and let's make a name for ourselves, lest we be scattered abroad on the surface of the whole earth."

Here, man decided to build a nation (a name), a capitol (a city) for that nation, and a new religion (a tower) separate from God's plan.

God saw that mankind would not only grow in his evil as he had done before but, in their unity, they would be able to do things that were "godlike." It is obvious that either all men would succumb to their desires or be killed. The kingdom God was threatened, and man was scattered.

Genesis 11:5-9
Yahweh came down to see the city and the tower, which the children of men built. Yahweh said, "Behold, they are one people, and they all have one language, and this is what they begin to do. Now nothing will be withheld from them, which they intend to do. Come, let's go down, and there confuse their language, that they may not understand one another's speech." So Yahweh scattered them abroad from there on the surface of all the earth. They stopped building the city. Therefore its name was called Babel, because there Yahweh confused the language of all the earth....

Their difference in language would ultimately separate them. This would also allow for a tension between nations in order to keep each in check preventing the one world government which would rise at the end. Though wars would come, God would use them to bring others to salvation based on his reputation as we see in the story of Rahab and her faith in the Lord God.

The Judgment in the Rapture

The next big event in redemptive history is the gathering of the saints in the air which is commonly referred to as the rapture of the church.

1 Corinthians 15:52
In a moment, in the twinkling of an eye, at the last trumpet. For the trumpet will sound and the dead will be raised incorruptible, and we will be changed.

As with Sodom and Gomorrah, God will not administer His justice to the innocent. Instead, the Innocent is removed. So, God will remove His church from this time of judgment and with them His restrainer the Holy Spirit who resides in them.

1 Corinthians 6:19-20
Or don't you know that your body is a temple of the Holy Spirit who is in you, whom you have from God? You are not your own, for you were bought with a price. Therefore glorify God in your body and in your spirit, which are God's.

Viewing the rapture from our self-defense point of view, God will defend His saints by delivering them from the harm which will be brought on by the one called the anti-Christ and the judgment the Almighty will administer.

2 Thessalonians 2:7-8
For the mystery of lawlessness already works. Only there is one who restrains now, until he is taken out of the way. Then the lawless one will be revealed, whom the Lord will kill with the breath of his mouth, and destroy by the manifestation of his coming.

In the Rapture, the Lord protects His people from harm. Those who enter the time of tribulation refused to receive Christ before this time. Also, they are not a part of the "church age." They are referred to as "tribulation saints."

Revelation 6:9-11
When he opened the fifth seal, I saw underneath the altar the souls of those who had been killed for the Word of God, and for the testimony of the Lamb which they had. They cried with a loud voice, saying, "How long, Master, the holy and true, until you judge and avenge our blood on those who dwell on the earth?" A long white robe was given to each of them. They were told that they should rest yet for a while, until their fellow servants and their brothers, who would also be killed even as they were, should complete their course.

Once the Rapture occurs, the time of tribulation begins. The church age saints are defended and delivered.

The Judgment in the Tribulation

The tribulation period is divided into two parts. Each section of time is three and a half years long. The first half is referred to as the time of "Birth Pangs." The second is called "The Great Tribulation." For the purposes of this book, we will deal with these judgments during the tribulation as a whole.

As the tribulation is unfolding on earth, it is being initiated by specific events in heaven. In Revelation 4, the apostle John is taken up into heaven in a great vision. First, there is great rejoicing and worship in heaven which involves both men and angels. In chapter 5, a book appears which is the title deed of the earth, and a question is asked.

Revelation 5:1-2
I saw, in the right hand of him who sat on the throne, a book written inside and outside, sealed shut with seven seals. I saw a mighty angel proclaiming with a loud voice, "Who is worthy to open the book, and to break its seals?"

The answer comes in the form of a slain lamb.

Revelation 5:6
I saw in the middle of the throne and of the four living creatures, and in the middle of the elders, a Lamb standing, as though it had been slain, having seven horns and seven eyes, which are the seven Spirits of God, sent out into all the earth.

This is a depiction of the Lord Jesus Christ who through His death and resurrection has the power and authority to open the deed.

This deed has seven seals. The seventh seal brings seven trumpets being blown. The seventh trumpet brings seven bowls which are poured out. All of these represent judgments upon the earth before Christ returns in glory.

The first seal is opened and will lead to the others being opened in numerical order.

Revelation 6:1-3
I saw that the Lamb opened one of the seven seals, and I heard one of the four living creatures saying, as with a voice of thunder, "Come and see!" Then a white horse appeared, and he who sat on it had a bow. A crown was given to him, and he came out conquering, and to conquer. When he opened the second seal....

The seals involve the appearance of the Antichrist, anarchy and terrorism, a world-wide depression, famine, disease, the animal kingdom turning on man, and man killing his fellow man. Then a great earthquake will occur and the falling of the stars from heaven. Those on the earth become terribly afraid and flee for their lives.

Revelation 6:15-17
The kings of the earth, the princes, the commanding officers, the rich, the strong, and every slave and free person, hid themselves in the caves and in the rocks of the mountains. They told the mountains and the rocks, "Fall on us, and hide us from the face of him who sits on the throne, and from the wrath of the Lamb, for the great day of his wrath has come; and who is able to stand?"

The seventh seal announces the many trumpet judgments.

Revelation 8:1-2
When he opened the seventh seal, there was silence in heaven for about half an hour. I saw the seven angels who stand before God, and seven trumpets were given to them.

These will bring great devastation upon the earth.

The trumpets are blown, and the earth is pummeled with hail, fire, and blood which destroys one third of vegetation on the earth. Then, a huge mountain is thrown into the sea and one third of sea turns to blood. So, death is brought to a third of the sea creatures and ships. After this, a star breaks apart and tumbles into the streams of the earth making them bitter and killing many people. Then a third of the sun, moon, and stars are blackened causing a third of the day and night to be darkened. Then, a demonic invasion is unleashed from the abyss in the form of locusts who can inflict intense pain but do not kill. After this, four demons are loosed, and they gather the army of two hundred million soldiers as prophesied who kill a third of mankind. As the temple in heaven is opened, a great earthquake shakes the earth and lightning, thunder, and hail follow.

Then, the seventh trumpet announces the final seven bowl judgments. These judgments bring devastation to the earth before Christ's return.

Revelation 15:1
I saw another great and marvelous sign in the sky: seven angels having the seven last plagues, for in them God's wrath is finished.

First comes malignant sores upon men with the mark of the beast. The sea then turns to blood bringing death upon every living thing in the sea. The pouring out of another bowl leads to the fresh water being turned to blood also. Then, the sun flares up and scorches many upon the earth. After this comes darkness upon the kingdom of the beast. Then, three unclean spirits come forth from Satan, the beast, and the false prophets which gathers the nations for war. Finally, lightning and thunder with a great and powerful earthquake comes. Many cities fall, islands flee away, mountains break apart, and a plague of hail descends upon the world.

All these judgments are poured out upon man because of his sin, and he is still unwilling to repent.

Revelation 16:8-11
The fourth poured out his bowl on the sun, and it was given to him to scorch men with fire. People were scorched with great heat, and people blasphemed the name of God who has the power over these plagues. They didn't repent and give him glory. The fifth poured out his bowl on the throne of the beast, and his kingdom was darkened. They gnawed their tongues because of the pain, and they blasphemed the God of heaven because of their pains and their sores. They still didn't repent of their works.

This sin brings forth great persecution upon the saints who cry out continually for justice.

Revelation 6:9-10
When he opened the fifth seal, I saw underneath the altar the souls of those who had been killed for the Word of God, and for the testimony of the Lamb which they had. They cried with a loud voice, saying, "How long, Master, the holy and true, until you judge and avenge our blood on those who dwell on the earth?"

When God's will for the number of martyrs that would glorify Him is completed, justice will finally be poured out and the murders will finally stop.

Revelation 6:11
A long white robe was given to each of them. They were told that they should rest yet for a while, until their fellow servants and their brothers, who would...be killed even as they were, should complete their course.

What does this mean concerning self-defense and the defense of others? These judgments upon mankind virtually end the murdering of God's people that had begun after the flood and was brought to its highest point in the tribulation period. This is God's defense of His people upon the earth among other purposes.

In Psalm 63, David fled from his son Absalom who stole his throne. The king writes of the coming victory as the Lord provides.

Psalm 63:8-11
My soul stays close to you.... But those who seek my soul to destroy it shall go into the lower parts of the earth. They shall be given over to the power of the sword. They shall be jackal food. But the king shall rejoice in God. Everyone who swears by him will praise him, for the mouth of those who speak lies shall be silenced.

These persecutors of God's anointed had to be stopped. God would defend David and his men as the defended themselves in battle. Their death would finally lead to his protection.

In the same way, the judgments of God are the ultimate defense of His people from those who desire to harm them. Here, we see the Lord defending Himself, His purposes, plan, those He loves, and the innocent. It is the triumph of many wars and battles that have raged from the beginning.

The Return of The Lord of Lords

After the judgments of the seals, trumpets, and bowls are completed, there is an announcement in heaven.

Revelation 19:1-2
After these things I heard something like a loud voice of a great multitude in heaven, saying, "Hallelujah! Salvation, power, and glory belong to our God; for his judgments are true and righteous. For he has judged the great prostitute, who corrupted the earth with her sexual immorality...he has avenged the blood of his servants...

Divine justice is administered for the persecutions of Christ's saints. What a great defense!

After the wedding feast with His saints, the Lord readies Himself for His return.

Revelation 19:11-13
I saw the heaven opened, and behold, a white horse, and he who sat on it is called Faithful and True. In righteousness he judges and makes war. His eyes are a flame of fire, and on his head are many crowns. He has names written and a name written which no one knows but he himself. He is clothed in a garment sprinkled with blood. His name is called "The Word of God."

The return of the Lord Jesus in His second coming is not the return of a triumphant king after victory in battle, but the coming of a powerful king with His armies to do battle. This is an important distinction.

Revelation 19:14-16
The armies which are in heaven followed him on white horses, clothed in white, pure, fine linen. Out of his mouth proceeds a sharp, double-edged sword, that with it he should strike the nations. He will rule them with an iron rod. He has on his garment and on his thigh a name written, "KING OF KING'S...LORD OF LORDS."

These armies are comprised of the saints who have died through the ages who have now been outfitted with glorified bodies and angels.

Matthew 16:27
For the Son of Man will come in the glory of his Father with his angels, and then he will render to everyone according to his deeds.

This will be the final battle. The Lord returns to take the earth for Himself and set up His kingdom for a thousand years.

As He returns, all the nations of the earth point their many weapons at Him and His armies to blast them out of the sky.

Revelation 19:18-21
That you may eat the flesh of kings... I saw the beast, and the kings of the earth, and their armies, gathered together to make war against him who sat on the horse, and against his army. The beast was taken, and with him the false prophet who worked the signs in his sight, with which he deceived those who had received the mark of the beast and those who worshiped his image. These two were thrown alive into the lake of fire that burns with sulfur. The rest were killed with the sword of him who sat on the horse, the sword which came out of his mouth. So, all the birds were filled with their flesh.

The leader of the world, the man of lawlessness, and the false prophet are thrown into the fire of hell and the battle begins.

The Lord of Lords battles the great forces of the earth and wins. The Lord ultimately defends Himself, His purposes, plan, His people whom He loves, and the innocent on earth and resurrected at His side.

The Judgment of the Sheep and Goats

The next event involves the ushering in of the saints who are alive into the kingdom. The unbelievers who may not enter are cast aside to await their final judgment.

Matthew 25:31-33
But when the Son of Man comes in his glory, and all the holy angels with him, then he will sit on the throne of his glory. Before him all the nations will be gathered, and he will separate them one from another, as a shepherd separates the sheep from the goats. He will set the sheep on his right hand, but the goats on the left.

The saints who are alive will enter the kingdom. This means that only believers enter the kingdom. All those unsaved who may attempt or have attempted to hurt them are removed to await their final judgment.

Therefore, this judgment is a powerful defense of God, His purposes and plan, and His holy people.

The Judgments in the Millennium

The next event will be the thousand-year reign of our Lord who will administer justice as he defends in His rule.

Revelation 20:6
Blessed and holy is he who has part in the first resurrection. Over these, the second death has no power, but they will be priests of God and of Christ, and will reign with him one thousand years.

During this reign, some of the children of the believers who originally inhabited the kingdom will be unbelievers. We know this because Satan is unleashed, and he gathers many unbelievers from the earth to overthrow the Lord Jesus. These must be the descendants of the original believers.

Revelation 20:7-9
And after the thousand years, Satan will be released from his prison, and he will come out to deceive the nations which are in the four corners of the earth, Gog and Magog, to gather them together to the war; the number of whom is as the sand of the sea. They went up over the width of the earth, and surrounded the camp of the saints, and the beloved city. Fire came down out of heaven from God and devoured them.

As a result, Christ will rule His kingdom with a rod of iron. This means that He will punish anyone attempting to harm Him or His people. He will protect His purposes and plans. This will be a powerful defense.

Revelation 19:15
Out of his mouth proceeds a sharp, double-edged sword, that with it he should strike the nations. He will rule them with an iron rod.

Not only does Christ battle with His sword to take over the rule of it, but He will use it to control the nations that are established.

To do this, He will bind Satan during this period. This binding of the serpent of old is a form of the defense of His person, purposes and plans, and His people.

HOW CHRISTIANS MAY DEFEND THEMSELVES AGAINST ATTACK

Revelation 20:1-3
I saw an angel coming down out of heaven, having the key of the abyss and a great chain in his hand. He seized the dragon, the old serpent, which is the devil and Satan, who deceives the whole inhabited earth, and bound him for a thousand years, and cast him into the abyss, and shut it, and sealed it over him, that he should deceive the nations no more, until the thousand years were finished. After this, he must be freed for a short time.

Here is a second powerful defense which is to bind Satan who controls the myriad of demons during the entire millennium.

Also, the curse upon the earth is rolled back so there is peace in the animal and human kingdoms. This is the period that Isaiah was speaking of in his prophecy.

Isaiah 11:6-9
The wolf will live with the lamb, and the leopard will lie down with the young goat, the calf, the young lion, and the fattened calf together; and a little child will lead them. The cow and the bear will graze. Their young ones will lie down together. The lion will eat straw like the ox. The nursing child will play near a cobra's hole, and the weaned child will put his hand on the viper's den. They will not hurt nor destroy in all my holy mountain; for the earth will be full of the knowledge of Yahweh, as the waters cover the sea.

So much more could be said, but I mention this for us to note another defensive move on the part of the Lord Jesus for His people. They will not have to be protected from any hostility from the animal kingdom.

The Judgment of the Final Offensive

At the end of the thousand years, the Devil is released from his prison in the abyss.

Revelation 20:7
And after the thousand years, Satan will be released from his prison.

At this time, he attempts a final offensive against Christ and His people.

Revelation 20:8-9
And he will come out to deceive the nations which are in the four corners of the earth, Gog and Magog, to gather them together to the war; the number of whom is as the sand of the sea. They went up over the width of the earth, and surrounded the camp of the saints, and the beloved city. Fire came down out of heaven from God and devoured them.

Christ's defense is swift and powerful.

Notice, His judgment and defense were also final eternally.

Revelation 20:10
The devil who deceived them was thrown into the lake of fire and sulfur, where the beast and the false prophet are also. They will be tormented day and night forever and ever.

Never again would the serpent of old disrupt God's purposes and plan or harm His people. This was His final defense.

The Judgment of the Great White Throne

The absolute final defense of God Himself, His purposes and plan, those He loves, and the innocent occurs on the Day of Judgment. First, Christ sits on His throne.

Revelation 20:11
I saw a great white throne...him who sat on it, from whose face the earth and the heaven fled away. There was found no place for them.

HOW CHRISTIANS MAY DEFEND THEMSELVES AGAINST ATTACK

Then, there is the judgment of the unsaved.

Revelation 20:12-15
I saw the dead, the great and the small, standing before the throne, and they opened books. Another book was opened, which is the book of life. The dead were judged out of the things which were written in the books, according to their works. The sea gave up the dead who were in it. Death and Hades gave up the dead who were in them. They were judged, each one according to his works.

Revelation 20:15
If anyone was not found written in the book of life, he was cast into the lake of fire.

Every unbeliever will be judged for every sin committed. This will include the evil and harm against God, His purposes and plan, and His people.

It appears that the demons will also be judged at this time.

2 Peter 2:4
For if God didn't spare angels when they sinned, but cast them down to Tartarus, and committed them to pits of darkness to be reserved for judgment.

Jude 6
Angels who didn't keep their first domain, but deserted their own dwelling place, he has kept in everlasting bonds under darkness for the judgment of the great day.

Matthew 25:41
Then he will say also to those on the left hand, 'Depart from me, you cursed, into the eternal fire which is prepared for the devil and his angels.

The demons will be cast into the lake of fire with the Devil.

This is the final defense and victory in the battle. Never again will the (unbelievers or demons) ever attempt to harm to us. We are eternally protected from them.

The Judgment of the Earth

The last hostile entity to God, His purpose and plans, and His people is the unredeemed earth.

Romans 8:19-22
For the creation waits with eager expectation for the children of God to be revealed. For the creation was subjected to vanity, not of its own will, but because of him who subjected it, in hope that the creation itself also will be delivered from the bondage of decay into the liberty of the glory of the children of God. For we know that the whole creation groans and travails in pain together until now.

This earth is hostile to us and must ultimately be redeemed as we are redeemed. This is the final defense, deliverance, and protection against harm.

This redemption comes in the form of destroying the old earth.

2 Peter 3:10
But the day of the Lord will come as a thief in the night; in which the heavens will pass away with a great noise, and the elements will be dissolved with fervent heat, and the earth and the works that are in it will be burned up.

Then, a new earth must be created.

Revelation 21:1
I saw a new heaven and a new earth: for the first heaven and the first earth have passed away, and the sea is no more.

HOW CHRISTIANS MAY DEFEND THEMSELVES AGAINST ATTACK

Finally, we will dwell forever in the presence of God.

Revelation 21:3
I heard a loud voice out of heaven saying, "Behold, God's dwelling is with people, and he will dwell with them, and they will be his people, and God himself will be with them as their God.

Now, everything is in place and never again will there need to be any defense or self-defense among men and angels.

Revelation 21:4
He will wipe away every tear from their eyes. Death will be no more; neither will there be mourning, nor crying, nor pain, any more. The first things have passed away."

As can be seen, the righteous judgments of the Lord God are a defense of Himself and His people either in this life, the life to come, or both. The death of the unrighteous and its resultant judgment delivers God's people from evil and harm. Death and redemption eternally deliver and protects the righteous from harm because believers are outfitted with supernatural bodies and an eternal state in the presence and safety of God. The judgment of Satan, his demons, and the wicked keep them forever locked up in torment which keeps them from ever harming God's holy ones. Judgment is the Lord God's ultimate defense of Himself, His many purposes and plan, and His people. It is the triumph of many wars and battles. God gains the victory and vanquishes His enemies forever. Just as God defends Himself (His purposes and plan), those He loves, and the innocent, He expects His children to do the same.

DEFENDING YOUR LIFE

Chapter 10

The Legal Allowance

Self-defense and the defense of others has always had a place in the governments and laws of mankind. One of the reasons we may defend ourselves and others is because the government expects and condones it under certain specific circumstances. Therefore, when we defend ourselves and others we are submitting to the laws of the land. The major exception would be when Christians must disobey a law to obey a divine command. The information in this chapter is an abridged version of a chapter in my companion book *Standing Your Ground, The Persecution of the Saints and How to Overcome It, A Biblical Handbook*. Please see that important book for the full discussion.

Their Human Identity

All governments that are in places of authority in cities, regions, or nations (doing good or even evil) on a continual basis are divinely established. This is clearly delineated by the apostle Paul. First, Paul identifies who these authorities are by using specific Greek terms. The primary term he uses is translated "authorities."

Romans 13:1-3
Let every soul be in subjection to the higher authorities, for there is no authority except from God, and those who exist are ordained by God. Therefore he [Christian] who resists the authority, withstands the ordinance of God; and those who withstand will receive to themselves judgment. For rulers are not a terror to the good work,

but to the evil. Do you desire to have no fear of the authority? Do that which is good, and you will have praise from the same.

Titus 3:1
Remind them to be in subjection to rulers and to authorities, to be obedient [to authorities - verb form], to be ready for every good work.

This word refers to "those who have the power of choice or the liberty of doing as one pleases." It is used of different types of authorities who are either divine, angelic, or human. We will focus on human authorities.

It is used of various kinds of authorities of different ranks in the military and society. It referred to a Roman Centurion who was a commander of one hundred soldiers.

Matthew 8:8-9
The centurion answered, "Lord, I'm not worthy for you to come under my roof. Just say the word, and my servant will be healed. For I am also a man under authority, having under myself soldiers. I tell this one, 'Go,' and he goes; and tell another, 'Come,' and he comes; and tell my servant, 'Do this,' and he does it."

It speaks of the authority of a provincial Roman governor.

Luke 20:20
They watched him...sent out spies, who pretended to be righteous, that they might trap him in something he said, so as to deliver him [Jesus] up to the power and authority of the governor.

Also, it referred to Herod rank and authority as the ruler of the Jewish nation.

Luke 23:7
When he found out that he was in Herod's jurisdiction, he sent him to Herod, who was also in Jerusalem during those days.

HOW CHRISTIANS MAY DEFEND THEMSELVES AGAINST ATTACK

It is utilized to describe the authority of Pilate, the Roman governor of Judea.

John 19:10
Pilate therefore said to him, "Aren't you speaking to me? Don't you know that I have power [authority] to release you, and have power [authority] to crucify you?"

The term was also used of the religious authorities of Jesus' day.

Acts 26:10
This I also did in Jerusalem. I both shut up many of the saints in prisons, having received authority from the chief priests, and when they were put to death I gave my vote against them.

When Paul described these authorities in Romans 13:1, he added "higher." This Greek word means "to stand out, rise above, be superior in rank, authority, or quality." This refers to authorities superior to the average man.

Second, these authorities are regional leaders. Another term that is used to refer to those to whom we are to obey is "governors." These are the rulers who have authority over the particular regions of a nation.

1 Peter 2:14
Or to governors, as sent by him for vengeance on evildoers and for praise to those who do well.

It referred to Pilate, the governor over the region of Judea, who gave the order to crucify Jesus.

Matthew 27:2
And they bound him, and led him away, and delivered him up to Pontius Pilate, the governor.

Also, Felix who succeeded Pilate as governor of the same region was identified with this term.

Acts 23:26
Claudius Lysias [the commanding officer in charge of Paul] to the most excellent governor Felix: Greetings.

Then, Festus who succeeded Felix was called "governor." Both these men held Paul for over two years each in custody.

Acts 26:30
The king rose up with the governor, and Bernice....

Third, these "authorities" would be rulers in general. The next Greek term is a general term for many different kinds of rulers. These would usually be men other than the ultimate authorities of the land or region.

Romans 13:3
For rulers are not a terror to the good work, but to the evil. Do you desire to have no fear of the authority? Do that which is good, and you will have praise from the same.

Titus 3:1
Remind them to be in subjection to rulers and to authorities, to be obedient, to be ready for every good work.

Also, the term was used to refer to religious officials.

Luke 8:41
Behold, there came a man named Jairus, and he was a ruler of the synagogue...fell...at Jesus' feet...begged him to come into his house.

John 3:1
Now there was a man of the Pharisees named Nicodemus, a ruler of the Jews. The same came to him by night, and said....

HOW CHRISTIANS MAY DEFEND THEMSELVES AGAINST ATTACK

It was used of local town officials.

Luke 12:58
For when you are going with your adversary before the magistrate, try diligently on the way to be released from him, lest perhaps he drag you to the judge, and the judge deliver you to the officer, and the officer throw you into prison.

Also, at times, this Greek term was used to refer to rulers of the nations in general of many ranks.

Matthew 20:25
But Jesus summoned them, and said, "You know that the rulers of the nations.

Acts 4:26
The kings of the earth take a stand, and the rulers take council together, against the Lord, and against his Christ.

So, authorities can be any official rank above us.

Second, Peter and Paul us the term translated "kings" to refers to all heads of nations that have full authority. This would be the supreme ruler or highest authority in land.

1 Peter 2:13
Therefore subject yourselves to every ordinance of man for the Lord's sake: whether to the king, as supreme.

1 Peter 2:17
Honor all men. Love the brotherhood. Fear God. Honor the king.

1 Timothy 2:1-2
I exhort [beseech, entreat] therefore, first of all, that petitions, prayers, intercessions, and givings of thanks, be made for all men: for kings and all who are in high places.... reverence.

Matthew 1:6
Jesse became the father of King David. David became the father of Solomon by her who had been Uriah's wife.

Matthew 18:23
Therefore the Kingdom of Heaven is like a certain king, who wanted to reconcile accounts with his servants.

Mark 6:22
When the daughter of Herodias herself came in and danced, she pleased Herod and those sitting with him. The king said to the young lady, "Ask me whatever you want, and I will give it to you."

Acts 12:1
Now about that time, King Herod stretched out his hands to oppress some of the assembly.

Though he had a different title, this Greek word would include emperors like Caesar in Rome. Of course, in modern times, the word would refer to presidents, prime ministers, and even dictators who are acting within their legal authority. Therefore, we should submit to them.

Finally, Peter speaks of human ordinances or laws created by those in authority.

1 Peter 2:13-14
Therefore subject yourselves to every ordinance of man for the Lord's sake: whether to the king, as supreme; or to governors, as sent by him for vengeance...and for praise to those who do well.

The word translated "ordinance" literally means in the Greek "creation."

Mark 10:6
But from the beginning of the creation, God made them male and female.

HOW CHRISTIANS MAY DEFEND THEMSELVES AGAINST ATTACK

Though it is used for creation almost everywhere else, in this context, it refers to the created laws, policies, or procedures created by kings and governors. Therefore, these refer to the numerous laws these authorities create. This would include the statutes and ordinances of towns, cities, states, regions, provinces, and nations. Saints do not get to pick and choose laws to obey.

Next, we are given the standard by which we judge the "divine legitimacy" of these superior authorities in Romans 13:1; that is, they must be "established." These governments must have been established in the past and continually set in place. We are not talking at all about authorities who are in the process of being "established" either by election or force. This is an important distinction. Once a superior authority is established and continually in place, then we must believe by faith that this is God's doing.

Romans 13:1
Let every soul be in subjection to the higher authorities, for there is no authority except from God, and those who exist are ordained [established] by God.

The verb translated "exist" is in the present tense indicating a continual "existence" in present time. This portion of the passage can best be translated, "those who are continually existing in the present are established by God." Authorities that are established by God are the ones who are in existence right now.

The other critical word in this passage is translated by the English word "ordained." The Greek word speaks of "putting something in order, stationing, arranging, or assigning a place to something; appointing one to a position of responsibility." It is an important word because it establishes the fact that God was involved in the process.

Luke used it to describe the selection, appointment, and establishment process of Paul and Barnabas to represent the church at the Jerusalem Council in Antioch.

Acts 15:2
Therefore when Paul and Barnabas had no small discord and discussion with them, they appointed Paul and Barnabas, and some others of them, to go up to Jerusalem to the apostles and elders about this question.

The word is in the perfect tense which denotes authorities who were selected, appointed, and established in the past with continuing results (their current existence) are the ones established by God. The verb is in the passive voice which means the ordaining happened to them by an outside force. Of course, this force was God. Though they think they were active in their establishment, actually they were passive. God is the one who established them. How can we possibly know? They still exist. This ordination by our Lord God does not legitimize wicked or despotic behavior which was used in past history by kings to force the people to accept their evil. The establishment by God is not a coronation; instead, it is an allowance.

Their Divine Purpose

These authorities are divinely authorized for a purpose.

Romans 13:1
Let every soul be in subjection to the higher authorities, for there is no authority except from God...those who exist...ordained by God.

The critical word in this passage is the verb "is." This is in the present tense and should be properly interpreted "for there is

HOW CHRISTIANS MAY DEFEND THEMSELVES AGAINST ATTACK

'continually existing' no authority except from God." If there is an authority that is currently in place, it is from God. This means they are divinely given authority.

This is a divine structure in society. It is part of the Lord God's blueprint to keep order and preserve life.

Romans 13:2
Therefore he who resists the authority, withstands the ordinance of God; and those who withstand will receive to themselves judgment.

The authorities administer divine judgment.

Romans 13:2
Therefore he who resists the authority, withstands the ordinance of God; and those who withstand will receive to themselves judgment.

Here, Paul explains that if we do not submit, then they will render a judgment and punishment. This is God's judgment.

They will praise those who do good on behalf of God.

Romans 13:3
For rulers are not a terror to the good work, but to the evil. Do you desire to have no fear of the authority? Do that which is good, and you will have praise from the same.

1 Peter 2:14
Or to governors, as sent by him for vengeance on evildoers and for praise to those who do well.

This praise for their good behavior is God's praise.

They provide a divine ministry and service for the Lord God. Among the responsibilities that they have, they are His instruments to administer His justice in the temporal world.

Romans 13:4
For he is a servant of God to you for good. But if you do that which is evil, be afraid, for he doesn't bear the sword in vain; for he is a servant of God, an avenger for wrath to him who does evil.

They bear a sword and will use it against people on behalf of God.

Romans 13:4
For he is a servant of God to you for good. But if you do that which is evil, be afraid, for he doesn't bear the sword in vain; for he is a servant of God, an avenger for wrath to him who does evil.

These authorities are God's avengers and instruments of His justice.

Romans 13:4
For he is a servant of God to you for good. But if you do that which is evil, be afraid, for he doesn't bear the sword in vain; for he is a servant of God, an avenger for wrath to him who does evil.

1 Peter 2:14
Or to governors, as sent by him for vengeance on evildoers and for praise to those who do well.

They bring God's vengeance upon men when they refuse to follow the laws.

They are always on call for service to God.

Romans 13:6
For this reason you also pay taxes, for they are servants of God's service, attending continually on this very thing.

The government has a divine sender. These authorities do not send themselves; they are sent by God.

HOW CHRISTIANS MAY DEFEND THEMSELVES AGAINST ATTACK

1 Peter 2:14
Or to governors, as sent by him for vengeance on evildoers and for praise to those who do well.

We must understand that the government is an instrument of defense on God's behalf.

Their Allowance of Self-Defense

The question now arises, "Do these purposes involve self-defense and the defense of others.?" Yes. Why is this? Their laws are to protect the society, but they can't be everywhere at every moment, so citizens will have to defend themselves. On a school yard, we may tell children to find a teacher if other children hit them. This is because they lack discernment, and they must be supervised by an adult at all times. Adults do not live in a school yard and authorities recognize that they do have the discernment to know the laws and what they can and cannot do to defend themselves. They do not have police everywhere within eyesight or earshot of all violence. As a result, self-defense and defending others may be necessary and lawful. Also, even on a schoolyard, we do not expect that children will allow themselves to be beaten without stopping the others from hurting them.

This is intuitive and obvious. In any society, if someone attempted to kill our family with a knife we would try and stop them. If we did not people would wonder what was wrong with us?

Now, does this change because we are Christians? No, it does not as we are discovering. The laws do not say that people may defend themselves and others except if they are Christians nor does the Bible as we are discovering.

Here is the thinking behind this discussion. If governments are established by God to protect citizens and all governments allow some kind of self-defense, it is from God. In the eyes of the law, the defender would be innocent and applauded for the bravery of physical protection. The authorities would claim justice was served and would give the defender praise. They would also say that the perpetrator received what he deserved which was God's wrath.

Our Divine Submission

We are told in Scripture that we must submit to authority. This is the normal course of behavior toward governments and their laws for Christians. Paul and Peter clearly command us to subject ourselves to higher authorities and their laws, policies, and ordinances. We find this in three passages where Paul and Peter use the exact same Greek term to speak of this submission.

Romans 13:1
Let every soul be in subjection to the higher authorities, for there is no authority except from God, and those who exist are ordained by God.

Romans 13:5
Therefore you need to be in subjection, not only because of the wrath, but also for conscience' sake.

1 Peter 2:13
Therefore subject yourselves to every ordinance of man for the Lord's sake: whether to the king, as supreme.

This verb means "to arrange under, to subordinate, to subject, to obey, to submit to another's control, or to yield to another's admonition." This term was also a military term meaning "to arrange [troop divisions] in a military fashion under the command of a leader."

In Romans 13:1, the verb translated "be in subjection" is in the present tense indicating constant action that should be continued. It could be translated, "Let us keep on being subjected to the higher authorities." Apparently, the Roman Christians were being submissive to those in authority, and Paul commands them to keep on submitting.

In Romans 13:5, Paul discusses the same truth again and adds a new aspect. The verb in this verse is in the middle voice. This speaks of an action upon ourselves. Therefore, Christians are to be subjecting themselves to the authorities and should not have been forced. In Peter's passage, the verb translated "subject" is in the aorist tense indicating that the readers of the letters of Peter were not subjecting themselves and needed to start. Here, we see the lack of consensus of obedience in the Body of Christ. Some of the saints were submitting, others had stopped and needed to begin again, and still others had to start for the first time.

Therefore, if we are to submit to government, then we should obey the law that allows people to defend themselves and others. This is utterly reasonable because again people will ask, "Why didn't you try and stop them?" What, if any, explanation could be satisfying?

So far, it can be argued that the standard for the saints in every land under every government is to obey all the laws of the land. Why is this important? In general, governments have always allowed its citizens to defend themselves. There have been differences in the circumstances that may warrant a legal action of self-defense, but it has always been present.

There may be controls on what weapons people may utilize for self-defense, but it has always been legal under certain circumstances. No one would deny this important reality and it is critical to our discussion.

What are those circumstances? Citizens are allowed to use the reasonable force needed to stop the attacker from harming them. They should not use any more force or any less force. The force and the weapon they choose is governed by what a reasonable person would do under the same circumstances. This might be an oversimplification, but it is the common thread of understanding. This is about as far as it can be taken without an attorney. The point is the government generally allows self-defense.

Since we are told to submit ourselves to them and obey their laws, then we may use self-defense or defend others. In fact, most governments and peoples will applaud heroic self-defense and the defense of others.

His Divine Examples

In fact, in the Holy Scriptures, we find some interesting examples of a leader commanding a group of God's people to defend themselves as a matter of law. In the book of Esther, we see a powerful example of this. You may remember that after the death of King Solomon, Israel was split into two kingdoms: Israel (ten tribes) and Judah (tribe of Judah and Benjamin). The prophets warned and warned God's people to cease from their idolatry and sin or God would bring a nation to conquer them. When they refused, God sent the Assyrians to conquer them. They did not kill all the peoples in those days but took most away into their lands to assimilate them into their nation under their authority. Then, the nation of Judah was warned but it did not heed the prophets, so the

HOW CHRISTIANS MAY DEFEND THEMSELVES AGAINST ATTACK

Babylonians who had conquered the empire of the Assyrians came and triumphed over the people of Judah. Then, the Babylonian Empire was conquered by the Persian Empire.

During this captivity the book of Esther was written to celebrate God's protection of his people against an evil man named Haman. After the King of Persia, Ahasuerus, was shamed by his wife, he sought another among the beautiful maidens of the land. After seeing Esther, a Jewish maiden, he chose her to be his new queen. Her uncle Mordecai would visit her often. Haman, a court official, loved the pomp and circumstance of his authority and demanded that Mordecai bow down to him. This Jewish man refused because he only bowed down to God. This infuriated Haman and he plotted to destroy not only Haman but the entire Jewish nation that were subject to them. Through a series of horrific lies, he was able to trick the king into issuing an edict to kill the Jews as he desired on a given day.

When Esther intervened on the Jews' behalf and outlined the plot and lies Haman had been telling King Ahasuerus, the ruler hung Haman on the gallows that had been built for Mordecai. The king rescinded the edict and commanded the Jews to defend themselves if it was necessary on that day. In Esther 8:11, the author describes it in this way,

Esther 8:11
In those letters, the king granted the Jews who were in every city to gather themselves together, and to defend their life, to destroy, to kill, and to cause to perish, all the power of the people and province that would assault them...and to plunder their possessions.

Then in Esther 9:16, the writer explains what happened,

Esther 9:16
The...Jews who were in the king's provinces gathered themselves

together, defended their lives, had rest from their enemies, and killed seventy-five thousand of those who hated them; but they didn't lay their hand on the plunder.

The people were attacked and obeyed the law by defending themselves. Yet, they did not feel that it was right according to God's holy law to plunder them. They were satisfied with simply defending themselves from their enemies. They knew self-defense and defense of others was God's way.

Years later, Cyrus became king of the Persian Empire and God told him to release his people from bondage. Ezra was released and then Nehemiah. Ezra would be the presiding priest over the people and Nehemiah would be the governor. When they returned to the land, some of the people who now lived there did not want the Jews to return. There was a series of appeals to Cyrus and hostility toward one another until Cyrus finally had decided to side with the Jews. They were allowed to rebuild their city and temple.

Nehemiah tells an interesting story about the difficulty they had with building the wall around the city for protection. Though Cyrus had supported them this did not necessarily mean all would comply. As a result, the Hebrews would have to not only have guards watch the workers, but the workers had to have a tool in one hand and a sword in another in case they were attacked to defend themselves. This was acceptable to the emperor.

When the Jews returned after seventy years in captivity, they were met with antagonism by the inhabitants and their offspring left behind and others in the land.

Nehemiah 4:7
But when Sanballat, Tobiah, the Arabians, the Ammonites, and the Ashdodites heard that the repairing of the walls of Jerusalem went

HOW CHRISTIANS MAY DEFEND THEMSELVES AGAINST ATTACK

forward, and that the breaches began to be filled, they were very angry; 8 and they all conspired together to come and fight against Jerusalem, and to cause confusion among us.

So, Nehemiah and those with him, prayed earnestly to God and set up a watch to protect themselves. Notice, they prayed and prepared to defend themselves.

Nehemiah 4:9
But we made our prayer to our God, and set a watch against them day and night because of them.

Nehemiah set up guards by families and encouraged all to be ready to defend their brothers, children, and wives.

Nehemiah 4:13-14
Therefore I set guards in the lowest parts of the space behind the wall, in the open places. I set the people by family groups with their swords, their spears, and their bows. I looked, and rose up, and said to the nobles, to the rulers, and to the rest of the people, "Don't be afraid of them! Remember the Lord, who is great and awesome, and fight for your brothers, your sons, your daughters, your wives, and your houses."

Then, to provide a proper defense of themselves and others, they worked, ate, and slept with a sword in their hands.

Nehemiah 4:16-17
From that time forth, half of my servants did the work, and half of them held the spears, the shields, the bows, and the coats of mail; and the rulers were behind all the house of Judah. Those who built the wall, and those who bore burdens loaded themselves; everyone with one of his hands did the work, and with the other held his weapon.

They expected God to protect and defend them as they protected and defended themselves and others.

Nehemiah 4:20
Wherever you hear the sound of the trumpet, rally there to us. Our God will fight for us."

If the battle had come, they certainly expected God and Cyrus' protection.

His National Law

When the Lord God established the laws of Israel, we have learned that codes and rules were set up which allowed and expected self-defense and the defense of others to occur. We have already studied this. Here are a few found in the Bible.

Exodus 22:2-3
If the thief is found breaking in, and is struck so that he dies, there shall be no guilt of bloodshed for him. If the sun has risen on him, he is guilty of bloodshed. He shall make restitution. If he has nothing, then he shall be sold for his theft.

If a thief in the dark breaks into a house, the owner may defend himself even to the point of death. It was dark so he could not determine the intentions beyond stealing. Also, the thief would know that the owner and his family would be home and would expect to do physical harm to the family to defend himself. In the daytime, he knows the thief expects no one to be home. The owner can identify his intentions and should be able to quickly determine whether his life and the life of others are threatened.

As we have seen, it is necessary to obey the governmental authorities. These governmental authorities inevitably have specific laws which state that under certain circumstances, their citizens may defend themselves and others. Therefore, we may defend ourselves and others based on these laws.

Chapter 11

The Son's Instruction

In this chapter, we will study the numerous teachings of Jesus, His warnings, His revelation of the Father, and His titles which all verify these truths concerning self-defense. In Chapter 12, we will study His directive to His disciples.

The Natural Assumption

Often, Jesus would utilize analogies from life to explain certain spiritual truths. The content of these stories and tales were born out of the real-life experiences of His audiences. This helped them understand the truths Jesus was teaching.

Truth in Analogies

For example, the Lord used a fishing analogy when he told his disciples that He was calling them to share the gospel and bring souls into the kingdom.

Matthew 4:18-19
Walking by the sea of Galilee, he saw two brothers: Simon, who is called Peter, and Andrew, his brother, casting a net into the sea; for they were fishermen. He said to them, "Come after me, and I will make you fishers for men."

Mark 1:16-17
Passing along by the sea...he saw Simon and Andrew the brother of Simon casting a net into the sea, for they were fishermen. Jesus said to them, "Come after me, and I will make you into fishers for men."

Here, Jesus said that He would make them fishers of men. He meant that as they threw their nets into the water, caught fish, and pulled them into the boat, they would do the same in evangelism. First, they would share the gospel throwing out its net. Then, they would capture men's souls as they believed in Jesus. Finally, they would draw them into the kingdom of God as they believed in Him.

When Jesus spoke of the different reactions people had toward the gospel, he used the analogy of seeds. A farmer threw out seeds to grow. Some seeds were thrown on the road, rocks, thorns, and good soil. Only the seeds thrown on the good soil grew.

Matthew 13:3-9
He spoke to them many things in parables, saying, "Behold, a farmer went out to sow. As he sowed, some seeds fell by the roadside, and the birds came and devoured them. Others fell on rocky ground, where they didn't have much soil, and immediately they sprang up, because they had no depth of earth. When the sun had risen, they were scorched. Because they had no root, they withered away. Others fell among thorns. The thorns grew up and choked them. Others fell on good soil, and yielded fruit: some one hundred times as much, some sixty, and some thirty. He who has ears to hear, let him hear."

Then, He explained the spiritual truth behind them.

Matthew 13:19-23
When anyone hears the word...and doesn't understand it, the evil one comes and snatches away that which has been sown in his heart. This is what was sown by the roadside. What was sown on the rocky places, this is he who hears the word and immediately with joy receives it; yet he has no root in himself, but endures for a while.... oppression or persecution arises because of the word, immediately he stumbles. What was sown among the thorns, this is he who hears

HOW CHRISTIANS MAY DEFEND THEMSELVES AGAINST ATTACK

the word, but the cares of this age and the deceitfulness of riches choke the word, and he becomes unfruitful. What was sown on the good ground, this is he who hears the word and understands it, who most certainly bears fruit and produces, some one hundred times as much, some sixty, and some thirty.

Only about a quarter of the ones who hear the gospel will genuinely respond and bear good works to prove it. Others will not believe, or believe for a short time but oppression, persecution, worries, or riches will cause them to eventually fall away.

It is assumed that the many aspects of farming to which Jesus referred were true to life. Why? If the Lord Jesus had not used truthful statements from physical life, how could the spiritual statements or truths be believed? If Jesus had said that the seeds were thrown into the ocean, the clouds, or even the pocket of a person, this would not match their real-life experience. There would be an immediate rejection by the hearers stating, "This makes no sense; farmers would never do that!" The entire analogy would break down and the teaching would be ignored. Instead, they were true to life comparisons that helped people understand what He was teaching. Because they were true to life, they were easily understood. In fact, nobody ever objected to the reality of the analogy, though they may have rejected the theological truth behind it. This is a critical understanding.

What about the comparison Jesus made between the whitewashed tombs in His day and the hypocrisy of the sect of the Pharisees?

Matthew 23:27
Woe to you, scribes and pharisees, hypocrites! For you are like whitewashed tombs...outwardly appear beautiful, but inwardly are full of dead men's bones...of all uncleanness.

If Jesus had told the Pharisees and Jewish leaders that they were like whitewashed stones, clean on the outside but full of dead men's bones, the analogy would have broken down and the point could not have been made. He would have been mocked and scorned and would have spent much of his time explaining why he had used an irrational analogy. Instead, He spoke of whitewashed tombs - a common experience.

Concerning the other analogies Jesus used, a real woman could lose a coin, light a lamp, search for the coin, and find it.

Luke 15:8
Or what woman, if she had ten...coins, if she lost one drachma coin, wouldn't light a lamp, sweep the house, and seek diligently until she found it?

A man could have found a treasure in a field, bought the field, and kept the treasure. Men are real. Treasures are real. Fields are real.

Matthew 13:44
Again, the Kingdom of Heaven is like a treasure hidden in the field, which a man found, and hid. In his joy, he goes and sells all that he has, and buys that field.

A son might have squandered his father's inheritance.

Luke 15:11-13
He said, "A certain man had two sons. The younger of them said to his father, 'Father, give me my share of your property.' He divided his livelihood between them. Not many days after...younger son gathered all of this together and traveled into a far country. There he wasted his property with riotous living.

A real man could have built his house upon the sand and see it wash away in a storm.

HOW CHRISTIANS MAY DEFEND THEMSELVES AGAINST ATTACK

Matthew 7:26-27
Everyone who hears these words of mine, and doesn't do them will be like a foolish man, who built his house on the sand. The rain came down, the floods came, and the winds blew, and beat on that house; and it fell — and great was its fall.

Of course, there are many more. All of these are true to life analogies which were utilized to teach spiritual principles. Jesus always used analogies that were commonplace and true to life.

As a result of this, we can find out much about life in ancient times by looking at the stories he told. In the analogies previously discussed, we can learn that seeds were thrown upon the ground to plant them, some people were fisherman who went out and caught fish, and tombs were painted white. If people lost coins, they would look for them. Treasures may be found in a field and fields could be purchased. People built houses and they could be built on sand or rocks.

In Luke 15, we have the story of the Prodigal Son which is another analogy Jesus used.

Luke 15:11-14
He said, "A certain man had two sons. The younger of them said to his father, 'Father, give me my share of your property.' So he divided his livelihood between them. Not many days after, the younger son gathered all of this together and traveled into a far country. There he wasted his property with riotous living. When he had spent all of it, there arose a severe famine in that country, and he began to be in need.

Luke 15:18-20
I will get up and go to my father, and will tell him, "Father, I have sinned against heaven, and in your sight. I am no more worthy to be called your son. Make me as one of your hired servants."'

"He arose, and came to his father. But while he was still far off, his father saw him, and was moved with compassion, and ran, and fell on his neck, and kissed him. The son said to him, 'Father, I have sinned against heaven and in your sight. I am no longer worthy to be called your son.'"

In the story, it is easy to see that a son could receive his inheritance before the father died. The hearers may have been appalled at the father giving the inheritance early, the son squandering it, and the father forgiving him, but they would not disagree with the fact that these things were from real life experiences.

Here is a second point. When Jesus spoke in analogies, He would point out the sin or wrongdoing of the characters in the story. In the one just mentioned, the son pronounced his own sin.

Luke 15:18-19
I will get up and go to my father, and will tell him, "Father, I have sinned against heaven, and in your sight. I am no more worthy to be called your son. Make me as one of your hired servants."

It was obvious who had wronged whom. This is critical.

In the story of the unforgiving servant, a king forgave his servant who owed the ruler a huge debt. This reminded the servant of a much lesser debt that another servant owed him. Because he was unwilling to forgive the debt as the king had forgiven him, the king judged and condemned the servant for the sin and threw him into prison.

Matthew 18:32-35
Then his lord called him in and said to him, "You wicked servant! I forgave you all that debt because you begged me. Shouldn't you also have had mercy on your fellow servant, even as I had mercy on

HOW CHRISTIANS MAY DEFEND THEMSELVES AGAINST ATTACK

you?" His lord was angry, and delivered him to the tormentors until he should pay all that was due to him. So my heavenly Father will also do to you, if you don't each forgive your brother from your hearts for his misdeeds.

So, Jesus spoke in true to life analogies and pointed out the sinful issues involved.

Here is a simple hermeneutical principle of interpretation concerning these analogies. The truth of the spiritual principle taught verifies the truth of the real-life analogy used unless it is clearly specified by the Lord and vice versa. We can assume that the real-life possibilities in the stories were true. We can assume both Jesus and the audience would have assumed it to be true, especially if no one objected to its veracity. If Jesus did not comment about actions taken by the characters as sinful in the story, we can also assume they were acceptable practices at the time.

Why is this so important to our subject? In some of the analogies the Lord used, he described self-defense and the defense of others and did not speak against them but acted as if they were assumed to be general practices of life and acceptable to all. In fact, self-defense and the defense of others was such a normal part of life, Jesus did not have to explain or qualify what He meant. When He utilized these analogies on defense, it was expected that self-defense or the defense of others would naturally occur, were acceptable, and expected.

To put it another way, self-defense and the defense of others was used as a common action in the Lord's instruction without a negative commentary to the contrary. This verifies their legitimacy. They were acceptable and expected. I call this an argument from "natural assumption." It is naturally assumed to be true and verified by Jesus' use in His teaching and the absence of any contrary facts, criticisms, or remarks.

Self-Defense in Analogies

In the following analogies the Lord used to teach spiritual truth, self-defense is assumed as a normal expected course of action when one was threatened.

The Analogy of the Strong and Stronger Man

The first analogy involves a comparison between an enemy intruder and a strong man protecting his person, home, and possessions. This is compared to the assault of the Lord Jesus upon the domain of the Devil. This analogy is recorded twice when given on one occasion and once when given on another. We will look at the shorter version first.

Matthew 12:29
Or how can one enter into the house of the strong man and plunder his goods, unless he first bind the strong man? Then he will plunder his house.

Mark 3:27
But no one can enter into the house of the strong man to plunder unless he first binds the strong man; then he will plunder his house.

Here is a simple but powerful natural assumption in this true to life story: One must bind the strong man before plundering his home. Why? He will defend himself. This is so obvious. No one would question this. Self-defense was a given.

Once this assumption was established, the comparison could then easily be made. Notice, the Lord Jesus presented the spiritual fact first, because the social fact was so obvious. Also, it seems reasonable to assume that Mark did not write the comparative statement because it was so utterly evident and his gospel was shorter, but Matthew did.

HOW CHRISTIANS MAY DEFEND THEMSELVES AGAINST ATTACK

Matthew 12:28
But if I by the Spirit of God cast out demons, then God's Kingdom has come upon you.

The people accused Him of casting out demons by Satan's power. His response was clear. He had bound the Devil and was now plundering His domain. How? He was casting out demons, doing miracles, and bringing people out of the dominion of darkness and into the kingdom of light.

The second incident which occurred much later is only recorded by Luke. Here, Jesus makes the same comparison but adds many important details which relate to our study of self-defense. In chapter 11, once again, Jesus is accused of casting out demons by Satan. He explained how illogical it was because Satan's house would be divided and would not be able to stand. Then to drive His point home, He speaks again of this true to life analogy describing how He is now plundering Satan's domain.

First, He makes the point that God's kingdom is here, and I am plundering the Devil's domain.

Luke 11:20
But if I by God's finger [as plunderer] cast out demons, then God's Kingdom has come to you.

Then, Jesus utilizes the analogy to compare His work with the plunderer. Jesus is "the stronger man" who conquers the strong man.

Luke 11:21-22
When the strong man, fully armed [with weapon (s)], guards his own dwelling, his goods are safe. But when someone stronger attacks him and overcomes him, he takes from him his whole armor in which he trusted [relied] and divides his plunder.

Jesus, who is stronger than the strong man, Satan, has come, attacked, and overcome Him. He has taken his weapons and armor. This is true and is verified by the fact that a stronger man could come, attack a strong man, overcome him, and take his weapons and armor away.

We can look at this analogy alone as a story about life in ancient times. This story is about a man who is prepared for an attack and defends himself. Though he was overcome in this violent encounter, self-defense and its elements are seen.

First, we have a strong man. The word translated "strong man" is one word in the Greek. It refers to someone who is "mighty, strong, or powerful (usually physically)." Though Christ may be using this word as a reference to the power of Satan, it could also be that the strong man became strong to protect himself. One's strength has always been the first line of defense against any attack. A strong man is more likely to be able to defend himself, his family, and many possessions against plunderers. This is obvious in life and in the story. Therefore, the only person who will be able to overcome this strong man is a stronger man.

Second, this strong man is fully armed. The two words translated "fully armed" is only one word in the Greek. It means "armed with weapons." The root word of this one is the Greek word for "weapons."

John 18:3
Judas then, having taken a detachment of soldiers and officers from the chief priests and the Pharisees, came there with lanterns, torches, and weapons.

Romans 6:13-14
Also, do not present your members to sin as instruments of unrighteousness, but present yourselves to God as alive from the

HOW CHRISTIANS MAY DEFEND THEMSELVES AGAINST ATTACK

dead, and your members as instruments [weapons] of righteousness to God. For sin will not have dominion...but under grace.

Romans 13:12
The night is far gone, and the day is near. Let's therefore throw off the deeds of darkness, and let's put on the armor [weapons] of light.

2 Corinthians 6:7
In the word of truth [Bible], in the power of God; by the armor of righteousness on the right hand and on the left.

2 Corinthians 10:4
For the weapons of our warfare are not of the flesh, but mighty before God to the throwing down of strongholds.

He had weapons. What weapons? In the latter part of verse 22, we see the word translated "armor." This word has the same root meaning "weapons" but has an adjective attached to the front meaning "all or whole." So, this compound word refers to "all one's weapons or one's whole armor."

This word is used by Paul in his description of the armor of God. Here, he compares spiritual weapons that we have in Christ with the physical armor of the Roman guards that were watching him in his first Roman imprisonment.

Ephesians 6:11
Put on the whole armor of God, that you may be able to stand against the wiles of the devil.

Ephesians 6:13
Therefore put on the whole armor of God, that you may be able to withstand in the evil day, and having done all, to stand.

In the following passage, Paul lists the different pieces of armor that a real-life soldier would carry.

Ephesians 6:10-18
Finally, be strong in the Lord, and in the strength of his might. Put on the whole armor of God, that you may be able to stand against the wiles of the devil....Therefore put on the whole armor of God, that you may be able to withstand in the evil day, and having done all, to stand [firm]....having the utility belt of truth...the breastplate of righteousness...fitted your feet [shoes] with the preparation of the Good News of peace...the shield of faith....the helmet of salvation, and the sword of the Spirit...with all prayer and requests [I like to think of this as the spear or lance], praying at all times...and being watchful...in all perseverance and requests for all the saints.

The only Roman weapon left out was the spear or lance which one could consider possibly prayer.

By the way, here Paul is describing a spiritually strong person wearing the full armor in order to defend himself or herself from the attacks of the Devil and his minions. Here is the same example as Luke 11:21-22. This is a strong man with armor defending himself.

Third, he is "guarding." The word in the Greek in this kind of context means "to keep watch over or to guard."

Luke 2:8
There were shepherds in the same country staying in the field, and keeping watch [guard] by night over their flock.

Acts 12:4
When he had arrested him, he put him in prison, and delivered him to four squads of four soldiers each to guard him, intending to bring him out to the people after the Passover.

Acts 23:35
"I will hear you fully when your accusers...arrive." He commanded that he be kept [guard] in Herod's palace.

HOW CHRISTIANS MAY DEFEND THEMSELVES AGAINST ATTACK

Acts 28:16
When we entered into Rome, the centurion delivered the prisoners to the captain of the guard, but Paul was allowed to stay by himself with the soldier who guarded him.

So, this strong man with his full armor was keeping watch. What was he really guarding? It was his home and goods.

Luke 11:21-22
When the strong man, fully armed [with weapon(s)], guards his own dwelling, his goods are safe.

The phrase "his own dwelling" refers to his home. Though Jesus uses a term that could refer to a "palace, sheepfold, as well as a home," in this passage, He uses the common word translated "house" the other time He told this story.

The word in Matthew 12 and Mark 3 refers to a house. Here are several examples of this use.

Matthew 2:11
They came into the house and saw the young child with Mary, his mother, and they fell down and worshiped him. Opening their treasures, they offered to him gifts: gold, frankincense, and myrrh.

Matthew 5:15
Neither do you light a lamp and put it under a measuring basket, but on a stand; and it shines to all who are in the house.

Matthew 7:26
Everyone who hears these words of mine and doesn't do them will be like a foolish man who built his house on the sand.

Mark 1:29
Immediately, when they had come out of the synagogue, they came into the house of Simon and Andrew, with James and John.

Mark 2:15
He was reclining at the table in his house, and many tax collectors and sinners sat down with Jesus and his disciples, for there were many, and they followed him.

This word establishes that this strong man is protecting his house and goods. He is not a guard or soldier watching for enemy attack on a palace but a common man.

So, he is protecting his goods. The Greek word translated "goods" refers to the possessions we own from the mundane and common to the expensive and luxurious. It refers to all that we would normally possess and protect.

Luke 12:15
He said..., "Beware! Keep yourselves from covetousness, for a man's life doesn't consist of the abundance of the things which he possesses."

Luke 14:33
So therefore whoever of you who doesn't renounce all that he has, he can't be my disciple.

Luke 19:8
Zacchaeus stood and said to the Lord, "Behold, Lord, half of my goods I give to the poor. If I have...exacted anything of anyone, I restore four times as much."

Acts 4:32
The multitude of those who believed were of one heart and soul. Not one of them claimed that anything of the things which he possessed was his own, but they had all things in common.

His goods are safe because the man is guarding them. The word "safe' is the usual Greek word for "peace." His goods are "peaceful, safe, secure, or quiet." Everything is peaceful.

HOW CHRISTIANS MAY DEFEND THEMSELVES AGAINST ATTACK

The goods are secure. Why? The strong man is guarding them with his house in full armor. This is not unusual or out of the ordinary. In fact, it is so common that everyone hearing the story could relate to it. It is a part of normal life.

Then, a plunderer attacks the homeowner. This thief and robber are physically much stronger than this strong man, has weapons mightier than his, and overcomes him. The man loses all he has.

Luke 11:21-22
"When the strong man, fully armed, guards his own dwelling, his goods are safe. But when someone stronger attacks him and overcomes him, he takes from him his whole armor in which he trusted, and divides his plunder. But when someone stronger attacks him and overcomes him, he takes from him his whole armor in which he trusted [relied], and divides his plunder.

The word translated "attack" is literally "to come upon." He comes upon him, not his house or goods but him. This is obvious but important. The man knew he would have to defend himself to keep his goods safe. The attacker knew he would have to attack him to plunder his home and goods. This is a normal course of life. This needs no discussion. It is obvious.

Then the attacker overcomes him because he is stronger. This is same Greek word as "strong" in "strong man" but in the comparative form. He is physically stronger or with more powerful weapons or both and overcomes him. The word translated "overcomes" means "to conquer, have victory over, or prevail." There is a fight, and the attacker prevails. The attacker came, the man defended himself as expected but lost. The attacker had superior strength and power and he was conquered. This is exactly how these things work in normal life. There is nothing out of the ordinary here.

Finally, this attacker "takes from him his whole armor in which he trusted [relied] and divides his plunder." The attacker robs him, steals his armor, and divides his goods up between others involved or sells them. The word "plunder" is a "pelt off an animal or the valuables off an enemy." This is easy to understand because this is exactly what an intruder would do.

Lastly, the strong man is left with nothing. His armor is gone, his goods have been taken, and he is defenseless. This is what would be expected to happen. This is why the strong man became strong. He gathers his armor and was guarding his own house. He needed to keep his possessions safe. If there were family or others in the house, he would be keeping them safe. Though the man lost, we can easily assume if a weaker man came, the weaker man would be overcome, and the strong man's goods would be safe. The strong man would have successfully defended himself. This is life as we know it.

We can see how clear this point is once carefully laid out. This is what people do once they have possessions which they perceive could be stolen. We are looking at this analogy in the reverse. Jesus plundering the Devil's domain with superior power is exactly the same as a stronger man then plundering a strong man's house. The analogy must be true or possibly within the realm of reality for the spiritual truth to be true.

All would have understood this analogy because it would be assumed without question that one would protect his own home and possessions. No one questioned His analogy and its truth born out of the normal course of life.

What does this teach us about self-defense in Christ's day? First, it was naturally assumed as appropriate. Second, people protect themselves and their possessions. Third, if they want their possessions safe, they must be stronger than the one who wants to steal them. This could be done through physical strength and through appropriate weaponry. The physical strength and weaponry must be greater than the one who wants our possessions. Our weaponry can be all the weapons being used at the time. We are expected to guard and keep secure what we possess. If we are overcome by a perpetrator, then the attacker will take our possessions and weaponry. For us to be overcome, we must be unable to stop our enemy.

The Analogy of the Thief and Robber

A second set of analogies utilized by the Lord Jesus is His references to the many actions of thieves and the importance of protecting against them to teach spiritual truth. As these true to life analogies confirm the truthfulness of the spiritual principles so the principles verify the true to life stories.

Here Jesus is speaking about the coming of the Lord. It will be like a thief in the night. People must be prepared for His coming as they would be for a thief coming in the night.

Matthew 24:43
But know this, that if the master of the house had known in what watch of the night the thief was coming, he would have watched, and would not have allowed his house to be broken into.

He makes a simple but powerful natural assumption. If the owner knew that a thief was coming, he would watch for him so as to defend his house. There is no other possibility except that the thief was coming to rob the house.

Another thief analogy legitimizing a defense of ourselves and others as a normal course of life is used in Luke chapter twelve. Here, the Lord explained the importance of storing up treasure in heaven rather than upon the earth.

Luke 12:33-34
Sell that which you have, and give gifts to the needy. Make for yourselves purses which don't grow old, a treasure in the heavens that doesn't fail, where no thief approaches, neither moth destroys. For where your treasure is, there will your heart be also.

As believers we are to put our hearts toward spiritual things that cannot be stolen by a thief. I mention this because this thief analogy is used several times with a critical implication: no matter how much we prepare to defend our possessions, a thief can come unexpectedly to steal them.

It is not the unexpectedness that concerns us in this critical analogy here but the assumed self-defense. Without the self-defense being naturally assumed, there is no point to the analogy. No one leaves their possessions out but protects them. Even with the protection, they can be stolen. So, put your heart in spiritual things where they are fully protected.

Another analogy utilized by the Lord is found a little later in the same chapter when Jesus teaches the Hebrew people that they must be ready for the day of judgment because it will come unexpectedly.

Luke 12:39-40
But know this, that if the master of the house had known in what hour the thief was coming, he would have watched, and not allowed his house to be broken into. Therefore be ready also, for the Son of Man is coming in an hour that you don't expect him.

Rather than discuss the truths Jesus is revealing, let us look at the real-life example He uses. The master or owner of a house needs to be ready and protect his home from a thief at all times. The thief will not announce himself. If for some reason the thief did announce himself, what would the master do? It is naturally assumed that he would have been prepared to defend his home against the thief. If self-defense was not naturally assumed, the analogy would break down.

Paul uses the same analogy in 1 Thessalonians.

1 Thessalonians 5:2-6
For you yourselves know well that the day of the Lord comes like a thief in the night. For when they are saying, "Peace and safety," then sudden destruction will come on them, like birth pains on a pregnant woman. Then they will in no way escape. But you, brothers, aren't in darkness, that the day should overtake you like a thief. You are all children of light and children of the day. We don't belong to the night, nor to darkness, so then let's not sleep, as the rest do, but let's watch and be sober.

Again, here is an argument from this natural assumption. People should be prepared to defend themselves if a thief comes in the night. In the same way, we must be prepared by living righteously and being sober and watchful for the day of the lord. When judgment day comes, we will escape its fury and not be overcome by it because we are prepared and watchful to defend ourselves against it.

Peter picks up this theme in his second letter.

2 Peter 3:10-11
But the day of the Lord will come as a thief in the night; in which the heavens will pass away with a great noise, and the elements will be dissolved with fervent heat, and the earth and the works that are in it will be burned up. Therefore since all these things will be destroyed like this, what kind of people ought you to be in holy living and godliness.

As people prepare to defend themselves against a thief in the night, we also must be prepared to defend ourselves from judgment day by holy and righteous living.

We see the same thing in Revelation chapter sixteen.

Revelation 16:15
Behold, I come like a thief. Blessed is he who watches, and keeps his clothes, so that he doesn't walk naked, and they see his shame.

Here, the Lord Christ describes the vigilance of righteous living and sober watching that Christians must have as they prepare for the coming judgment on the earth. The Lord calls unrighteous living being caught naked when the thief comes. In this analogy, it is naturally assumed every man would understand that one must be prepared to defend themselves when a thief comes unexpectedly. If not self-defense, why would people prepare and then watch for the thief?

When Christ spoke of His role as a shepherd, He utilized this thief analogy. In John 10, He compares Himself as the good shepherd to the shepherds of Israel who had allowed their sheep to be ravaged by spiritual wolves and thieves.

John 10:12-15
He who is a hired hand, and not a shepherd, who doesn't own the sheep, sees the wolf coming, leaves the sheep, and flees. The wolf snatches the sheep, and scatters them. The hired hand flees because he is a hired hand, and doesn't care for the sheep. I am the good shepherd. I know my own, and I'm known by my own; even as the Father knows me, and I know the Father. I lay down my life for the sheep.

Their shepherds acted like hirelings who would not protect the sheep by defending them, but He will with His own life.

In the entire passage, the Lord Jesus expects His listeners to assume that shepherds are to defend their flocks against thieves and wolves. Of course, this would require them also to defend themselves from attack when the wolves or thieves turned on them. If they did not assume this defense, then they would not have understood His role.

Finally, at His arrest, he contrasts Himself with a thief and asks why they would need to come with weapons they would use for a robber.

Matthew 26:55
In that hour Jesus said to the multitudes, "Have you come out as against a robber with swords and clubs to seize me? I sat daily in the temple teaching, and you didn't arrest me.

Mark 14:43
Immediately, while he was still speaking, Judas, one of the twelve, came -- and with him a multitude with swords and clubs, from the chief priests, the scribes, and the elders.

Luke 22:52
Jesus said to the chief priests, captains of the temple, and elders, who had come against him, "Have you come out as against a robber, with swords and clubs?

Why would they come out with swords and clubs to arrest a robber? He might resist them, and they will have to defend themselves. The robber would immediately think that their weapons are greater than his so he could not defend himself and win. As a result, he will give himself up. This dialogue hinges on the natural assumption of self-defense.

The Analogies in the Old Testament

These analogies of self-defense and defense of others to teach spiritual truth are also found in the Old Testament as well. In Proverbs, Solomon uses the natural assumption of self-defense as he discusses the plight of the lazy.

DEFENDING YOUR LIFE

Proverbs 6:10-11
A little sleep, a little slumber, a little folding of the hands to sleep: so your poverty will come as a robber, and your scarcity as an armed man.

This wise man is comparing slothful people to those who are unprepared for an attack. Just like an attack by a robber on a road or an armed man in one's path comes suddenly and in great terror, so will poverty come to the lazy. Here is the natural assumption that people should be prepared to defend themselves. In the analogy, it is assumed.

In the Psalms, David uses self-defense analogies to speak of God's protection in many different ways.

In Psalm 35, he speaks of the Lord defending him against his enemies as one would defend another with weapons.

Psalm 35:1-2
Contend, Yahweh, with those who contend with me. Fight against those who fight against me. Take hold of shield and buckler, and stand up for my help. Brandish the spear and block those who pursue...Tell my soul, "I am your salvation."

To understand this comparison, we would have to picture a man defending himself or others with armor and weapons that would work against an attack. We can naturally do this.

Over and over in the psalms the help of the Lord is seen as a shield in front of His holy people whom He loves for their protection. This clearly demonstrates that shields were used to defend themselves and others.

Psalm 3:3
But you, Yahweh, are a shield around me, my glory, and the one who lifts up my head.

HOW CHRISTIANS MAY DEFEND THEMSELVES AGAINST ATTACK

Psalm 18:1-3
I love you, Yahweh, my strength. Yahweh is my rock, my fortress, and my deliverer; my God, my rock, in whom I take refuge; my shield, and the horn of my salvation, my high tower. I call on Yahweh, who is worthy to be praised; and I am saved from my enemies.

Psalm 18:30
As for God, his way is perfect. Yahweh's word is tried. He is a shield to all those who take refuge in him.

Psalm 18:35
You have also given me the shield of your salvation. Your right hand sustains me. Your gentleness has made me great.

Psalm 28:7
Yahweh is my strength and my shield. My heart has trusted in him, and I am helped. Therefore my heart greatly rejoices. With my song I will thank him.

Psalm 35:2
Take hold of shield and buckler, and stand up for my help.

Psalm 84:9
Behold, God our shield, look at the face of your anointed.

Psalm 84:11
For Yahweh God is a sun and a shield. Yahweh will give grace and glory. He withholds no good thing from those who walk blamelessly.

Psalm 89:18
For our shield belongs to Yahweh, our king to the Holy One of Israel.

Psalm 144:2
My loving kindness, my fortress, my high tower, my deliverer, my shield, and he in whom I take refuge, who subdues my people under me.

In all of these passages, God is portrayed as our shield of protection, He is our defense against enemies and those who oppress us. When this concept of "the Lord is my shield" is used, all knew (military or non-military) that a shield is for self-defense or the defense of others. This is clearly a natural assumption. The inspired writers only had to write the word "shield", and all would know what he meant.

As can be seen through the use of these many analogies of self-defense, it was a natural assumption. To defend goods or friends, one would stand guard over them with weapons and physical prowess enough to keep them safe. One would have to be prepared and watchful for thieves, robbers, and armed men who come violently and ferociously at any time to attack their flocks, possessions, or loved ones.

The Divine Warning

In the many encounters that Jesus had with authorities and others, He threatened them with what He could have done or what He would eventually do to defend Himself. These words must be viewed as warnings of what He could have at His first coming and eventually will have at His second coming as He defends Himself and others.

The Demonstrations of Potential Power

First, He gave them demonstrations of His power and what He could have done had it not been His time to sacrifice His life for the sins of humankind.

A crowd of people had come to arrest the Lord, perhaps a thousand people made up of Jewish leaders, temple police,

HOW CHRISTIANS MAY DEFEND THEMSELVES AGAINST ATTACK

and a cohort of Roman soldiers carrying swords and spears. Accompanying them were a mob carrying clubs. Rather than wait for them to come to Him, Jesus walked up to the crowd and asked for the name of the person they were looking for.

When Jesus said His Holy name "I AM," which is the name of God, they immediately fell to the ground.

John 18:5-6
They answered him, Jesus of Nazareth." Jesus said to them, "I am he." Judas also, who betrayed him, was standing with them. When therefore he said to them, "I am he," they went backward, and fell to the ground.

All the leaders, police, soldiers, and mob fell backward. This was Jesus' way of saying, "I am handing myself over to you! If I wanted to, I could defend myself with the simple word of my mouth."

The Declarations of Potential Power

Second, the Lord Jesus gave clear warnings of what He or His Father could have done to defend Him against all the violent accusations and eventual murder.

After the crowd got up and attempted to lay hands on Jesus, Peter defended Jesus by thrusting his sword at Malchus and cutting off the ear of the High priest's slave. After Jesus healed his injured ear, He made a powerful declaration to Peter in the hearing of the crowd.

Matthew 26:53
Do you think that I couldn't ask my Father, and he would even now send me more than twelve legions of angels?

This was not only to assure Peter that God was in control, but that God had many angels who could be sent at any moment to deliver Him. This was also a veiled threat to the crowd who thought that they were in charge and there was nothing Jesus could do.

Pilate becomes concerned when Jesus is called the King of the Jews and questions Him about this claim.

John 18:33-35
Pilate therefore entered again into the Praetorium, called Jesus, and said to him, "Are you the King of the Jews?" Jesus answered him, "Do you say this by yourself, or did others tell you about me? Pilate answered, "I'm not a Jew, am I? Your own nation and the chief priests delivered you to me. What have you done?"

Jesus answers with a veiled threat.

John 18:36
Jesus answered, "My Kingdom is not of this world. If my Kingdom were of this world, then my servants would fight, that I wouldn't be delivered.... But now my Kingdom is not from here."

What was Jesus implying in this statement? He was a king of another realm, and He had an army at His service who would fight for Him. A second implication is that they are ready for His command. He may look defenseless but is not. Again, this is a veiled threat letting Pilate know that He is allowing this.

The Announcement of Coming in Power

Third, He warned them that He would be coming in the future to defend Himself in great glory and power with many angels. The implication is this, "You leaders may think I am

HOW CHRISTIANS MAY DEFEND THEMSELVES AGAINST ATTACK

defenseless now, but I am not. I will return to defend myself when this is all over."

After His arrest, Caiaphas, the high priest, demanded that Jesus declare whether or not He was the Son of God.

Matthew 26:62-63
The high priest stood up and said to him, "Have you no answer? What is this that these testify against you?" But Jesus stayed silent. The high priest answered him, "I adjure you by the living God that you tell us whether you are the Christ, the Son of God."

Jesus responded with a definitive answer in the language of the day and then He issued a veiled warning. This warning of the Lord would have been clearly understood.

Matthew 26:64
Jesus said to him, "You have said so. Nevertheless, I tell you, after this you will see the Son of Man sitting at the right hand of Power, and coming on the clouds of the sky."

Notice, Jesus says the right hand of power, not love. Not only does Jesus claim to be the Son of God but explains that He will return in judgment on the clouds to defend Himself. The phrase "right hand of power" meant the right hand of God and He would be coming again in that power. The Jews knew exactly what He meant.

When the Lord stood before the Sanhedrin (the Jewish Council), He made the same veiled threat as Luke records.

Luke 22:66-70
As soon as it was day, the assembly of the elders of the people was gathered together, both chief priests and scribes, and they led him away into their council, saying, "If you are the Christ, tell us." But he said to them, "If I tell you, you won't believe, and if I ask, you

will in no way answer me or let me go. From now on, the Son of Man will be seated at the right hand of the power of God." They all said, *"Are you then the Son of God?"* He said to them, *"You say it, because I am."*

Here again Jesus admits to being the Son of God. After this is all over, He will be seated at the Almighty's right hand. The right hand refers to God's power. Jesus will be the instrument of God's power.

This was a serious but veiled threat with the implication that He would return to defend Himself and judge them. Therefore, these words authenticate the Lord's acceptance of self-defense and the defense of others. This would have to occur at another time because His hour to die had come.

Now to demonstrate that Jesus believed in the same truth of self-defense and the defense of others, we will study His revelation of the Father.

The Son's Communication

Since self-defense and the defense of others ultimately involves violence, people will distinguish between the Lord God's words and actions in the Old Testament and the Lord Jesus' words and actions in the New Testament. In a variety of ways both interpretive and theological, they will explain away many of the passages that I have already dealt with by insinuating that Jesus was a "gentler and kinder" God. They will simply ignore the Old Testament and focus on the Lord Jesus as the compassionate healer of the New Covenant. Yet, was there really a difference between the Father in the Old Testament and the Son in the New Testament regarding their words, actions, and messages? The answer is found in the opening words of the book of Hebrews.

HOW CHRISTIANS MAY DEFEND THEMSELVES AGAINST ATTACK

Hebrews 1:1-4
God, having in the past spoken to the fathers through the prophets at many times and in various ways, has at the end of these days spoken to us by his Son, whom he appointed heir of all things, through whom also he made the worlds. His Son is the radiance of his glory, the very image of his substance, and upholding all things by the word of his power, who, when he had by himself purified us of our sins, sat down on the right hand of the Majesty on high, having become as much better than the angels as the more excellent name he has inherited is better than theirs.

One of the purposes for which Christ came was to reveal the Father. The Lord Jesus explained that His words and actions came from the Father. Everything that the Son said and did what the Father told Him to say and do. He did nothing apart from this critical purpose that He Himself annunciated to His disciples and the general population.

John 3:34
For he whom God has sent speaks the words of God; for God gives the Spirit without measure.

John 4:34
Jesus said to them, "My food is to do the will of him who sent me and to accomplish his work.

John 5:19
Jesus therefore answered them, "Most certainly, I tell you, the Son can do nothing of himself, but what he sees the Father doing. For whatever things he does, these the Son also does likewise.

John 5:36
But the testimony which I have is greater than that of John, for the works which the Father gave me to accomplish, the very works that I do, testify about me, that the Father has sent me.

John 9:4
I must work the works of him who sent me while it is day. The night is coming, when no one can work.

John 10:36-38
Do you say of him whom the Father sanctified and sent into the world, "You blaspheme," because I said, "I am the Son of God?" If I don't do the works of my Father, don't believe me. But if I do them, though you don't believe me, believe the works, that you may know and believe that the Father is in me, and I in the Father.

John 12:50
I know that his commandment is eternal life. The things therefore which I speak, even as the Father has said to me, so I speak."

John 14:10
Don't you believe that I am in the Father, and the Father in me? The words that I tell you, I speak not from myself; but the Father who lives in me does his works.

The Son in the New Testament

Therefore, the Son communicated His Father's truths in words and actions in the New Testament. This would include truths concerning self-defense and the defense of others if the Father had commanded it.

Why? The Father in the Old Testament was the same Lord God as the Father in the New Testament. His nature, power, and attributes do not change. His truths do not change. This is called the attribute of immutability.

Malachi 3:5-6
I will come near to you to judgment.... For I, Yahweh, don't change; therefore you, sons of Jacob, are not consumed.

HOW CHRISTIANS MAY DEFEND THEMSELVES AGAINST ATTACK

Numbers 23:19
God is not a man, that he should lie, nor a son of man, that he should repent. Has he said, and he won't do it? Or has he spoken, and he won't make it good?

This means that we can rely on everything the Father said in the Old Testament about Himself and what He desires His children to do. This would include His truths concerning the defense of ourselves, those we love, and the innocent.

Since Jesus came to communicate the truths of the Father, then He would have communicated the same unchanging truths. Then the question must be asked, "Did the Son have to communicate every truth that was already communicated in the Old Testament by the same Father? No, He did not. Then a second question must also be asked, "Would the new truth Jesus revealed contradict the truths already revealed? This answer is also obvious; it cannot contradict any truth already revealed. Why? God, the Father, cannot lie and the same God was communicating in the New Testament as in the Old.

In John 17:17, the Son, Jesus, makes a simple but powerful statement.

John 17:17
Sanctify them in your truth. Your word is truth.

All of God's Word is truth. It cannot by its nature contradict itself. It all comes from the Spirit of God.

John 14:26
But the Counselor, the Holy Spirit, whom the Father will send in my name, will teach you all things, and will remind you of all that I said to you.

So, how could the new truth Jesus revealed disagree with the previously revealed truth when God's truth does not change? The apparent "kinder and gentler approach" that the Lord Jesus exhibited did not in any way have to do with the truth He revealed.

The Son in the Old Testament

Not only did the Son reveal the words and actions of the Father in the New Testament, but He often did the same in the Old Testament. It is important to understand that Jesus appeared in a preincarnate state in the Old Testament and spoke and acted on behalf of the Father. This included the defense of the Father, the people He loves, and the innocent. In His appearances in the Old Testament, we will simply highlight the ones that dealt specifically with defense rather than all mentioned.

In John 8, the Jewish authorities were rejecting Christ and claiming that their salvation was due to their father being Abraham. Jesus explains that their father is not Abraham because they would not be rejecting Him if he had been. Why? Jesus had appeared to Abraham.

John 8:55-56
You have not known him [the Father], but I know him. If I said, 'I don't know him,' I would be like you, a liar. But I know him and keep his word. Your father Abraham rejoiced to see my day. He saw it, and was glad."

Here, Jesus claimed to have appeared to Abraham. When could this have been?

Of course, it would have been the appearance of the Lord God to Abraham in human form before the Lord was to have destroyed Sodom and Gomorrah.

HOW CHRISTIANS MAY DEFEND THEMSELVES AGAINST ATTACK

Genesis 18:1-3
Yahweh appeared to him by the oaks of Mamre, as he sat in the tent door in the heat of the day. He lifted up his eyes and looked, and saw that three men stood near him. When he saw them, he ran to meet them from the tent door, and bowed himself to the earth, and said, "My lord, if now I have found favor in your sight, please don't go away from your servant.

Here, God appears with two angels. During this conversation, God promises him a son though he and Sarah were beyond childbirth years. Abraham also makes a plea for the innocent as God reveals the impending destruction of Sodom and Gomorrah to save his nephew. In this discussion, God agrees to save the innocents in the city which were only Lot and his family. Then the two angels travel to Sodom.

This is the appearance that the Jews would have known the Lord was referring to as Jesus spoke of Abraham seeing His day. Notice, God is going to judge Sodom and Gomorrah which is His defense of His purposes and plan. Abraham questioned God as to His defense of the innocent in that city. So, here Jesus is claiming to have communicated the truths about God to Abraham in a preincarnate appearance which had everything to do with defense.

Second, Jesus claimed to have existed before Abraham.

John 8:57-58
The Jews therefore said to him, "You are not yet fifty years old! Have you seen Abraham?" Jesus said to them, "Most certainly, I tell you, before Abraham came into existence, I AM."

When He states this, He refers to the identification of God's true name "I AM THAT I AM" that God gave to Moses at the burning bush. Here, the Lord is claiming to have appeared to their most revered prophet, Moses, as God.

Moses discusses this event in Exodus.

Exodus 3:2-6
Yahweh's angel appeared to him in a flame of fire out of the middle of a bush. He looked, and behold, the bush burned with fire, and the bush was not consumed. Moses said, "I will go now, and see this great sight, why the bush is not burned." When Yahweh saw that he came over to see, God called to him out of the middle of the bush, and said, "Moses! Moses!" He said, "Here I am." He said, "Don't come close. Take off your sandals, for the place you are standing on is holy ground." Moreover he said, "I am the God of your father, the God of Abraham, the God of Isaac, and the God of Jacob."

Here, Moses identifies the speaker as Yahweh's "angel" which means "messenger." Then, this "messenger" identifies Himself as "Yahweh" which means "I AM" or "I AM THAT I AM." The Lord Jesus is claiming to have been that very messenger that day. The "I AM" refers to His eternal existence.

The Jews knew exactly what Jesus was claiming to have been the God of the burning bush. This is the reason they picked up stones to kill Him on the spot. This was blasphemy of the highest order. Of course, it was not actual blasphemy because He was God.

John 8:59
Therefore they took up stones to throw at him, but Jesus was hidden, and went out of the temple, having gone through the middle of them, and so passed by.

Notice, the Son of God communicated the words and actions of the Father at the burning bush. What did Jesus appearing on behalf of the Father command Moses to do? He demanded that Moses go and lead His people out of Egypt. We have already seen in another chapter that this redemption from Egypt was God's greatest act of defense in the Old Testament!

HOW CHRISTIANS MAY DEFEND THEMSELVES AGAINST ATTACK

Later Paul identifies Jesus as the one who led the people through the wilderness and provided for them in every way.

1 Corinthians 10:1-4
Now I would not have you ignorant, brothers, that our fathers were all under the cloud, and all passed through the sea; and were all baptized into Moses in the cloud and in the sea; and all ate the same spiritual food; and all drank the same spiritual drink. For they drank of a spiritual rock that followed them, and the rock was Christ.

Once again, the Son of God appeared for the Father and led the people in the Shekinah glory which was the pillar of fire by night and the cloud of light by day. He led them through the Red Sea, through the desert, he provided manna and water for them. He was their rock of protection and support. Is this not defense of those whom God loves and the innocent? Was not Israel at the forefront of His plans for His Messiah to come?

So, we see the Son communicating the words and actions of the unchanging Father with His unchanging truth in both Testaments. As Jesus communicated for the Father, the truths of defense were definitely a part. We must remember that the Son was the exact representation of the Father including His words and actions. In Colossians, the apostle Paul explains it in a different way.

Colossians 1:17-19
He is before all things, and in him all things are held together. He is the head of the body, the assembly, who is the beginning, the firstborn [prominent one] from the dead, that in all things he might have the preeminence. For all the fullness was pleased to dwell in him.

Jesus had all the fullness of the Father in Him. Therefore, if the Father defended Himself, His people that He loved, and the innocent and desired His children to do the same, then His exact image and fullness would communicate that.

As we can see, Jesus was the exact representation of the Father who revealed His words and works. This would include self-defense and the defense of others. We see this demonstrated in the Lord Christ's many names, titles, and designations which refer to not only His Old Testament appearances but also His first and second comings.

The Lord Jesus appears as a "gentler, kinder God" because there are two comings of the Messiah. The first coming was as a suffering servant for the sins of men and the second will be as a conquering warrior.

Isaiah 53:3-5
He was despised and rejected by men, a man of suffering and acquainted with disease....pierced for our transgressions...

1 Samuel 2:10
Those who strive against Yahweh shall be broken to pieces.... He will give strength to his king, and exalt the horn of his anointed."

The difference in these two comings is the reason for the seeming difference in the Son's words and actions between the two Testaments. Yet, the names, titles, and designations speak of the defense of Himself, those He loves, and the innocent.

The Son's Designations

The numerous names, titles, and descriptions of the Son of God refer to His defense, deliverance, and protection. These would refer to His many Old Testament appearances and the Lord's first and second comings.

HOW CHRISTIANS MAY DEFEND THEMSELVES AGAINST ATTACK

The Advocate

Christ is our advocate to the Father. When we sin, Jesus will essentially come to our defense before the Father so stay His wrath. It is not difficult to conceive of Jesus advocating for our protection as we pray to the Father in His name.

1 John 2:1-2
My little children, I write these things to you so that you may not sin. If anyone sins, we have a Counselor with the Father, Jesus Christ, the righteous. And he is the atoning sacrifice for our sins, and not for ours only, but also for the whole world.

The Authority

Jesus has authority over all things and is supreme above all. This means He has the authority to protect His brethren and He will.

Matthew 28:18
Jesus came to them and spoke to them, saying, "All authority has been given to me in heaven and on earth.

The Blessed and Only Potentate

In this passage, Jesus is referred to as the coming king and Lord at His Second Coming. He is ruler of all. At His coming, the Lord will administer His justice, defend Himself, and His people.

1 Timothy 6:14-15
That you keep the commandment without spot, blameless, until the appearing of our Lord Jesus...which in its own times he will show, who is...blessed and only Ruler, the King of kings, and Lord of lords.

He alone has immortality, dwelling in unapproachable light, whom no man has seen...to whom be honor and eternal power....

The Bridegroom

Jesus is called the groom and His church the bridegroom. As husbands love and protect wives, so Christ does the same.

Matthew 9:15
Jesus said to them, "Can the friends of the bridegroom mourn as long as the bridegroom is with them? But the days will come when the bridegroom will be taken away from them, and then they will fast."

The Consolation of Israel

When Jesus was born, he came to be the comfort for Israel. They were under the dominion of Rome, in bondage to man-made rules, and lost in unbelief. Jesus came to deliver them spiritually the first time and physically the second time.

Luke 2:25
Behold, there was a man in Jerusalem whose name was Simeon. This man was righteous and devout, looking for the consolation of Israel, and the Holy Spirit was on him.

The Deliverer

The deliverance of Jesus Christ in defense of His brethren is from the wrath of the Father. Yet, Jesus will also deliver His brethren from harm.

Psalm 18:2
Yahweh is my rock, my fortress, and my deliverer; my God, my rock,

in whom I take refuge; my shield, and the horn of my salvation, my high tower.

1 Thessalonians 1:10
And to wait for his Son from heaven, whom he raised from the dead: Jesus, who delivers us from the wrath to come.

The Door of the Sheepfold

Jesus refers to Himself as the door of the sheepfold. This indicates that He decides who He lets into His kingdom and protects His sheep from harm. Though this may usually be spiritual, believers cannot deny that they depend upon their shepherd for protection from physical harm.

John 10:7
Jesus therefore said to them again, "Most certainly, I tell you, I am the sheep's door."

The Faithful and True

The Lord Jesus is faithful and true to keep His promises. One of these is to protect His sheep to the end. He will do what He promised.

Revelation 19:11
I saw the heaven opened, and behold, a white horse, and he who sat on it is called Faithful and True. In righteousness he judges and makes war.

The Great High Priest

As our high priest, Jesus understands our difficulties and

will come to our aid in times of trouble. The temptations we experience, when harm comes, incites us to rely on ourselves or some sinful solution, but we must trust Christ to help.

Hebrews 4:14-15
Having then a great high priest who has passed through the heavens, Jesus, the Son of God, let's hold tightly to our confession. For we don't have a high priest who can't be touched with the feeling of our infirmities, but one who has been in all points tempted like we are....

The Head of the Church

Jesus is the head of His church and we can trust Him to protect us as our leader.

Ephesians 5:23-24
For the husband is the head of the wife, as Christ also is the head of the assembly, being himself the savior of the body. But as the assembly is subject to Christ, so let the wives also be to their own husbands in everything.

The Immanuel

Jesus is God with us. He is all that God is and is with us. Since God is a defender of His people, Christ will do the same.

Isaiah 7:14
Therefore the Lord himself will give you a sign. Behold, the virgin will conceive...bear a son...name Immanuel [God with us].

Matthew 1:22-23
Now all this has happened.... "Behold, the virgin shall be with child, and shall give birth to a son. They shall call his name Immanuel," which is, being interpreted, "God with us."

The Judge

The judgement of God is a form of self-defense of His plans, purposes, and people.

Acts 10:42-43
He commanded us to preach to the people and to testify that this is he who is appointed by God as the Judge of the living and the dead. All the prophets testify about him, that through his name everyone who believes in him will receive remission of sins."

The King of Kings

The Lord Christ is the King of all kings upon the earth. He rules and controls all things on earth and in the heavenly places. We depend on Him to protect us against individual, city, regional, and national harm.

Revelation 17:14-15
These will war against the Lamb, and the Lamb will overcome them, for he is Lord of lords, and King of kings, and those who are with him are called chosen and faithful. He said to me, "The waters which you saw, where the prostitute sits, are peoples, multitudes, nations, and languages."

The King of the Jews

As the King of the Jews, Jesus will spiritually save the Jews who believe in Him now. Next, He will set up His kingdom for a thousand years to fulfill the promises of God in the past to the Jews.

Matthew 2:2
Where is he who is born King of the Jews? For we saw his star in the east, and have come to worship him.

The Way, Truth, and Life

Jesus is the only way to heaven. He is the truth about God revealed in bodily form and eternal life is found in Him. Though eternal life is seen as a gracious gift from God, is it not the ultimate deliverance from harm (God defending us)?

John 14:5-7
Thomas said to him, "Lord, we don't know where you are going. How can we know the way?" Jesus said to him, "I am the way, the truth, and the life. No one comes to the Father, except through me. If you had known me, you would have known the Father also....

The Lion of the Tribe of Judah

The Lion is a majestic and ferocious animal which has no animal predator due to its size and strength. It is a symbol of royalty and leadership in the Scriptures. This speaks of Christ's authority, power, and leadership over all of creation. The Lord comes from the promised Messianic line of Abraham through Judah. The Lord Jesus Christ is fully able to protect His people. Like the power of a lion, we have this kind of power with us.

Revelation 5:5
One of the elders said to me, "Don't weep. Behold, the Lion who is of the tribe of Judah, the Root of David, has overcome: he who opens the book and its seven seals."

The Lord of All

The word "lord" means "master". The Lord Jesus is master of the entire universe. He can always be depended upon to come to our aid in our affliction and trouble.

HOW CHRISTIANS MAY DEFEND THEMSELVES AGAINST ATTACK

Acts 10:36
The word which he sent to the children of Israel, preaching good news of peace by Jesus Christ — he is Lord of all.

The Lord of Glory

The glory of God refers to the nature, attributes, and power of God expressed and on display. One of the ways in which Christ will put His glory on display at His Second Coming is in judgment. Here, He will defend His people and put away all His enemies. He is the glorious Lord Jesus in whom we can depend.

1 Corinthians 2:8
Which none of the rulers of this world has known. For had they known it, they wouldn't have crucified the Lord of glory.

The Lord of Lords

Christ is above all rulers of the earth. Jesus is the Ruler and Master of all Masters. His people must trust Him in time of trouble. He has the authority and power to defend and deliver them.

1 Timothy 6:15
Which in its own times he will show, who is the blessed and only Ruler, the King of kings, and Lord of lords.

The Mediator

As our advocate, Christ is the great mediator between God, the Father, and His brethren. God will desire to protect His children because Christ died for them.

1 Timothy 2:5
For there is one God, and one mediator between God and men, the man Christ Jesus.

The Messiah

The Messiah came to defend and deliver His people spiritually and supernaturally the first time. The second time He will deliver them from temporal and supernatural forces.

John 1:41
He first found his own brother, Simon, and said to him, "We have found the Messiah!" (which is, being interpreted, Christ).

The Hope

We know our hope in the most difficult circumstances is our Lord Jesus who will be our deliverer either in this life or the life to come. He defends His people.

1 Timothy 1:1
Paul, an apostle of Jesus Christ according to the commandment of God our Savior and the Lord Jesus Christ our hope.

The Prince of Life

Jesus is the Prince of life. The Lord is the ruler over our physical lives and eternal lives. He is in control of all and defends us.

Acts 3:15
And killed the Prince of life, whom God raised from the dead, to which we are witnesses.

The Risen Lord

Christ can deliver us even from death because He has risen from the dead and conquered death. Who could ultimately harm us?

Luke 24:33-34
They rose up that very hour, returned to Jerusalem, and found the eleven gathered together, and those who were with them, saying, "The Lord is risen indeed, and has appeared to Simon!"

The Savior

The Lord Jesus saved and delivered us from the penalty of sin which was physical and spiritual death. Now, when we die, we enter into heaven. This is the most important defense.

Luke 2:10-12
The angel said to them, "Don't be afraid, for behold, I bring you good news of great joy which will be to all the people. For there is born to you today, in David's city, a Savior, who is Christ the Lord. This is the sign...find a baby wrapped in...cloth, lying in a feeding trough."

The Son of Man

The Son of Man speaks of not only Christ's humanity but is used by the Lord to refer to His future coming in glory. As we have seen, this coming is a time of ultimate defense of His Father, and His plans and purposes, His people, and Christ Himself.

Mark 14:62
Jesus said, "I am. You will see the Son of Man sitting at the right hand of Power, and coming with the clouds of the sky."

The Son of the Most High

The Son of the God Most High also means He is above all else. This is incredibly important for God's defense of His people. Who can come against us whom He cannot stop? Who can attempt evil or harm upon us with His superior power and supremacy?

Luke 1:32
He will be great and will be called the Son of the Most High. The Lord God will give him the throne of his father David.

The Victorious One

What victory has our Lord Jesus brought? He has battled the forces of evil and overcame them all. Therefore, we also will overcome all evil and spend an eternity in heaven. Is this not the greatest defense of all?

Revelation 3:21
He who overcomes, I will give to him to sit down with me on my throne, as I also overcame...sat down with my Father on his throne.

1 John 5:5
Who is he who overcomes the world, but he who believes that Jesus is the Son of God?

In this chapter, we have studied the numerous teachings of Jesus, His warnings, His revelation of the Father, and His Titles which all verify these truths concerning self-defense. In the next chapter, we will study His directive to His disciples.

Chapter 12

The Lord's Directive

Now, we come to some of the most important passages in the entire Scriptures concerning self-defense. This involves the direct commands of the Lord Jesus on the subject. We saw in a previous chapter that the disciples carried staffs for self-defense against robbers or wild animals. Now, we come to a discussion of our self-defense from persecutors. The Lord's instruction on this topic encompasses three major events in the gospel accounts. They were the sending of the twelve, the seventy to preach, and His preparation of the disciples for His impending departure.

The first two times, they were proclaiming the kingdom while He was with them and supported by the crowds. The third time, Jesus would soon be gone, and the disciples would have to change their strategy to protect themselves. We will look at each individually. We will begin by setting the stage.

The Initial Reaction of the Crowds

The Son's direction begins with the initial reaction of the crowds which welcomed His miracles and message.

The Welcoming of The Son

The Lord Jesus was welcomed by great crowds wherever He went because He healed them with mighty miracles. They came to Him in droves.

Matthew 4:23-25
Jesus went about...Galilee, teaching in their synagogues, preaching the Good News of the Kingdom, and healing every disease...sickness among the people. The report about him went out into all Syria. They brought to him [Jesus] all who were sick, afflicted with various diseases and torments, possessed with demons, epileptics, and paralytics; and he healed them. Great multitudes from Galilee, Decapolis, Jerusalem, Judea, and from beyond the Jordan followed him.

Matthew 7:28
When Jesus had finished saying these things, the multitudes were astonished at his teaching.

Matthew 9:8
But when...multitudes saw it, they marveled and glorified God, who had given such authority to men.

Matthew 9:33
When the demon was cast out, the mute man spoke. The multitudes marveled, saying, "Nothing like this has ever been seen in Israel!"

Matthew 12:15
Jesus...withdrew from there. Great multitudes followed him; and he healed them all.

Matthew 12:23
All the multitudes were amazed, and said, "Can this be the son of David?"

Matthew 15:31
So that the multitude wondered when...saw the mute speaking, the injured healed, the lame walking, and the blind seeing – and they glorified the God of Israel.

Matthew 20:27-29
Whoever desires to be first among you shall be your bondservant,

HOW CHRISTIANS MAY DEFEND THEMSELVES AGAINST ATTACK

even as the Son of Man came not to be served, but to serve, and to give his life as a ransom for many." As they went out from Jericho, a great multitude followed him.

Until finally, the Lord Jesus and His disciples rode into Jerusalem amid celebration and praise from the crowds.

Matthew 21:8-9
A...great multitude spread their clothes on the road. Others cut branches from the trees and spread them on the road. The multitudes who went in front of him, and those who followed, kept shouting, "Hosanna to the son of David! Blessed is he who comes in the name of the Lord! Hosanna in the highest!"

Usually, the disciples accompanied Jesus as He and they proclaimed the gospel and baptized the converts. John, the apostle, records it in John chapter four.

John 4:1-3
"Therefore when the Lord knew that the Pharisees had heard that Jesus was making and baptizing more disciples than John [The Baptist] (although Jesus himself didn't baptize, but his disciples), he left Judea, and departed into Galilee."

So, at first all was well.

The Peaceful Proclamation of the Disciples

When Jesus sent the disciples to cities to prepare the way for Him and preach the gospel, they traveled peacefully.

Luke 9:51-53
It came to pass, when the days were near that he should be taken up, he intently set his face to go to Jerusalem and sent messengers before his face. They went and entered into a village of the Samaritans, so

as to prepare for him. They didn't receive him, because he was traveling with his face set toward Jerusalem.*

Though in this instance, the cities were unwilling to receive Jesus, we still see the pattern He used with His disciples. Even though they were not accepted, they were never in danger.

This peaceful period occurred because it was not the time for His death on the cross. His great moment of persecution determined by the Father had not yet come.

John 7:6-8
Jesus therefore said to them [His brothers], "My time has not yet come, but your time is always ready.... its works are evil. You go up to the feast. I am not yet going up to this feast, because my time is not yet fulfilled.

John 7:30
They sought therefore to take him. No one laid a hand on him, because his hour had not yet come.

Eventually, the time did come, and real persecution was about to begin not just for Jesus but also for His disciples.

John 12:23
Jesus answered them, "The time has come for the Son of Man to be glorified."

Mark 14:41
He came the third time, and said to them, "Sleep on now, and take your rest. It is enough. The hour has come. Behold, the Son of Man is betrayed into the hands of sinners."

Matthew 26:45-46
Then he came to his disciples and said to them, "Are you still sleeping and resting? Behold, the hour is...at hand."

The Original Directive to Depend

During this peaceful time, Jesus sent the disciples out to proclaim the gospel. Before the Lord did this, He provided some very specific instructions for them to follow. These rules and the changes that came later are critical to our discussion.

The Initial Sending of the Twelve

It was during the time of the popular reception of Jesus by the multitudes that our first two incidents occur. As was mentioned, Jesus sent His disciples on short term excursions to prepare the people for His arrival and to train them to preach the gospel themselves.

We do not know how many times this occurred or how long these short-term missionary trips lasted. There were two trips recorded with very specific instructions to His disciples that are included by the writers of the gospels. Since they are similar, we can assume these governed their behavior at this time of popularity and peace.

The first incident occurred as Jesus was near the end of His Galilean ministry. His disciples had been with Him for some time. They were ready to preach and proclaim the truth on their own with the miracles that verified them. So, Jesus called them and gave them the authority they would need to do what He was doing. This incident was recorded by Matthew and Luke.

Matthew 10:1
He called to himself his twelve disciples, and gave them authority over unclean spirits, to cast them out, and to heal every disease and every sickness.

Luke 9:1-2
He called the twelve...and gave them power and authority over all demons, and to cure diseases....sent them forth to preach the kingdom of God, and to heal the sick.

Mark writes that Jesus sent them out in pairs.

Mark 6:6-7
He marveled because of their unbelief. He went around the villages teaching. He marveled because of their unbelief. He went around the villages teaching. He called to himself the twelve, and began to send them out two by two; and he gave them authority over the unclean spirits. So, the Lord commissions these twelve men to travel in twos and preach God's kingdom, heal the sick...diseased...cast out demons.

The Twelve's Dependence

The Lord Jesus gave specific instructions as to whom they would speak, where they would go, what they should bring, and how they should behave.

He began His instructions by commanding them to speak to only the Jews. They were not to go to the Samaritans or the Gentiles.

Matthew 10:5-6
Jesus sent these twelve out, and commanded them, saying, "Don't go among the Gentiles...don't enter into any city of the Samaritans. Rather, go to the lost sheep of the house of Israel."

Jesus required them to go to the Jews only because the Lord God had promised the Jews that the Messiah would come and bring the fulfillment of all His promises. Then the Jews would share it with the people of the world.

HOW CHRISTIANS MAY DEFEND THEMSELVES AGAINST ATTACK

Matthew 15:22-24
Behold, a Canaanite woman came...and cried, saying, "Have mercy on me, Lord...son of David. My daughter is...vexed with a demon." But he answered...not a word. His disciples came and begged him, saying, "Send her away; for she cries after us." But he answered, "I wasn't sent to anyone but the lost sheep of the house of Israel."

When the nation rejected Him as the promised Messiah, He would go to sheep of another fold which would be the rest of mankind, the Gentiles.

John 10:16
I have other sheep, which are not of this fold. I must bring them also, and they will hear my voice. They will become one flock with one shepherd.

Matthew 28:18-20
Jesus came to them and spoke to them, saying, "All authority has been given to me in heaven and on earth. Go, and make disciples of all nations, baptizing...in the name of the Father...the Son and of the...Spirit, teaching them to observe all things which I commanded you. Behold, I am with you always...to the end of the age." Amen.

Then, the Lord told His disciples to "freely give" as they had received. Here, the Lord Jesus Christ was authorizing the disciples to do miracles as He did.

Matthew 10:8
Heal the sick, cleanse the lepers, and cast out demons. Freely you received, so freely give.

They were to be as generous in their miracles and preaching as God had been generous to the twelve of them.

After this, Jesus described exactly what they may or may not bring on their preaching mission and the reason for it.

This instruction is what we will focus on in our study because Jesus will change these instructions as He nears the cross which is critical to our discussion of self-defense.

Matthew 10:10
Take no bag for your journey, neither two coats, nor shoes, nor staff: for the laborer is worthy of his food.

Here, Jesus alludes to the Levitical law concerned itself with not holding back what people had earned.

Leviticus 19:13
You shall not oppress your neighbor, nor rob him. The wages of a hired servant shall not remain with you all night until the morning.

This came from a farming analogy by Moses in Deuteronomy.

Deuteronomy 25:4
You shall not muzzle the ox when he treads out the grain.

Paul refers to this very instruction by Jesus when he writes to the Corinthians.

1 Corinthians 9:9-10
For it is written in the law of Moses, "You shall not muzzle an ox while it treads out the grain." Is it for the oxen that God cares, or does he say it assuredly for our sake? Yes, it was written for our sake, because he who plows ought to plow in hope, and he who threshes in hope should partake of his hope.

Here, the apostle explains his right to earn money from the preaching of the gospel which he had not exercised in their church.

When Paul describes the elder who labors in the word and doctrine, he states that the elder is worthy of wages.

HOW CHRISTIANS MAY DEFEND THEMSELVES AGAINST ATTACK

1 Timothy 5:18
For the Scripture says, "You shall not muzzle the ox when it treads out the grain." And, [another] "The laborer is worthy of his wages."

The "muzzling of the ox" was an analogy from farming and ranching in ancient times. As the powerful ox was treading upon the wheat to separate the grain from the stalk and chaff, he would eat some of it. This would cost the owner of the field some of his earnings, so he would muzzle the ox. Here God presents an important principle. He did not want the animal muzzled but wanted it to reap a benefit from its own labor. In the Lord God's plan, the worker (man or animal) should receive the benefits from his or its own labor which is found in the Levitical law.

So, Jesus continues with a series of instructions which will allow them to practice this principle. This means that His disciples must financially depend upon their hearers of the gospel to provide them shelter, food, and other essentials as they shared the gospel. This would teach them to depend upon the Lord for sustenance.

How would this actually work itself out? Would they ask for money from the people to whom they were speaking or what? Jesus provides the answer in great detail which can be summed up with "bring what you have and ask for the rest." Money would not have to be exchanged at all; instead, all their basic needs would be met by the people responding to the gospel and through their dependence on God.

Now, what would these disciples need as they traveled and preached the kingdom of God? They would need food, clothing, shoes, shelter, a staff, and some money to replace anything that was consumed or worn out. So, the Lord Jesus commands them not to purchase any of these necessities, but only to take what they already had and no money to replace them. This would be the responsibility of the hearers of their message.

These instructions are recorded in three of the gospels but not by John. As we discuss these, we must keep in mind that Jesus did not speak in a series of statements. He was like you and I having real conversations of which the inspired writers would describe in different ways. Some would leave out one thing and others would insert something else He said. Yet, all of them would have been in His instruction.

First, we will consider the account of the apostle Matthew in chapter ten of his book.

Matthew 10:9-10
Don't take any gold, silver, or brass in your money belts. Take no bag for your journey, neither two coats, nor shoes, nor staff: for the laborer is worthy of his food [his support].

At first, this sounds like Jesus is telling His disciples to take nothing on their trip but to live off those who hear the gospel. He can't mean this because it would be absolutely absurd since they could not travel in bare feet and with no initial food or money.

Then what is Jesus saying? The Greek word translated "take" can also mean "to acquire, obtain, or purchase." He is simply telling them not to obtain, purchase, or acquire anything extra for their journey than the bare necessities they already had. If they did, how would they be able to live off the gospel? How would they be able to obtain wages and benefits from their preaching? He is saying that they should take what little money they had, the bag and a few items of clothes, one coat or tunic (an undergarment for cold weather), shoes they already had, and a staff. If they wore out, then it would be provided by their hearers.

Here is a paraphrase of the true translation with the correct meaning.

Matthew 10:9-10
Don't acquire, purchase, or obtain any extra gold, silver, or brass and put it in your money belts. Acquire, obtain, or purchase no extra bag for your journey, neither two coats, nor shoes, nor staff: for the laborer is worthy of his food [his support].

I presented Matthew's account first because the other two would not make sense without it. For Mark and Luke use the same verb translated "take."

In Mark 6:8-9, Mark provides his account.

Mark 6:8-9
He commanded them that they should take nothing for their journey, except a staff only: no bread, no wallet, no money in their purse, but to wear sandals, and not put on two tunics.

Now, we will insert the correct meaning of "take" with the added word "more" to aid in our understanding.

Mark 6:8-9
He commanded them that they should acquire, obtain, or purchase nothing more for their journey, except a staff only if they didn't have one or it was broken: no extra bread, no extra wallet, no extra money in their purse, but to wear sandals, and not put on two tunics.

Again, they would not need to purchase anything extra for their travels. They would not need to be concerned about food, money, or a second tunic (for cold weather in case the other wore out) because a workman is worthy of his wages (being provided for). Instead, they should take the basics: sandals, a tunic, and a staff. We might say, "Take nothing extra for the journey than what you have."

In Luke's account we see the same theme.

Luke 9:3
He said to them, "Take nothing for your journey — neither staffs, nor wallet, nor bread, nor money; neither have two coats apiece."

They were not to take additional supplies. They did not need any extra staffs, money, food, or an additional undergarment. Why? The people to whom they would be preaching would provide the things they would need if they wore out because a workman is worthy of his wages. Here is the paraphrase of the translation.

Luke 9:3
Jesus said to them, "Acquire, obtain, or purchase nothing more for your journey — neither an extra staff, nor an extra wallet, nor additional bread, nor extra money; neither have two coats apiece."

Why? The people they shared the gospel with would provide their food, money, and shelter. They were not to purchase any more items because they were to live off the gospel. It was important for them to learn that they could depend on God for their daily needs.

How would they be provided for? How would this occur? In the accounts of the three gospels, the Lord Jesus Christ explains this process whereby they will obtain their necessary provisions during this ministry.

Matthew 10:11
Into whatever city or village you enter, find out who in it is worthy; and stay there until you go on.

Mark 6:10
He said to them, "Wherever you enter into a house, stay there until you depart from there."

HOW CHRISTIANS MAY DEFEND THEMSELVES AGAINST ATTACK

Luke 9:4
Into whatever house you enter, stay there, and depart from there.

Here, Jesus explains that the person who hears their message and is willing to take them in, that is where they will stay. They do not need to be going from house to house choosing the one with better accommodations. The worthy household would be the ones who responded to their gospel message.

An example of this worthiness was the woman Lydia. She responded to the apostle Paul's message in Philippi, and she opened her home to them.

Acts 16:14-15
A certain woman named Lydia, a seller of purple, of the city of Thyatira, one who worshiped God, heard us. The Lord opened her heart to listen to the things which were spoken by Paul. When she and her household were baptized, she begged us, saying, "If you have judged me to be faithful to the Lord, come into my house and stay." So she persuaded us.

These are the people the disciples of the Lord Jesus were to find wherever they went. These gracious people would need to provide for them.

Next, if the disciples were not welcomed, then they would perform a ceremonial gesture that would warn those that rejected them that they were done with them and would no longer preach the gospel to them. Three of the gospel writers, Matthew, Mark, and Luke, mention this.

Matthew 10:12-14
As you enter into the household, greet it. If the household is worthy, let your peace come on it, but if it isn't worthy, let your peace return to you. Whoever doesn't receive you, nor hear your words, as you go out of that house or that city, shake off the dust from your feet.

Mark 6:11
Whoever will not receive you nor hear you, as you depart from there, shake off the dust that is under your feet for a testimony against them.

Luke 9:5
As many as don't receive you, when you depart from that city, shake off even the dust from your feet for a testimony against them.

Also, to shake the dust off their feet would be a symbol of taking their greeting back.

Then, the Lord Jesus discloses the judgment on the cities who did not receive His disciples.

Matthew 10:15
Most certainly I tell you, it will be more tolerable for the land of Sodom and Gomorrah in the day of judgment than for that city.

Sodom and Gomorrah were never visited by the disciples of Jesus who gave them an opportunity directly to repent of their sins. These people who refused to listen to His disciples will have the greater judgment.

After this, the Lord warned His disciples of the coming persecution that they would endure. Before, He had spoken of Himself, now they would also experience it. This was a warning for the future. Though this is a lengthy portrayal, we will only look at the first few verses.

Matthew 10:16-18
Behold, I send you out as sheep among wolves. Therefore be wise as serpents, and harmless as doves. But beware of men: for they will deliver you...to councils...synagogues they will scourge you....you will be brought before governors and kings for my sake...a testimony to them and to the nations.

This persecution did not occur until much later. This future aspect is critical because Jesus discusses these instructions at the last supper. Then He changes them. Why? The coming persecution would begin at His arrest.

Finally, the disciples were sent out. When they returned, there was great rejoicing among them as they reported what had occurred.

Mark 6:30
The apostles gathered themselves together to Jesus...they told him all things, whatever they had done, and whatever they had taught.

Luke 9:10
The apostles, when they had returned, told him what things they had done. He took them, and withdrew apart to a deserted place of a city called Bethsaida.

There is no indication that they had experienced any kind of persecution. Instead, there is every indication that everything went incredibly well. The Lord God was at work through them, and they knew it. This gave them great confidence and excitement for what God was doing. The Almighty One was working through them!

The Additional Sending of the Seventy

The second event is similar to the first, except it involves seventy others and not the disciples. Sometime later, at the end of His Judean ministry, Jesus appoints seventy others and gave them similar instructions.

Luke 10:1
Now after these things, the Lord...appointed seventy others, and sent them two by two ahead of him...where he was about to come.

The Son's Similar Instructions to the Seventy

This time the Lord issues His warning of coming persecution first then gave His instructions.

Luke 10:3
Go your ways. Behold, I send you...as lambs among wolves.

Jesus then presents a similar set of instructions for these other disciples to follow.

Luke 10:4
Carry no purse, nor wallet, nor sandals. Greet no one on the way.

Of course, He is not telling them to leave their shoes behind with their money and wallets; instead, He is asserting that they are to bring "no extra" money or shoes.

The Lord continues with His instructions which were the same as He had given previously.

Luke 10:7-8
Into whatever house you enter, first say, "Peace be to this house." If a son of peace is there, your peace will rest on him; but if not, it will return to you. Remain in that same house, eating and drinking the things they give, for the laborer is worthy of his wages. Don't go from house to house. Into whatever city you enter, and they receive you, eat the things that are set before you.

The Lord explains the same principle to follow: a workman is worthy of his wages. They should be supported by the people with whom they are sharing the gospel. They are to greet the home or return their greeting depending on the hospitality and the welcome of their message. These seventy disciples were not to be going house to house looking for the very best accommodations they could find; but instead, they should

HOW CHRISTIANS MAY DEFEND THEMSELVES AGAINST ATTACK

stay wherever someone had offered and eat what is placed before them.

Luke indicates that these seventy other disciples were also given the same message to proclaim wherever they went and the same power to heal.

Luke 10:9
Heal the sick who are therein, and tell them, "God's Kingdom has come near to you."

Then if anyone did not respond, their dust was to be shaken off.

Luke 10:10
But into whatever city you enter, and they don't receive you, go out into its streets and say, Even the dust from your city that clings to us, we wipe off against you. Nevertheless know this, that God's Kingdom has come near to you.

Here the Lord gives them a warning they are to proclaim as they shake off the dust of their feet. Here again, this was probably what the twelve also did.

After the Lord issues a declaration of judgment on several cities, Luke records the return of the seventy.

Luke 10:17-18
The seventy returned with joy, saying, "Lord, even the demons are subject to us in your name." He said to them, "I saw Satan having fallen like lightning from heaven."

Notice first, there was rejoicing which means they did not encounter any persecution. As with the twelve, persecution was coming in the future. Also, Jesus speaks of Satan being thwarted in his efforts to stop these seventy. The power of

God was so incredibly decisive over Satan's power in this missionary trip that it was like him being thrown out of heaven like a lightning bolt out of the sky. It was sure and quick. Since Satan is the main source behind all persecution and was thrown down, they did not experience the kinds of threats that they would in the future. Their authority had been given by the authority of the one above the Devil.

The Growing Disdain of the Leaders

As His following and popularity grew, so did the disdain of the leaders of Israel. They could not seize Him because they feared the crowds. There simply were too many people who would be watching! Though they grew in their animosity, so did the crowds in their admiration. The leaders became more and more threatened and jealous by His powerful message and immense popularity.

The Initial Concern of the Jews

As Jesus preached and He healed, a concern about Him from the leadership grew. He was becoming popular and a possible threat to their power.

Matthew 21:46
When they sought to lay hold on him, they feared the multitudes, because they took him for a prophet.

Mark 12:12
They tried to seize him, but they feared the multitude; for they perceived that he spoke the parable against them. They left him....

Luke 20:19
The chief priests and the scribes sought to lay hands on Him that

very hour, but they feared the people -- for they knew He had spoken this parable against them.

There were some moments when the Lord so incited them that they sought to kill Him on the spot, but He escaped.

Luke 4:28-30
They were...filled with wrath in the synagogue, as they heard these things; and they rose up, and threw him out of the city, and led him to the brow of the hill that their city was built on, that they might throw him off the cliff. But he [Jesus], passing through the midst of them, went his way.

The Avoidance of The Son

Jesus used many methods to avoid being captured until the time the Father had determined. Sometimes, the Lord Jesus remained in public among the crowds so the leaders could not seize Him. After the Lord cleansed the temple a second time, He was teaching in the temple and Luke comments on the intentions of the Jewish leaders.

Luke 19:47-48
He was teaching daily in the temple, but the chief priests and the scribes and the leading men among the people sought to destroy him. They couldn't find what they might do, for all the people hung on to every word that he said.

At times, Jesus would withdraw from the crowd to avoid confrontation.

Matthew 12:14-15
But the Pharisees went out, and took counsel against him, how they might destroy [assassinate] him. Jesus, perceiving that, withdrew from there. Great multitudes followed him; and he healed them all.

Among other approaches, Jesus asked those He cured not to tell anyone which they did not always follow.

Mark 1:43-44
He strictly warned him, and immediately sent him out, and said to him, "See you say nothing to anybody, but go show yourself to the priest, and offer for your cleansing the things which Moses commanded, for a testimony to them."

We consistently see Jesus avoiding the leaders and those who desired to seize Him. Many prophecies had to be fulfilled in a specific order and on a specific timetable to demonstrate He was truly the Son of God. If arrested, all would be ruined.

The Protection of the Disciples

During His three years of ministry, the focus was on Him. The crowds looked to Him for healing and the leaders tried to stop Him. No one was paying attention to the disciples who were under the direct protection of their Master anyway. The Lord explained this early in His ministry.

John 6:39
This is the will of my Father who sent me, that of all he has given to me I should lose nothing, but should raise him up at the last day.

The Lord described His protection in His priestly prayer.

John 17:12
have kept those whom you have given me. None of them is lost except While I was with them in the world, I kept them in your name. I the son of destruction, that the Scripture might be fulfilled.

He demonstrated this at His arrest. He was protecting His disciples physically as well as spiritually.

HOW CHRISTIANS MAY DEFEND THEMSELVES AGAINST ATTACK

John 18:8-9
Again therefore he asked them, "Who are you looking for?" They said, "Jesus of Nazareth." Jesus answered, "I told you that I am he. If therefore you seek me, let these go their way," that the word might be fulfilled which he spoke, "Of those whom you have given me, I have lost none."

The Changing Situation of the Twelve

As the disdain grew, the threat to Jesus and the disciples also grew. This meant that their strategy in sharing the gospel would also have to change. It could not remain as if all were well when hostility was coming. They would have to face the fact that ultimately everything in their lives was about to change, and they needed to be ready to face the new dangers that would come.

The Warning of a Coming Change

In this last event at His last Passover meal, things were about to dramatically change. The shadow of the cross was upon Him which meant the persecution He had predicted was coming. When Jesus was alive the focus of the leaders was to stop Jesus but soon their focus would be on stopping His disciples. Their world would become a dangerous one as those who killed Jesus would now turn their attention to them. They would not be shaking the dust off their feet but running for their lives. Satan would not be falling from the sky but would be given "permission to sift them like wheat."

As a result, the Lord Jesus must reverse His instructions to the disciples. They would no longer be able to depend on the basic self-defense of a staff; instead, they would need the power of a sword. The staff would not be enough. It just could not deal with the persecution that would be coming.

In this new set of instructions, in which the Lord Jesus connects to the other two, we find the confirmation by Jesus that defense of self and others is an acceptable and God-ordained approach to persecution under certain conditions. Physical defense of self and others had always been the approach of God and His people Israel. It had not been necessary for Jesus and His disciples to defend themselves though it was most certainly possible. As we saw with Jesus' natural assumptions on self-defense, the possibility was there. Now, it would become reality and they would need to become stronger men with the main weapon of the day - the sword.

The Final Meal with the Disciples

This last event entails His last meal, last words, and last actions before He was arrested, beaten, and crucified. After this, the disciples would be on their own and needed some important guidance.

The Service That Would Be Necessary

First, the Lord demonstrates the service they would need to show one another after He left.

John 13:5
Then he poured water into the basin, and began to wash the disciples' feet and to wipe them with the towel that was wrapped around him.

Then, He teaches them to do the same to each other.

John 13:14-15
If I then, the Lord and the Teacher, have washed your feet, you also ought to wash one another's feet. For I have given you an example, that you should also do as I have done to you.

The Betrayal That Would Come

Next, the Lord declared that someone at their table would betray Him.

John 13:18
I don't speak concerning all of you. I know whom I have chosen. But that the Scripture may be fulfilled, "He who eats bread with me has lifted up his heel against me."

This person would not be a servant of theirs because he only had his interests in mind. Jesus knew that he would unleash the coming persecution of His disciples that He predicted.

Each of the disciples began to question Him wondering if it was him. Then Jesus identified Judas as the betrayer.

John 13:26-30
Jesus therefore answered, "It is he to whom I will give this piece of bread when I have dipped it." So when he had dipped the piece of bread, he gave it to Judas, the son of Simon Iscariot. After the piece of bread, then Satan entered into him. Then Jesus said to him, "What you do, do quickly." Now nobody at the table knew why he said this to him. For some thought, because Judas had the money box, that Jesus said to him, "Buy what things we need for the feast," or that he should give something to the poor. Therefore having received that morsel, he went out immediately. It was night.

This unloving, selfish, now Satan-possessed disciple left the room to prepare for his evil act.

The Love That Would Be Necessary

Now the eleven were there alone with Jesus for His final moments. We are not told why but perhaps the departure of Judas prompted a discussion of their past behavior towards the Lord and who He regarded as greatest in His kingdom. This implies that they all felt that though Judas had fallen, they would not fall.

Their mindset is easy to discern. They would stand with Him no matter whom He faced and what the outcome. They verbally repeated this fact to the Lord several times that evening.

Next, this compelled the Lord to return to His example of service and how this servant attitude would be the key to a greatness in His kingdom.

Luke 22:24-30
A dispute also arose among them, which of them was considered to be greatest. He said to them, "The kings of the nations lord it over them...those who have authority over them are called 'benefactors.' But not so with you. But one who is the greater among you, let him become as the younger, and one who is governing, as one who serves. For who is greater, one who sits at the table, or one who serves? Isn't it he who sits at the table? But I am among you as one who serves. But you are those who have continued with me in my trials. I confer on you a kingdom, even as my Father conferred on me, that you may eat and drink at my table in my Kingdom. You will sit on thrones, judging the twelve tribes of Israel."

They all would equally reign with Him on twelve thrones, but now they needed to serve one another which would include protection and self-sacrifice. When the persecution came, this would be an important hope that they must cling to amid such horrifying and terrible dangers they would face.

The Coming Departure of the Lord

After this, Jesus once again explains that He is going away.

John 13:33
Little children, I will be with you a little while longer. You will seek me... Where I am going, you can't come,' so now I tell you.

This prompts Jesus to provide for them their most important and critical response to His leaving them: love. He declares His love for them and that they were to love one another as He had loved them (after he had gone).

John 13:34-35
A new commandment I give...that you love one another, just like I have loved you; that you also love one another. By this everyone will know that you are my disciples, if you have love for one another."

During their coming hard times without Him, they must care for one another. Would they love one another enough to stick together, serve and protect each other in the coming danger which He is about to describe?

This caused a question to arise in Peter's mind concerning the words of Jesus.

John 13:36
Simon Peter said to him, "Lord, where are you going?" Jesus answered, "Where I am going, you can't follow now, but you will follow afterwards."

Peter inquired as to where the Lord Jesus Christ was suddenly going. The Lord explained that where He was going, they could not follow (His persecution which led to His death), but they would follow later (due to their own persecution and death). They would follow Him into the same fate.

The Coming Sifting of the Disciples

After this, Peter, as always, made an inquiry of the Lord.

John 13:37
Peter said to him, "Lord, why can't I follow you now?...

Peter was not understanding what the Lord was saying nor were the disciples. As a result, the Lord Jesus clarifies the last portion of His statement concerning the disciples following after Him later.

Luke 22:31-32
The Lord said, "Simon, Simon, behold, Satan asked to have you [plural: disciples], that he might sift you [implied] as wheat.

The Lord Jesus addresses Peter but is speaking about all the disciples. We know this because the pronoun "you" is in the plural. This is important. The disciples believe that they will stand with Jesus no matter what happens. Unfortunately, Jesus issues them a warning.

Satan is coming to test them. He calls Peter "Simon." This was his name before Christ. This occurred usually when he behaved contrary to God's ways in the flesh. He repeats his name and uses the word "behold" which in the Greek means "Look! Listen! This indicates that He has something serious to say. He refers to the Devil by the word "Satan" which means "adversary."

The phrase "asked to have" is just one word in the Greek meaning "to ask, beg to have something for oneself or to desire to have power over another." So, the Lord is saying essentially, "Simon, listen, I am saying this to you in the weakness of you flesh. The adversary has begged God to have power over you eleven and has received permission to toss all of you up and down as if you were wheat having your chaff (impurities) sifted out.

This should have rattled the disciples to their very core but as we will see they remained confident. The Devil was going to turn his attention to them. He was going to focus on them. They were going to be sifted like Satan sifted Job. The wheat was thrown up and the chaff, weeds, and impurities would be caught by the wind leaving only the pure grain behind.

Then, the Lord Jesus turns His attention to Peter who was bold enough to ask why he couldn't follow Jesus right away. He was going to have a special sifting.

Luke 22:32
But I prayed for you [Simon], that your faith wouldn't fail. You, when once you [Simon] have turned again, establish your brothers."

Peter's sifting would be so difficult that his faith itself might fail. So, the Lord prayed especially for him. Though Simon Peter had amazing confidence in his flesh, he was about to be tested in ways he could not possibly understand. Then, he was to strengthen his brothers after he had been restored.

When did this actual sifting occur? For all the disciples it began when they fled out of fear at the arrest of Jesus and would continue throughout their lifelong ministries. For Peter is would begin at His denial of Christ as he followed Him to the courtyard of the high priest.

The Ignorant Confidence of the Eleven

Then, Peter responds with a powerful declaration. Part of it is recorded by Luke and the other part by John.

Luke 22:33
He said to him, "Lord, I am ready to go with you both to prison and to death!"

John 13:37
Peter said to him, "Lord, why can't I follow you now? I will lay down my life for you."

When Peter made this declaration, was he speaking for the disciples also? The answer is provided later on at the Mount of Olives. Here Peter again pledged his loyalty to the Lord.

Matthew 26:35
Peter said to him, "Even if I must die with you, I will not deny you." All of the disciples also said likewise.

Mark 14:31
But he spoke all the more, "If I must die with you, I will not deny you." Likewise, they all said so.

Here, he declares that he will die with Christ if necessary. No matter what, he will never deny the Lord.

The other disciples were in full agreement. They would stand up to those who would attempt to harm Jesus. They would not abandon the Lord Jesus as Judas did. Implied here is self-defense.

How would they be able to lay down their life for Jesus without expecting to defend Him in some way? Someone doesn't lay down a life by just standing next to Him and being killed. Peter is proclaiming that he will defend the Lord Jesus physically or be killed trying, if necessary. What about the other disciples? They all agreed. They would stand together and defend Him. If He went down, they would all god down with Him. This was the reality they would endure for Him.

The Warning of The Impending Denial

To demonstrate just how foolish it was to think that they would stand up for Him as they pondered this in the safety of the upper room that night, Jesus questioned his loyalty and issued him a warning.

John 13:38
Jesus answered him, "Will you lay down your life for me? Most certainly I tell you, the rooster won't crow until you have denied me three times.

Notice, Jesus uses the word "behold" again. Peter did not fully comprehend the full impact of the Lord's statement so He will put it simply, "Peter, you will deny me three times." The words "truly, truly" signal this will happen and should not be brushed aside as if it was only conjecture. The Lord now speaks to Peter in His new name (the Christian who will turn back to Him) and explains that it the sifting will occur this very night before morning and that he will deny the Lord not once but three times!

The New Directive to Defend

As the departure of the Lord Jesus Christ grew more and more imminent, the situation was becoming increasingly dangerous. This required new instructions.

The Reversal of the Lord's Instructions

After this, the Lord Jesus looks beyond their initial sifting to their proclamation of the gospel and the persecution they will experience. As a result, He must reverse the instructions that He had given them prior to His impending death. Why? All was about to change in a very dangerous way.

First, the Lord Jesus refers to the prior instructions that they had been following throughout the three years of their ministry.

Luke 22:35
He said..."When I sent you...without purse [money belt], and wallet, and shoes, did you lack anything?" They said, "Nothing."

These prior mandates were their marching orders. Workmen were worthy of their wages so the disciples should live off the gospel. These men would be welcomed into the homes of the worthy and stay there. Therefore, they wouldn't need to take any additional possessions with them. Then He asked them if they were ever in need of anything during this preaching time. Of course, they indicated were not.

Now, Jesus must change these marching orders.

Luke 22:36
Then he said to them, "But now, whoever has a purse, let him take it, and likewise a wallet. Whoever has none, let him sell his cloak, and buy a sword.

What was Jesus saying? In the past, they wouldn't need any additional supplies, but now they must take a purse with money, a bag with clothes and supplies, and sell a cloak and buy a sword.

The Instruction of Future Self Defense

Notice, the Lord Jesus says, "Now." This word means "at the present time." This contrasts their past actions which it is necessary to change, and it must be done right now. Then, He essentially states, "I told you not to bring any extra items but just what you had. Now, take additional supplies along."

The most important supply was now "a sword." How do we know this? Jesus said that they should sell their cloaks to get a sword, if they did not have one. This was the garment that they wore over the tunic. This garment was the clothing that was always worn. The tunic was put on underneath it in the winter. He is referring to the extra garment they should take along with them now that things have changed. If they do not have a sword, they should get one because it would be better for them if they were wearing worn out clothes and be able to protect themselves than have proper clothing and not be able to do this. The Lord said, "if." This implies some of the disciples had swords and would not need to purchase them. The possession of a sword was now at this present time in these new circumstances necessary and urgent.

The Necessity of a Roman Sword

What did Jesus mean by this word translated "sword?" The Greek word is utilized in the New Testament for Roman swords. These were the swords used in the time of the New Testament. In Ephesians 6, the apostle Paul was in his first Roman imprisonment. As he describes the spiritual power we have to contend with the forces of evil, he uses an analogy of battle and the armor a Roman soldier wears to fight. Since he is chained to a Roman guard with full armor, this is the perfect comparison.

As he compares each piece of their physical armor with spiritual weapons, he comes to the power we have through the Scriptures and refers to it as a "sword." This is critical.

Ephesians 6:17
And take the helmet of salvation, and the sword of the Spirit, which is the word of God.

This is the same word that Jesus uses in His instructions at the last supper.

This Roman sword was eighteen to twenty-four inches. It was not a large knife or dagger. It was a short sword carried in a sheath at the side and used for hand-to-hand combat. It had sharp edges on both sides. When two combatants faced each other up close in battle, it was thrust into the face, neck, or between the shoulder blades for a kill.

When the crowd came to arrest Jesus, they were carrying swords. The writers of the gospels used the very same Greek word to describe the "swords" that were carried by many.

Matthew 26:47
While he was still speaking, behold, Judas, one of the twelve, came, and with him a great multitude with swords and clubs, from the chief priest and elders of the people.

Matthew 26:55
In that hour Jesus said to the multitudes, "Have you come out as against a robber with swords and clubs to seize me? I sat daily in the temple teaching, and you didn't arrest me.

Mark 14:43
Immediately, while he was still speaking, Judas, one of the twelve, came -- and with him a multitude with swords and clubs, from the chief priests, the scribes, and the elders.

Luke 22:52-53
Jesus said to the chief priests, captains of the temple, and elders, who had come against him, "Have you come out as against a robber, with swords and clubs? When I was with you in the temple daily....

HOW CHRISTIANS MAY DEFEND THEMSELVES AGAINST ATTACK

Who would have been carrying those swords? Certainly, the swords would have been carried by the Roman guards and temple police.

John 18:12
So the detachment the commanding officer, and the officers of the Jews, seized Jesus and bound him.

The "detachment" would have been 600 Roman soldiers with a commanding officer. The "officers of the Jews" would have been the Temple police. These would be the Jewish version of city police.

Some citizens would have had them also. This is obvious from the fact that Jesus told them to buy a sword and two swords were in the upper room. If they were illegal, Jesus would not have given this command. Then, when Peter drew his sword, he was not rebuked for carrying an illegal weapon. Why? It was not illegal. It was perfectly legal to carry a sword. It was the use of it that would have been regulated.

Luke 22:36
Then he said to them, "But now, whoever has a purse, let him take it, and likewise a wallet. Whoever has none, let him sell his cloak, and buy a sword.

Luke 22:38
They said, "Lord, behold, here are two swords." He said to them, "That is enough."

John 18:11
Jesus therefore said to Peter, "Put the sword into its sheath. The cup which the Father has given me, shall I not surely drink it?"

So, it can easily be assumed there were private citizens who carried swords for protection.

We see this same sword mentioned in many places in the New Testament. In Acts 12, Luke describes the apostle James being executed by a sword. Of course, this this was a Roman sword carried by soldiers.

Acts 12:2
He killed James, the brother of John, with the sword.

In Acts 16, while Paul was in a Philippian jail, an earthquake occurred. When the jailor thought that all his prisoners had escaped, he attempted to commit suicide with his sword, but Paul stopped him.

Acts 16:27
The jailer, being roused out of sleep and seeing the prison doors open, drew his sword and was about to kill himself, supposing that the prisoners had escaped.

The Philippian jailor would have been executed for allowing the prisoners to escape, so the jailor decided to take his own life with his sword, but Paul saved him. This "sword" refers to the same Roman sword.

In Matthew 10, the Lord uses the same word to describe the war he would bring in a family as one chose to follow him, and another chose to reject Him. This will be like using a sword to start a war.

Matthew 10:34-39
Don't think that I came to send peace on the earth. I didn't come to send peace, but a sword. For I came to set a man at odds against his father, and a daughter against her mother, and a daughter-in-law against her mother-in-law. A man's foes will be those of his own household. He who loves father or mother more than me is not worthy of me; and he who loves son or daughter more than me isn't worthy of me. He who doesn't take his cross and follow after me isn't

HOW CHRISTIANS MAY DEFEND THEMSELVES AGAINST ATTACK

worthy of me. He who seeks his life will lose it; and he who loses his life for my sake will find it.

Loyalty to Him would bring a sword into a family. Belief in Him and rejection of Him would divide them. This division would cut relationships apart and there would be numerous casualties.

In Luke 21, the Lord uses this word to speak of the future killing of believers in persecution.

Luke 21:24
They will fall by the edge of the [Roman] sword, and will be led captive into all the nations. Jerusalem will be trampled... by the Gentiles, until the times of the Gentiles are fulfilled.

This apocalyptic prophesy speaks of a sword as the symbol of war, killing, and death.

In Romans 8, the apostle Paul uses the sword as a symbol of the threat of death and actual death a sword brings.

Romans 8:35
Who shall separate us from the love of [Jesus] Christ? Could oppression, or anguish [extreme distress] or persecution, or famine, or nakedness, or peril, or sword?

Once again, the word "sword" is the same word and refers to death by sword or even death in general.

In Hebrews 4, the Bible is compared to the doubled-edged Roman sword.

Hebrews 4:12
For the word of God is living and active, and sharper than any two-edged sword, piercing even to the dividing of soul and spirit, of both

joints and marrow, and is able to discern the thoughts and intentions of the heart.

Here, Paul compares the Scriptures with a Roman sword. It is sharper and is able to do deep and intricate surgical slicing of the soul.

In Hebrews 11, the author speaks of faith standing against the physical sword of battle and death.

Hebrews 11:34
Quenched the power of fire, escaped the edge of the sword, from weakness were made strong, grew mighty in war...caused foreign armies to flee.

Then in verse 37, the inspired writer provides more examples.

Hebrew 11:37
They were stoned. They were sawn apart. They were tempted. They were slain with the sword. They went around in sheep skins and in goat skins; being destitute, afflicted, ill-treated."

These believers battled with a real sword, found victory with a sword, ran from a sword, were sawn in two by a sword, or killed by a sword. These are the same words that Jesus uses.

In John's vision in Revelation, the sword is used by one on a red horse to take peace from the earth.

Revelation 6:4
Another came...a red horse. To him who sat on it was given power to take peace from the earth, and that they should kill one another. There was given to him a great sword.

Here, we have a great supernatural sword. It is so strong and powerful that it can take peace from the earth. The sword is so potent that it can leave mankind only with war which it also symbolizes.

In Revelation 13, the sword is used by the antichrist or man of lawlessness (first beast) to force people into submission to him or be killed. Here, the sword represents the power and authority to take a life.

Revelation 13:10
If anyone is to go into captivity, he will go into captivity. If anyone is to be killed with the sword, he must be killed. Here is... endurance and the faith of the saints.

Here, we discover that true believers will demonstrate their faith and endurance in Him through death. This death is by a sword.

A second beast (the false prophet) rises and convinces the nations to consolidate. This brings the countries under one world government. In verse 14, John describes how they will have to worship the antichrist or be killed with the sword.

Revelation 13:14
He deceives my own people who dwell on the earth because of the signs he was granted to do in front of the beast; saying to those who dwell on the earth, that they should make an image to the beast who had the sword wound and lived.

Here again, we see the same word Jesus used as a physical sword bringing captivity and death. Of course, at that time it may be a much more sophisticated weapon.

Finally, in the parallel passages that describe the "sword" that Peter takes in response to the instructions of Jesus make it clear that it is a Roman sword. The purpose of this sword was for combat.

Matthew 26:51
Behold, one of those who were with Jesus stretched out his hand, and drew his sword, and struck the servant of the high priest, and struck off his ear.

Matthew 26:52
Then Jesus said to him, "Put your sword back into its place, for all those who take the sword will die by the sword."

Mark 14:47
But a certain one of those who stood by drew his sword, and struck the servant of the high priest, and cut off his ear.

John 18:10
Simon Peter therefore, having a sword, drew it, and struck the high priest's servant, and cut off his right ear. The servant's name was Malchus.

John 18:11
Jesus therefore said to Peter, "Put up the sword into its sheath. The cup which the Father has given me, shall I not drink it?"

One last comment on the sword. Some believe that it was a large knife or dagger because one verse in the Septuagint (Greek translation of the Old Testament). These people say that the Hebrew word for knife or dagger is translated using the Greek word that Jesus used. Therefore, Jesus meant knife or dagger. This is not true.

Genesis 22:10
Abraham stretched out his hand, and took the knife to kill his son.

This makes no sense because there is no other word in the Greek to translate it. This is the word they had to use. Every use of the word in the New Testament refers to a sword, not a knife. Knives are not referred to in the New Testament at all.

They simply refuse to believe that the Lord Jesus Christ actually instructed His disciples to carry a weapon, and this is the very best that they can provide for evidence, but they are mistaken.

Why is this discussion so critical? When Jesus told them to always have a sword with them when they went out to minister, what did He mean? What could He have meant? First, we must establish the fact that the Lord Jesus was really referring to a sword and that in every instance it was a Roman sword. Second, we must ask what is the purpose of a sword? The sword was used for only two purposes: to deter or stop people from killing you or to kill them.

For what reason would the disciples need this kind of weapon? Each of them had a staff as we have seen. Why were these rods no longer enough? Had the crime rate risen to such an extent that a sword was needed for safety? Of course not. Had the local animal population become more dangerous? Were they suddenly going to prey on travelers in a more menacing way? It could not be. Would they need food which they could not purchase and would have to hunt and kill? This could not be true. What had changed?

The Reason for The Sword's Necessity

Let us go back to the context to see the explanation the Lord Jesus provides for His new instructions. The Lord was talking about leaving, the disciples could not go where He would be going until much later (future persecution), and Satan was now allowed to sift all of them. This indicates that ordinary staffs would no longer be enough for self-defense. What the disciples were about to encounter was far too ominous. This coming persecution would require swords.

Luke 22:37
For I tell you that this which is written must still be fulfilled in me: "He was counted with transgressors." For that which concerns me has an end.

Here, Jesus quotes a very familiar passage to the Jews. It was a Messianic passage which identified the coming redeemer.

Isaiah 53:12
Therefore will I give him a portion with the great, and he will divide the plunder with the strong; because he poured out his soul to death...was numbered with the transgressors; yet he bore the sin of many, and made intercession for the transgressors.

Notice, the coming Messiah would be "numbered with the transgressors." He will be considered a criminal, be treated like a criminal, and be among criminals by God. Why? He "bore the sin of many." He died to pay the penalty for sin.

Though Jesus was considered a criminal, treated like a criminal, and was among criminals by men which may be a part of identifying Him according to this prophecy, the main feature was God as judge, jury, and executioner. God would now see Him in the light of the sins of men and kill Him using the Jews to do it in their unrepentant, unbelieving condition.

His time had come to fulfill this critical prophecy and it would be fulfilled. It was going to happen. As a result, they would need swords for protection.

What is the connection? The Lord's death would be the beginning of the real persecution of the disciples. His death would bring a change in the people's attitude toward the disciples which would lead to their persecution. This can be immediately seen in the death of James, the first of the twelve apostles to be martyred for their faith.

HOW CHRISTIANS MAY DEFEND THEMSELVES AGAINST ATTACK

Acts 12:1-3
Now about that time, King Herod stretched out his hands to oppress some of the assembly. He killed James, the brother of John, with the sword. When he saw that it pleased the Jews, he proceeded to seize Peter also. This was during the days of unleavened bread.

The murder of James made the people happy and glad. They gave their approval to Herod's actions. This made him then arrest Peter who would have also been martyred had God not determined to intervene in his defense with angelic help.

The swords that they were to buy, if they did not have one, were for the future persecution. It was to defend against the persecutors. The people will desire to kill them, and they were now being given permission to respond to persecutors in self-defense. The disciples would have known that they were to defend themselves against robbers and others but what about persecutors? Are the followers of the Lord allowed to defend themselves because they are Christians? Yes, they can.

Persecutors are not protected from God's natural, human, or governmental laws. His followers do not have to stand in front of their persecutors and be killed. Jesus, as we will see, did not do this. Though He came to sacrifice Himself for our sins on the cross, He displayed His power and warned them of His authority to resist if His time had not come as we will see. Here is the key: if the Lord Jesus had not said this, when persecution came, they would not have known what to do. Now, they knew they could resist.

Again, it is important to note what was not said. Jesus did not say, "Men, the crime rate has risen to such an extent that a sword is now needed for safety!" He did not declare, "Men, the local animal population has become more dangerous and preying upon travelers more often, so begin to carry swords to protect yourself!" He said that He was going to now fulfill the prophecy stating that God was going to now count Him among transgressors, and He would die. He would now be seen by the people as a criminal, treated as a criminal, killed like a criminal, and so would they. So, it is time to take a sword because they were not going to be welcomed like they were in their previous days of ministry. The Devil will not be thrown down like he was lightning; but instead, the serpent will be given reign over the earth for a particular period of time.

The Clear Understanding of the Eleven

What did the disciples understand Christ to be saying? As we look at the next verse, it becomes clear.

Luke 22:38
They said, "Lord, behold, here are two swords." He said to them, "That is enough."

Notice first that "they" said, not Peter alone! The disciples in unison or almost unison see two swords in the room and shout, "Behold." They all understood the same thing. This is important. Whatever Jesus meant they all got it. There was no dissension among the eleven as to what Jesus had been saying about carrying swords and his coming death. It was clear. Previously, we saw that all the disciples were in agreement that though Jesus Christ had indicated that they were all going to stumble and fall away, they were determined to prove Him wrong. They would die for Him! In their minds, they would already have swords in hand and be defending Jesus. This would be a given.

Here the word translated "behold" is used to draw the Lord's full attention to the "swords" and to demonstrate their astonishment at the supposed coincidence. He was talking about their need for swords and there were two right there in front of them. Had they not noticed or had both appeared supernaturally? The word "behold" is a clear confirmation of the fullness of their understanding of what Jesus just said. As a result, let us take a moment to focus on this word.

This word "behold" can be used to indicate astonishment and amazement. We would yell, "Look!" This word is used so often we will simply look at the uses by the author himself in this one gospel (Luke).

The word signaled supernatural events or appearances.

Luke 2:10
The angel said to them, "Don't be afraid, for behold, I bring you good news of great joy which will be to all the people.

Luke 9:30
Behold, two men talked with him, who were Moses and Elijah.

Luke 24:4
It happened, while they were greatly perplexed about this, behold, two men stood by them in dazzling clothing.

It was utilized to heighten the attention when truths of great importance were about to be given.

Luke 13:29-30
They will come from the east, west, north, and south, and will sit down in God's Kingdom. Behold, there are some who are last who will be first, and there are some who are first who will be last.

Luke 7:27
This is he...it is written, "Behold, I send my messenger before your face, Who will prepare your way before you."

Luke 18:31
He took the twelve aside, and said to them, "Behold, we are going up to Jerusalem…all the things that are written through the prophets concerning the Son of Man will be completed.

It was used for warnings of danger that may be coming one's way.

Luke 10:3
Go your ways. Behold, I send you out as lambs in the midst of wolves.

Luke 13:35
Behold, your house is left to you desolate. I tell you, you will not see me, until you say, "Blessed is he who comes in the name of the Lord!"

Luke 22:31-32
The Lord said, "Simon, Simon, behold, Satan asked to have you, that he might sift you as wheat, but I prayed for you, that your faith wouldn't fail. You, when once you have turned again, establish your brothers."

Luke 23:29
For behold, the days are coming in which they will say, 'Blessed are the barren, the wombs that never bore, and the breasts that never nursed.

This term was used to express unexpected occurrences or ones that would startle people.

Luke 1:44-46
For behold, when the voice of your greeting came into my ears, the baby leaped in my womb for joy! Blessed is she who believed, for there will be a fulfillment of the things which have been spoken to her from the Lord!" Mary said, "My soul magnifies the Lord.

Luke 2:48
When they saw him, they were astonished, and his mother said to him, "Son, why have you treated us this way? Behold, your father and I were anxiously looking for you."

Luke 22:47
While he was still speaking, behold, a multitude, and he who was called Judas, one of the twelve, went in front of them. He came near to Jesus to kiss him.

The word was also utilized to declare commitments that were considered very serious.

Luke 1:38
Mary said, "Behold, the handmaid of the Lord; be it to me according to your word." The angel departed from her.

It was used to signify the occurrence of a supernatural, divine miracle.

Luke 1:31
Behold, you will conceive in your womb, and bring forth a son, and will call his name "Jesus."

Luke 1:36
Behold, Elizabeth, your relative, also has conceived a son in her old age; and this is the sixth month with her who was called barren.

Luke 5:12
It happened, while he was in one of the cities, behold, there was a man full of leprosy. When he saw Jesus, he fell on his face, and begged him, saying, "Lord, if you want to, you can make me clean."

Luke 14:1-4
When he went into the house of one of the rulers of the Pharisees on a Sabbath to eat bread, they were watching him. Behold, a certain man who had dropsy was in front of him. Jesus, answering, spoke to

the lawyers and Pharisees, saying, "Is it lawful to heal on the Sabbath?" But they were silent.

It called attention to amazing blessings.

Luke 1:48
For he has looked at the humble state of his handmaid. For behold, from now on, all generations will call me blessed.

Luke 6:23
Rejoice in that day, and leap for joy, for behold, your reward is great in heaven, for their fathers did the same thing to the prophets.

Finally, it promoted powerful declarations that some may make and want recognized.

Luke 2:34
And Simeon blessed them, and said to Mary, his mother, "Behold, this child is set for the falling and the rising of many in Israel, and for a sign which is spoken against."

Luke 10:19
Behold, I give you authority to tread on serpents...scorpions, and over all the power of the enemy. Nothing will in any way hurt you.

Luke 13:7
He said to the vine dresser, "Behold, these three years I came seeking fruit on this fig tree, and found none. Cut it down. Why does it waste the soil?"

Luke 13:32
He said to them, "Go and tell that fox, 'Behold, I cast out demons and perform cures today and tomorrow, and the third day I complete my mission.'"

Luke 18:28
Peter said, "Look, we...left everything, and followed you."

Luke 22:21
But behold, the hand of him who betrays me is with me on the table.

It was not a word one just said! So, when the disciples said "behold" it was out of this astonishing amazement that there were two swords near, and Jesus was just talking about them.

Right after the eleven were told to purchase swords, they see two placed in the upper room. Some will say, "They were carrying them." Then what would be the point of saying, "Behold!" If they had already had these swords, they would be no need for this kind of word.

Jesus mentions the important need for swords, and they suddenly notice two swords in the room and proclaim, "Jesus, look here are two swords!" It is better to assume that the two swords were either left there by the owner of the room or were miraculously put there at that particular moment. We do not know but we do know that they suddenly noticed them and shouted, "Look!"

The Affirmation of the Sword's Sufficiency

Then, Jesus makes an important response.

Luke 22:38
They said, "Lord, behold, here are two swords." He said to them, "That is enough."

The response is literally in the Greek, "It is enough." What does He mean by this? The word translated "enough" has the idea of "sufficient or adequate for a purpose." Jesus had just said that they should buy swords right now. So, He was affirming the fact that the two swords were sufficient for their purpose for the events of the evening. Jesus knows that the disciples will attempt to defend Him. He knows that Peter will strike a servant's ear.

The Lord knows that He will do a miracle to heal it right in front of the people. He knows that He will need to teach the disciples one more lesson in regard to the use of the sword. Though they would not be defending Him tonight because His time had come, He must get the swords into their hands so they will not forget to get one when He leaves. Otherwise, why would the swords even be in this narrative? It would not make sense.

Some say that the Lord was disgusted with the lack of understanding of the disciples and in exasperation said, "It is enough!" They contend that He was making this statement, "I have had enough with your ignorance." This could not be the intended meaning. First of all, he had just stated that they needed to purchase swords because He was about to fulfill the prophecy of being named with transgressors. Then, they saw the swords. When did the disciples even have time to exasperate Him?

Second, the word "enough" is never used in this way. It is always translated "enough" with the meaning "sufficient for its purpose, adequate, and enough." The only other use is with crowds or numbers of people and meant a "sufficient or large amount" with the usual translation "many."

Third, the word Luke uses describing the Lord's making of this statement is the verb "to say." It has no emotion attached to it. If Luke wanted to describe His exasperation, we would expect a different verb because the phrase "it is enough" conveys no emotion. The people who make this assertion do not want to think that Jesus would speak about self-defense, but He did. Once He mentioned the importance of purchasing a sword, it is poor exegesis to try and "interpret it away."

Lastly, if the Lord Jesus had been exasperated, He would have noticed Peter taking up the sword, putting the sheath on his waist, and carrying it to Gethsemane. Yet, we do not see the Lord Jesus chastising Peter. He does not say, "Peter, go put that sword away. You completely misinterpreted what I was trying to say." Later, when Peter does use it, the Lord Jesus merely tells him to put it away. Jesus does not rebuke him for having it in the first place. Throughout the discussion the misunderstanding that He was trying to correct was their over confidence standing up for Him in the light of the sifting that was about to happen. In fact, it was the overconfidence of Peter that almost brought on a blood bath not the sword.

The Laying Down of His life and Theirs

After this injunction, Jesus and the disciples partake of the Passover meal and Jesus institutes this meal as a memorial of His death. Then, Jesus explained to the eleven disciples once again that He was leaving, and they should not be troubled.

John 14:1-4
"Don't let your heart be troubled. Believe in God. Believe also in me. In my Father's house are many mansions. If it weren't so, I would have told you. I am going to prepare a place for you. If I go and prepare a place for you, I will come again, and will receive you to myself; *that where I am, you may be there also. Where I go, you know, and you know the way."*

Then Jesus presents another lesson on love. This time the Lord speaks of His death for them and their deaths for each other.

John 15:12-13
This is my commandment, that you love one another, even as I have loved you. Greater love has no one than this that someone lay down his life for his friends.

What did Jesus mean by this? Was He speaking of the meeting of needs sacrificially or referring to defending each other?

First, we know He meant the actual physical laying down of His life in death for them. He had mentioned this many times using the same phrase.

John 10:11
I am the good shepherd. The good shepherd lays down his life for the sheep.

John 10:15
Even as the Father knows me, and I know the Father. I lay down my life for the sheep.

John 10:17
Therefore the Father loves me, because I lay down my life, that I may take it again.

John 10:18
No one takes it away from me, but I lay it down by myself. I have power to lay it down, and I have power to take it again. I received this commandment from my Father."

Second, Peter had used the same phrase also previously after Jesus had said He was going away.

John 13:37
Peter said to him, "Lord, why can't I follow you now? I will lay down my life for you."

Luke 22:33
He said to him, "Lord, I am ready to go with you both to prison and to death!"

Both statements were made in the same declaration. Peter

meant he would lay down his physical life to defend the Lord to the death if necessary.

Why would the Lord Jesus utilize the same phrase in this context metaphorically and not literally without explaining what He meant? Also, how will they lay down their physical lives for each other? What is the context in the upper room? He was leaving and they were to purchase swords. It was self-defense and the defense of each other. So, even here the Lord Jesus is again speaking of self-defense.

Some might say, "Perhaps, Jesus was explaining how they must love each other by sacrificing in deed and truth." They will then quote John's exhortation in his first letter. In chapter 3, John describes the essence of love being not just empty words but in actions also.

1 John 3: 16-18
By this we know love, because he laid down his life for us. And we ought to lay down our lives for the brothers. But whoever has the world's goods and sees his brother in need, then closes his heart of compassion against him, how does God's love remain in him? My little children, let's not love in word only, or with the tongue only, but in deed and truth.

In this passage, John is merely taking this commandment of the Lord Jesus and applying beyond the actual context to the life of the church. That is all. This one use does not negate the context in which Jesus used it. Otherwise, the Lord would have said clearly explained that He meant just meeting needs. He would not have allowed Peter to have said what he had said several times. He would have responded, "Peter, I am talking about you meeting each other's needs, not physically laying your life down in the defense of each other. Forget about the two swords, go buy some food." Yet, this is not what was said by the Lord Jesus Christ.

The Warning of Coming Persecution Again

Then, the Lord continues with another warning about the coming persecution in the sight of the swords!

John 15:18
If the world hates you, you know...it...hated me before it hated you.

John 15:20
Remember the word that I said to you: "A servant is not greater than his lord." If they persecuted me, they will also persecute you. If they kept my word, they will keep yours....

John 16:1-2
These things have I spoken to you, so that you wouldn't be caused to stumble. They will put you out of the synagogues. Yes, the time comes that whoever kills you will think that he offers service to God.

Sandwiched in between these warnings, Jesus promises the Spirit will come to help testify of Him in persecution.

John 15:26-27
When the Counselor has come, whom I will send to you from the Father, the Spirit of truth, who proceeds from the Father, he will testify about me. You will also testify, because you have been with me from the beginning.

This does not refer to witnessing for the Lord at any time, but more importantly sharing the gospel in a court of law.

Now, Jesus makes a profound statement.

John 16:4
But I have told you these things...when the time comes, you may remember that I told you about them. I didn't tell you these things from the beginning, because I was with you.

HOW CHRISTIANS MAY DEFEND THEMSELVES AGAINST ATTACK

Did this last statement refer to everything He had said at the last supper or just the few previous words? No, it concerns everything He had said, including the taking up of the sword and loving each other to the point of laying down his life for another. Jesus was leaving them, and they were on their own. They needed to be prepared for the worst.

John 16:6
But because I have told you these things, sorrow...filled your heart.

Sorrow had filled their hearts because there was darkness ahead for them as they perceived it. The Lord also predicted a sorrow that is coming from His death and their persecution.

John 16:20
Most certainly I tell you, that you will weep and lament, but the world will rejoice. You will be sorrowful, but your sorrow will be turned into joy.

Eventually, as they see the Lord work powerfully, joy will fill them. Now, Jesus explains the coming sifting.

John 16:32-33
Behold, the time is coming, yes, and has now come, that you will be scattered, everyone to his own place, and you will leave me alone. Yet I am not alone...the Father is with me. I have told you these things, that in me you may have peace. In the world you have oppression...cheer up! I [Jesus] have overcome the world.

Though this appeared as if it were a message of despair, it was actually a message of future blessing and victory. They will be scattered but will turn back to Him. He will resurrect and come back to them.

So, with the swords in view, He describes their coming sorrow, scattering, and oppression. Yet, there will be joy later because they will see Him again. Then, Jesus prays to the Father a long, powerful prayer in their hearing. In this prayer, He asks the Father for protection in the future.

John 17:13-15
But now I come to you, and I say these things in the world, that they may have my joy made full in themselves. I have given them your word. The world hated them, because they are not of the world, even as I am not of the world. I pray not that you would take them from the world, but that you would keep them from the evil one.

Here the disciples hear that the world hates them, and they will not be removed from the world. Instead, the Evil One will attack them. Though His prayer of protection may have reassured them, the Lord just stated that they were going to be attacked by Satan himself!

So, the Lord had just told them that He was leaving them, they should all now have swords for protection (a staff is no longer enough). They should love one another to the point of laying their lives down for the others because the world will hate them and will bring sadness and oppression. The Devil will be behind it all and they will initially be scattered while Christ endures His death alone. Then, they sang a hymn and departed.

Matthew 26:30
When they had sung a hymn, they went out to the Mount of Olives.

Mark 14:26
When they had sung a hymn, they went out to the Mount of Olives.

Now, the most difficult part is about to be faced by the disciples. They leave for the Mount of Olives and the Garden of Gethsemane. Here are the disciples walking with the Lord Jesus. They have their staffs in hand and at least two swords.

Peter is now carrying one of them. They have been told that Jesus will be facing death, and they will be sifted like wheat. Yet, they are all determined to stand with Christ and fight for Him if necessary. They are willing to put their lives on the line, but they are sorrowful because Jesus is leaving them.

When they arrive, Jesus once again warns them that they will be sifted and will not stand with Him but be scattered.

Matthew 26:30-32
Then Jesus said to them, "All of you will be made to stumble because of me tonight, for it is written, 'I will strike the shepherd, and the sheep of the flock will be scattered.' But after I am raised up, I will go before you into Galilee.'"

Jesus quotes Zechariah 13:7. They would have been familiar with this Messianic passage. The Lord God will strike Jesus tonight. The sword is coming, and they will be scattered. The Lord will turn against His "little ones," the disciples. Finally, though they will scatter, Jesus will return and meet them in Galilee! God is still in charge.

The Disciples' Reassurance of Their Defense

Even though He just told the eleven that they would run for their lives as God fulfills His prophecy, they will not have it. In their minds, this scenario is simply not going to happen if they can help it.

Luke 22:33
But Peter answered him, "Even if all will be made to stumble because of you, I will never be made to stumble."

Once again, Peter reiterates his claim to loyalty, courage, and love probably as he clutched his sword now hanging from his waist. Jesus predicts that they "will be made" to stumble. Peter declares that no one will ever make Him fail to stand with Christ.

Peter leaves the disciples behind and declares even if all of those standing stumbles, he will not. He will not be scattered, and he will not deny Him. He will watch all the others run for their lives, but he will be standing side by side with the Lord. Jesus must have shaken his head in disbelief and makes the same prediction again.

Matthew 26:34
Jesus said to him, "Most certainly I tell you that tonight, before the rooster crows, you will deny me three times."

Once again, Jesus makes the firm assertion that Peter will absolutely deny the Lord even though he was so confident in standing for Jesus no matter what came his way. Confidence is not enough against the forces of evil.

Here, the disciples confirm that Peter's feelings were their feelings, and his commitments were their commitments.

Matthew 26:35
Peter said to him, "Even if I must die with you, I will not deny you." All of the disciples also said likewise.

Here the disciples must speak their minds because Peter had just insinuated that they would stumble. They now declare with Peter that there be no stumbling tonight. Every disciple vowed his allegiance and determination to stand strong no matter what. Mark confirms this.

Mark 14:31
But he spoke all the more, "If I must die with you, I will not deny you." Likewise, they all said so.

The disciples are prepared to die with Him. Is it logical that they mean they will just stand next to Him and be killed? No. They will fight to defend Him unto death, if necessary.

The Need to Watch and Pray

Then, the Lord Jesus left the eight of them and took Peter, James, and John with Him. The Lord leaves the three at the edge of a garden on the mountain and enters to pray alone.

Mark 14:33-34
He took with him Peter, James, and John, and began to be greatly troubled and distressed. He said to them, "My soul is exceedingly sorrowful, even to death. Stay here, and watch."

Now things become dire because the demeanor of the Lord changes. Suddenly, He is agitated, distressed, troubled, and exceedingly sorrowful. Rather than go through all the details of this section, we will only consider what is relevant to the topic of this book. As Jesus wrestled with God in prayer, the disciples grew in their sadness over His leaving them. It increased to such a point that it exhausted them, and they fell asleep.

Luke 22:45-46
When he rose up from his prayer, he came to the disciples, and found them sleeping because of grief, and said to them, "Why do you sleep? Rise and pray that you may not enter into temptation."

Mark 14:37-39
He came and found them sleeping, and said to Peter, "Simon, are you sleeping? Couldn't you watch one hour? Watch and pray, that you not enter into temptation. The spirit indeed is willing, but the flesh is weak." Again he went away, and prayed, saying the same words.

Here Jesus again calls Peter by his old name and chastises him for falling asleep, but they couldn't help it. They were so sorrowful that their bodies were shutting down. Their spirits were willing, but their flesh was weak. The sorrow of the Lord poured over them, and their sorrow exhausted them.

Notice, Jesus told them to watch and pray so they did not enter into temptation. What were they to watch for that would cause such temptation? It would be the danger that was coming. Rather than the danger causing them to stand up and fight for Him, it would cause them to flee from fear. Three times Jesus came and gave them His final warning.

The Disciples' Action to Defend

The instructions have been given, the willingness of the disciples was demonstrated, now it was time for action.

The Arrival of the Betrayer and the Mob

Finally, the time had arrived.

Matthew 26:46
Arise, let's be going. Behold, he who betrays me is at hand.

Mark 14:41-42
Arise, let us be going. Behold, he who betrays me is at hand.

The mob had come with Judas, the betrayer. Immediately the disciples joined Him. There, the eleven were standing with Jesus. They were exhausted, on edge, filled with sorrow, and scared. Rolling around in their minds were the warnings of their Lord. He was leaving and the disciples could not follow

HOW CHRISTIANS MAY DEFEND THEMSELVES AGAINST ATTACK

Him into His death but would have to face theirs later. They did not know when. The Devil had been granted permission to sift all of them. They knew what Satan had done to Job so what would he do to them? Twice Jesus had predicted that they would stumble, fall, and scatter while Peter, their own leader, would deny Him three times.

The Lord Jesus had told them that they should all have swords for protection because staffs would no longer be enough to ward off the danger. They had two which He said was sufficient. They were told that their love for one another could mean even laying down their lives in death. The world now hated them and would kill them and think they were serving God. Would that happen tonight?

Yet, they had vowed to the Lord that they would not let Him leave without them. They refused to face death later. It would be now or never. The disciples had decided that they would take the sifting and determined not to stumble, fall, and scatter. Though everyone did not possess swords, they would face their enemies with two swords and nine staffs in hand. If it were necessary to demonstrate their love through laying their lives on the line, they would do it. They were ready to do battle with a hating world that desired to kill the one they loved the most. They would overcome their sorrow, fear, and exhaustion, and fight for their Lord. When the dust cleared tonight no matter what happened, they would still be standing with Him or laying on the ground dead with Him.

As they stood there, more and more people came until it was a multitude. They arrived carrying lanterns, torches, swords, and clubs. Though there was a full moon that night and all would be able to see, they would be ready just in case Jesus attempted to escape among the olive trees. With the lanterns and torches, then swords and clubs, this must have rattled the disciples. What was going on? The crowd was not a mob of bystanders and malcontents. They were a carefully orchestrated group of people capable of plotting His capture, finding Him, and seizing Jesus in the dead of night. Also, they were perfectly willing to do it illegally and in the utmost of secrecy. These were bad men with bad intentions.

Who was there? There were priests and elders. Not all of them came, but a good representation. The top officials were not going to get "their hands dirty" in case something went awry. The High priest at the time had sent his number one personal servant Malchus to view the scene and report back to him.

Luke 22:52
Jesus said to the chief priests, captains of the temple, and elders, who had come against him, "Have you come out as against a robber, with swords and clubs?"

To handle the arrest and a possible violent outbreak, these Jewish leaders had enlisted the aid of the temple guards and a Roman cohort with a commanding officer.

John 18:3
Judas then, having taken a detachment [cohort] of soldiers and officers [temple guards] from the chief priests and...Pharisees, came there with lanterns, torches, and weapons.

John 18:12
So the detachment [cohort], the commanding officer, and the officers of the Jews seized Jesus and bound him.

The Roman cohort could have consisted of 480-600 soldiers. Both the leaders and the Romans would have been worried about the same thing: a riot among the people. Though they were arresting Jesus before dawn, they could not be sure things would not get out of hand. The Romans did not like to interfere with the affairs of the Jews unless violence broke out or its potential presented itself.

Judas had decided upon a simple, single sign. A symbol of the depth of his betrayal. He would identify Christ using the "kiss of a friend" when he was an enemy.

Mark 14:44-45
Now he who betrayed him [Judas] had given them a sign, saying, "Whoever I will kiss, that is he. Take him, and lead him away safely." When he had come, immediately he came to him, and said, "Rabbi! Rabbi!" and kissed him.

So, what did he do? This demon-possessed man who had been in the inner circle with the Son of God, boldly walked straight up to the Lord of Lords and the King of Kings and in front of the eleven kissed him as a friend with a prolonged hug of false affection. This was not the kiss of an inferior who would kiss the hand, nor a slave who would kiss the foot, it was the kiss of an equal. That kiss became a powerful and despicable gesture of the great wickedness and betrayal that was in his heart and was now being displayed for everyone to see. Judas would identify Jesus with a warm greeting.

The disciples must have been amazed and dumbfounded at the same time! Inside this evil man was the Devil Himself.

Luke 22:48
But Jesus said to him, "Judas, do you betray the Son of Man with a kiss?"

Once Judas had greeted Him, Jesus asked Him if he was betraying a friend with a kiss and then addressed the crowd. He asked whom they were seeking, and they responded that it was Jesus of Nazareth. Then the Lord uttered, "I AM."

The Demonstration of Power by The Son

When those words He had often used to identify Himself with the Father were spoken (I AM), the entire multitude fell to the ground with great force. The disciples must have been astonished once again to view the great display of power Jesus had. Perhaps, this even filled them with great boldness. Maybe their time had come to stand with the Lord. After they got up, Jesus asked them once again who they were seeking, and they answered, "Jesus of Nazareth." Again, the Messiah identified Himself with "I AM." Here the disciples saw Jesus for who He was the great "Yahweh" of the Old Testament. They were in the presence of the Son of God. They would stand and defend Him! Their minds had been made up, this only encouraged them more.

The Son's Protection of The Eleven

Then the Son of God stood up for the twelve to protect and defend them from this crowd.

John 18:8-9
Jesus answered, "I told you that I am he. If therefore you seek me, let these go their way," that the word might be fulfilled which he spoke, "Of those whom you have given me, I have lost none."

He told Judas and the mob to leave His disciples alone and let them leave. This fulfilled an important prophecy He Himself had made in His prayer to the Father hours before and on two previous occasions. Not one of His disciples would be lost under His care.

John 17:12
While I was with them in the world, I kept them in your name. Those

whom you have given me I have kept. None of them is lost, except the son of perdition, that the Scripture might be fulfilled.

John 6:39
This is the will of my Father who sent me, that of all he has given to me I should lose nothing, but should raise them up at the last day.

John 6:40
This is the will of the one who sent me, that everyone who sees the Son, and believes in him, should have eternal life; and I will raise him up at the last day."

John 6:44
No one can come to me unless the Father who sent me draws him, and I will raise him up in the last day.

John 10:28
I give eternal life to them. They will never perish, and no one will snatch them out of my hand.

Notice, Jesus was defending the disciples with his power. He had just knocked the multitude down and then requested that they not lay a hand on His disciples.

This demonstration of supernatural power would have made them follow His request. Is this not a physical defense of Himself and His disciples? The message was clear, I can drop all of you at any moment. If you touch my disciples, you will be sorry!

The Disciples' Defensive Actions

The disciples were off the hook, Jesus had defended them, and they could go, but they did not move! They were not leaving the side of their Lord. It is important to note here that there is a good chance that Peter, and the other disciples would not have anticipated an arrest. It was against Jewish law to arrest anyone at night. They also had been with Jesus all along and knew he had done nothing wrong.

Even with the multitude of leaders, officers, guards, and soldiers nothing was being done according to the law that they all knew. They did not know what would or could happen, but they knew they were not going to leave the side of Jesus. Then things turned sour very quickly, almost in a heartbeat.

Matthew, an eyewitness, and Mark, receiving his record from Peter described what happened next.

Matthew 26:50
Jesus said to him, "Friend, why are you here?" Then they came and laid hands on Jesus, and took him.

Mark 14:46
They laid their hands on him, and seized him.

The two words these gospel writers use is "laid hands on" and "seized." The first word means "to put hands on or to throw oneself upon" and the other means "to hold, even to restrain." Someone decided that they had spoken enough and rushed past Judas and grabbed the Lord and began to restrain Him physically.

According to John, the Lord Jesus knew exactly what was going to happen, but the disciples did not. They did not have divine knowledge.

John 18:4
Jesus therefore, knowing all the things that were happening to him, went out, and said to them, "Who are you looking for?"

HOW CHRISTIANS MAY DEFEND THEMSELVES AGAINST ATTACK

When they grabbed Jesus, it suddenly dawned on them that the time Jesus had been discussing had finally arrived for their defense unto death.

Luke 22:49
When those who were around him saw what was about to happen, they said to him, "Lord, shall we strike with the sword?"

Not just Peter but all the disciples anxiously asked if this was the time to "strike with the sword?" Their intention was to defend the Lord just as they had been taught in their new instructions. The word translated "see" is not to just see with the eyes, but with the understanding.

It suddenly dawned on them that this night-time crowd, who had come to them secretly, were going to illegally arrest Him. Would Christ be killed on the spot? Would they try and whisk Him away and He would never be seen again? Would He rot in some Roman dungeon for the rest of His life? The disciples would not let this happen. They were prepared to act.

Immediately, the disciples went into a self-defense, "lay down their lives" mode. They saw the swords and clubs, the Jewish leaders, the Temple guards, and Roman soldiers, but it didn't matter. Something was seriously wrong! Jesus had done nothing evil or illegal. How dare they touch the Lord? Everything was now clear in their minds. So, they all ask Jesus if they should strike with the sword. This word "strike" is a powerful, violent word. It means "to smite, strike down, kill, or slay." So, they cried out, "Lord, shall we strike with the sword?"

Stephen uses the word in Acts 7:24, when he describes Moses striking down the Egyptian that was beating one of his Hebrew brethren.

Acts 7:24
Seeing one of them suffer wrong, he defended him, and avenged him who was oppressed, striking the Egyptian.

It is used in Acts 12:23 of the angel striking King Herod as he paraded around the city as the crowds yelled, "the voice of a god and not a man."

Acts 12:23
Immediately an angel of the Lord struck him, because he didn't give God the glory. Then he was eaten by worms and died.

They would not be scattered tonight! Satan would not sift them! The world would not kill them! They refused to be scattered! Instead, they would strike them down before the crowd could strike their Lord and Master down. So many thoughts would have been racing through their minds as they stood with the Lord at that moment. Together, probably in a deep gasp in unison they cried, "Should we strike with the sword?" In essence, they are asking if the time had come to follow the new instructions for ministry. Is it now that the sword should be used to kill? Is it now that they need to defend themselves and Jesus?" Once again, Peter decided to take the lead. Why not? He was the boldest of the group. He knew exactly what to do and was prepared to do it. No one would take His Lord without a fight. He was not going to allow the sifting Jesus had predicted. He had told the Lord that he would lay down his life and he meant it.

As Peter's heart pounded and his adrenaline flowed, he did not wait for an answer. He was sure the time had come. He drew his sword and thrust it at a key recognizable figure in the crowd, Malchus. He was the slave of Caiaphas the high priest. Peter knew the high priest and knew that he was not there, but Malchus was up close and personal listening and viewing every detail to report this illegal activity back to his boss. Most likely, Malchus was one of those who seized Jesus. His very hands were on "the Christ, the Son of the living God."

Though Peter was an accomplished fisherman, he was not a trained swordsman. Still, he would know all the basics of thrusting a Roman sword and not swinging it. The Lord Jesus would never have allowed them to have a sword that they were incapable of using.

As we have discussed, the Roman sword was for battle up close and personal. It was thrust deeply into the face, neck, or the shoulder blades. The apostle Peter would have known Malchus represented the high priest behind this evil plot upon their Lord and went in for the kill.

The Son's Request to Allow the Arrest

Instead, his ear was cut off which was all planned by the sovereign Lord Jesus. Should we dare to assume Jesus was in anyway surprised by this? Of course not.

John 18:10
Simon Peter therefore, having a sword, drew it, and struck the high priest's servant, and cut off his right ear. The servant's name was Malchus.

Luke records the Lord's answer and the servant's healing.

Luke 22:51
But Jesus answered, "Let me at least do this" — and he touched his ear, and healed him.

This small clause "Let me do this" is made up of three Greek words which have been sorely mistranslated. When a phrase or sentence would be difficult to translate literally word for word, the translators had to make a choice. This choice would be an interpretation of the phrase or sentence rather than its actual literal meaning. This is fine in instances where the interpretation is correct but not when it is grossly in error.

What the Lord is saying to the disciples is, "Allow this to happen [even this]." This is mistranslated by some as "Stop! No more of this." This interpretation sounds like Jesus is chastising Peter for what he had just done. This is not the case at all! The words Jesus used are literally in this order, "Permit until this one." The verb "permit" means exactly that "to permit or allow" something to happen before something else or after something else occurs.

Every instance in the New Testament is translated almost exclusively "permit." In Matthew 24, Jesus speaks of a homeowner who wouldn't allow a thief to break in if he had known.

Matthew 24:43
But know this, that if the master of the house had known in what watch the thief was coming, he would have watched, and would not have allowed [permitted] his house to be broken into.

In Luke 4, Jesus would not allow the demons to speak of Him.

Luke 4:41
Demons also came out from many, crying out, and saying, "You are the Christ, the Son of God!" Rebuking them, he did not allow [permitted] them to speak, because they knew that he was the Christ.

In Acts 14, it states that God allows nations to walk in their own ways.

Acts 14:16
Who in the generations gone by allowed [permitted] all the nations to walk in their own ways.

HOW CHRISTIANS MAY DEFEND THEMSELVES AGAINST ATTACK

In Acts 16, the Holy Spirit would not allow Paul to go into Bithynia.

Acts 16:7
When they had come opposite Mysia, they tried to go into Bithynia, but the Spirit didn't allow [permitted] them.

In Acts 19, the disciples would not allow Paul to go into the theater and face shouting unbelievers. They thought it was too dangerous.

Acts 19:30
When Paul wanted to enter into the people, the disciples didn't allow [permitted] him.

In Acts 23, the horsemen were allowed to accompany Paul to Caesarea for protection.

Acts 23:32
But on the next day they left the horsemen to go with him and returned to the barracks.

In Acts 27, to lighten a sinking ship Paul was on the soldiers cut away the ropes of the boat and allowed them to fall off.

Acts 27:32
Then the soldiers cut...ropes of the boat...let [permitted] it fall off.

Then in Acts 27, they cast off the anchors and permitted them to stay in sea.

Acts 27:39-40
When it was day, they didn't recognize the land, but they noticed a certain bay with a beach, and they decided to try to drive the ship onto it. Casting off the anchors, they left [permitted] them in the sea, at the same time untying the rudder ropes. Hoisting up the foresail to the wind, they made for the beach.

In Acts 28, when Paul was bitten by a snake the natives of the island thought justice would not allow him to live.

Acts 28:4
When the natives saw the creature hanging from his hand, they said one to another, "No doubt this man is a murderer, whom, though he has escaped...yet Justice has not allowed [permitted] to live."

In 1 Corinthians 10, Paul explains that God is faithful and will not allow you to be tempted above what you are able.

1 Corinthians 10:13
No temptation has taken you but such as man can bear. God is faithful, who will not allow [permitted] you to be tempted above what you are able but will with the temptation make also the way of escape, that you may be able to endure it.

So, the verb means "permit or allow." Since it is in the present active imperative tense, the Lord Jesus was giving the disciples a command. The Lord Jesus Christ was actually saying, "Disciples, permit it until this one [incident] is over." This implies so much! The Lord Jesus was giving them the responsibility of deciding when in the future they would defend themselves but this one time He wants it allowed. He will be gone after "this one [incident]."

This fits perfectly with everything we have seen thus far and what Jesus says and does next which is to first heal the ear that was severed.

Luke 22:51-53
But Jesus answered, "Let me at least do this" -- and he touched his ear, and healed him.

This was His second miracle in a short time in front of a huge crowd. Everyone must have been completely astonished.

HOW CHRISTIANS MAY DEFEND THEMSELVES AGAINST ATTACK

Some wonder why Peter was not arrested. Why would he be? The Jews knew they were acting illegally. They wanted Jesus dead quickly. They did not have time for a lengthy trial concerning what Peter had done. Besides, Malchus' ear was restored. The Romans did not want to start something. The disciples would not have spoken up, he was doing what they were about to do.

Also, the apostle Peter was acting legally in self-defense. Malchus was right there in the center of the entire affair. He had no authority to lay his hands on the Lord and be involved with the act. All the Jews wanted was to arrest Jesus and get out of there before anyone woke up. They had to have Jesus arrested, tried, sentenced, dead, and buried by sunset of that very day according to the law.

Deuteronomy 21:22-23
If a man have committed a sin worthy of death, and he be put to death, and you hang him on a tree; his body shall not remain all night on the tree, but you shall surely bury him the same day; for he who is hanged is accursed of God; that you don't defile your land which Yahweh your God gives you for an inheritance.

Annas and Caiaphas with the Sanhedrin leadership were already making preparations for His arrival.

Next, Jesus tells Peter that he should put back the sword into its sheath.

John 18:11
Jesus therefore said to Peter, "Put up the sword into its sheath. The cup which the Father has given me, shall I not surely drink it?"

Notice, Jesus does not say, "What are you doing with the sword? We never take up arms!" He did not say this because He knew Peter had the sword and needed to use it in self-defense and the defense of his brothers but not at this "one time or incident."

The Reasons for the Allowance

Then, the Lord Jesus provides four reasons why Peter and the disciples should permit this to happen and not take up the sword in self-defense. It is difficult to determine in what order Jesus gave these reasons based on the four accounts, but the reasons remain the same. First, taking up the sword in defense of self and others at this particular time was not the will of the Lord God.

John 18:11
Jesus therefore said to Peter, "Put the sword into its sheath. The cup which the Father has given me, shall I not surely drink it?"

Here, in the Lord's rhetorical question is implied, "This cup is the cup from my Father, and I must drink it." He uses the same terminology He used when He prayed for the Father to take the cup away and then bowed to His will to accept it. This cup was the Lord's to bear in order to lay down His life for them. Peter must allow Him to drink it and not lay down their lives for Him at this time in this incident.

Second, they should permit the arrest at this time because the prophecies concerning it must be fulfilled.

Matthew 26:54
How then would the Scriptures be fulfilled that it must be so?"

The prophecies concerning the events from the arrest to His death and resurrection had to be fulfilled. Though the Lord's disciples could and should defend Him, these fulfillments were the priority because they proved that He was the Son of

HOW CHRISTIANS MAY DEFEND THEMSELVES AGAINST ATTACK

God. These prophecies include the well-known passages in Isaiah 53 and Psalm 22 among many others.

Third, Peter and the other disciples must permit this one event to occur because the Father would be defending Him against such a massive multitude of oppressors if this cup was not for Him to drink right then and there.

Matthew 26:53
Or do you think that I couldn't ask my Father, and he would even now send me more than twelve legions of angels?"

Here, the Lord describes a massive angelic army the Father would send against this large group of soldiers and guards if the time had not been right for Him to die.

Finally, Jesus tells the disciples that taking up the sword now was suicidal.

Matthew 26:52
Then Jesus said to him, "Put your sword back into its place, for all those who take the sword will die by the sword."

What does Jesus mean by this statement? To understand the passage, we must take a close look at the Greek grammar.

The verb "to die" which means "to destroy, perish, or die." It is in the future tense which means that the action is being done in the future after the taking up of the sword. It is in the middle voice rather than the active voice indicating that they will be doing the destruction to themselves by initiating a fight they could not win. If He had used the active voice, it would have indicated that they will destroy others with the sword and the passive would indicate they will die by the sword of others. The verb "take" is an aorist participle which indicates that the action is occurring before the main future verb. It could be literally translated, "For the ones taking up a sword, they will destroy themselves [by themselves]." The emphasis is on their own destruction.

Why? In this context, the many guards and soldiers had swords and some in the crowd had clubs which would require several legions of angels to stop. If they took up the sword now, they would be killing themselves off. They would basically be committing suicide. This is not God's way!

The Lord's Affirmation of Peter's Response

Notice, when Jesus speaks to Peter, He does not use his secular name. Why? This is critical to understanding self-defense. That name is reserved for a moment Peter is in the wrong. Here Peter was not in the wrong. Peter, not Simon, was doing the right thing, but it was at the wrong time. This was not the sifting that the Lord was referring to in His last discourse with Peter when He called Him Simon.

The sifting had not occurred at this moment because Peter was not wrong in doing what he did to protect Jesus, he was simply uninformed. This was due to the Lord desiring one more miracle that would go straight to the high priest who would condemn Him! Now, he and all those in the multitude would be without excuse on judgment day. Malchus would return to his master and describe the incredible miracle that Jesus had done even as he was condemning Him to death! What a glorious display of His power and God's control! It also was another opportunity to believe in Him.

As a side note, if what Peter had done was not a proper defense, then why was he bold enough to follow Jesus into the courtyard of Caiaphas. Why did the people accuse him of being with Jesus but not the cutting off of Malchus' ear?

HOW CHRISTIANS MAY DEFEND THEMSELVES AGAINST ATTACK

Matthew 26:69
Now Peter was sitting outside in the court, and a maid came to him, saying, "You were also with Jesus, the Galilean!"

No fear out of Peter for the offense and no accusation.

Jesus wanted all the parties involved to learn when to defend themselves and when not to. The Lord wanted us to be able to distinguish between the right and wrong time to defend oneself against persecutors. When outnumbered, we cannot take up the sword because it would be as if we are killing ourselves. Secondly, it was not necessary to defend themselves, because they had just been released. Peter and the disciples were told to leave, but they didn't. Third, when we know it is God's will to accept a certain death, we must accept it. The Lord's death was very a certain death. Their death would have been a certain death if they took up the sword.

This was allowed to happen for all the others to see that, once again, Jesus had great power but was relinquishing it to them because no one takes the life of the Son of God, unless He lays it down for them. The crowd falling down at His identification and the healing of Malchus' ear were powerful miracles that would resonate in their memories for their entire lives. Now, Jesus turns his attention to the crowd.

The Lord's Indictment of the Mob

Now, Jesus indicts the crowd for their illegal activity of arresting Him without cause as they would do a robber.

Matthew 26:55
In that hour Jesus said to the multitudes, "Have you come out as against a robber with swords and clubs to seize me? I sat daily in the temple teaching, and you didn't arrest me.

They were doing it at night as if they had caught a thief in the act. Yet, He had been their daily teaching in front of the whole world, and they never arrested Him. Why? He had done nothing wrong! They were committing an illegal act in secret with no charges! Then John records what happened next.

John 18:12
So the detachment, the commanding officer, and the officers of the Jews, seized Jesus and bound him.

So, they seized and bound Him, and the disciples took off.

Matthew 26:56
"But all this... happened, that the Scriptures of the prophets might be fulfilled." Then all the disciples left him, and fled.

They left and fled. There was nothing left for them to do. From that moment on, everything Jesus said was coming true. The sword would definitely now be needed to protect themselves from persecution but not tonight. Tonight, would have only brought a blood bath upon themselves.

Chapter 13

The Certain Urgency

Throughout biblical history, people have always had a certain urgency in preparing for the defense of themselves and others. Individuals, families, clans, tribes, cities, regions, and nations sought to build and develop weapons to protect themselves and others.

The Defense of the Staff

When we study the people of Israel and their basic weapon of defense, we discover that it was the staff. Every male carried a staff. It was used first for protection against man and animals. Only secondarily was it used for other purposes. Though somewhat obvious when pointed out, yet it often goes unnoticed. In any discussion of ancient Jewish life, it must be noted that carrying staffs was a common Jewish practice. This was not the sole custom of shepherds as some might think. It was quite typical among the Hebrews to carry staffs for a variety of uses including protection.

The Staff in the Old Testament

We literally see the staff throughout the Bible. It is not just with shepherds as we will see. The staff is one of those objects, not noticeable or discussed, but was an intricate part of Jewish life. Though its significance is not directly discussed, it was incredibly important. We will begin our study of the "staff" with a discussion of the actual terms used.

The Hebrew Terms

An ancient staff used by common people was a thick stick of wood which was cut to various sizes. There are several Hebrew words that refer to the staff and other types of rods or sticks that could be used for a variety of purposes. It is important to note that these different Hebrew terms are translated with different English words depending on the context and the particular translator. Yet, these terms are used interchangeably as we would use synonyms in the English language to refer to the same object but perhaps to bring out certain nuances of meaning. It is critical to note that, at times, two Hebrew words are used in the same sentence to refer to the same instrument.

Often, the Hebrews would use parallel phrases in order to emphasize a particular truth, idea, or concept as a result they would use synonymous terms. When this occurs, the English translator will use "rod", "scepter", and "staff." These do not refer to necessarily different objects, but simply the reference to the same "staff" with its different symbolic meanings.

Except in a few obscure passages, there is no reason to believe that anything other than a staff is referenced. The concept of a "rod" as a separate more combative "club" as distinguished from a staff comes from one popular writer's conception of his childhood experience among shepherds. In Psalm 23:4, David speaks to this truth.

Psalm 23:4
Even though I walk through the valley of the shadow of death, I will fear no evil, for you are with me. Your rod and your staff, they comfort me.

He interprets the first Hebrew word as a club and the second as a staff claiming that shepherds always carried both. This is not the case. Though he references his past experience, there is absolutely no indication that shepherds carried more than one implement.

Here the psalmist is looking at God as shepherd through the lenses of the various uses of the staff and utilizes a parallel approach. How would God's staff comfort him? It was used for protection, examination, discipline, and was a symbol of his presence, direction, and care. Two different instruments are not envisioned here, but different aspects of God's care for us who gives comfort. Two synonyms are used by the writer to bring emphasis to the truth. Before this writer wrote his book, it was always interpreted this way.

The Common Occurrence

A staff was carried by every man throughout ancient times. Because they could be made quickly and easily, they were available to all. Other weapons, such as the sword, would have to be purchased.

The best Old Testament example of the common use of the staff is found in the description by Moses in the great story of the Exodus from Egypt. God's people had been slaves for seventy years and the Lord sent Moses to free them. Each time Pharaoh refused; God sent a powerful plague upon the land. Finally, after the ninth divine disaster, God determined that He would take the first born of every Egyptian family in the land. To exempt themselves from this "angel of death," the Hebrews were to put lamb's blood around the door to mark their home for protection.

Before this event occurred, God commanded His people to commemorate this great act of deliverance. They were to do this through the celebration of the Passover meal annually.

The Passover meal was to bring to the remembrance of every Jew what God had done to redeem them. This foreshadowed the coming of His Messiah.

In Exodus 12, the Lord through Moses shares aspects of this meal.

Exodus 12:11
This is how you shall eat it: with your belt on your waist, your shoes on your feet, and your staff in your hand; and you shall eat it in haste: it is Yahweh's Passover.

Notice, they were to eat the meal with the basic instruments of travel: belt, sandals, and staff. The belt held up the long tunic to walk, the sandals protected the feet, and the staff was used for their family's protection, the tending of their family's animals, and other uses. They would eat ready to leave. God mentions the staff because it was one of the essentials of the life of the Hebrews.

When Judah refused to follow God's law of inheritance by giving his son to Tamar, his other son's widow, Tamar took action. She disguised herself as a prostitute and stood on the side of the road in the path Judah took.

For her services, Judah promised a young goat. Since he did not have it on hand, he gave her his signet ring, his cord, and his staff. These were the basic and essential items a man carried. The signet ring had engraved on it the family seal to verify legal transactions. The staff often had a top with a personalized image. The three would be used to identify him.

In Genesis 38:18, Moses records what happened.

Genesis 38:18
He said, "What pledge will I give you?" She said, "Your signet and

HOW CHRISTIANS MAY DEFEND THEMSELVES AGAINST ATTACK

your cord, and your staff that is in your hand." He gave them to her, and came in to her, and she conceived by him.

The point is Judah was carrying a staff.

In Genesis 32, as Jacob envisions a difficult encounter with his estranged brother Esau on his way home to his father Abraham's land, he begs God for divine protection. He begins his prayer with praises for the Lord's blessing over the years with his uncle Laban.

Genesis 32:10
I am not worthy of the least of all the lovingkindnesses, and of all the truth, which you have shown to your servant; for with just my staff I passed over this Jordan…now I have become two companies.

Here, he indicates that he had begun his stay with only the most common and simplest of possessions: his staff. Now, he had so much more.

This staff is mentioned by the author of Hebrews in chapter eleven.

Hebrews 11:21
By faith, Jacob, when he was dying, blessed each of the sons of Joseph, and worshiped, leaning on the top of his staff.

In Exodus 7, when Aaron assisted Moses in bringing the plagues on Egypt, he asked Aaron to use his staff which was something every man carried.

Exodus 7:9-10
When Pharaoh speaks to you, saying, ''Perform a miracle!' then you shall tell Aaron, 'Take your rod [staff], and cast it down before Pharaoh, that it become a serpent.' Moses and Aaron went into Pharaoh, and they did so, as Yahweh had commanded: and Aaron

cast down his rod [staff] before Pharaoh and before his servants, and it became a serpent.

When the sorcerers of Pharaoh saw this, they also had staffs and turned them into serpents.

Exodus 7:11-12
Then Pharaoh also called for the wise men and the sorcerers. They also, the magicians of Egypt, did the same thing with their enchantments. For they each cast down their rods, and they became serpents; but Aaron's rod swallowed up their rods.

Of course, their serpents were eaten by Aaron's. Then Aaron used his staff to turn the Nile into blood.

One of the most interesting stories in Scripture is the ass of Balaam speaking to him in Numbers 22. An angel whom Balaam did not see had halted the donkey in his tracks to prevent the prophet Balaam from prophesying falsely for money. When Balaam struck him with his staff, the donkey rebuked him.

Numbers 22:27
The donkey saw Yahweh's angel, and she lay down under Balaam. Balaam's anger burned, and he struck the donkey with his staff.

The passage describes the striking of the donkey three times. Balaam was a prophet for hire, not a shepherd, yet he carried a staff as all men did.

In Zechariah 11, when the Lord commanded Zechariah to prophecy concerning His coming Messiah, He described His ministry with the use of two rods or staffs. He named one "Favor" and the other "Unity" for God's Messiah [Jesus] would bring blessing, favor, and unity among His people. The staff was such a common "tool" that it was used metaphorically in

HOW CHRISTIANS MAY DEFEND THEMSELVES AGAINST ATTACK

the inspired speaking, teaching, and writing of the prophets. They knew the readers would understand exactly what was being said without explanation.

Zechariah 11:10
I took my staff Favor, and cut it apart, that I might break my covenant that I had made with all the peoples. He cut the staff called "Favor" in half to symbolize God's destruction of Israel after they rejected His Messiah.

Zechariah 11:14
Then I cut apart my other staff, even Union, that I might break the brotherhood between Judah and Israel.

The second staff indicated the scattering and disunity that would result. Since Israel rejected the Messiah, they would be no more. Of course, we know this occurred in 70 AD when the nation was torn apart by the Romans. In our discussion, it is not the prophecy that is important; it is the availability and use of the staff for his prophecy. These would be familiar objects to His people and well understood when they were named and then broken.

Prophets also carried staffs like other men. In 2 Kings 4, when Elisha decided to raise the Shunamite's son from the dead, his initial step was to send his servant Gehazi ahead of him and lay Elisha's staff upon the child's head.

2 Kings 4:29
Then he said to Gehazi, Gird up your loins, and take my staff in your hand, and go your way: if you meet any man, Don't greet him; and if anyone greets you, don't answer him again: and lay my staff on the face of the child.

Though it took the prophet himself laying on top of the child to raise him, we have once again, the use of a staff.

In Isaiah 36, the prophet warns the people of God not to trust in Pharaoh's might rather than His power.

Isaiah 36:6
Behold, you trust in the staff of this bruised reed, even in Egypt, which if a man leans on it, it will go into his hand and pierce it. So is Pharaoh king of Egypt to all who trust in him.

A staff would often be made from a hollow, straight reed. Trusting in Pharaoh to help them against their enemy was like leaning on one of these reeds which broke and cut the hand. They could not rely on him but should rely on God. This would be understood by the average person because the staff was so common.

The staff was considered as much a staple of daily life as bread was. As a result, the term "staff of bread" came to mean the people's supply of its most basic food: bread. In Psalm 105. the Psalmist reviews how God brought a famine on the land in the time of Joseph and describes it with this analogy in mind.

Psalm 105:16
He called for a famine on the land. He destroyed the food supplies [literally staff of bread].

In Isaiah 3, Isaiah predicts the destruction of Judah with a play on words using staff and its root word.

Isaiah 3:1
For, behold, the Lord, Yahweh of Armies, takes away from Jerusalem and from Judah supply and support, the whole supply of bread, and the whole supply of water.

The Hebrew word for staff can mean "support." The root word means "supply." So, the prophet is warning the Hebrew people that their whole staff or support of staples, its full supply of bread and water will be gone! This word play was easily understood because the staff was so common.

In Ezekiel, the prophet issues a similar warning. This time to Jerusalem.

Ezekiel 4:16
Moreover he said to me, "Son of man, behold, I will break the staff of bread in Jerusalem: and they shall eat bread by weight, and with fearfulness; and they shall drink water by measure, and in dismay."

Ezekiel 5:16
When I shall send on them the evil arrows of famine, that are for destruction, which I will send to destroy you: and I will increase the famine on you, and will break your staff of bread.

Ezekiel 14:13
Son of man, when a land sins against me by committing a trespass, and I stretch out my hand on it, and break the staff of its bread, and send famine on it, and cut off from it man and animal.

All of these passages demonstrate the common use of the staff through the daily necessity of bread

The Primary use

The staff was utilized primarily for self-defense and the defense of others. It could readily become a weapon to protect oneself.

The Staff as Defense in Common Use

A powerful illustration of the use of the staff for protection was the incident that occurred between David and Goliath.

Though David was a shepherd, he carried with him the humble common instruments of defense.

In 1 Samuel 17, when young David faced Goliath, he had two weapons in his hand: his staff and his sling.

1 Samuel 17:40
He took his staff in his hand, and chose for himself five smooth stones out of the brook, and put them in the pouch of his shepherd's bag which he had. His sling was in his hand; and he came near to the Philistine.

The staff was used for battle close up while the sling was utilized for combat at a distance. The warrior Goliath was so huge that distant combat would be David's only hope. Notice, the great warrior's reaction.

1 Samuel 17:42-44
When the Philistine looked around and saw David, he disdained him; for he was but a youth, and ruddy, and had a good looking face. The Philistine said to David, "Am I a dog, that you come to me with sticks?" The Philistine cursed David by his gods. The Philistine said to David, "Come to me, and I will give your flesh to the birds of the sky and to the animals of the field."

The Philistine mocked David because he was not a seasoned warrior bringing a warrior's weapons against him. Instead, he was a commoner with a common weapon (staff). The word translated "stick" is the Hebrew word meaning "staff." The sling was probably out of sight and unexpected.

Since the staff would not work against this giant, David used his sling. This killed the giant.

1 Samuel 17:49-50
David put his hand in his bag, took a stone, and slung it, and struck

the Philistine in his forehead. The stone sank into his forehead, and he fell on his face to the earth. So David prevailed over the Philistine with a sling and with a stone, and struck the Philistine and killed him; but there was no sword David's hand.*

I mentioned this story because it demonstrates that the staff was the basic weapon of a common man verses the weapons of a soldier.

David carried a sling together with the staff for combat with animals. When Saul attempted to put his armor on David, it didn't feel right, and David rejected it.

1 Samuel 17:38
Saul dressed David with his clothing. He put a helmet of bronze on his head, and he clad him with a coat of mail. 39 David strapped his sword on his clothing and he tried to move, for he had not tested it. David said to Saul, "I can't go with these, for I have not tested them." Then David took them off.

The young man had already explained that the staff and sling was enough to kill large animals with the help of the Lord.

1 Samuel 17:34-37
David said to Saul, "Your servant was keeping his father's sheep; and when a lion or a bear came and took a lamb out of the flock, I went out after him, struck him, and rescued it out of his mouth. When he arose against me, I caught him by his beard, struck him, and killed him. Your servant struck both the lion and the bear. This uncircumcised Philistine shall be as one of them, since he has defied the armies of the living God." David said, "Yahweh, who delivered me out of the paw of the lion and out of the paw of the bear, will deliver me out of the hand of this Philistine."

Here, the sling would have been used to injure and stop the beasts and the staff to finish them off.

The Staff as Defense in Combat

Since the staff was used for daily protection by common folk, sometimes, it had to be used by those who must engage in combat.

In 2 Samuel 23, one of David's men used a staff to fight in hand-to-hand combat against a warrior's spear.

2 Samuel 23:21
He killed a huge Egyptian, and the Egyptian had a spear in his hand; but he went down to him with a staff, and plucked the spear out of the Egyptian's hand, and killed him with his own spear.

It is described again in 1 Chronicles 11:23. here the author uses the same Hebrew word.

1 Chronicles 11:23
He killed an Egyptian, a man of great stature, five cubits high. In the Egyptian's hand was a spear like a weaver's beam; and he went down to him with a staff, plucked the spear out of the Egyptian's hand, and killed him with his own spear.

Some translators want to translate the word to "club," but it is never used that way. Plus, how valiant would it be to fight a spear-wielding soldier with a club? The use of the staff would have demonstrated great skill and courage. Also, how would one "pluck" or "snatch" a spear away from a man with a club half the size? The point of the story is this: one of David's bold and courageous men took an ordinary staff and went after this huge Egyptian and defeated him with his own spear! He would have had to disarm him with the staff first.

The common staff could easily be cut sharp at one end and used much like a spear for the lowest rank of troops who could not afford other kinds of weapons.

HOW CHRISTIANS MAY DEFEND THEMSELVES AGAINST ATTACK

In Habakkuk 3, the prophet is reviewing the story of the Lord God's great deliverance of Israel from the Egyptian army.

Habakkuk 3:14
You pierced the heads of his warriors with their own spears [staffs]. They came as a whirlwind to scatter me, gloating as if to devour the poor in secret (DEJ).

Here the normal words for spear are not used; instead, he uses the word staff." Yet, it is utilized in the context of battle.

Speaking of the Egyptians, their army came to destroy His people Israel as easy as one would destroy or devour the poor without anyone seeing. He is saying that the Israelites were so weak, that the Egyptians would only have needed their most common weapon of defense which was their staff to destroy them." Here, the staff is mentioned as a weapon.

We see this also used in a list of various weapons given in Ezekiel 39:9. In this passage, the prophet is speaking of the seven-year tribulation. The armies that are against the Lord who have invaded Israel will be so defeated by God's fury as seen in earthquakes, pestilence, and hailstorms of fire and brimstone that they will have to burn their weapons for fuel.

Ezekiel 39:9
Those who dwell in the cities of Israel shall go out, and shall make fires of the weapons and burn them, both the shields and the bucklers, the bows and the arrows, and the staffs, and the spears, and they shall make fires of them seven years (DEJ).

Some desire to translate the word "staffs" by "war clubs," but this word is never used or translated this way. It is best understood as staffs used as the most minimal of weapons when this was all some may have had.

The Secondary Uses

The staff was a part of daily life because not only was it used for protection, but it had other daily uses.

The Picking Up of Objects

In 1 Samuel 14, Jonathon was waiting to enter the battle with Israel and grew hungry. So, he used his staff to pick up some honey to eat.

1 Samuel 14:27
But Jonathan didn't hear when his father commanded the people with the oath. Therefore he put out the end of the staff who was in his hand, and dipped it in the honeycomb, and put his hand to his mouth; and his eyes brightened (DEJ).

This was against his father's injunction. There was to be no eating until he had had revenge on his enemies. Anyone who did would die. Then Saul found out.

1 Samuel 14:43
Then Saul said to Jonathan, "Tell me what you have done!" Jonathan told him, and said, "I certainly did taste a little honey with the end of the staff that was in my hand; and behold, I must die."

So, the staff had this useful purpose.

The Carrying of Objects

Of course, one could carry fruit or other objects on a staff.

Numbers 13:23
They came to the valley of Eshcol, and cut down from there a branch

with one cluster of grapes, and they bore it on a staff between two. They also brought some of the pomegranates and figs.

This was one of the simple uses of the staff.

The Crushing of Plants

In Isaiah 28, the prophet compares the wisdom of God's dealing with Israel as a farmer wisely deals with his crops. Each stage of growing is done with discernment and care.

Isaiah 28:27
For the dill are not threshed with a sharp instrument, neither is a cart wheel turned over the cumin; but the dill is beaten out with a stick, and the cumin with a rod.

The staff whether small or large, cut or full size, could be used to beat the dill and then to crush the cumin into powder carefully. He did not have to use a sharp instrument.

The Counting with a Marker

The staff was used as a marker to keep track of a count. In Leviticus 27, it describes a staff used for counting.

Leviticus 27:32
All the tithe of the herds or the flocks, whatever passes under the rod [staff], the tenth shall be holy to Yahweh.

Sheep would pass under the staff to count every tenth one.

In Ezekiel 20, it is symbolically used to speak of checking for false believers (rebels) as a shepherd checked for flaws among his sheep as each passed under his staff.

Ezekiel 20:37
"I will cause you to pass under the rod, and I will bring you into the bond of the covenant."

God said that He would be checking and counting the true sheep who were His.

The Stabilization of a Cane or Crutch

The staff was utilized to help stabilize people who had incurred injuries. In Exodus 21, it is found in a law given by Moses.

Exodus 21:18-19
If men quarrel and one strikes the other with a stone, or with his fist, and he doesn't die, but is confined to bed; if he rises again and walks around with his staff, then he who struck him shall be cleared: only he shall pay for the loss of his time, and shall provide for his healing until he is thoroughly healed.

In Zechariah 8, it is used of the aged to aid them in their feebleness.

Zechariah 8:4-6
Yahweh of Armies says: "Old men and old women will again dwell in the streets of Jerusalem, every man with his staff in his hand for very age [due to old age]." The streets of the city will be full of boys and girls playing in its streets." Yahweh of Armies says: "If it is marvelous in the eyes of the remnant of this people in those days, should it also be marvelous in my eyes?" says Yahweh of Armies.

Here, the prophet foretells the Lord God's blessing after their Israel's impending captivity. The Almighty God of Israel will restore His people and the streets of Jerusalem will be filled with young and old alike.

HOW CHRISTIANS MAY DEFEND THEMSELVES AGAINST ATTACK

The Shoveling of Earth

If needed, the staff could be utilized for digging a well. In Numbers 21, the people of God sang a song praising Him for water He had provided for them.

Numbers 21:18
The well, which the princes dug, which the nobles of the people dug, with the scepter [rods], and with their poles [staffs].

In this passage, two different words are used for staff which are synonyms. This is used for emphasis.

The Symbolization of Divine Authority

The staff was utilized to direct or participate in miracles symbolizing the leader's divine authority.

In Exodus 4, the leader Moses turned was told by God that He would use his staff to direct His miracles against Pharaoh.

Exodus 4:17
You shall take this rod [staff] in your hand, with which you shall do the signs.

It was with this staff that Moses brought the ten plagues upon Egypt to free God's people.

When the people of God were in the wilderness desperate to get across the Red Sea to escape the approaching army of Egypt, Moses used his staff to initiate the miracle.

Exodus 14:16
Lift up your rod [staff], and stretch out your hand over the sea, and divide it…Israel shall go into the middle of the sea on dry ground.

In Exodus 17, Moses kept his staff in the air and the people of God were able to miraculously defeat the Amalekites.

Exodus 17:9
Moses said to Joshua, "Choose men for us, and go out, fight with Amalek. Tomorrow I will stand on the top of the hill with God's rod in my hand."

When Aaron's authority was challenged by some of the leaders of Israel, his staff budded miraculously and the other rods representing the other tribes did not.

Numbers 17:8
On the next day, Moses went into the tent of the testimony; and behold, Aaron's rod for the house of Levi had sprouted, budded, produced blossoms, and bore ripe almonds.

The Designation of Rulership

In ancient societies, ornate staffs were signs of authority and rulership.

In Judges 5, Deborah and Barak described the peoples who came out of Israel's tribes to fight with them.

Judges 5:14
Those...root is in Amalek came out of Ephraim, after you, Benjamin, among your peoples. Governors come down out of Machir. Those who handle the marshal's staff [Literally: staff of office] came out of Zebulun.

Officials came out of various parts of the land and had their symbolic designations of leadership. These ornate staffs designating leadership positions were often translated with the English word "scepter" for the Hebrew.

In Numbers 24, Balaam utters a prophecy of the coming Messiah.

Numbers 24:17
I see him, but not now. I see him, but not near. A star will come out of Jacob. A scepter [ruler] will rise out of Israel, and shall strike through the corners of Moab, and break down all the sons of Sheth."

Here scepter would have indicated a ruler carrying a ruler's staff or rod.

In Psalm 45, the psalmist speaks of the rule of God using the term.

Psalm 45:6
Your throne, God, is forever and ever. A scepter [ruler's staff] of equity is the scepter [ruler's staff] of your kingdom.

Two these are the same word in the Hebrew referring to the staff of a ruler. Thus, the ruler would lead in God's equity, fairness, and uprightness.

In Psalm 108, the Lord speaks of His Messiah coming from the line of Judah which is symbolized by the staff.

Psalm 108:8
Gilead is mine. Manasseh is mine. Ephraim also is my helmet. Judah is my scepter [ruler's staff].

In Amos 1, the term translated "staff" or "scepter" refers to the ruler who carries it.

Amos 1:5
"I will break the bar of Damascus, and cut off the inhabitant from the valley of Aven, and him who holds the scepter from the house of Eden...people of Syria shall go into captivity to Kir," says Yahweh.

Amos 1:8
"I will cut off the inhabitant from Ashdod, and him who holds the scepter from Ashkelon; and I will turn my hand against Ekron; and the remnant of the Philistines will perish," says the Lord Yahweh.

Here God speaks of two different rulers and refers to them as those who carry the scepter (staff) for that country.

In Zechariah 10, the inspired prophet gives a warning to the leader of Egypt.

Zechariah 10:11
He will pass through the sea of affliction, and will strike the waves in the sea, and all the depths of the Nile will dry up; and the pride of Assyria will be brought down, and the scepter of Egypt will depart.

Once again, the Hebrew word for staff is translated scepter because it refers to a ruler. This common instrument carried by every man became a symbol of power when carried by a king!

The Rod of Discipline

We know that the staff could be used to strike people usually in discipline.

In Exodus 21, the Lord speaks of a chastening between a master and servant.

Exodus 21:20
If a man strikes his servant or his maid with a rod [staff], and he dies under his hand, he shall surely be punished.

The master gets angry at the servant for something he or she has done and strikes him with a staff. Though this is not self-

HOW CHRISTIANS MAY DEFEND THEMSELVES AGAINST ATTACK

defense, it shows the staff being used for striking. If it is used for offense, it can also be used for defense.

In Proverbs 22, Solomon speaks of the staff as a rod of fury. This implies striking someone.

Proverbs 22:8
He who sows wickedness reaps trouble, and the rod of his fury will be destroyed.

The Symbol of National Power

The staff is utilized to describe the attack, battle, subduing, and oppression of one nation by another through weaponry. It was a symbol of the great power in a nation's arsenal. In Isaiah 10, the prophet warns Israel that the Assyrians will come and destroy them as God's instruments, yet God will eventually deliver them.

Isaiah 10:24
Therefore the Lord, Yahweh of Armies, says "My people who dwell in Zion, don't be afraid of the Assyrian, though he strike you with the rod, and lift up his staff against you, as Egypt did."

Here Hebrew synonyms are used to describe the power of a nation for destruction symbolized by the staff.

To understand the next few passages, one must remember that after Solomon, Israel divided into two kingdoms. The first was Israel made up of ten tribes and Judah made up of the tribe by its name and Benjamin. The prophets warned Israel if they continued to defy the Lord, He would bring Assyria against them. If Judah continued to defy the Lord after He had disciplined Israel, God would raise up the Babylonians to conquer them. Both happened.

In Isaiah 10, the Lord explains to His people that Assyria will be used by God to discipline them, but they will not do it for this purpose. The Assyrians will do it out of pride and world domination. Then God will punish them also.

Isaiah 10:15
Should an ax brag against him who chops with it? Should a saw exalt itself above him who saws with it? As if a rod should lift those who lift it up, or as if a staff should lift up someone who is not wood.

The Lord God is saying that He is lifting up their staff and rod of destruction and they cannot exalt themselves because they are the staff not the wielder of the staff, God is.

In Jeremiah 48, Jeremiah prophesies the annihilation of Moab. When they are destroyed, people will speak of their former power and beauty.

Jeremiah 48:17
All you who are around him, bemoan him, and all you who know his name; say, how is the strong staff broken, the beautiful rod!

In Isaiah 10, God speaks of the coming powerful army of Assyria who will destroy Israel, yet God will eventually deliver them from His instruments of discipline. He will not leave them in their despair forever.

Isaiah 10:24
Therefore the Lord, Yahweh of Armies, says "My people who dwell in Zion, don't be afraid of the Assyrian, though he strike you with the rod, and lift up his staff against you, as Egypt did."

Notice, the rod and staff (synonyms) are used as a symbol of authority as the ruler lifts up his staff to signal a charge and then brings his staff down to pummel his enemies with the strength of his armies and weaponry.

HOW CHRISTIANS MAY DEFEND THEMSELVES AGAINST ATTACK

In Isaiah 14, the prophet now warns Judah that Babylon will be coming to destroy them. They were not to worry because one day the Lord would turn on Babylon for their pride, arrogance, and viciousness. Then Israel will take up a taunt against them.

Isaiah 14:5
Yahweh has broken the staff of the wicked, the scepter of the rulers.

Notice once again, the synonyms and parallel phrases used to emphasize the demolition of their great strength symbolized by their staffs.

In Ezekiel 19, the prophet is describing the power and wisdom of Jerusalem before they were destroyed, and their king dragged away in hooks by Babylon. In verses 11-12, Ezekiel portrays their former wise rulers and magistrates as a strong tree whose scepter (staff) and rods (symbol of their power) came from strong branches and now are broken and demolished by Babylon.

Ezekiel 19:11-12
It had strong rods [staffs] or the scepters (staffs) of those who bore rule, and their stature was exalted among the thick boughs, and they were seen in their height with the multitude of their branches But it was plucked up in fury, it was cast down to the ground, and the east wind dried up its fruit: its strong rods [staffs] were broken off and withered; the fire consumed them.

In Isaiah 9:4, Isaiah speaks of the oppression of the nations that the Messiah will relieve in His coming, The Lord God will come in power to defend His people once and for all.

Isaiah 9:4
For the yoke of his burden, and the staff of his shoulder, the rod of his oppressor, you have broken as in the day of Midian.

All of these passages use two different Hebrew words to emphasize the power and might of a nation symbolized in its staff used as a scepter of rule.

The Symbol of Divine Power

In fact, God utilizes the same symbolism when He speaks of His power and might. It is utilized to demonstrate His discipline and punishment which would have involved the striking, hurting, and even death of others.

As Isaiah warns Israel of the coming Assyrian army to discipline and punish them for their sin, God calls them His rod and staff.

Isaiah 10:5
Alas…the rod of my anger…staff in whose hand is my indignation!

Isaiah 10:26
Yahweh of Armies will stir up a scourge against him, as in the slaughter of Midian at the rock of Oreb. His rod will be over the sea, and he will lift it up like he did against Egypt.

In Exodus 14, the staff refers to the Lord God's destruction of the Egyptian army in the Red Sea.

Exodus 14:26-28
Yahweh said to Moses, "Stretch out your hand over the sea, that the waters may come again on the Egyptians, on their chariots, and on their horsemen." Moses stretched out his hand over the sea, and the sea returned to its strength when the morning appeared; and the Egyptians fled against it. Yahweh overthrew the Egyptians in the midst of the sea. The waters returned, and covered the chariots and the horsemen, even all Pharaoh's army that went in after them into the sea. There remained not so much as one of them.

In Genesis 49, Jacob is blessing his sons and prophecies the rule of God's Messiah in power and great might (referring to His staff) which will be demonstrated by the obedience of the nations.

Genesis 49:9-10
Judah is a lion's cub. From the prey, my son, you have gone up. He stooped down, he crouched as a lion, as a lioness. Who will rouse him up? The scepter will not depart from Judah, nor the ruler's staff from between his feet, until he comes to whom it belongs. To him will the obedience of the peoples be.

The great future king and Messiah will be from the tribe of Judah. In Psalm 2:9, the Father speaks to His Son.

Psalm 2:9
You shall break them with a rod [staff] of iron. You shall dash them in pieces like a potter's vessel.

The Staff in the New Testament

Though the staff is not mentioned as prominently in the New Testament as the Old, it had much the same purposes and uses.

The Greek Terms

In the Greek language, two terms are used in reference to the staff. As in the Hebrew, two synonyms are used and translated differently depending on the context and the translator but refer to the common staff. There was a different term for a club which was carried by the mob among those who came to arrest Jesus rather than by army. This will be discussed in another section of this chapter.

The Old Testament Reference in the New

There are many ways to demonstrate how the staff was still a common occurrence in the first century. In this section, we will discover that passages from the Old Testament with the staff as an intricate part of the understanding were provided without explanation. This could only be possible if the staff was still a common instrument in daily life.

In Hebrews 1, the author is explaining the superiority of Jesus as compared to angels because He was the Son who was given rule.

Hebrews 1:8
But of the Son he says, "Your throne, O God, is forever and ever. The scepter of uprightness is the scepter of your Kingdom.

Psalm 45:6-7
Your throne, God, is forever and ever. A scepter...is the scepter of your kingdom. You have loved righteousness, and hated wickedness. Therefore God, your God, has anointed you with the oil of gladness above your fellows.

In chapter 9, the inspired writer mentions the items that were in the ark which included Aaron's signature staff that budded to demonstrate God was with Him.

Hebrews 9:4
Having a golden altar of incense, and the ark of the covenant overlaid on all sides with gold, in which was a golden pot holding the manna, Aaron's rod that budded, and the tablets of the covenant.

Numbers 17:5
It shall happen that the rod of the man whom I shall choose shall bud. I will make the murmurings of the children of Israel, which they murmur against you, cease from me."

Numbers 17:8
On the next day, Moses went into the Tent of the Testimony; and behold, Aaron's rod for the house of Levi had sprouted, budded, produced blossoms, and bore ripe almonds.

Numbers 17:9-11
Moses brought out all the rods from before Yahweh to all the children of Israel. They looked, and each man took his rod. Yahweh said to Moses, "Put back the rod of Aaron before the covenant, to be kept for a token against the children of rebellion; that you may make an end of their complaining against me, that they not die." Moses did so. As Yahweh commanded him, so he did.

His Hebrew readers would have been familiar with the staff and its use as a symbol of a man, his family, or tribe.

In Hebrews 11, the author mentions Jacob blessing his sons on his death bed.

Hebrews 11:21
By faith, Jacob, when he was dying, blessed each of the sons of Joseph, and worshiped, leaning on the top of his staff.

Genesis 47:31
Israel said, "Swear to me," and he swore to him. Then Israel bowed himself on the bed's head.

Though this was not commented on by Moses, it obviously was passed down verbally. The aged leaning on their staff for support would have been a common occurrence.

The Common Use in the New Testament

The staff is mentioned in the instructions of the Lord as He sent out His disciples because every male had one.

Luke 9:3
He said to them, "Take nothing [more] for your journey — neither staffs, nor wallet, nor bread, nor money; neither have two coats apiece."

The Staff is mentioned in the final instructions of the Lord as He prepared His disciples for His departure as compared to a sword.

Luke 22:36
Then he said to them, "But now, whoever has a purse, let him take it, and likewise a wallet. Whoever has none, let him sell his cloak, and buy a sword.

In the book of Revelation, John speaks of Jesus ruling the nations with a staff (rod) of iron.

Revelation 12:5
She gave birth to a son, a male child, who is to rule all the nations with a rod of iron. Her child was caught up to God, and to his throne.

Revelation 19:15
Out of his mouth proceeds a sharp, double-edged sword, that with it he should strike the nations. He will rule them with an iron rod.

Both a staff and iron were used in ancient times and would have immediately been understood as a "strong and fierce rule."

The Primary use

The most important passages referring to the primary use of the staff also point to its common use. Though we will cover the following passages in much more detail in another chapter, we will touch on them here. Three of the writers of

HOW CHRISTIANS MAY DEFEND THEMSELVES AGAINST ATTACK

the gospels record the words of the Lord Jesus to His disciples concerning the use of a staff as they initially ventured out into the world to preach the gospel. When Jesus decided to send His twelve disciples out on a short missionary endeavor, He instructed them concerning what to bring and not bring.

In Mark 6, we have one record of these instructions.

Mark 6:8-10
He commanded them that they should take nothing for their journey, except a staff only: no bread, no wallet, and no money in their purse, but to wear sandals, and not put on two tunics. He said to them, "Wherever you enter into a house, stay there until you depart from there."

Here His disciples were to follow the biblical mandate that a worker is worthy of his support and rely on the people to whom they were preaching for support. They were to bring only a few necessities: sandals, a tunic, and a staff. The rest would be provided for as they trusted God. They were not to acquire any new supplies.

In Matthew 10, this apostle provides some added details.

Matthew 10:9-11
Don't take [purchase or acquire] any gold, silver, or brass in your money belts. Take [acquire] no bag for your journey, neither two coats, nor shoes, nor staff: for the laborer is worthy of his food. Into whatever city or village you enter, find out who in it is worthy; and stay there until you go on.

Jesus here is not contradicting Himself, but simply explaining they were to take what they had and not acquire additional supplies.

Luke describes the instructions from his perspective.

Luke 9:3-4
He said to them, "Take nothing for your journey — neither staffs, nor wallet, nor bread, nor money; neither have two coats apiece. Into whatever house you enter, stay there, and depart from there."

Though this sounds as if Jesus is telling them not to take these items, we can see from Matthew and Mark that he is actually commanding them to take no more than what they had. They were not to purchase any more items because they had the right to live off the gospel.

I present these passages for your consideration because they demonstrate that the disciples and even Jesus Himself would have been carrying staffs as every man did at the time. This custom was so assumed and such a natural part of life that it would not be mentioned unless it directly pertained to the purposes of the inspired writers.

In the twentieth century, there was a period of time where men and woman wore hats. It was a basic aspect of their clothing and style. They would not necessarily mention it unless it pertained in some way their writing. We might be reading an account of that time, and it would be mentioned in passing as the staff was and go almost unnoticed, yet the wearing of hats like the carrying of staffs was an intricate part their lives.

The Staff as Defense in Common Use

The Jews in the New Testament were under Roman rule. If problems occurred, the Romans would become involved in the protection of the people. Nevertheless, as with modern police, they cannot always arrive on time and often did not become involved. So, having a staff allowed the common people to defend themselves and their loved ones.

HOW CHRISTIANS MAY DEFEND THEMSELVES AGAINST ATTACK

In Acts 21, Paul had been mobbed near the temple because someone accused him of bringing a Gentile into the restricted area though they were mistaken. As a result, the Roman army intervened.

Acts 21:30-33
All the city was moved and the people ran together. They seized Paul and dragged him out of the temple. Immediately the doors were shut. As they were trying to kill him, news came up to the commanding officer...that all Jerusalem was in an uproar. Immediately he took soldiers and centurions and ran down to them. They, when they saw the chief captain and the soldiers, stopped beating Paul. Then the commanding officer came near, arrested him, commanded him to be bound with two chains, and inquired who he was and what he had done.

Yet, as Stephen discovered, the Romans did not always come to the aid of someone in danger.

Acts 7:57-60
But they cried out with a loud voice and stopped their ears, then rushed at him with one accord. They threw him out of the city and stoned him. The witnesses placed their garments at the feet of a young man named Saul. They stoned Stephen as he called out, saying, "Lord Jesus, receive my spirit!" He kneeled down, and cried with a loud voice, "Lord, don't hold this sin against them!" When he had said this, he fell asleep.

When this happened to Jesus in Nazareth, the Lord had to use supernatural power to escape their grip. There was no other way.

Luke 4:28-30
They were all filled with wrath in the synagogue, as they heard these things. They rose up, threw him out of the city, and led him to the brow of the hill that their city was built on, that they might throw him off the cliff. But he, passing through the middle...went his way.

DEFENDING YOUR LIFE

Paul described the many dangers inherent in traveling as he explained to the Corinthians his qualifications for ministry. Some of those qualifications involved facing the dangers of traveling in the first century to preach the gospel.

2 Corinthians 11:26
I have been in travels often, perils of rivers, perils of robbers, perils from my countrymen, perils from the Gentiles, perils in the city, perils in the wilderness, perils in the sea, perils among false brothers.

Most of the dangers would have required a weapon. The staff would have been the common one to possess.

In His story of the Good Samaritan, Jesus provides an example of the dangers of robbers who steal from and beat their victims.

Luke 10:30
Jesus answered, "A certain man was going down from Jerusalem to Jericho, and he fell among robbers, who both stripped him and beat him, and departed, leaving him half dead."

Though this story was fiction, it was realistic fiction based on real life possibilities.

In John 10, Jesus spoke of thieves who came to steal sheep.

John 10:1
"Most certainly, I tell you, one who doesn't enter by the door into the sheep fold, but climbs up some other way, is a thief and a robber.

Though, the Lord is speaking spiritually here, it was based on real life experiences.

There were also dangers of wild animals which would be included in Paul's "perils in the wilderness" and "perils in the cities." One example can be found the interaction with Jesus and the Canaanite woman.

Matthew 15:22-28
Behold, a Canaanite woman came…saying, "Have mercy on me, Lord, you son of David! My daughter is severely possessed by a demon!" But he answered her not a word. His disciples came and begged him, saying, "Send her away; for she cries after us." But he answered, "I wasn't sent to anyone but the lost sheep of the house of Israel." But she came and worshiped him, saying, "Lord, help me." But he answered, "It is not appropriate to take the children's bread and throw it to the dogs." But she said, "Yes, Lord, but even the dogs eat the crumbs which fall from their masters' table." Then Jesus answered her, "Woman, great is your faith! Be it done to you even as you desire." And her daughter was healed from that hour.

The dogs referred to were not pets as we think of them today but wild dogs who roamed the city and countryside. Of course, there were always wild animals to contend with.

As can be seen, the necessity of a staff to protect oneself against minor difficulties was still necessary.

The Disciples' Intentions

One incident among the disciples may indicate their expectation to defend Jesus with staffs in hand. When Jesus had received message that Lazarus was sick, He purposely remained where He was to allow Lazarus to die. After two days, Jesus announced that they should travel to Judea. Then the disciples immediately reacted by asking a question.

John 11:8
The disciples told him, "Rabbi, the Jews were just trying to stone you, and are you going there again?"

Jesus did not respond to the question but explained that Lazarus was asleep and needed to be wakened. The disciples thought He meant that Lazarus was physically asleep rather than dead. This puzzled them. Could Lazarus just recover with Jesus being put in great danger of death? Once Jesus revealed that He was speaking of physical death, Thomas made an amazing declaration.

John 11:16
Thomas therefore, who is called Didymus, said to his fellow disciples, "Let's go also, that we may die with him."

What could Thomas have really meant? Did he mean that they would follow Jesus, and all stand around and watch Him be stoned? Did he think they would follow Him and all stand with Him passively while they all were stoned? I suggest that he would have meant that they would all go and stand with Him and defend themselves, if necessary. This would not have been a legal trial; it would be a mob desiring to stone him as soon as they saw the Lord. It is most likely that they proceeded with staffs in hand to defend our Lord against a mob attack. Thomas expected to lose that battle and die with Christ.

The Secondary Uses

Though we do not see the staff mentioned as much in the New Testament, we can assume it was used in the same ways as the Old Testament. Here are a few examples.

The Picking Up of Objects

It is interesting to note that when Jesus was on the cross and became thirsty, it was a staff with a sponge on the top that was used to give Him vinegar to drink.

Matthew 27:48
Immediately one of them ran, and took a sponge, and filled it with vinegar, and put it on a reed [staff], and gave him a drink.

Mark 15:36
One ran, and filling a sponge full of vinegar, put it on a reed [staff], and gave it to him to drink, saying, "Let him be. Let's see whether Elijah comes to take him down."

So, the staff was utilized to pick up objects in the first century as well.

The Measuring as a Rod

Because of the length and its common use, the staff could be used to measure objects of various lengths. There are two illustrations of this use in Revelation.

In Revelation 11, John describes using the staff to measure the heavenly temple which was another of the uses of a staff by the people.

Revelation 11:1
A rod like a staff was given to me. Someone said, "Rise, and measure God's temple, and the altar, and those who worship in it" (DEJ).

Here the first word "rod" is the material the staff would have been made out of which is a reed. So, John measured with a staff made from a reed.

Revelation 21:15-16
He who spoke with me had for a measure, a golden reed [staff], to measure the city, its gates, and its walls. The city is square, and its length is as great as its width. He measured the city with the reed [staff], twelve thousand twelve stadia. Its length, width, and height are equal. Its wall is one hundred forty-four cubits...angel.

Once again, a staff was used to measure the New Jerusalem. It is referred to by the material from which it was commonly made.

The Symbolism of Divine Authority

As in Israel's history, the staff continued to be used to speak of authority and power. In Revelation, we have seen it used to refer to divine authority.

Revelation 2:27
He [Christ] will rule them with a rod of iron, shattering them like clay pots.

Revelation 12:5
She gave birth to a son [Christ], a male child, who is to rule all the nations with a rod of iron. Her child was caught up to God, and to his throne.

Revelation 19:15
Out of his mouth proceeds a sharp, double-edged sword, that with it he should strike the nations. He [Christ] will rule them with an iron rod.

The Designation of Rulership

As in Hebrew history, the staff continued to be used to designate rulership. In Revelation, it refers to the rulership believers will have in the Millennium. In chapter 2, Jesus tells the church at Thyatira that if they persist in their faith and obedience, He will allow them to rule with Him.

Revelation 2:26-27
He who overcomes, and he who keeps my works to the end, to him I

will give authority over the nations. He will rule them with a rod [staff] of iron, shattering them like clay pots; as I also have received of my Father.*

The point of this chapter is to demonstrate that the staff has always been carried by Jewish men and was carried by the disciples. Though it had many uses, the main use would be for self-defense.

The Distinction from a Club

There are two Greek words used interchangeably for the staff. Yet, when the Lord Jesus was arrested by the Jewish leaders, the temple police, and a mob, the mob was carrying clubs (a different Greek word).

Matthew 26:55
In that hour Jesus said to the multitudes, "Have you come out as against a robber with swords and clubs to seize me? I sat daily in the temple teaching, and you didn't arrest me."

Mark 14:48
Jesus answered them, "Have you come out, as against a robber, with swords and clubs to seize me?"

Luke 22:52
Jesus said to the chief priests, captains of the temple, and elders, who had come against him, "Have you come out as against a robber, with swords and clubs?"

The Jewish leaders would not have been carrying clubs; they would leave the arrest up to the temple police. This group would have been carrying swords. The mob of malcontents, troublemakers, and rabble rousers would have grabbed some wood or branches and taken off with the crowd.

The Greek word translated "club" refers to the "sticks that are made from trees." A club would have been cut off a branch, quickly shaped, and taken to commit their mayhem.

The Acquisition of a Staff

The reason a man could carry a staff was due to the fact it was readily available. It can be made from common elements. If one desired the top portion of the staff to be more ornate or stronger, it could be forged by the village blacksmiths out of metal.

The Building with Common Elements

The staff could be a branch cut from a tree.

In this passage, we see Jacob cutting rods from a tree to produce a breeding result among his sheep. Though Jacob was not using the rods for a staff, this is how they were made.

Genesis 30:37-38
Jacob took to himself rods of fresh poplar, almond, and plane tree, peeled white streaks in them, and made the white appear which was in the rods. He set the rods which he had peeled opposite the flocks in...troughs where the flocks came to drink. They conceived when they came to drink.

In the prophecy against the princes of Israel, he compares them to a dry branch though they came from a fruitful one.

Ezekiel 19:10-11
Your mother was like a vine in your blood, planted by the waters. It was fruitful and full of branches by reason of many waters. It had strong branches for the scepters of those who ruled.

Ezekiel 19:13-14
Now it is planted in the wilderness, in a dry and thirsty land. Fire has gone out of its branches. It has devoured its fruit, so that there is in it no strong branch to be a scepter to rule.

Though this is an analogy, we can see that a strong branch would be chosen to cut into a rod for use as protection.

The staff could be cut from a reed.

Reeds were not as strong but plentiful and could be cut quickly and used for many purposes.

Isaiah 36:6
Behold, you trust in the staff of this bruised reed, even in Egypt, which if a man leans on it, it will go into his hand and pierce it. So is Pharaoh king of Egypt to all who trust in him.

Ezekiel 29:6
All the inhabitants of Egypt will know that I am Yahweh, because they have been a staff of reed to the house of Israel.

Notice, reeds could be bruised more easily than tree branches, but they are more readily available.

The Carving of a Crest or Symbol

The staff could be personalized for a particular person so it could be identified. After Tamar dressed up as a prostitute, she required Judah to give her his signet ring, cord, and staff. The signet ring had the personal symbol on it which is pressed in hot wax to seal documents. The cord was most likely a special bracelet made of woven interlocking small cords. The staff would have been carved with the name and symbol of the person. All three would have been easily identifiable.

Genesis 38:25
When she was brought out, she sent to her father-in-law, saying, "I am with child by the man who owns these." She also said, "Please discern whose these are — the signet, and the cords, and the staff."

If Judah hadn't recognized the three objects, she would have been disgraced and possibly stoned. He did recognize them and declared that Tamar was more righteous than he. Why? He would not give her his youngest son to raise up offspring.

When Aaron's priestly authority was challenged by Israel's people, God caused the rod with Aaron's name on it to bud. This reaffirmed Aaron's standing before God.

Numbers 17:3
You shall write Aaron's name on Levi's rod. There shall be one rod for each head of their fathers' houses.

Numbers 17:6
Moses spoke to the children of Israel; and all their princes gave him rods, for each prince one, according to their fathers' houses, a total of twelve rods. Aaron's rod was among their rods.

He carved the rod of Levi with his name. Rods were able to be carved in order to identify them.

The Forging with Metals

The staff became a symbol of rulership and was referred to as a scepter. Some kings had their scepters forged from gold.

Esther 5:2
When the king saw Esther the queen standing in the court, she obtained favor in his sight; and the king held out to Esther the golden scepter.... So Esther came near, and touched the top of the scepter.

HOW CHRISTIANS MAY DEFEND THEMSELVES AGAINST ATTACK

Esther 8:4
Then the king held out to Esther the golden scepter. So Esther arose, and stood before the king.

In Revelation, Jesus will rule with a rod of iron. This could be only metaphorical or even possibly with iron itself which would be forged by a blacksmith.

Revelation 19:15
Out of his mouth proceeds a sharp, double-edged sword, that with it he should strike the nations. He will rule them with an iron rod. He treads the wine press of the fierceness of the wrath of God, the Almighty.

Iron spoke of strength, power, and wrath.

The Defense with Weapons

Besides the staff, weapons of various kinds are found all throughout the Scriptures. They are mentioned as far back as Genesis 3 after man's fall. Once Adam and Eve were thrown out of the garden, God placed an angel with a flaming sword to protect its entrance.

Genesis 3:23-24
Therefore Yahweh God sent him out from the garden of Eden, to till the ground from which he was taken. So he drove out the man; and he placed cherubim at the east of the garden of Eden, and a flaming sword which turned every way, to guard the way to the tree of life.

He could not allow the couple to eat of the Tree of Life and remain in their sin forever.

At the end of chapter 4, the inventor of the first weapons made of bronze and iron is identified.

Genesis 4:19-22
Lamech took two wives: the name of the first one was Adah, and the name of the second one was Zillah. Adah gave birth to Jabal, who was the father of those who dwell in tents and have livestock. His brother's name was Jubal, who was the father of all who handle the harp and pipe. Zillah also gave birth to Tubal Cain, the forger of every cutting instrument of bronze and iron. Tubal Cain's sister was Naamah.

The final weapon is utilized at the return of Christ.

Revelation 19:11-16
I saw the heaven opened, and behold, a white horse, and he who sat on it is called Faithful and True. In righteousness he judges and makes war. His eyes are a flame of fire, and on his head are many crowns. He has names written and a name written which no one knows but he himself. He is clothed in a garment sprinkled with blood. His name is called "The Word of God." The armies which are in heaven followed him on white horses, clothed in white, pure, fine linen. Out of his mouth proceeds a sharp, double-edged sword, that with it he should strike the nations. He will rule them with an iron rod. He has on his garment and on his thigh a name written, "KING OF KINGS, AND LORD OF LORDS."

The Lord Jesus Christ returns with a sword coming out of His mouth and does battle with the evil forces of men and the demons behind them.

The Purpose of Their Creation

Weapons can be used offensively and defensively. Yet, as we ponder the human condition, it becomes so obvious that weapons are always created and developed for safety first. It is not the desire to attack others that is foremost on the mind of men, rather it is the compulsion to protect themselves and

HOW CHRISTIANS MAY DEFEND THEMSELVES AGAINST ATTACK

those they love from attack. As we saw in the initial chapters, murder is on the heart of some men but defending oneself is in the heart of all men.

The Bible is filled with face-to-face violent confrontations, skirmishes, and wars where weapons are used for defense. The creation and use of these weapons clearly demonstrate that self-defense and the defense of others is an anticipated necessity on an individual, regional, and national level. A few examples should suffice.

When Nehemiah returned to the land after the Babylonian captivity, he desired to build the wall around their new city. The wall was a necessary protection from enemies or those will wrong intentions. So, he went out to survey the damage.

Nehemiah 2:13
I went out by night by the valley gate, even toward the jackal's well, then to the dung gate, and inspected the walls of Jerusalem, which were broken down, and its gates were consumed with fire.

Once he saw the destruction, he realized that the Hebrews who had returned were virtually without any defense.

Nehemiah 2:17
Then I said to them, "You see the bad situation that we are in, how Jerusalem lies waste, and its gates are burned with fire. Come, let's build up the wall of Jerusalem, that we won't be disgraced."

The disgrace he had spoken about involved many issues, one of which was their inability to defend themselves. Sanballat, the regional leader, mocked it.

Nehemiah 4:1
But when Sanballat heard that we were building the wall, he was angry, and was very indignant, and mocked the Jews.

The mockery involved how weak and small it was.

Nehemiah 4:3
Now Tobiah the Ammonite was by him, and he said, "What they are building, if a fox climbed up it, he would break down their stone wall."

Nehemiah and the returning people began work on it.

Nehemiah 4:6
So we built the wall; and all the wall was joined together to half its height: for the people had a mind to work.

Of course, the Gentiles who were living in the land were not happy that the Jews were back and building their city again.

Nehemiah 4:7
But when Sanballat, Tobiah, the Arabians, the Ammonites, and the Ashdodites heard that the repairing of the walls of Jerusalem went forward, and that the breaches began to be filled, they were very angry.

What was Nehemiah's reaction? Should they just love them? Meet their needs? No, they prepared to defend all that were involved.

Nehemiah 4:13-16
Therefore I set guards in the lowest parts of the space behind the wall, in the open places. I set the people by family groups with their swords, their spears, and their bows. I looked, and rose up, and said to the nobles, to the rulers, and to the rest of the people, "Don't be afraid of them! Remember the Lord, who is great and awesome, and fight for your brothers, your sons, your daughters, your wives, and your houses." When our enemies heard that it was known to us, and God had brought their counsel to nothing, all of us returned to the

wall, everyone to his work. From that time forth, half of my servants did the work, and half of them held the spears, the shields, the bows, and the coats of mail; and the rulers were behind...house of Judah.

Notice, the people were equipped with weaponry besides a personal staff. When Jonathon's friendship with David had deepened, he gave him some of his personal weapons to this man of God.

1 Samuel 18:4
Jonathan stripped himself of the robe...and gave it to David with his clothing, even including his sword, his bow, and his sash.

This gave David not only a wardrobe in which to enter the court but more suitable protection for his new status in Saul's court after conquering Goliath.

2 Kings 3:21
Now when all the Moabites heard that the kings had come up to fight against them, they gathered themselves together, all who were able to put on armor, young and old, and stood on the border.

The Defense of Individuals

In our discussion of weapons, we will concern ourselves first with the numerous weapons created for individuals to defend themselves found in the Bible. There will be no need to describe them since they are well known.

The Axe

Ezekiel 26:9
He will set his battering engines against your walls, and with his axes he will break down your towers.

The Bow, Arrow, and Quiver

Genesis 27:3
Now therefore, please take your weapons, your quiver and your bow, and go out to the field, and get me venison.

The Breastplate

Isaiah 59:17
He put on righteousness as a breastplate, and a helmet of salvation on his head. He put on garments of vengeance for clothing, and was clad with zeal as a mantle.

Coat of Mail

1 Samuel 17:38
Saul dressed David with his clothing. He put a helmet of bronze on his head, and he clad him with a coat of mail.

The Buckler (Small Hand Shield)

Psalm 35:1-2
Contend, Yahweh, with those who contend with me.... Take hold of shield and buckler, and stand up for my help.

The Chariot

Judges 4:2-3
Yahweh sold them into the hand of Jabin king of Canaan, who reigned in Hazor...The children of Israel cried to Yahweh, for he had nine hundred chariots of iron; and he mightily oppressed the children of Israel for twenty years.

The Greaves (Leg Armor)

1 Samuel 17:6
He had bronze shin armor on his legs [greaves] and a bronze javelin between his shoulders.

The Helmet

2 Chronicles 26:14
Uzziah prepared for them, even for all the army, shields, spears, helmets, coats of mail, bows, and stones for slinging.

The Mace (Possible Reference)

Habakkuk 3:13
You went out for the salvation of your people, for the salvation of your anointed. You crushed the head of the land of wickedness. You stripped them head to foot. Selah.

The Shield

2 Chronicles 12:10
King Rehoboam made shields of bronze in their place, and committed them to the hands of the captains of the guard, who kept the door of the king's house.

The Sling

Judges 20:16-17
Among all these soldiers…seven hundred chosen men…Every one of them could sling a stone at a hair and not miss. The men of Israel, besides Benjamin, were counted four hundred thousand men…war.

The Spear

2 Chronicles 11:11-12
He fortified the strongholds, and put captains in them, and stores of food, oil and wine. He put shields and spears in every city, and made them exceedingly strong. Judah and Benjamin belonged to him.

The Sword

Genesis 34:25
On the third day, when they were sore, two of Jacob's sons, Simeon and Levi, Dinah's brothers, each took his sword, came upon the unsuspecting city, and killed all the males.

Exodus 15:9
The enemy said, 'I will pursue. I will overtake. I will divide the plunder. My desire will be satisfied on them. I will draw my sword. My hand will destroy them.'

The Torch

Nahum 2:3
The shield of his mighty men is made red. The valiant men are in scarlet. The chariots flash with steel in the day of his preparation, and the pine spears are brandished.

The Horses and Horsemen

Hosea 2:18
In that day I will make a covenant for them with the animals of the field, and with the birds of the sky, and with the creeping things of the ground. I will break the bow, the sword, and the battle out of the land, and will make them lie down safely.

The Defense of Cities

The cities protected themselves with various structures which alerted them to an enemy's presence and then to keep the enemy out.

The Great Walls

Ezekiel 4:3
Take for yourself an iron pan, and set it for a wall of iron between you and the city. Then set your face toward it. It will be besieged, and you shall lay siege against it. This shall be a sign to the house of Israel.

Deuteronomy 28:52
They will besiege you in all your gates until your high and fortified walls in which you trusted come down throughout all your land....

The Watchtowers

Psalm 18:2
Yahweh is my rock, my fortress, and my deliverer; my God, my rock, in whom I take refuge; my shield, and the horn of my salvation, my high tower.

The Tower Weapons

2 Chronicles 26:14-15
The children of Benjamin gathered themselves together...to go out to battle against the children of Israel. In Jerusalem, he made devices, invented by skillful men, to be on the towers and on the battlements, with which to shoot arrows and great stones. His name spread far abroad, because he was marvelously helped until he was strong.

The Acquisition of These Weapons

The weapons were so important for defense that they were constantly being obtained in a variety of ways.

The Invention of Weaponry

Often weapons had to be invented because nations did not obviously share them with their enemies. Uzziah, the king, invented weapons and fortified Judah with them.

2 Chronicles 26:15
In Jerusalem, he made devices, invented by skillful men, to be on the towers and on the battlements, with which to shoot arrows and great stones. His name spread far abroad, because he was marvelously helped until he was strong.

This is just one illustration concerning the invention of many of the weapons in the Bible.

The Purchase of Weaponry

Weapons, especially horses and chariots for battle were purchased from others.

2 Chronicles 1:16-17
The horses which Solomon had were brought out of Egypt and from Kue. The king's merchants purchased them from Kue. They brought up and brought out of Egypt a chariot for six hundred pieces of silver, and a horse for one hundred fifty. They also exported them to the Hittite kings and the Syrian kings.

Notice, the kings had merchants who made purchases for them. Weapons would have been an essential one.

HOW CHRISTIANS MAY DEFEND THEMSELVES AGAINST ATTACK

We saw that Jesus told His disciples to purchase a sword, since things would become dangerous after His departure.

Luke 22:36
Then he said to them, "But now, whoever has a purse, let him take it, and likewise a wallet. Whoever has none, let him sell his cloak, and buy a sword."

So, some weapons had to be purchased if enough could not be acquired or if superior ones were needed.

The Tribute of Weaponry

Weapons were sometimes presented as tribute to a ruler from another country. Here is one description of some of the tribute brought by people around the world in order to honor Solomon.

1 Kings 10:25
Year after year, every man brought his tribute, vessels of silver, vessels of gold, clothing, armor, spices, horses, and mules.

So, tribute was another way to obtain weapons. This would allow the acquisition of unique weapons they may not have had.

The Plunder of Weaponry

Weapons were confiscated as plunder in war. The people of Israel were told to take plunder after they had won battles against certain nations and not others. Of course, weapons most likely would have been taken in any case. Can anyone imagine conquering an army and then leaving the weapons, especially ones they had not seen before?

Deuteronomy 20:14
But the women, the little ones, the livestock, and all that is in the city, even all its plunder, you shall take for plunder for yourself. You may use the plunder of your enemies, which Yahweh...given you.

Here is a simple example.

2 Samuel 8:4
David took from him one thousand seven hundred horsemen and twenty thousand footmen. David hamstrung all the chariot horses, but reserved of them for one hundred chariots. Lord teaches hand to war.

Obviously, once warriors were killed on the battlefield, why wouldn't they confiscate their weapons?

The Building of Weaponry

Weapons were constantly being built as threats increased and they were destroyed or taken on the battlefield. Hezekiah made weapons when Sennacherib came to war against him.

2 Chronicles 32:5
He took courage, built up all the wall that was broken down, and raised it up to the towers, with the other wall outside...strengthened Millo in David's city, and made weapons and shields in abundance.

Defense was always on their minds.

As can be seen many weapons were invented, purchased, accepted as tribute, and taken as plunder for protection and defense because it was an anticipated necessity in an evil world. Therefore, self-defense and the defense of others is a legitimate practice against the possibility of murder.

Chapter 14

The Biblical Significance

Self-defense and the defense of others is a valid approach to dealing with violence because it has a prominent place in both our scriptural history and theology.

The Historical Precedence

The greatest deed that is proclaimed in Israel's history from the Old Testament is God's deliverance of Israel from Egypt. This event was considered a great moment of redemption. In fact, it was a great act of defense. God defended Israel from the bondage of the Egyptians.

The Celebration of the Deliverance

When Pharaoh would not release His people after so many plagues, the Lord God sent the angel of death to kill the first-born child in every household. He spared the Hebrews from this threat and told them to celebrate this momentous event as the Passover annually.

Leviticus 23:4-5
These are the set feasts of Yahweh, even holy convocations, which you shall proclaim in their appointed season. In the first month, on the fourteenth day...in the evening, is Yahweh's Passover.

This historic moment of the Lord God's defense of His people warranted a great annual celebration.

The Recitation by Moses

In Deuteronomy 6, before Israel was to enter the Promised Land, Moses gives them a series of commands.

Deuteronomy 6:21
Then you shall tell your son, 'We were Pharaoh's slaves in Egypt. Yahweh brought us out of Egypt with a mighty hand.

The Lord God's mighty hand involved the ultimate defense of Israel which involved much bloodshed.

As Moses prepares Israel to enter the Promised Land, he mentions this significant event numerous times.

Deuteronomy 7:8
But because Yahweh loves you, and because he would keep the oath which he swore to your fathers, has Yahweh brought you out with a mighty hand, and redeemed you out of the house of bondage, from the hand of Pharaoh king of Egypt.

Deuteronomy 11:3
And his signs, and his works, which he did in the midst of Egypt to Pharaoh the king of Egypt, and to all his land.

Deuteronomy 29:2
Moses called to all Israel, and said to them, You have seen all that Yahweh did before your eyes in the land of Egypt to Pharaoh, and to all his servants, and to all his land.

Deuteronomy 34:11
In all the signs and the wonders, which Yahweh sent him to do in the land of Egypt, to Pharaoh, and to all his servants, and to all his land.

This was a critical moment for Israel.

The Dedication of the First-Born

The Lord God required every first-born to be dedicated to Him because He killed the first-born of the Egyptians to defend His people and free them.

Numbers 3:13
For all the firstborn are mine. On the day that I struck down all the firstborn in the land of Egypt I made holy to me all the firstborn in Israel, both man and animal. They shall be mine. I am Yahweh.

Numbers 8:17
For all the firstborn among the children of Israel are mine, both man and animal. On the day that I struck all the firstborn in the land of Egypt, I sanctified them for myself.

Every family was faced with the remembrance of God's defense of His people with the dedication of their first born.

The Reference in Time

We see the historical significance of this deliverance when time is discussed in reference to bringing His people out of Egypt.

Numbers 1:1
Yahweh spoke to Moses in the wilderness of Sinai, in the Tent of Meeting, on the first day of the second month, in the second year after they had come out of the land of Egypt, saying.

1 Kings 6:11
In the four hundred and eightieth year after the children of Israel had come out of the land of Egypt, in the fourth year of Solomon's reign over Israel, in the month Ziv, which is the second month, he began to build Yahweh's house.

The Continual Divine Reference

The Lord Almighty will often refer to His deliverance of the Hebrews when He spoke to the nation of Israel. Therefore, God continually referenced His defense of them in Egypt.

1 Samuel 2:27
A man of God came to Eli, and said to him, "Yahweh says, 'Did I reveal myself to the house of your father, when they were in Egypt in bondage to Pharaoh's house?'"

1 Kings 8:16
Since the day that I brought my people Israel out of Egypt, I chose no city out of all the tribes of Israel to build a house, that my name might be there; but I chose David to be over my people Israel.

Isaiah 10:26
Yahweh of Armies will stir up a scourge against him, as in the slaughter of Midian at the rock of Oreb. His rod will be over the sea, and he will lift it up like he did against Egypt.

The Concern of Other Nations

When the Philistines had captured the ark and God had wreaked so much havoc upon them, they decided to return it. They discussed among themselves what kind of offering they should send with it based on God's defense of His people in Egypt. Some of them did not desire to offer something and were rebuked by others. In 1 Samuel 6, the author describes this indictment.

1 Samuel 6:6
Why then do you harden your hearts, as the Egyptians and Pharaoh hardened their hearts? When he had worked wonderfully among them, didn't they let the people go, and they departed?

HOW CHRISTIANS MAY DEFEND THEMSELVES AGAINST ATTACK

When the spies from Joshua came to Jericho, Rahab and her people had heard of what the Lord God had done in Egypt and were afraid.

Joshua 2:9-11
She said to the men, "I know that Yahweh has given you the land, and that the fear of you has fallen upon us, and that all the inhabitants of the land melt away before you. For we have heard how Yahweh dried up the water of the Red Sea before you, when you came out of Egypt; and what you did to the two kings of the Amorites, who were beyond the Jordan, to Sihon and to Og, whom you utterly destroyed. As soon as we had heard it, our hearts melted, and there wasn't any more spirit in any man, because of you: for Yahweh your God, he is God in heaven above, and on earth beneath.

The nations all knew that the God of the Hebrews defends His people.

The Event Remembered

In Nehemiah 9, when Nehemiah returned to the land of Israel and finally built the wall around the city after a long absence in captivity, they celebrated. In their prayers, they proclaimed His deliverance from Egypt.

Nehemiah 9:9-10
You saw the affliction of our fathers in Egypt, and heard their cry by the Red Sea, and showed signs and wonders against Pharaoh, and against all his servants, and against all the people of his land; for you knew that they dealt proudly against them, and made a name for yourself, as it is today. You divided the sea before them, so that they went through the middle of the sea on the dry land; and you cast their pursuers into the depths, as a stone into the mighty waters.

This great defense of Israel was called to mind as God's great demonstration of His power and might.

In Romans 9, when Paul argued that the Lord God has mercy on whom He desires, the apostle brings up this mighty event.

Romans 9:17-19
For the Scripture says to Pharaoh, "For this very purpose I caused you to be raised up, that I might show in you my power, and that my name might be published abroad in all the earth." So then, he has mercy on whom he desires, and he hardens whom he desires. You will say...to me, "Why does he still find fault? For who withstands his will?"

The Inspired Praise

In the inspired songs and prayers of Israel, one will often find praise to God for either His direct defense of the psalmist personally or His defense of the nation of Israel collectively. We will even find praise for victory in self-defense. These may involve very violent events in their histories. These psalms became the songs of both Old and New Testament saints.

The Praise for Many Deliverances from God

In Psalm 135, the Psalmist speaks of the great exodus of Israel and other victories God brought as He defended His nation.

First, he opens with a praise.

Psalm 135:1
Praise Yah! Praise Yahweh's name! Praise him, you servants of Yahweh.

Then in verses 8-12, he lists victories God wrought for them.

HOW CHRISTIANS MAY DEFEND THEMSELVES AGAINST ATTACK

Psalm 135:8-12
Who struck the firstborn of Egypt, both of man and animal; Who sent signs and wonders into the middle of you, Egypt, on Pharaoh, and on all his servants; who struck many nations, and killed mighty kings, Sihon king of the Amorites, Og king of Bashan, and all the kingdoms of Canaan, and gave their land for a heritage, a heritage to Israel, his people.

We see the same in the next psalm. In Psalm 136, the inspired author begins with the Lord God's "good, loving, and kind" nature.

Psalm 136:1
Give thanks to Yahweh, for he is good; for his loving kindness endures forever.

He then explains how God's goodness, love, and kindness led to many victories in battle.

Psalm 136:10-21
To him [Lord God] who struck down the Egyptian firstborn; For his lovingkindness endures forever; And brought out Israel from among them; For his lovingkindness endures forever; With a strong hand, and with an outstretched arm; For his lovingkindness endures... To him who divided the Red Sea apart; For his lovingkindness endures forever; Made Israel to pass through the midst...his lovingkindness endures forever; But overthrew Pharaoh and his host in the Red Sea; For his lovingkindness endures forever: To him who led his people through the wilderness; For his lovingkindness endures...To him who struck great kings; For his lovingkindness endures forever; And killed mighty kings; For his lovingkindness endures forever: Sihon king of the Amorites; For his lovingkindness endures forever; Og king of Bashan; For his lovingkindness endures forever; And gave...land as an inheritance...his lovingkindness endures forever.

Then he concludes with a powerful proclamation of the Lord God's defense of the nation of Israel.

Psalm 136:24
And has delivered us from our adversaries; For his lovingkindness endures forever.

The Praise of David for Deliverance

King David fled from his son Absalom who had taken over his throne. In the wilderness, he and his men were hiding out from Absalom's army. The king knew that a fierce battle was eminent, and he was already praising God for His defense of the rightful king. David begins with praise.

Psalm 63:1-5
God, you are my God. I will earnestly seek you. My soul thirsts for you. My flesh longs for you, in a dry and weary land, where there is no water. So I have seen you in the sanctuary, Watching your power and your glory. Because your lovingkindness is better than life, My lips shall praise you. So I will bless you while I live. I will lift up my hands in your name. My soul shall be satisfied as with the richest food. My mouth shall praise you with joyful lips.

He remembers how God had defended him in the past so many times.

Psalm 63:6-7
When I remember you on my bed and think about you in the night watches…been my help. I will rejoice in the shadow of your wings.

As a result of His past protection, he would rely on Him in the present.

Psalm 63:8
My soul stays close to you. Your right hand holds me up.

Then the king declares his expectation that the Lord God will deliver him in this difficult circumstance.

HOW CHRISTIANS MAY DEFEND THEMSELVES AGAINST ATTACK

Psalm 63:9-11
But those who seek my soul, to destroy it, shall go into the lower parts of the earth. They shall be given over to the power of the sword. They shall be jackal food. But the king shall rejoice in God. Everyone who swears by him will praise him, For the mouth of those who speak lies shall be silenced.

David knew the Lord would work through him and his men to gain the kingdom back. The Lord would defend them as they were defending themselves.

In Psalm 18, David had just been delivered from pursuit of Saul. Saul had attempted to kill the future king in violation of God's direct command. Now, he was dead and David was full of joy.

Psalm 18:1-3
I love you, Yahweh, my strength. Yahweh is my rock, my fortress, and my deliverer; my God, my rock, in whom I take refuge; my shield, and the horn of my salvation [deliverance], my high tower. I call on Yahweh, who is worthy to be praised...I am saved [delivered] from my enemies.

In verse 3-5, he praises God for defending him.

Psalm 18:3-5
I call on Yahweh, who is worthy to be praised; and I am saved from my enemies. The cords of death surrounded me. The floods of ungodliness made me afraid. The cords of Sheol were around me. The snares of death came on me.

Then in verse 34-35, David continues his song.

Psalm 18:34-35
He teaches my hands to war, so that my arms bend a bow of bronze. You have also given me the shield of your salvation. Your right hand [power] sustains me. Your gentleness has made me great.

David was fleeing for his life and the Lord God gave Him the strength to be a great warrior and defend himself. The power of God sustained him in time of battle. He fought but knew God would fight with him.

During his run from Saul, David was not a soldier in active duty. He had been a great soldier in the past but was now functioning as a private citizen. Though he would not kill Saul because he was still God's king on the throne, he certainly killed many others in self-defense and attributed it to the Lord's power. God is praised for this.

The Praise of Others for Deliverance

There are many other places in the Scriptures which praise God for His deliverance.

Exodus 18:9-10
Jethro rejoiced for all the goodness which Yahweh had done to Israel, in that he had delivered them out of the hand of the Egyptians. 10 Jethro said, "Blessed be Yahweh, who has delivered you out of the hand of the Egyptians, and out of the hand of Pharaoh; who has delivered the people from under the hand of the Egyptians."

Jeremiah 20:12-13
But Yahweh of Armies…let me see your vengeance on them, for I have revealed my cause to you. Sing to Yahweh! Praise Yahweh, for he has delivered the soul of the needy from the hand of evildoers.

Psalm 34:17
The righteous cry, and Yahweh hears, and delivers them out of all their troubles.

Psalm 34:19
Many are the afflictions of the righteous, but Yahweh delivers him out of them all.

Psalm 97:10
You who love Yahweh, hate evil! He preserves the souls of his saints. He delivers them out of the hand of the wicked.

Psalm 107:6-8
Then they cried to Yahweh in their trouble, and he delivered them out of their distresses. he led them also by a straight way, that they might go to a city to live in. Let them praise Yahweh for his loving kindness, for his wonderful deeds to the children of men!

As can be seen, God's defense of His people fills the praises of His people both in the Old and New Testaments. We see this in real life as God protects us from of evil and harm.

The Faith-Based Examples

The defending of oneself or others can be a faith-based act worthy of reward. In the "Hall of Faith" in Hebrews chapter eleven, many acts of defense are applauded by the author and used as examples of faith.

The Faith of Those Who Left Egypt

In Hebrews 11, it describes the act of faith that the people of God demonstrated when leaving Egypt,

Hebrews 11:29
By faith, they passed through the Red Sea as on dry land. When the Egyptians tried to do so, they were swallowed up.

This act of faith depended upon the Lord God to deliver them. God's act was to miraculously separate the waters. Their act of faith was to defend themselves by rushing onto the dry land believing that the walls would remain up.

The Faith of Rahab

In Hebrews 11, Rahab acted in faith by defending herself and her family in Jericho from the Israelite army that God was sending to defeat them.

Hebrews 11:31
By faith, Rahab the prostitute, didn't perish with those who were disobedient, having received the spies in peace.

She received the spies because of her faith. Yet, she was also defending herself from the harm their God was about to do.

The Faith of Israel's Leaders

Then in Hebrews 11, the author acknowledges leaders who went into battle to protect themselves and their nation.

Hebrews 11:32-34
What more shall I say? For the time would fail me if I told of Gideon, Barak, Samson, Jephthah, David, Samuel, and the prophets. Who, through faith subdued kingdoms, worked...righteousness, obtained promises, stopped the mouths of lions, quenched the power of fire, escaped the edge of the sword, from weakness were made strong, grew mighty in war, and caused foreign armies to flee.

These people saw great power in endurance and deliverance.

The Faith of the Courageous Sufferers

Finally, in Hebrews 11:35-40, the inspired author describes others who had to face the persecution and could not defend themselves due to the overwhelming odds against them.

Hebrews 11:35-40
Others were tortured, not accepting their deliverance, that they might obtain a better resurrection. Others were tried by mocking and scourging, yes, moreover by bonds and imprisonment. They were stoned. They were sawn apart. They were tempted. They were slain with the sword. They went around in sheep skins and in goat skins; being destitute, afflicted, ill-treated (of whom the world was not worthy), wandering in deserts, mountains, caves, and the holes of the earth. These all, having had testimony given to them through their faith, didn't receive the promise, God having provided some better thing concerning us, so that apart from us they should not be made perfect.

Their acts of faith were to endure and be delivered from their persecution through death. This was God's final defense.

The Baptist's Omission

In this section, we will consider the testimony of the last and greatest of the Old Testament prophets: John the Baptist. This forerunner of the Lord Jesus Christ is crucial in our study of self-defense because a group of soldiers asked him what they must do to repent and what John said and did not say provides us insight concerning his views on self-defense and the defense of others. Of course, this is certainly not the only argument for self-defense nor is it the most critical. Yet, his reaction and response to these soldiers certainly provides evidence that self-defense and the defense of others are holy and righteous deeds.

Included in this chapter will be the reaction and response of Jesus and His disciples to the various soldiers they also encountered during the course of their ministries and what was said and not said, done and not done. When one comes to hear the gospel and an important element of it is repentance and the turning of one's life around for the Lord Jesus, it will be interesting to note whether their soldiering or military service became an issue.

The question is simple: did they rebuke soldiers for being soldiers or defending themselves as soldiers and did they require repentance of this action for salvation. In Romans 13, Paul explains their function.

Romans 13:3-4
For rulers are not a terror to the good work, but to the evil. Do you desire to have no fear of the authority? Do that which is good, and you will have praise from the same, for he is a servant of God to you for good. But if you do that which is evil, be afraid, for he doesn't bear the sword in vain; for he is a servant of God, an avenger for wrath to him who does evil.

These servants of God who bear the sword (soldiers, police officers, etc.) derive their authority ultimately from God. He uses them to establish order, stop evil, and encourage good.

In 1 Peter 2, the apostle agrees with Paul.

1 Peter 2:13-14
Therefore, subject yourselves to every ordinance of man for the Lord's sake: whether to the king, as supreme; or to governors, as sent by him for vengeance on evildoers and for praise to those who do well.

These men and women provide God's judgment on evil and His praise on good. Obviously, this is not perfectly done because they are not perfect people. Yet, they are not only servants of God and human authorities, but real people!

First, we should make a distinction between soldiers acting as agents of the government and also acting as individuals.

HOW CHRISTIANS MAY DEFEND THEMSELVES AGAINST ATTACK

When soldiers are in battle, they are not only defending their nation but also themselves as well. When police officers are engaged in a gun battle, they are not only defending their city but themselves as well. When firefighters are fighting a fire in a home, they are not only defending the home's occupants but themselves as well. If all of them weren't, then they could simply die in the line of duty without any thought of their well-being.

Yet, they are not simply robots acting at the command of some higher authority but real people who must look out for their own well-being as well. If the soldiers or officers had to kill someone in order to protect their own lives, they would not say that they did it to protect the citizens of a nation or city, they would say they were protecting themselves as real people. This is an important difference and should be kept in mind as we discuss the words and actions of John the Baptist, Jesus, and the Disciples.

Who was John the Baptist and what authority did he have which would make what he said and did not say so critical to our discussion? Since he is such a familiar character in Scripture, we will only discuss the most relevant points to establish his spiritual authority to say what he said and do what he did.

The name "John the Baptist" meant "John the Immerser." This distinguished him from other John's not only in the Bible but in those days where there were no last names. People were usually designated by the city they were from (Jesus of Nazareth, Saul of Tarsus), the father they had (James and John, Sons of Zebedee, Simon Bar Jonah), or even some other designation (Simon the Zealot, Matthew the Tax-Gatherer). John immersed people in water and it was by this that he was well known. Of course, the fact that he preached repentance was the key to his ministry.

His Angelic Call

Zacharias and Elizabeth were John's righteous parents and were given his call to ministry by an angel. These two holy people had no children because Elizabeth was barren at first. Zacharias prayed to the Lord for her to conceive. Periodically, Zacharias, as a Levitical priest, would be ordered to serve in the temple.

While he was in the midst of serving, Gabriel, an angel of God, appeared to him to provide an answer to his prayer and announce his future son's role in the coming of the long-awaited Messiah.

Luke 1:13
But the angel said to him, "Don't be afraid, Zacharias, because your request has been heard, and your wife, Elizabeth, will bear you a son, and you shall call his name John."

After this angelic appearance, Zacharias questioned the possibility of a barren woman conceiving and was struck mute by the angel until the boy was born.

Luke 1:20
Behold, you will be silent and not able to speak, until the day that these things will happen, because you didn't believe my words, which will be fulfilled in their proper time.

Then, Luke describes the reaction to the people as they verified this miraculous birth and John's status.

Luke 1:22
When he came out, he could not speak to them, and they perceived that he had seen a vision in the temple. He continued making signs to them and remained mute. When the day had approached for his birth, the mother and father indicated that their son would be name

John (God is gracious). The people thought that was odd since no one in among his relatives had that name.

After this, the historian provides the people's response.

Luke 1:65-66
All who heard them laid them up in their heart, saying, 'What then will this child be?' The hand of the Lord was with him. His father Zacharias was filled with the Holy Spirit, and prophesied, saying.

This was not a one-time reaction, but continual conversation throughout the land. So, when John came baptizing, they would know this was no ordinary man.

His Devout Life

John lived a life devoted to the Lord God. He was filled with the Spirit all the days of his life and lived a life separated from the things of the world. He lived a life that he did not have to live as just an ordinary believer but desired to live as a spokesman for God. This authenticated his message.

In Luke 1:15, the angel described exactly what John would be like.

Luke 1:15
For he will be great in the sight of the Lord, and he will drink no wine nor strong drink. He will be filled with the Holy Spirit, even from his mother's womb.

Notice, he will not drink strong wine or strong drink. He would not be a drinker.

In Luke 7:33-34, the Lord Jesus compared His reputation to John's among the pharisees.

Luke 7:33-34
For John the Baptizer came neither eating bread nor drinking wine, and you say, "He has a demon." The Son of Man has come eating and drinking, and you say, "Behold, a gluttonous man, and a drunkard; a friend of tax collectors and sinners!"

Jesus made an important point. If the Jewish leaders opposed a person, they would twist whatever the person did to look sinful. John lived a life separate from the people and Jesus lived a life among the people. Both were accused of sin when neither were guilty. They said that John lived such an austere life that he must be demon-possessed. Perhaps, this was like the man among the tombs.

Matthew 8:28
When he came to the other side, into the country of the Gergesenes, two people possessed with demons met him there, coming forth out of the tombs, exceedingly fierce, so that no man could pass by....

Jesus drank the wine mixed with water (the staple drink of the day - wine killed the bacteria, etc.) and ate regular meals and he was a glutton and a drunk. I bring this up to simply mention the wholly separate and holy life that John lived. This was not for normal believers. John had a special task from God, and this demanded a lifestyle that would make people stand up and take-notice.

In Matthew 3:4, the author describes his lifestyle with some details.

Matthew 3:4
Now John himself wore clothing made of camel's hair, with a leather belt around his waist. His food was locusts and wild honey.

In Mark 1, Mark tells us that John the Baptist lived in the wilderness. This was a dessert rather than a forest.

HOW CHRISTIANS MAY DEFEND THEMSELVES AGAINST ATTACK

Mark 1:44
And said to him, "See you say nothing to anybody, but go show yourself to the priest, and offer for your cleansing the things which Moses commanded, for a testimony to them."

So, John lived in the wilderness and wore clothing that was simple, almost uncomfortable. He ate what he could find in the wilderness which was locusts and wild honey. He kept himself separate from the evil practices of the world and the temptations of people.

It was a lifestyle of self-sacrifice not self-indulgence. Then when he came, he preached a message of repentance. He lived a life where constant repentance would not be necessary. People would not point their finger at John and say, "Wasn't he in the tavern the other night?"

Also, he was filled with the Spirit from his mother's womb. When Mary went to visit Elizabeth, who was now six months pregnant, something miraculously occurred. Mary arose in those days and went into the hill country with haste, into a city of Judah, and entered into the house of Zacharias and greeted Elizabeth. When Elizabeth heard Mary's greeting, the baby leaped in her womb, and Elizabeth was filled with the Holy Spirit.

Luke 1:41
When Elizabeth heard Mary's greeting, the baby leaped in her womb; and Elizabeth was filled with the Holy Spirit. be a fulfillment of the things which have been spoken to her from the Lord!"

When this happened, Elizabeth began to share the good news with Mary. John had been filled with the Spirit and leaped in her womb when he heard Mary's voice. He was already identifying the Messiah to his own mother. It was probably here that the Spirit came upon John and never left.

So, when John spoke, people would have sensed the Spirit at work in him.

His Prophetic Significance

The ministry of John was foretold in the Old Testament and fulfilled through him in the New Testament. First, John himself testified as to who he was. In John 1:23, the apostle John records John the Baptist's own words.

John 1:23
He said, "I am the voice of one crying in the wilderness, 'Make straight the way of the Lord,' as Isaiah the prophet said."

The other three gospel writers identify John the Baptist as fulfilling the ancient prophecies.

Matthew 3:3
For this is he who was spoken of by Isaiah the prophet, saying, 'The voice of one crying in the wilderness, make ready the way of the Lord. Make his paths straight."

Mark 1:2-3
As it is written in the prophets, "Behold, I send my messenger before your face, who will prepare your way before you. The voice of one crying in the wilderness, 'Make ready the way of the Lord! Make his paths straight!'"

Luke 3:4
As it is written in the book of the words of Isaiah the prophet, "The voice of one crying in the wilderness, 'Make ready the way of the Lord. Make his paths straight.'"

Though Isaiah is primarily mentioned, there were actually two prophecies of the forerunner of the Messiah.

HOW CHRISTIANS MAY DEFEND THEMSELVES AGAINST ATTACK

In Isaiah 40, though Isaiah is initially speaking of the return of the Jewish people from their Babylonian captivity, it has a Messianic significance.

Isaiah 40:3
The voice of one who calls out, "Prepare the way of Yahweh in the wilderness! Make a level highway in the desert for our God."

Malachi also speaks of John's ministry.

Malachi 3:1
"Behold, I send my messenger, and he will prepare the way before me; and the Lord, whom you seek, will suddenly come to his temple; and the messenger of the covenant, whom you desire, behold, he comes!" says Yahweh of Armies.

Here, Malachi makes a distinction between the messenger who prepares the way (John the Baptist) and the messenger of the covenant (Jesus).

Then in Malachi 4, the prophet identifies this messenger as Elijah.

Malachi 4:5-6
Behold, I will send you Elijah the prophet before the great and terrible day of Yahweh comes. He will turn the hearts of the fathers to the children, and the hearts of the children to their fathers, lest I come and strike the earth with a curse.

Though this refers to Elijah, the angel Gabriel alludes to John's ministry in his prediction.

Luke 1;17
He will go before him in the spirit and power of Elijah." Then Jesus actually explains that had the people of Israel accepted Him as Messiah, John would have fulfilled that prophecy.

Matthew 11:12-15
From the days of John, the Baptizer until now, the Kingdom of Heaven suffers violence, and the violent take it by force. For all the prophets and the law prophesied until John. If you are willing to receive it, this is Elijah, who is to come. He who has ears to hear....

The coming of John the Baptist fulfilled prophecy. He knew it, Jesus knew it, John told people about it, and the gospels wrote of it. When the people inquired as to who John was, they had thought he was Elijah. They knew this prophecy and understood that he was fulfilling it.

His Kingdom Status

In Luke 1, the angel Gabriel speaks of John's importance in the kingdom.

Luke 1:15
For he will be great in the sight of the Lord, and he will drink no wine nor strong drink. He will be filled with the Holy Spirit, even from his mother's womb.

In Matthew 11, Jesus described John greatness.

Matthew 11:11
Most certainly I tell you, among those who are born of women there has not arisen anyone greater than John the Baptizer; yet he who is least in the Kingdom of Heaven is greater than he.

Here Jesus is comparing the people of the Old Covenant with the people of the New. John was the greatest of the Old Testament saints in terms of status as the forerunner of Jesus, yet any New Covenant saint will be greater because the New Covenant was much greater. Not only was John the greatest in God's Old Covenant Kingdom, but he was sent from God.

HOW CHRISTIANS MAY DEFEND THEMSELVES AGAINST ATTACK

In John 1, the apostle John makes a powerful statement about this forerunner.

John 1:6
There came a man, sent from God, whose name was John.

This is not simply a passing comment. He is declaring that this person was sent directly from God to do His work. He had a God-ordained position as a forerunner of Jesus Christ. When someone sent from God speaks and acts, their words and actions are from God.

His Prophetic Office

John the Baptist was the last of the many prophets of the Old Testament. In Luke 1, Zacharias, his father, prophesied that his son would be a prophet.

Luke 1:76
And you, child, will be called a prophet of the Most High, for you will go before the face of the Lord to prepare his ways.

As a prophet of the Most High God, He had the responsibility of identifying the Messiah.

John was the one who was to identify that Jesus was the Messiah.

John 1:7-8
The same came as a witness, that he might testify about the light, that all might believe through him. He was not the light, but was sent that he might testify about the light.

So, he prepared hearts for the light to come and then gave witness that Jesus was the light.

God confirmed to John that Jesus was the Messiah and then John confirmed it to the whole world. As John was baptizing, The Lord Jesus came and asked to be baptized by him, but John objected to this.

Matthew 3:13-17
Then Jesus came from Galilee to the Jordan to John, to be baptized by him. But John would have hindered him, saying, "I need to be baptized by you, and you come to me?" But Jesus, answering, said to him, "Allow it now, for this is the fitting way for us to fulfill all righteousness." Then he allowed him. Jesus, when he was baptized, went up directly from the water: and behold, the heavens were opened to him. He saw the Spirit of God descending as a dove, and coming on him. Behold, a voice out of the heavens said, "This is my beloved Son, with whom I am well pleased."

This was once again a communication to John as a prophet and to Jesus as the Messiah. Notice, John implies that Jesus was sinless because he did not have to be baptized and should have been baptizing him. Yet, Jesus wanting to fulfill all of the law desired this to happen. Once he was immersed, then our God confirmed His Sonship through the heavens opening, a descent of the Holy Spirit in the form of a dove, and the voice of God declaring who Jesus was.

We see later that John began declaring that Jesus was God's lamb who would die for men's sins.

John 1:29
The next day, he saw Jesus coming to him, and said, "Behold, the Lamb of God, who takes away the sin of the world!"

Then in verses 30-34, John the Baptist describes in detail that great moment of confirmation by the Father and the Spirit concerning the Son. This powerful message must have been preached many times after this.

John 1:30-34
This is he of whom I said, "After me comes a man who is preferred before me, for he was before me." I didn't know him, but for this reason I came baptizing in water: that he would be revealed to Israel. John testified, saying, "I have seen the Spirit descending like a dove out of heaven, and it remained on him. I didn't recognize him, but he who sent me to baptize in water, he said to me, 'On whoever you will see the Spirit descending, and remaining on him, the same is he who baptizes in the Holy Spirit.' I have seen, and have testified that this is the Son of God." Again, on the next day, John was standing with two of his disciples, and he looked at Jesus as he walked, and said, "Behold, the Lamb of God!"

John identified Jesus as the Messiah at other times also.

John 1:35-36
Again, the next day, John was standing with two of his disciples, and he looked at Jesus as he walked, and said, "Behold, the Lamb of God!"

John's testimony of the light was simple and clear: Jesus was the sinless Messiah, Son of God, and the lamb who would be sacrificed for the sins of the world.

His Divine Ministry

In Luke 1, Zacharias, John's father, prophesied that his son would be a prophet.

Luke 1:76
And you, child, will be called a prophet of the Most High, for you will go before the face of the Lord to prepare his ways.

Here his father even defines his divine ministry. He would be preparing the people for the coming of the Lord.

The angel described his ministry in Luke 1.

Luke 1:16-17
He will turn many of the children of Israel to the Lord, their God. He will go before him in the spirit and power of Elijah, "to turn the hearts of the fathers to the children," and the disobedient to the wisdom of the just; to prepare a people prepared for the Lord."

How did John ready the people for the coming of Jesus? He prepared them in several ways. He proclaimed the coming kingdom of God, the arrival of the Savior, the judgment of sin, and the need for repentance and confession.

Matthew, the Tax-gather describes these truths.

Matthew 3:1-2
In those days, John the Baptizer came, preaching in the wilderness of Judea, saying, "Repent, for the Kingdom of Heaven is at hand!"

Then, he adds this.

Matthew 3:6
They were baptized by him in the Jordan, confessing their sins.

His Demonstration of Its Necessity

John the Baptist was a prophet who had righteous parents, an angelic call, a miraculous conception, lived a devout life, had great kingdom status, a prophetic office, and a divine ministry. When He spoke, it mattered. It is important to our study of self-defense and the defense of others because he encountered a group of soldiers who asked him an important question. What he said and did not say adds much to our understanding of the Lord God's perspective on defense. It's not always what is said that matters.

HOW CHRISTIANS MAY DEFEND THEMSELVES AGAINST ATTACK

When he was preaching, he knew that many of the people thought that they were saved simply because they were Jews and Abraham was their father. They needed only to follow the detailed prescriptions of their leaders to be righteous. John stood against this false notion. Luke records the incident.

Luke 3:7-9
He said therefore to the multitudes who went out to be baptized by him, "You offspring of vipers, who warned you to flee from the wrath to come? Therefore produce fruits worthy of repentance, and don't begin to say among yourselves, 'We have Abraham for our father;' for I tell you that God is able to raise up children to Abraham from these stones! Even now…. Every tree…that doesn't produce good fruit is cut down, and thrown into the fire.'"

Their Jewish lineage was not enough to save them from God's judgment for their sins. The outward confession would not be enough to be delivered from the Lord's condemnation. True repentance had to be demonstrated. It had to produce fruit.

This led to an immediate question among the crowds. This is the question Luke records.

Luke 3:10-11
The multitudes asked him, "What then must we do?" He answered them, "He who has two coats, let him give to him who has none. He who has food, let him do likewise."

When asked, John said that they could begin with kind deeds to neighbors. Then specific groups of individuals desired to know exactly what John thought they should do?

Luke 3:12-13
Tax collectors also came to be baptized, and they said to him, "Teacher, what must we do?" He said to them, "Collect no more than that which is appointed to you."

Some soldiers were listening and began to wonder what they should do. In Luke 3, Luke describes the scene.

Luke 3:14
Soldiers also asked him, saying, "What about us? What must we do?" He said to them, "Extort from no one by violence, neither accuse anyone wrongfully. Be content with your wages."

Luke does not identify who the soldiers were, so it is better not to speculate. We do know that they were soldiers in active duty in combat roles. In fact, to identify them Luke uses a verb form (participle), not a noun. This particular word can best be translated "while soldiering, warring, doing battle, in active service."

In the first part of 1 Corinthians 9:7, when Paul argues that a minister of the gospel deserves wages, he looks into the world to make a comparison and asks, "What soldier ever serves at his own expense?"

1 Corinthians 9:7
What soldier ever serves at his own expense? Who plants a vineyard, and doesn't eat of its fruit? Or who feeds a flock, and doesn't drink from the flock's milk?

Here the words "soldier serves" are one word which is a verb in the Greek. It is better translated, "Who soldiers, (or wars, or battles, or is in active military service) at his own expense." Here Paul is speaking of real soldiers in active duty.

In 2 Corinthians 10:3, he uses the word to speak of spiritual warfare.

2 Corinthians 10:3-4
For though we walk in the flesh, we don't wage war according to the flesh; for the weapons of our warfare are not of the flesh....

HOW CHRISTIANS MAY DEFEND THEMSELVES AGAINST ATTACK

Here the verb is translated "wage war."

Now, we can easily translate the passage in Luke 3:14.

Luke 3:14
Soldiers also asked him, saying, "What about us? What must we do?" He said to them, "Extort from no one by violence, neither accuse anyone wrongfully. Be content with your wages."

It was "those waging war" who asked the question.

We see the same phrase in 1 Timothy 1:18 in the instruction of Paul to Timothy concerning his dealing with error and false doctrine in the church.

1 Timothy 1:18
This instruction I commit to you, my child Timothy, according to the prophecies which led the way to you, that by them you may wage the good warfare.

In James 4:1, James identifies the quarreling and conflicts among the Christians in the churches as "warring."

James 4:1
Where do wars and fightings among you come from? Don't they come from your pleasures that war in your members?" They were warring together.

So, this word is incredibly powerful in describing the real activity that these people were engaged in. They were in active service waging war. Some commentators go so far as to say that they may have been a unit marching to battle who had stopped to hear John. This is how strong the word is.

The verb translated "asked" in the English has a Greek ending which indicates it has a third person pronoun. The best translation is "They were asking while soldiering." These active-duty soldiers who were participating in battles, killing, and wars at that moment were questioning the Baptist as to how they could show their repentance. This is critical because they were in the midst of battles and war. How should they show their true sorrow and repentance over their sin? How should they turn toward righteousness?

John's answer involves three typical sins that those in governmental authority, who were carrying weapons and were used to fighting battles and war, should no longer stop engage in.

In Luke 3:15, Luke provides the Baptist's response.

Luke 3:15
He said to them, "Extort from no one by violence, neither accuse anyone wrongfully. Be content with your wages."

He begins with extortion. The phrase "extort from no one by violence" is all one word in the Greek which literally means a "to shake thoroughly, to make to tremble, to terrify, to agitate, to extort from one by intimidation money or other property." It portrays the idea of soldiers with their swords in hand threatening someone to get something from them. The people were afraid of soldiers because they had weapons and there were so many of them. These armored warriors would take full advantage of this.

The second phrase, "accuse anyone wrongly," is also one word meaning "to accuse wrongfully, to attack by malicious devices, to exact money wrongfully, to extort from, defraud." This deals with soldiers who threatened to bring false accusations upon a person if they did not comply with their wishes. It could also mean that they were lying about people to get revenge, extort, perhaps even to solve an investigation in a timely fashion. There are many reasons why those in authority with weapons might lie about someone.

The third phrase is "be content with your wages." The word translated "wages" refers to compensation for something one does." Here it means of course the wages a soldier earns plus the bed and board. It is everything the military provides to compensate them.

In 1 Corinthians 9:7, Paul argues that a minister of the gospel deserves wages. So, he looks into the world to make a comparison and asks a question.

1 Corinthians 9:7
What soldier ever serves at his own expense? Who plants a vineyard, and doesn't eat of its fruit? Or who feeds a flock, and doesn't drink from the flock's milk?

The word "expenses" is the same as "wages." The idea is that wages deal with expenses. The military provides for their expenses in life.

In Romans 6:23, Paul compares death to a wage.

Romans 6:23
For the wages of sin is death, but the free gift of God is eternal life in Christ Jesus our Lord.

One earns the wage of death by sinning. One receives the gift of life by believing, so wages are earned. To demonstrate repentance, these soldiers should be content with their pay and the provisions given to them. The Greek word translated "content" means "to be strong in, satisfied in, contented in." They are to find contentment and satisfaction in their wages. They do not need to be looking for more which will cause the other two evil deeds: extortion and lies.

In Hebrews 13:5, the author speaks to this issue concerning the general population.

Hebrews 13:5
Be free from the love of money, content with such things as you have, for he has said, "I will in no way leave you, neither will I in any way forsake you." He is basically telling these soldiers in active duty to be content with what they military has provided them.

Notice, out of all the ways that soldiers could demonstrate real repentance leading to salvation, John the Baptist chose these three issues. Now, we will consider what he did not say. Sometimes what someone does not say is as critical as what someone does say, especially if he is a great prophet of God.

When asked what they needed to do for repentance, he did not say, "Quit the military and find a peaceful profession." He did not shout, "Stay in the military, but get a desk job." John didn't tell them to stop killing, defending themselves, or being violent toward others in battle." This great prophet of God had his chance to tell them to leave the military and did not. Why? Soldiers are defending the nation and themselves in battle. This is self-defense in its most biblical display.

In Matthew 8:8-13, Jesus healed a centurion's servant and called him a great man of faith. Luke described Cornelius as a righteous man and Peter brought him to Christ in Acts 10. They did not tell either to stop being soldiers. Paul used them as analogies to the Christian life and ministry (1 Corinthians 9:7; Philippians 2:25; 2 Timothy 2:3-4; Philemon 1:2).

Self-defense and the defense of others was involved in the greatest event in Jewish history, found in the praises of God's people, and John the Baptist, Jesus, and Peter confirmed it by not condemning the act of soldiering, and Paul used it in his teaching. Here is more evidence of its legitimacy.

HOW CHRISTIANS MAY DEFEND THEMSELVES AGAINST ATTACK

Chapter 15

The Equal Access

As the different instances of self-defense and the defense of others were being studied, several truths began to emerge. For God's people to be able to appropriately defend, they must have the ability to stop the violence and end the threat. By necessity, this would require a weapon that is equal or superior to the weapons of the ones threatening us.

First, every person should possess a weapon for defense and not expect God to miraculously save them. Second, if we have different weapons, then we must have the superior ones. Third, if we have equal weapons, then we must have superior skills to wield those weapons. Fourth, if new weapons emerge that can overcome ours, we must gain access to those or similar weapons. Fifth, once we gain access, we must build the skills to use them in a superior manner than those who may threaten us.

Sixth, if a town, city, region, state, or nation wants to limit our access to weapons they will need to be able to defend us themselves not only as quickly and securely as we are able but in a superior way. Seventh, if they desire to limit our access to weapons, it will be necessary to place safeguards just in case they themselves become a threat to us. Is this not a possibly? Of course, it is, and we should always be prepared for action. Eighth we must continually be assessing the very possible threatening situations we might encounter in order for us to be prepared with the best weapons. Ninth, to impede an attack and allow the time for us to ready ourselves with weapons, we must be surrounded by barriers. Tenth, when outnumbered, if we think we can be saved by surrender, we should surrender and not bring a bloodbath upon ourselves if it will save our lives.

The Weapons and Skills Needed

Here are several principles found in the Scriptures which indicate that we must have equal access to weaponry in order to defend ourselves and others.

The Necessity of a Weapon

First, every person should possess a weapon for defense and not expect God to miraculously save them.

The Common Use of a Staff

Every Hebrew carried a staff for protection. In our chapter on the subject, we demonstrated that the staff was not only commonplace but essential to life.

When every Hebrew left Egypt, they were to take the staff among other essential items.

Exodus 12:11
This is how you shall eat it: with your belt on your waist, your sandals on your feet, and your staff in your hand; and you shall eat it in haste: it is Yahweh's Passover.

This did not change in the time of Christ. When the Lord was describing the things, they should bring for their preaching tour, he mentioned the staff.

HOW CHRISTIANS MAY DEFEND THEMSELVES AGAINST ATTACK

Mark 6:8
He commanded them that they should take nothing for their journey, except a staff only: no bread, no wallet, no money in their purse.

So, it is critical to be prepared for attack with a basic weapon which could be a cane, baseball bat, pepper spray, keys with a something on it that can inflict pain, a rod, small knife, or ax, a hammer or something of that nature. Then they must be watchful and on guard.

The Availability of the Sword

In both the Old and New Testaments, we have seen that God's people had access to weapons beyond the staff. The most common was the sword. This was obviously available to all.

We recently discussed the necessity for the Hebrews with Nehemiah to protect themselves.

Nehemiah 4:13
Therefore I set guards in the lowest parts of the space behind the wall, in the open places. I set the people by family groups with their swords, their spears, and their bows.

Nehemiah 4:18
Among the builders, everyone wore his sword at his side, and so built. He who sounded the trumpet was by me.

Notice, there was no one running around desperately looking for a sword. They all had swords.

When Jesus indicated that he was leaving them and they needed additional protection, what did he tell them? He told them to buy a superior weapon which was a sword.

Luke 22:36
Then he said to them, "But now, whoever has a purse, let him take it, and likewise a wallet. Whoever has none, let him sell his cloak, and buy a sword."

Notice, the disciples did not protest because it was illegal, unavailable, or too expensive. Therefore, everyone should make sure that a better weapon is available have a form of protection if they need it. Each Christian must assess the danger level in the neighborhood, city, region, and nation they live in. If the danger level calls for it, then they should purchase a gun, machete, or something above the basic level.

A Superior Weapon

Second, if we have different weapons, then we must have the superior ones.

As has been observed, people cannot defend themselves and others from harm unless they have a weapon which has the power to overcome the weapon of the one attempting to physically hurt them or others. Since this is an obvious truth, we will take a look at only a few illustrations of this important principle.

In Judges 4, Jabin, King of Canaan, was able to keep control of Israel because they had many chariots of iron.

Judges 4:3
The children of Israel cried to Yahweh, for he had nine hundred chariots of iron; and he mightily oppressed the children of Israel for twenty years.

The children of Israel committed idolatry and the Lord God allowed the king to conquer the land, but he did it by allowing

HOW CHRISTIANS MAY DEFEND THEMSELVES AGAINST ATTACK

a superior army with the superior armor and weapons to do battle with his people and lose.

In 2 Kings 6, the Syrians came to conquer Israel, and all were afraid because they had a superior army and weapons.

2 Kings 6:14
Therefore he sent horses, chariots, and a great army there. They came by night, and surrounded the city.

God intervened by making the Syrians think that Israel had an even bigger army and they fled.

2 Kings 7:6
For the Lord had made the army of the Syrians to hear the sound of chariots, and the sound of horses, even the noise of a great army; and they said to one another, "Behold, the king of Israel has hired against us the kings of the Hittites and the kings of the Egyptians to attack us." Therefore they arose and fled in the twilight, and left their tents, and their horses, and their donkeys, even the camp as it was, and fled for their life.

In the story of the strong man and the attacker, the strong man was fully armed.

Luke 11:21-22
When the strong man, fully armed [with weapon (s)], guards his own dwelling, his goods are safe. But when someone stronger attacks him and overcomes him, he takes from him his whole armor in which he trusted [relied], and divides his plunder.

Notice, the attacker was "stronger" in that he had either better weapons or better skills.

Christians should acquire weapons that are superior to the ones that may attack them. This will prepare us for a proper defense. God's people were always prepared for attack with the best weapons they could create or acquire. If they cannot acquire better weapons, they must develop better skills.

An Equal Weapon with A Superior Skill

Third, if we have equal weapons, then we must have superior skills to wield those weapons.

As has been observed, people cannot defend themselves and others from harm unless they have a weapon which has the power to overcome the weapon of the one attempting to physically hurt them or the others. If this is not possible, they must have an equal or lesser weapon but with superior skill. This is how God has chosen to normally work.

In the following passages, the various skills of the warriors are noted. Why? They could use them in battle and win.

2 Chronicles 25:5
Moreover Amaziah gathered Judah together, and ordered them according to their fathers' houses, under captains of thousands and captains of hundreds, even all Judah and Benjamin. He counted them from twenty years old and upward, and found that there were three hundred thousand chosen men, able to go out to war, who could handle spear and shield.

1 Chronicles 12:2
They were armed with bows, and could use both the right hand and the left in slinging stones and in shooting arrows from the bow. They were of Saul's relatives of the tribe of Benjamin.

1 Chronicles 5:18
The sons of Reuben, the Gadites, and the half-tribe of Manasseh, of valiant men, men able to bear buckler and sword, and to shoot with

HOW CHRISTIANS MAY DEFEND THEMSELVES AGAINST ATTACK

bow, and skillful in war, were forty-four thousand seven hundred sixty, that were able to go out to war.

Why would this be important? Though they were trusting in God, they developed skills for war because this is how God usually works.

Remember the powerful words of David.

Psalm 18:34
He teaches my hands to war, so that my arms bend a bow of bronze.

They not only relied on the Lord God for battle but relied on the development of their skills.

Would individual self-defense be any different? Isn't battle really individual self-defense ultimately soldier to soldier? Or would a group to group, army to army be different? No, it is the same with the same parameters only on a larger scale.

Another example is David facing Goliath. Did God do a great miracle when David killed Goliath, or did God use David's skill with the sling? When Saul questioned his ability to fight Goliath, David did not say that he would just trust in God. He explained that he had fought a lion and a bear with God's help.

1 Samuel 17:33
Saul said to David, "You are not able to go against this Philistine to fight with him; for you are but a youth, and he a man of war from his youth."

1 Samuel 17:37
David said, "Yahweh, who delivered me out of the paw of the lion and out of the paw of the bear, will deliver me out of the hand of this Philistine." Saul said to David, "Go! Yahweh will be with you."

At the time, David could not even wear Saul's armor, let alone wield his weapons.

1 Samuel 17:37-38
David said, "Yahweh, who delivered me out of the paw of the lion and out of the paw of the bear, will deliver me out of the hand of this Philistine." Saul said to David, "Go! Yahweh will be with you." Saul dressed David with his clothing. He put a helmet of bronze on his head, and he clad him with a coat of mail. 39 David strapped his sword on his clothing and he tried to move, for he had not tested it. David said to Saul, "I can't go with these, for I have not tested them." Then David took them off.

Saul was not going to send David out weaponless but gave him his weapons.

Since David was unable to wield the armor and weaponry, he took the weapons that he knew the Lord God could use. Why? David had developed great skills in their use and knew they would do the job as the Lord worked.

1 Samuel 17:40
He took his staff in his hand, and chose for himself five smooth stones out of the brook, and put them in the pouch of his shepherd's bag which he had. His sling was in his hand; and he came near to the Philistine.

So, he depended upon his sling and His God to overcome the greater weapons, skills with the weapons, and experience in combat that Goliath possessed.

1 Samuel 17:5-7
A champion out of the camp of the Philistines named Goliath of Gath, whose height was six cubits and a span went out. He had a helmet of bronze on his head, and he wore a coat of mail; and the weight of the coat was five thousand shekels of bronze. He had bronze shin armor on his legs and a bronze javelin between his shoulders.

HOW CHRISTIANS MAY DEFEND THEMSELVES AGAINST ATTACK

The staff of his spear was like a weaver's beam; and his spear's head weighed six hundred shekels of iron. His shield bearer...before him.

1 Samuel 17:33
Saul said to David, "You are not able to go against this Philistine to fight with him; for you are but a youth, and he a man of war from his youth."

David was not a soldier when he stood in front of Goliath; instead, he was a shepherd who had developed skills with a sling that he would use against Goliath. Hand to hand combat with a miracle from the Lord was not how he killed the fierce animals and would not be how he killed Goliath. With the sling and a good aim, David could remain far enough away to kill Goliath without being engaged in actual battle which he would lose. So, David ran toward Goliath trusting God while God used his skills to find victory.

1 Samuel 17:49-51
David put his hand in his bag, took a stone and slung it, and struck the Philistine in his forehead. The stone sank into his forehead, and he fell on his face to the earth. So David prevailed over the Philistine with a sling and with a stone, and struck the Philistine and killed him; but there was no sword David's hand. Then David ran, stood over the Philistine, took his sword, drew it out of its sheath, killed him, and cut off his head with it. When the Philistines saw that their champion was dead, they fled.

Though we know God was at work, we do not see a direct miracle. Of course, the people on both sides would have attributed the felling of a giant warrior by a young shepherd as miraculous at the same time as acknowledging David's skill with a sling which was a recognized weapon at the time.

Why didn't the army simply pray and ask God to strike Goliath down on the spot? They most likely prayed that God would provide someone to step up and take the challenge rather than praying God would strike Goliath down. This is God's usual approach to defense unless He desires to do a miracle to glorify His name.

The Acquisition of New Weapons

Fourth, if new weapons emerge that can overcome ours, we must gain access to those or similar weapons.

As has been observed, people cannot defend themselves and others from harm unless they have a weapon which has the power to overcome the weapon of the one attempting to physically hurt them or the others. As a result, God's people were creating or acquiring new weapons as the weapons of their enemies became more dangerous.

As we saw, all weapons were invented, purchased, made, given as tribute, or taken as plunder. When David ran from Saul, he headed to Nob and arrived at the tabernacle. When he asked the high priest, Ahimelech, if there was a weapon available, he gave him the sword of Goliath.

1 Samuel 21:8
David said to Ahimelech, "Isn't there here under your hand spear or sword? For I haven't brought my sword or my weapons with me, because the king's business required haste." The priest said, "Behold, the sword of Goliath the Philistine, whom you killed in the valley of Elah, is here wrapped in a cloth behind the ephod. If you would like to take that, take it; for there is no other except that here." David said, "There is none like that. Give it to me."

How did the sword of Goliath end up in the tabernacle? First, after killing Goliath, David took the sword of this great warrior as plunder.

HOW CHRISTIANS MAY DEFEND THEMSELVES AGAINST ATTACK

1 Samuel 17:54
David took the head of the Philistine and brought it to Jerusalem, but he put his armor in his tent.

Second, David was glad to obtain the sword since it was like no other because it was obviously larger. Though the sword is not mentioned, much of the armor is and it was massive.

1 Samuel 17: 5
He had a helmet of bronze on his head, and he wore a coat of mail; and the weight of the coat was five thousand shekels of bronze. He had bronze shin armor on his legs and a bronze javelin between his shoulders. The staff of his spear was like a weaver's beam; and his spear's head weighed six hundred shekels of iron. His shield bearer went before him.

Not only was Goliath superior in height, strength, and build, but he had huge armor. This weaponry was much larger than the average military issue. Now, David had in his hands the superior sword of Goliath with his own experience to defend himself against the many soldiers of King Saul.

We saw that Jesus told His disciples to purchase a sword, since things would become dangerous after His departure. and a staff would not be enough. They needed something superior.

Luke 22:35-36
He said to them, "When I sent you out without purse, wallet, and sandals, did you lack anything?" They said, "Nothing." Then he said to them, "But now, whoever has a purse, let him take it, and likewise a wallet. Whoever has none, let him sell his cloak, and buy a sword."

So, some weapons had to be purchased if enough could not be acquired or if superior ones were needed.

As in today's world, ancient peoples were always making, creating, and acquiring new weapons that would be superior or equal to the weapons of the many peoples they must defend themselves against. This can be done on an individual, regional, and national basis.

The Attainment of New Skills

Fifth, once we gain access, we must build the skills to use them in a superior manner than those who may threaten us with the same weapons.

As has been observed, people cannot defend themselves and others from harm unless they have a weapon which has the power to overcome the weapon of the one attempting to physically hurt them or the others. If this is not possible, they must have an equal or lesser weapon but with superior skill. Then, when the skills of those who desire to harm us increase, we must also increase our skills. This is how God has chosen to normally work.

In Amos, the prophet asserts the coming defeat of Israel and Judah due to their sins. He describes some of the skills that were so valued in battle and that they would not deliver him. This simply meant that God would send an army with even better skills.

Amos 2:15
Neither shall he stand who handles the bow; and he who is swift of foot won't escape; neither shall he who rides the horse deliver himself.

In 1 Chronicles 5. the inspired author describes the powerful army that went against the Hagrites. Notice, he mentions the skills that were valued when they went to war.

HOW CHRISTIANS MAY DEFEND THEMSELVES AGAINST ATTACK

1 Chronicles 5:18
The sons of Reuben, the Gadites, and the half-tribe of Manasseh, of valiant men, men able to bear buckler and sword, and to shoot with bow, and skillful in war, were forty-four thousand seven hundred sixty, that were able to go out to war.

These skills that are mentioned were formidable in battle and would have given them a tremendous advantage in one-to-one combat or with others on the battlefield.

When David faced Goliath, it was discovered that though Goliath had superior armor and even experience, David had superior skills in a weaker weapon and with the help of the Lord felled the giant.

1 Samuel 17:34-36
David said to Saul, "Your servant was keeping his father's sheep; and when a lion or a bear came and took a lamb out of the flock, I went out after him, struck him, and rescued it out of his mouth. When he arose against me, I caught him by his beard, struck him, and killed him. Your servant struck both the lion and the bear. This uncircumcised Philistine shall be as one of them, since he has defied the armies of the living God."

The skills he had developed was used powerfully by God. So, to appropriately defend against equal weapons, we must develop more skills in the use of those same weapons to be able to overcome an attacker.

A Superior Defense by Government

Sixth, if a town, city, region, state, or nation wants to limit our access to weapons they will need to be able to defend us themselves not only as quickly and securely as we are able but in a superior way.

As has been observed, people cannot defend themselves and others from harm unless they have a weapon which has the power to overcome the weapon of the one attempting to physically hurt them or others. Sometimes, this is not possible by the general populace. As a result, governments are created to protect the people from violence wherever their people may dwell within a certain location.

Romans 13: 3-4
For rulers are not a terror to the good work, but to the evil. Do you desire to have no fear of the authority? Do that which is good, and you will have praise from the authority, for he is a servant of God to you for good. But if you do that which is evil, be afraid, for he doesn't bear the sword in vain; for he is a servant of God, an avenger for wrath to him who does evil.

The bearing of the sword would both deter a murder from occurring and stop it if it does. The crime could be murder or another violent action. For a government to be more effective than the average citizen, they must be able to defend the citizenry in a greater way than the citizenry could defend themselves or they would not be necessary. Often, we will see the words "To protect and to serve" on the side of a police car. This is what they are supposed to do.

A Safeguard Against A Government's Threat

Seventh, if they desire to limit our access to weapons, it will be necessary to place safeguards in case they themselves become a threat to us. Is this not a possibly? Of course, it is, and we should be prepared for action.

As has been observed, people cannot defend themselves and others from harm unless they have a weapon which has the power to overcome the weapon of the one attempting to physically hurt them or others. This includes a government who requires us to disobey God. Once we have determined that we must defy the law to obey a divine command, we may defend ourselves from death. Unfortunately, this becomes difficult because they will quickly overcome us and then we will bring a bloodbath upon ourselves. In this case, we must submit.

In Nehemiah, the cupbearer to the king of the Medo-Persian empire sent him to construct the wall of Jerusalem but the ruler of the people next door in Samaria opposed him. Sanballat began to prepare his armies for an attack upon the Jews. What was their defensive response? Every Jew prepared to defend himself and his family.

Nehemiah 4:13
Therefore I set guards in the lowest parts of the space behind the wall, in the open places. I set the people by family groups with their swords, their spears, and their bows.

Nehemiah 4:18
Among the builders, everyone wore his sword at his side, and so built. He who sounded the trumpet was by me.

Though this is another government, it's clear they took up their weapons to defend themselves.

They used swords because it would come to hand-to-hand combat if they were attacked.

The Importance of Continual Assessment

Eighth we must continually be assessing the very possible threatening situations we might encounter in order for us to be prepared with the best weapons.

DEFENDING YOUR LIFE

As we have seen, God's people have always set guards to watch for attack after intense preparation.

When Uzzah became king of Judah, he immediately began to build up the defenses of his kingdom.

2 Chronicles 26:9-15
Moreover Uzziah built towers in Jerusalem at the corner gate, at the valley gate, and at the turning of the wall, and fortified them. He built towers in the wilderness, and dug out many cisterns, for he had much livestock; in the lowland also, and in the plain. He had farmers and vineyard keepers in the mountains and in the fruitful fields, for he loved farming. Moreover Uzziah had an army of fighting men, who went out to war by bands, according to the number of their reckoning made by Jeiel the scribe and Maaseiah the officer, under the hand of Hananiah, one of the king's captains. The whole number of the heads of fathers' households, even the mighty men of valor, was two thousand six hundred. Under their hand was an army, three hundred seven thousand five hundred, who made war with mighty power, to help the king against the enemy. Uzziah prepared for them, even for all the army, shields, spears, helmets, coats of mail, bows, and stones for slinging. In Jerusalem, he made devices, invented by skillful men, to be on the towers and on the battlements, with which to shoot arrows and great stones. His name spread...abroad, because he was marvelously helped until...strong.

They had guards to constantly assess the state of danger they were in and what may be coming.

When Hezekiah was informed that Sennacherib, King of Assyria, came to fight Judah. As they were coming, Hezekiah prepared to watch for the attack and then to fight.

2 Chronicles 32:1-2
After these things and this faithfulness, Sennacherib king of Assyria came, entered into Judah, and encamped against the fortified cities,

HOW CHRISTIANS MAY DEFEND THEMSELVES AGAINST ATTACK

and intended to win them for himself. When Hezekiah saw that Sennacherib had come...he was planning to fight against Jerusalem.

2 Chronicles 32:5-8
He took courage, built up all the wall that was broken down, and raised it up to the towers, with the other wall outside, and strengthened Millo in David's city, and made weapons and shields in abundance. He set captains of war over the people, and gathered them together to him in the wide place at the gate of the city, and spoke encouragingly to them, saying, "Be strong and courageous. Don't be afraid or dismayed because of the king of Assyria, nor for all the multitude who is with him; for there is a greater one with us than with him. 8 An arm of flesh is with him, but Yahweh our God is with us to help us and to fight our battles." The people rested themselves on the words of Hezekiah king of Judah.

As we saw in Nehemiah, they set up guards and took their weapons with them as they worked and played.

Nehemiah 4:13
Therefore I set guards in the lowest parts of the space behind the wall, in the open places. I set the people by family groups with their swords, their spears, and their bows.

Nehemiah 4:18
Among the builders, everyone wore his sword at his side, and so built. He who sounded the trumpet was by me.

Even before the need arose, they were prepared for danger. When and if the danger comes, they will be watching for it and will not be surprised. Therefore, we must be constantly assessing the state of danger and preparing for it by the accumulation of weapons, skills, or both.

Finally, we have seen that a Jewish man always carried a staff for his protection and others. Of course, he would watch for danger as he walked. Therefore, everyone should have a form of protection that they carry with them regularly.

If we realize that a possible enemy may have weapons that we do not, then we may need to purchase additional weapons or gain new skills in the use of our old weapons or the new ones. This is up to individual assessments.

This can be seen in the story of the strong man and the stronger one by Jesus. This concerns a thief that breaks into a man's house with the owner possessing armor. Here is a common experience that all would have understood. A man protects his household. He does this by being "armed" with a weapon. Notice, he describes it as "fully" armed. This means with enough power to stop the expected enemy.

Luke 11:21-22
When the strong man, fully armed [with weapon (s)], guards his own dwelling, his goods are safe. But when someone stronger attacks him and overcomes him, he takes from him his whole armor in which he trusted [relied], and divides his plunder.

The attacker had either better weapons, better skills, or both. We need to make sure that we can attain better weapons if we feel they are needed. If we can't obtain them, we must develop additional skills.

The Building of Protective Barriers

Ninth, to impede an attack and allow the time for us to ready ourselves with weapons, we must be surrounded by barriers.

In Deuteronomy, Moses recounts the numerous victories they had in the wilderness. He mentions the conquering of the land of Bashan. The Lord empowered them to overcome all of their fortifications.

Deuteronomy 3:3-6
So Yahweh our God also delivered into our hand Og, the king of Bashan, and all his people. We struck him until no one was left to him remaining. We took all his cities at that time. There was not a city which we didn't take from them: sixty cities, all the region of Argob, the kingdom of Og in Bashan. All these were cities fortified with high walls, gates, and bars, in addition to a great many villages without walls. We utterly destroyed them, as we did to Sihon king of Heshbon, utterly destroying every inhabited city, with the women and the little ones.

The word translated "fortified" means to "to gather, restrain, fence, fortify, make inaccessible, enclose, or to cut off." Moses focuses on these fortifications because they are meant to keep attackers out. They were diverse (walls, gates, bars), solid, and high. Basically, it would take huge weapons and much manpower or a divine being to overcome them.

The walls of Jericho had to be brought down for Jericho to be conquered. The walls did what they were supposed to do, keep attackers out. Divine power had to overcome them.

When the friends of the paralytic attempted to bring the friend into the house Jesus was preaching in, they could not reach Him because of the crowd. So, they went up the stairs to the roof and dug their way through. Then, they lowered him down.

Mark 2:1-5
When he entered again into Capernaum after some days, it was heard that he [Jesus] was at home. Immediately many were gathered together, so that there was no more room, not...around the door; and he spoke the word to them. Four people came, carrying a paralytic to

him. When they could not come near to him for the crowd, they removed the roof where he was. When they had broken it up, they let down the mat that the paralytic was lying on. Jesus, seeing their faith, said to the paralytic, "Son, your sins are forgiven you."

The homes in Jewish ancient times had a wall around it with a gate to enter into an outdoor courtyard which then had steps to the roof of the home. The door on the roof would have been locked. The people secured their homes from attack, so they had to dig their way through the roof.

So, having a barrier between us and attackers is important. Also, the securing of doors and gates with locks are a critical protection.

In summary, for us, as God's people, to be able to defend ourselves, those we love, and the innocent, we must have the ability to stop the violence and end the threat. By necessity, this requires weapons and skills superior to those threatening us.

Chapter 16

The Scriptural Consistency

In this book, we have learned that we, as Christians, may defend ourselves, those we love, and the innocent from all those who desire to do physical harm to us with just two exceptions. First, if we have committed a crime, the governing authorities functioning within their jurisdiction are the only ones we may not defend ourselves against. Second, in the chapter on the Son's instruction, we learned that if taking up arms will result in a bloodbath upon ourselves and those we are with, we should not engage in physical self-defense. Of course, we may sacrifice our lives to save the lives of others.

I have waited till the end of the book to consider the many biblical passages which seem to teach something other than self-defense and the defense of all others in all circumstances by Christians. In this way, we can simply review some of the material in this book, my companion book, and some new material to see the full and complete picture of how self-defense is scripturally consistent with all passages of the Bible. The discrepancies only seem to be contradicting the biblical truths and passages presented when in reality, they are not but are in complete harmony with each other and these critical truths.

Even the casual reader will notice that there have been no real distinctions made concerning who we defend ourselves against and who we may not except for the two reasons given above. This is due to a lack of distinctions in the Bible. In the Scriptures an attacker is an attacker. It does not really matter whether the person is a stranger attempting to rob and kill us at gunpoint, a known enemy with a knife to our throats, or a persecutor with a rifle pointed at us demanding we renounce Christ, all may be defended against without distinction. Why? The Bible makes no distinction.

There are some believers who will object to self-defense and the defense of others against those in one or more of these three categories using bible verses which appear to support their conclusions. In this chapter, we will discuss these critical passages and will discover they are in compete harmony with each other and the defense against all attackers with the two exceptions.

Before we begin, let us consider this question, "Why are there so many opinions about this topic among Christians?" The answer is biblical ignorance. I do not mean this in a critical way but simply that Christians in general do not know what the Bible says on every subject. Of course, this leads to inappropriate thinking which comes from an ignorance of the total teaching of the Bible on the subject. The Lord Jesus and the apostles were continually dealing with this same lack of knowledge on a variety of subjects.

1 Thessalonians 4:13
But we don't want you to be ignorant, brothers, concerning those who have fallen asleep, so that you don't grieve like the rest, who have no hope.

In this instance, the ignorance led some to grieve far too much for the loss of a believer. The ignorance which concerns the defense of ourselves and others has a much greater impact because it can mean the difference between life and death.

Where does the biblical ignorance concerning self-defense and the defense of others come from? The main source is the lack of teaching on the subject by pastor-teachers, evangelists,

HOW CHRISTIANS MAY DEFEND THEMSELVES AGAINST ATTACK

and other teachers in the church. In Ephesians 4, the apostle presents the responsibility of pastor-teachers and evangelists who have been given to the church.

Ephesians 4:11-12
He [Christ] gave some to be apostles; and some, prophets; and some, evangelists; and some, shepherds and teachers; for the perfecting of the saints, to the work of serving, to the building up of the body of Christ.

Here, Paul explains that they are "to perfect" which means "to equip" the saints for the work of service. The Pastor-teacher equips the saints for service to one another in the church and the evangelist to the work of service in the world (believer to unbeliever). This equipping must involve persecution and the many responses to it by true believers. This automatically necessitates instruction on self-defense and the defense of others where others (unbelievers) attempt to harm believers due to the gospel (persecution) or another reason.

Other teachers in the church could and should pick up the mantle and teach on this important subject. In 1 Corinthians 12, Paul listed some of the gifted saints.

1 Corinthians 12:28-29
God has set some in the assembly: first apostles, second prophets, third teachers, then miracle workers, then gifts of healings, helps, governments, and various kinds of languages. Are all apostles? Are all prophets? Are all teachers? Are all miracle workers?

Teachers are those who have the gift of teaching. These are not "teachers in education" necessarily but those believers gifted to understand, teach, and apply the Scriptures.

So, why is there so little teaching on this important subject? First, it requires a study of all the Scriptures and the blending of the instruction of the Old and New Testaments. It also involves the interpretation of difficult passages in the Holy Scriptures. For example, most commentators virtually ignore the passages concerning Peter and his use of a sword.

Second, since most pastors of the past determined to focus on expository (verse by verse) sermons and commentaries as resources, they do not have the time to put into this extensive topical study. In fact, most commentaries, Bible dictionaries, and encyclopedias mention very little on these passages and topics. Today, since many pastors of the church focus on the proclamation of the good news to the unsaved and positive, inspirational sermons to the saved in one sermon package, there is no place for instruction on this topic.

In the past, these huge topics were left up to the "gifted teachers" in seminaries or authors of books. Unfortunately, many of these kinds of teachers focus on theological matters concerning the Trinity, end times, and others but not self-defense and the defense by believers. If an author or pastor dealt in anyway with the topic, it would be repeated over and over because the pastor had to rely on someone else to do it. Unfortunately, that "someone else" may be wrong because they relied on "someone else."

This brought many leaders to leave it up to the individual consciences of those in their congregation. This becomes the "catch all dumping ground" for difficult subjects. Like a "junk drawer" in the home, self-defense and the defense of others was left to a series of fragment passages put together in a wide variety of ways by a host of believers and non-believers alike. When needed, they would open the drawer grab the first the thing they saw and attempt to solve the problem. This leaves the topic to the hodgepodge opinions based on a variety of sermons they have heard, books they have read, and the human reasoning of their own minds. Like a puzzle missing

HOW CHRISTIANS MAY DEFEND THEMSELVES AGAINST ATTACK

pieces they attempt to piece it together without the picture on the cover of the box. This leads to all kinds of distorted images of self-defense and the defense of others. These images may not only be wrong but are often comical. One believer thought that they could defend those they loved but not themselves. How does this make sense?

We see the result of this kind of thinking in the book of Judges where in Judges 21:25, it says, "In those days there was no king in Israel. Everyone did that which was right in his own eyes." When the people are left to themselves with no teaching from the gifted then it only brings sin, division, and bad theology.

Another reason for the saints' ignorance on the subject comes from hardened hearts. They are unwilling to believe the Bible's teaching on the subject when presented to them. This was the difficulty the two men on the road to Emmaus struggled with.

Luke 24:25-28
He said to them, "Foolish men, and slow of heart to believe in all that the prophets have spoken! Didn't the Christ have to suffer these things and to enter into his glory?" Beginning from Moses and from all the prophets, he explained to them in all the Scriptures the things concerning himself. They came near to the village where they were going, and he acted like he would go further.

Some hold on to certain teachings because it makes sense to them and are unwilling to submit to the Bible.

The ignorance could come from listening to some very persuasive teachers who were wrong in their understanding. In Galatians 2, Paul discussed the coming of a false group of brethren (Judaizers) who believed that a Gentile must be circumcised among other practices to be saved. They were so persuasive that both Peter and Barnabas stopped eating with the church's Gentiles because they were not following Jewish dietary laws.

Galatians 2:11-14
But when Peter came to Antioch, I resisted him to his face, because he stood condemned. For before some people came from James, he ate with the Gentiles. But when they came, he drew back and separated himself, fearing those who were of the circumcision. And the rest of the Jews joined him in his hypocrisy, so that even Barnabas was carried away with their hypocrisy. But when I saw that they didn't walk uprightly according to the truth of the Good News, I said to Peter before them all, "If you, being a Jew, live as the Gentiles do, and not as the Jews do, why do you compel the Gentiles to live as the Jews do?

Though Paul called this a form of hypocrisy, it was also out of ignorance due to a powerful persuasion of the Judaizers who had come into the church. Remember, Peter had the vision that let Peter know that the Gentiles were being offered the kingdom separate from becoming Jews.

The Corinthians misunderstood many truths because they were wrapped up in the wisdom of the world. Paul exhorts them to follow him because he was teaching the wisdom of God. The apostle explains to them that they were following the wisdom of the world and not the wisdom of God.

1 Corinthians 2:6-8
That your faith wouldn't stand in the wisdom of men…. That your faith wouldn't stand in the wisdom of men, but in the power of God. We speak wisdom, however, among those who are full grown, yet a wisdom not of this world nor of the rulers of this world who are coming to nothing. But we speak God's wisdom in a mystery, the wisdom that has been hidden, which God foreordained before the worlds for our glory…none of the rulers of this world has known… had they known it, they wouldn't have crucified the Lord of glory.

The key reason Christians believe we should not defend ourselves against persecutors is due to the misunderstanding of the words and actions of Jesus and the apostles.

The Defense Against Strangers

Some believe that we should not defend ourselves against any attacker. This idea is based on certain misunderstandings of the words of Jesus. They object to self-defense and the defense of others because they believe Jesus taught this which simply is not true. These objections and the passages that accompany them are in no particular order.

The Shining of the Light

Some will say that the actions of God in the Old Testament do not involve believers because we belong to the New. Yet, the truth remains the same because the difference comes in who now brings the light of salvation. Once the Lord God called a nation to Himself the message was passed through Abraham. How the salvation message was shared in the Old Testament determined many of the actions of God including His defense and protection.

The National Light

In the Old Testament God revealed the truth about Himself through Israel to the nations. How God dealt with His people was watched by the nations surrounding them. From this, the people outside Israel believed. Much of this revelation had to do with war; that is, God defended His people and others saw it and believed. Rahab is a perfect example of this truth.

DEFENDING YOUR LIFE

When Israel entered the land of Canaan, the first stop was Jericho. When he sent spies to Jericho, they were welcomed by Rahab. Why? She believed in their God. How? God's defense of Israel against the Egyptians and their enemies in the wilderness, and the victories that came were told and retold all over the world including Jericho.

Joshua 2:9-13
She said to the men, "I know that Yahweh has given you the land, and that the fear of you has fallen upon us, and that all the inhabitants of the land melt away before you. For we have heard how Yahweh dried up the water of the Red Sea before you, when you came out of Egypt; and what you did to the two kings of the Amorites, who were beyond the Jordan, to Sihon and to Og, whom you utterly destroyed. As soon as we had heard it, our hearts melted, and there wasn't any more spirit in any man, because of you: for Yahweh your God, he is God in heaven above, and on earth beneath. Now therefore, please swear to me by Yahweh, since I have dealt kindly with you, that you also will deal kindly with my father's house, and give me a true sign; and that you will save alive my father, my mother, my brothers, and my sisters, and all that they have, and will deliver our lives from death."

Due to her faith, Rahab hid the spies and then asked them to protect her and her family when Israel attacked the city.

This was an act of faith confirmed by James, the brother of Jesus, and the author of Hebrews.

James 2:25
In the same way, wasn't Rahab the prostitute also justified by works, in that she received the messengers and sent them out another way?

Hebrews 11:31
By faith, Rahab the prostitute didn't perish with those who were disobedient, having received the spies in peace.

HOW CHRISTIANS MAY DEFEND THEMSELVES AGAINST ATTACK

Salvation through reputation was not the only way God spread the news about Himself. Ruth, a Moabitess, found her knowledge through her mother-in-law Naomi (a Jew).

Ruth 1:16
Ruth said, "Don't urge me to leave you, and to return from following you, for where you go, I will go; and where you stay, I will stay. Your people will be my people, and your God my God."

So, war was not the only way, but a significant way in which God presented Himself to an idolatrous world.

The Church's Light

When Jesus came, the Jews rejected Him and their light as a nation was turned off. The gospel was offered to the Gentiles directly and the church as a new light was born. This church was made up of both Jews and Gentiles who would share the gospel within a nation. Therefore, the need for miraculous victories by the nation of Israel was no longer necessary.

The Rule of Rome

In the Old Testament, God ruled His nation Israel through priests, prophets, and kings. The world was a difficult and chaotic place filled with warring nations who would have to be prepared for attack at any time. By the time of Christ, Rome was in control of much of the known world. The people, including Jesus, lived under the order and peace established by Roman rule. There were soldiers in every city and region to keep the peace. Therefore, the need for constant national self-defense or even individual defense was not as necessary as before, though it still existed.

The Love of Neighbor

In Matthew 22, the Lord commented on the two greatest commandments. One of them was "love your neighbor."

Matthew 22:39
A second likewise is this, "You shall love your neighbor as yourself."

Some think that self-defense is not truly "loving our neighbor" because it is harming the one that we are defending ourselves or others against. They might ask, "How can Christians love their neighbors if they are harming them?" To answer this question, we must pose another, "What about the one we are defending? Isn't he or she our neighbor also?"

When we consider how self-defense and the defense of others harmonizes with the biblical truth of loving one's neighbor, we must view it from two different perspectives. The first perspective is from the one being harmed (ourselves or others) and secondarily from those perpetrating the harm (others).

In John 15, Jesus told His disciples that the greatest way to show love to a friend is to lay down one's life for him.

John 15:12-13,
This is my commandment, that you love one another, even as I have loved you. Greater love has no one than this, that someone lay down his life for his friends.

The Lord was describing what He was about to do for them. He would lay down His life as a sacrifice for their sins and they were to do the same for each other.

As we saw earlier in this book, their protection of each other is also in view. In this simple statement, Jesus provides a powerful truth. Though some might like to spiritualize this statement to mean any sacrifice of one's life which might refer to time, energy, or problem-solving, this is not what the Lord meant. This does not stand up to its straightforward meaning. To sacrifice one's life for another means to give up one's life to protect another. It is a life for a life.

In our minds, we can understand how powerful this truth is. We immediately conjure up someone throwing themselves in front of a bullet and being killed. Or perhaps, we can see in our minds eye, someone pushing us out of the way of an oncoming car and being killed himself. We conjure up the image of a firefighter rescuing a child from a burning building as they fall to the ground and die from smoke inhalation.

Whatever image comes to mind, it almost always will be a life for a life. This is the sacrifice of one's life to protect another. This is the "defense of others." To protect others from danger and harm is an act of love toward neighbors.

What about the love of ourselves? The Scriptures assume the love of self but condemns selfishly loving oneself to the exclusion of others. God has put within a person through the conscience a love of self which leads to not only self-care but self-preservation which causes self-defense!

Ephesians 5:28-30
Even so husbands also ought to love their own wives as their own bodies. He who loves his own wife loves himself. For no man ever hated his own flesh; but nourishes and cherishes it, even as the Lord also does the assembly; because we are members of his body, of his flesh and bones.

Here, Paul explains that it is natural to nourish and cherish our bodies (selves) and we should also do the same with our spouses. As just mentioned, this includes self-preservation. Using this principle then, we would protect ourselves from danger and should do the same for our spouses. No one could argue the contrary.

In the Lord's powerful story of the Good Samaritan, Jesus is asked to identify one's neighbor. So, he tells a story of three men who walk by a Samaritan man who has become the victim of robbers.

Luke 10:33-35
But a certain Samaritan, as he traveled, came where he was. When he saw him, he was moved with compassion, came to him, and bound up his wounds, pouring on oil and wine. He...brought him to an inn, and took care of him. On the next day, when he departed, he took out two denarii, gave them to the host, and said to him, "Take care of him. Whatever you spend beyond that, I will repay you when I return."

In the story, he describes the third person who came by as the one who met his needs.

Jesus asks a question to get to the very heart of the issue.

Luke 10:36-37
Now which of these three do you think seemed to be a neighbor to him who fell among the robbers?" He said, "He who showed mercy on him." Then Jesus said to him, "Go and do likewise."

The Lord identifies the neighbor from the view of one whose needs were being met and not from the one meeting the needs. In His story, the Lord Christ does not bring up the robbers but the victim and how the man protected him from additional harm.

The showing of love did not begin with the perpetrators of evil but the victim of their evil and protecting him. In the same way, when considering the loving of our neighbors, we must consider first the demonstration of loving them in our defense of them. Who would really consider the robbers first? If the victim's true neighbor had stumbled upon him while he was being robbed, would we not expect the man to have defended him? Of course, we would. He would have been dismayed if the man asked to meet the needs of the robbers.

Then the question arises, "How can this be showing love to the neighbor who is attempting to harm us or others?" Most likely, he would now be considered an "enemy" and not a neighbor. Nevertheless, let us consider him as a neighbor also. The answer comes in the answer to these questions, "Which is a more wicked act? Is it the intent to harm or the actual harming?" Obviously, it is the actual harming of a person. When Jesus spoke of "adultery of the heart" it did not come with the stipulation that it broke the marriage bond, only physical infidelity could do that.

Matthew 5:27
You have heard that it was said, "You shall not commit adultery;" but I tell you that everyone who gazes at a woman to lust after her has committed adultery with her already in his heart.

Matthew 5:31
It was also said, "Whoever shall put away his wife, let him give her a writing of divorce," but I tell you that whoever puts away his wife, except for the cause of sexual immorality, makes her an adulteress; and whoever marries her when she is put away commits adultery.

Here, Jesus condemns both adultery of the heart and actions but only the actions sever the bond. This then brings a greater judgment. Whenever judgment is mentioned in the Bible, it is always mentioned as a judgment of deeds. When the Lord Jesus Christ spoke of either the judgment of the saved or the unsaved, He did not mention motives. He spoke first of the deeds that will be examined.

DEFENDING YOUR LIFE

John 5:28-29
Don't marvel at this, for the hour comes in which all who are in the tombs will hear his voice, and will come out; those who have done good, to the resurrection of life; and those who have done evil, to the resurrection of judgment.

Yet, we will have our motives examined. It usually occurs with the doing of "good deeds" for sinful motives.

1 Corinthians 4:5
Therefore judge nothing before the time, until the Lord comes, who will both bring to light the hidden things of darkness, and reveal the counsels of the hearts. Then each man will get his praise from God.

Romans 2:14-16
For when Gentiles who don't have the law do by nature the things of the law, these, not having the law, are a law to themselves, in that they show the work of...law written in their hearts, their conscience testifying with them, and their thoughts among themselves accusing or else excusing them in the day when God will judge the secrets of men, according to my Good News, by Jesus Christ.

In Corinthians, Paul speaks of judging the inner motives of believers, but in Romans, the apostle refers to unbelievers.

Speaking in general, Solomon adds this important truth to his wisdom literature.

Proverbs 21:27
The sacrifice of the wicked is an abomination – how much more, when he brings it with a wicked mind!

Proverbs 16:2
All the ways of a man are clean in his own eyes; but Yahweh weighs the motives.

We know that the writers often appealed to their motives.

HOW CHRISTIANS MAY DEFEND THEMSELVES AGAINST ATTACK

1 Thessalonians 2:4
But even as we have been approved by God to be entrusted with the Good News...not as pleasing men, but God, who test our hearts.

2 Corinthians 9:7
Let each man give according as he has determined in his heart, not grudgingly or under compulsion, for God loves a cheerful giver.

James 4:3
You ask, and don't receive, because you ask with wrong motives, so that you may spend it on your pleasures.

As we can see, motives are important and are judged as well as the deeds. How does this affect the actual loving of our neighbor who is attempting to hurt us or others? Let us consider this scenario also. If we, through self-defense, stop someone from harming or killing another then they will not have to face judgment for the act because we stopped them. They will be judged for their desires not their actions.

This is much like a person telling another who is about to kill someone, "Don't do it or the punishment will be much worse!" In the end, these people are being saved from a greater judgment. Would this not be a great act of love?

Both the neighbor who is the victim and the neighbor who is the perpetrator of evil can be loved best by the victim simply defending himself or someone coming to his rescue and stopping the attacker before the murder occurs.

The Natural Assumption

Some say, "Since self-defense and the defense of others is not clearly taught in the New Testament, Christians should not engage in it." Yet, we have already seen that it was a given. It was assumed as we saw in the use of analogies by Jesus.

Luke 11:21-23
When the strong man, fully armed [with weapon (s)], guards his own dwelling, his goods are safe. But when someone stronger attacks him and overcomes him, he takes from him his whole armor in which he trusted [relied], and divides his plunder. "He that is not with me is against me. He who doesn't gather with me scatters.

It would not be unusual for someone to have weapons to protect their family and goods. The people understood self-defense so they could understand the teaching of the Lord.

The Confusion of Miracles vs. Providence

Some believe that we do not need to defend ourselves or others against attackers because God will come to our rescue miraculously. This comes from a confusion between God's work through miracles and His work through providence. We have already seen that God works through people as they defend themselves and will work through circumstances to protect us. This is the Lord God's usual pattern. God's help usually comes from our human effort as He works through us or our circumstances which prevent or stop the attack. First, we will study the purpose of miracles, how God uses them, and their connection to God's providence.

The Miracles in Battle as Witness to Nations

The Lord decided to bring His light to the world through a nation. So, He called out a specific lineage to create the nation of Israel. He laid out national, ceremonial, and moral laws which demonstrated to the world that the God of Israel was not only the true God but different from their many false idols. Sometimes, He used the testimony of people such as with Naomi witnessing to Ruth. Naomi and her husband lived in Moab. Her sons married Moabite women. When both died, Naomi traveled to Israel and told the women to go back to their own homes. Ruth did not want to leave because she now believed in the God of Israel.

Ruth 1:8-10
Naomi said to her two daughters-in-law, "Go, return each of you to her mother's house. May Yahweh deal kindly with you, as you have dealt with the dead and with me. May Yahweh grant you that you may find rest, each of you in the house of her husband." Then she kissed them, and they lifted up their voices, and wept. They said to her, "No, but we will return with you to your people."

Ruth chose to stay with Naomi and follow the true God.

Ruth 1:14-16
They lifted up their voices and wept again; then Orpah kissed her mother-in-law, but Ruth stayed with her. She said, "Behold, your sister-in-law has gone back to her people and to her god. Follow your sister-in-law." Ruth said, "Don't urge me to leave you, and to return from following you, for where you go, I will go... Your people will be my people, and your God my God.

Naomi's sharing of the message of the true God was in the backdrop of God's demonstrating the veracity of who He is by putting on display His glory through military victories. Over and over Israel won great battles with God's assistance indirectly or directly since their miraculous exit from Egypt. His reputation spread throughout the world, and some came to God through this testimony.

This can be clearly seen in the story of Rahab. Jericho was the first city Joshua had to conquer when the people of Israel entered the promised land. Normally, the army would give a city the chance to give themselves up to spare the lives of the inhabitants. This is what Moses commanded the people of Israel at the border of the promised land.

Deuteronomy 20:10-12
When you draw near to a city to fight against it, then proclaim peace to it. It shall be, if it gives you answer of peace and opens to you, then it shall be that all the people who are found therein shall become forced laborers to you, and shall serve you. If it will make no peace with you, but will make war against you, then you shall besiege it.

So, when Rahab, one of the city's citizens, discovered that the army of Israel was about to go to war with them, she knew that the true God was on their side. How? She had heard the stories of Israel's victories. She knew that the true God must be with them and believed in Him.

As a result, she helped the spies so they would protect her and her family because spiritually they had believed in the true God.

Joshua 2:9-13
She said to the men, "I know that Yahweh has given you the land, and...the fear of you has fallen upon us, and that all the inhabitants of the land melt away before you. For we have heard how Yahweh dried up the water of the Red Sea before you, when you came out of Egypt; and what you did to the two kings of the Amorites, who were beyond the Jordan, to Sihon and to Og, whom you utterly destroyed. As soon as we had heard it, our hearts melted, and there wasn't any more spirit in any man, because of you: for Yahweh your God, he is God in heaven above, and on earth beneath. Now therefore, please swear to me by Yahweh, since I have dealt kindly with you, that you also will deal kindly with my father's house, and give me a true sign; and that you will save alive my father, my mother, my brothers, and my sisters, and all that they have, and will deliver our lives...death."

HOW CHRISTIANS MAY DEFEND THEMSELVES AGAINST ATTACK

When Gentile people heard of God's miraculous works in defending Israel, their light was shining.

Psalm 67:1-6
May God be merciful to us, bless us, and cause his face to shine on us. Selah. That your way may be known on earth, and your salvation among all nations, let the peoples praise you, God. Let all the peoples praise you. Oh let the nations be glad and sing for joy, for you will judge the peoples with equity, and govern the nations on earth. Selah. Let the peoples praise you, God. Let all the peoples praise you. The earth has yielded its increase. God...will bless us.

Though somewhat prophetic, this prayer demonstrates God's method of portraying His existence on earth. This was the special revelation that coincided with His general revelation in creation, conscience, and common grace (blessings for all to enjoy on earth).

As we have seen in the previous chapters, the Lord God occasionally did powerful miracles to defend His people but usually they had to do the actual fighting themselves. Again, here is Moses encouraging his people.

Deuteronomy 20:1-4
When you go out to battle against your enemies, and see horses, chariots, and a people more numerous than you, you shall not be afraid of them; for Yahweh your God is with you, who brought you up out of the land of Egypt. It shall be, when you draw near to the battle, that the priest shall approach and speak to the people, and shall tell them, "Hear, Israel, you draw near today to battle against your enemies. Don't let your heart faint! Don't be afraid, nor tremble, neither be scared of them; for Yahweh your God is he who goes with you, to fight for you against your enemies, to save you."

It is the same way as we defend ourselves and others. God will defend us as we defend ourselves.

The Miracles to Confirm the Prophets

God performed miracles during two great periods of time in the Old Testament. The first period was Moses and Joshua to confirm their authority to speak for God.

Exodus 4:1-5
Moses answered, "But, behold, they will not believe me, nor listen to my voice; for they will say, 'Yahweh has not appeared to you.'" Yahweh said to him, "What is that in your hand?" He said, "A rod." He said, "Throw it on the ground." He threw it on the ground, and it became a snake; and Moses ran away from it. Yahweh said to Moses, "Stretch out your hand, and take it by the tail." He stretched out his hand, and took hold of it, and it became a rod in his hand. "This is so that they may believe that Yahweh, the God of their fathers, the God of Abraham, the God of Isaac, and the God of Jacob, has appeared to you."

Then, God performed miracles during a second period of time when the Lord God desired to confirm His prophets as spokesman for Him. These powerful miracles were done primarily through Elijah and Elisha. Though we do not have the record of Elijah's commissioning by God, we do see Elijah almost immediately prophesying that it would not rain for three years, and it did not. Many other miracles came after this one.

1 Kings 17:13-15
Elijah said to her, "Don't be afraid. Go and do as you have said; but make me a little cake from it first, and bring it out to me, and afterward make some for you and for your son. For Yahweh, the God of Israel says, 'The jar of meal will not run out, and the jar of oil will not fail, until the day that Yahweh sends rain on the earth.'" She went and did according to the saying of Elijah; and she, and he, and her house, ate many days. The jar of meal didn't run out, and the jar of oil didn't fail, according to Yahweh's word...he spoke by Elijah.

We have the record of Elisha's commissioning by Elijah. After receiving Elijah's mantle and viewing his supernatural departure from the earth, Elisha began performing miracles which confirmed his prophetic office.

2 Kings 2:13-15
He also took up Elijah's mantle that fell from him, and went back, and stood by the bank of the Jordan. He took Elijah's mantle that fell from him, and struck the waters, and said, "Where is Yahweh, the God of Elijah?" When he also had struck the waters, they were divided apart, and Elisha went over. When the sons of the prophets who were at Jericho facing him saw him, they said, "The spirit of Elijah rests on Elisha." They came to meet him....

This ushered in the period of the prophets setting the stage for their numerous prophetic writings.

Though God occasionally performed miracles in battle and in prophecy, this was not the usual action God took. Instead, the Lord God would through the armies of Israel as they battled, and the prophets spoke.

The Miracles to Confirm the Gospel

The third period of miracles occurred with the coming of Christ, His apostles, and the gifts of the Spirit to confirm the gospel and lay the foundation for the church.

The miracles of Christ demonstrated His deity and the true message of His gospel.

Hebrews 1:1-2
God, having in the past spoken to the fathers through the prophets at many times and in various ways, has at the end of these days spoken to us by his Son, whom he appointed heir of all things....

John 5:36-37
But the testimony which I have is greater than that of John, for the works which the Father gave me to accomplish, the...works that I do, testify about me, that the Father has sent me. The Father himself, who sent me, has testified about me. You have neither heard his voice at any time, nor seen his form.

The miracles by the apostles demonstrated that they had the same gospel and confirmed the deliverance of the final revelation of God to the world.

Hebrews 2:3-4
How will we escape if we neglect so great a salvation — which at the first having been spoken through the Lord, was confirmed to us by those who heard, God also testifying with them, both by signs and wonders, by various works of power and by gifts of the Holy Spirit, according to his own will?

While the apostles delivered the doctrine of the church, the Holy Spirit empowered other believers through the spiritual gifts to teach and confirm those doctrines miraculously.

1 Corinthians 12:4-11
Now there are various kinds of gifts, but the same Spirit. There are various kinds of service, and the same Lord. There are various kinds of workings, but the same God, who works all things in all. But to each one is given the manifestation of the Spirit for the profit of all. For to one is given through the Spirit.... But the one and the same Spirit produces all of these, distributing to each one separately as he desires.

These gifts either pertained to revelation or miracles and were no longer needed when the canon was completed.

1 Corinthians 13:8
Love never fails. But where there are prophecies, they will be done

away with. Where there are various languages, they will cease. Where there is knowledge, it will be done away with. For we know in part and we prophesy in part; but when that which is complete has come, then that which is partial will be done away with.

Since the end had been revealed and curses were given to those who added to these books, the need for revelation or miracles also ceased. As the revelation of God was coming to an end so did these gifts.

Revelation 22:18-19
I testify to everyone who hears the words of the prophecy of this book, if anyone adds to them, may God add to him the plagues which are written in this book. If anyone takes away from the words of the book of this prophecy, may God take away his part from the tree of life, and out of the holy city, which are written in this book.

Therefore, if the necessity comes for us, as believers, to defend against attack, we should take action as we depend upon the Lord and not expect the Lord God to do something miraculous as we do nothing.

The Miracles through Answered Prayer

This does not mean God does not do miracles anymore. It simply means that those who can do miracles at will no longer exist. Instead, we see the saints praying for miracles and God answering their prayers as was the case with Peter.

Acts 12:3-5
When he saw that it pleased the Jews, he proceeded to seize Peter also…. When he [Herod] had arrested him, he put him in prison, and delivered him to four squads of four soldiers…intending to bring him out…after the Passover. Peter therefore was kept in the prison, but constant prayer was made by the assembly…for him.

Acts 12:7
And behold, an angel of the Lord stood by him, and a light shone in the cell.

The saints prayed and God answered. This is the Lord God's usual pattern when His children cannot defend themselves against their enemies.

The Miracles through Providence

Finally, the Lord God primarily works today through his providence. This means that He will change circumstances to defend us. We saw this when Saul had surrounded David in the wilderness of Moan. All seemed lost. Then, God provoked the Philistines to attack Israel a distance away and Saul had to curtail his pursuit of David and go to battle the Philistines.

1 Samuel 23:25-28
When Saul heard that, he pursued David in the wilderness of Maon. Saul went on this side of the mountain, and David and his men on that side of the mountain; and David hurried to get away for fear of Saul; for Saul and his men surrounded David and his men to take them. But a messenger came to Saul, saying, "Hurry and come; for the Philistines have made a raid on the land!" So Saul returned from pursuing David, and went against the Philistines. Therefore they called that place Sela Hammahlekoth.

Here, David and his men did not sit in the desert and wait for God to take action. This would be ridiculous. David engaged in battle and depended on the assistance of the Lord and He provided in His providence. This is important to believers because it means that we cannot and should not wait for God to miraculously work and not defend ourselves. We should defend ourselves, those we love, and the innocent as we let the Lord God work through us.

An Example of Defense with Divine Help

As we have observed, people cannot defend themselves and others from harm unless they take the action necessary to do this. When they take this action, they trust in God to help them. Defending men in action, while God empowers them is His normal way.

This can be clearly seen in Psalm 127.

Psalm 127:1-2
Unless Yahweh builds the house, they who build it labor in vain. Unless Yahweh watches over the city, the watchman guards it in vain. It is vain for you to rise up early, to stay up late, eating the bread of toil, for he gives sleep to his loved ones.

Here the author means that man alone cannot build a house or guard a city without the help of the Lord God. Both must be involved in these important processes. The author could not possibly mean that our Almighty God would do it alone, could he? He could not, because it doesn't make sense.

The author is explaining the importance of not relying totally on ourselves and our own efforts or we will work and watch and work and watch relentlessly. There needs to be some rest also. If we trust in Him as we toil, we will sleep well.

Then the psalmist continues is his story of God's blessing and protection. He does this by blessing us with children. In this portion, it is implied that we can rest because God has sent our children to help with the building, the watching, and eventually the defending.

Psalm 127:3-5
Behold, children are a heritage of Yahweh. The fruit of the womb is his reward. As arrows in the hand of a mighty man, so are the

children of youth. Happy is the man who has his quiver full of them. They won't be disappointed when they speak with their enemies....

Notice, he ends with speaking to his enemies in the gate. In ancient times, children were important because they helped in the affairs of the family from an early age. They brought joy and happiness, but, more importantly, the boys brought much needed protection. They were like arrows or weapons of defense in the hands or under the control of their father.

A man has enemies in the city who will be careful because he has sons to protect him. The sons of many families will protect all in the city. The Lord works as we work, and God protects and defends as we protect and defend.

In this psalm, David explains how God functions when he must defend himself and his people.

Psalm 18:34
He teaches my hands to war, so that my arms bend a bow of bronze. You have also given me the shield of your salvation. Your right hand sustains me. Your gentleness has made me great.

God was there as he was learning how to defend in war. God will be there when he fights with the bow, but he must fight.

In Psalm 44, the psalmist describes the times that the Lord God protected them as they fought.

Psalm 44:1-3
We have heard with our ears, God; our fathers have told us what work you did in their days, in the days of old. You drove out the nations with your hand, but you planted them. You afflicted the peoples, but you spread them abroad. For they didn't get the land in possession by their own sword, neither did their own arm save them; but your right hand...because you were favorable to them.

HOW CHRISTIANS MAY DEFEND THEMSELVES AGAINST ATTACK

Then he explains the importance of not relying on their weapons and skills as warriors.

Psalm 44:4-8
God, you are my King. Command victories for Jacob! Through you, we will push down our adversaries. Through your name, we will tread down those who rise up against us. For I will not trust in my bow, neither will my sword save me. But you have saved us from our adversaries, and have shamed those who hate us. In God we have made our boast all day long. We will give thanks to your name forever. Selah.

Could this possibly mean that they would put down their weapons and ask God to protect them? Of course not. It refers to them wielding their weapons as they rely on God to guide them, strengthen them, and keep them focused.

We know this because in the second portion of the psalm, God has stopped doing this and they have lost battle after battle. The armies were wielding their weapons and fighting with all their might but without His help.

Psalm 44:9-16
But now you rejected us, and brought us to dishonor, and don't go out with our armies. You make us turn back from the adversary. Those who hate us take plunder for themselves. You have made us like sheep for food, and have scattered us among the nations. You sell your people for nothing, and have gained nothing from their sale. You make us a reproach to our neighbors, a scoffing and a derision to those who are around us. You make us a byword among the nations, a shaking of the head among the peoples. All day long my dishonor is before me, and shame covers my face, at the taunt of one who reproaches and verbally abuses, because of the enemy and the avenger.

As can be seen, the psalmist is stating that the armies of Israel fought, and God was with them. Now, He is not. There is no indication that they put their weapons down and waited for a miracle.

Throughout this book, we have seen God occasionally do great miracles on behalf of Israel. Yet, most of the time, they fought knowing that He was with them. It never occurred to anyone that they should just wait for a miracle of defense rather than defend with God's help.

The Command to Make Peace

Some will object to self-defense and the defense of others because in numerous places in the New Testament, believers are told that they are to make peace with people. We are to be the peacemakers. How can we become peacemakers through violence? Of course, this refers to peacemaking between God and man through the gospel primarily, but we are also told to be at peace with men. This would refer to living peacefully with others and not solving problems violently.

Romans 12:18
If it is possible, as much as it is up to you, be at peace with all men.

Romans 14:19
So then, let's follow after things which make for peace, and things by which we may build one another up.

Hebrews 12:14
Follow after peace with all men, and the sanctification without which no man will see the Lord.

James 3:18
Now…righteousness is sown in peace by those who make peace.

HOW CHRISTIANS MAY DEFEND THEMSELVES AGAINST ATTACK

1 Peter 3:11
Let him turn away from evil and do good. Let him seek peace and pursue it.

We must make peace with others because our God is a God of peace.

1 Corinthians 14:33
For God is not a God of confusion, but of peace, as in all the assemblies of the saints.

1 Thessalonians 5:23
May the God of peace himself sanctify you completely. May your whole spirit, soul, and body be preserved blameless at the coming of our Lord Jesus Christ.

2 Thessalonians 3:16
Now may the Lord of peace himself give you peace at all times in all ways. The Lord be with you all.

If the Lord Jesus is called the Prince of Peace and the Holy Spirit brings peace, then how can this coincide with physical violence?

Isaiah 9:6
For a child is born to us. A son…given…and the government will be on His shoulders. His name will be called Wonderful Counselor, Mighty God, Everlasting Father, Prince of Peace.

Galatians 5:22-23
But the fruit of the Spirit is love, joy, peace, patience, kindness, goodness, faith, gentleness, and self-control. Against such things there is no law.

Yet, there seems to be a paradox. Though God is called a God of peace, He is also referred to as a God of war. Can He be a God of peace and war?

DEFENDING YOUR LIFE

Exodus 15:1-3
Then Moses and the children of Israel sang this song to Yahweh, and said, "I will sing to Yahweh, for he has triumphed gloriously. He has thrown the horse and his rider into the sea. Yah is my strength and song. He has become my salvation. This is my God, and I will praise him; my father's God, and I will exalt him. Yahweh is a man of war. Yahweh is his name.

How can this be? How can God be someone of peace and war? The answer is not all that complicated. It simply means that God seeks peace but at times it must be done through war.

The Lord God seeks peace in His love, grace, and mercy, but He must also desire war at times in His righteousness, holiness, and justice. God desires peace among men but also knows that men are sinful. He will not make peace at any cost.

In the church at Corinth, there was chaos in their assembly because they had been blessed with many people who had the "showy" gifts and they wanted to use them at every gathering.

1 Corinthians 14:12
So also you, since you are zealous for spiritual gifts, seek that you may abound to the building up of the assembly.

As a result, there were divisions and conflict in the assembly.

1 Corinthians 1:9-10
God is faithful, through whom you were called into the fellowship of his Son, Jesus Christ, our Lord. Now I beg you, brothers, through the name of our Lord, Jesus Christ, that you all speak the same thing, and that there be no divisions among you, but that you be perfected together in the same mind and in the same judgment.

So, Paul takes a general divine truth and applies it very specifically to the Corinthian chaos.

HOW CHRISTIANS MAY DEFEND THEMSELVES AGAINST ATTACK

1 Corinthians 14:33
For God is not a God of confusion, but of peace...in all the assemblies of the saints.

1 Corinthians 14:40
Let all things be done decently and in order.

Here, Paul explains that our God is a God of peace and as a result, He desires things to be done decently and in order.

Why? God is a God of peace; order and decency brings that peace. We can take this same truth and apply it to society. We have learned previously that God had created structures in society to administer His justice. These structures bring peace.

Violence upon others brings much confusion, indecency (dishonorable behavior), and disorder. This brings no peace. Self-defense and the defense of others will deter those who intend harm not to engage in it or stop it. This brings peace. An important fact must be considered at this point which is appealing and compromising on evil will not bring a peace that is acceptable to both parties because the appeaser will find peace at a great compromise of their well-being. The fact that we can war on an individual, regional, or national level will deter evil and violence from occurring and bring peace.

The Concept of Pacifism

Some will object because they believe that the Bible teaches pacifism. Though the concept of non-violence sounds utterly religious and devout, its origins do not arise from the Bible. It comes from Leo Tolstoy's actions in Russia and Gandhi's protests in India. It came to its most popular form in America through the leader Martin Luther King Jr. and his non-violent movement. Since this man is celebrated annually, Christians are continually reminded of his powerful non-violent, pacifist approach. So, this is not a criticism of the technique that he used but an analysis of its biblical validity.

What is meant by a "non-violent" approach? Nonviolence involves being harmless to ourselves and others under every condition. It bears the idea of hurting people is unnecessary to achieve an outcome. It usually carries the idea that if people hurt us or others, we should not defend ourselves in anyway with a violent action but accept the violence upon us or the others they desire to harm.

This idea grows out of the protest movement and can be effective in keeping some people from turning a protest into a violent and chaotic confrontation. No one should desire protestors to be violent to get their message across, but what if the response by those around them is violent? Can those peaceful protestors defend themselves? What if the protestors were followers of Christ and the violent responders were not? Should they allow themselves to be hurt and even killed at someone's pleasure?

The answer is "non-violence under any condition" is not biblical. It is not taught in the Old or New Testaments. There is a place for violence in the defense of ourselves and others. Christians may defend themselves against physical harm. This does not mean that they may become the aggressors. As we have seen in the case of Abraham's rescue of Lot, we may become the aggressors when the defense is a rescue. This is a form of defense when one must deliver others from harm.

The misunderstanding of many of these critical passages have given some Christians the false idea that Jesus was a pacifist. They have never taken a closer look at what the Lord did to forestall His arrest, the veiled demonstrations of His power, and the declarations that the Father's allowance.

HOW CHRISTIANS MAY DEFEND THEMSELVES AGAINST ATTACK

Since the world admires these brave men for choosing not to resist violence but to always remain passive no matter what comes their way, they have become the symbol of the ultimate religious response. Naïve Christians have picked this image of pacifism and superimposed it upon our blessed Lord Jesus. The true image of Jesus was not the humble dying man on the cross but the resurrected glorious Lord coming in power at His return.

Revelation 19:11-17
I saw the heaven opened, and behold, a white horse, and he who sat on it is called Faithful and True. In righteousness he judges and makes war. His eyes are a flame of fire, and on his head are many crowns. He has names written and a name written which no one knows but he himself. He is clothed in a garment sprinkled with blood. His name is called "The Word of God." The armies which are in heaven followed him on white horses, clothed in white, pure, fine linen. Out of his mouth proceeds a sharp, double-edged sword, that with it he should strike the nations. He will rule them with an iron rod. He treads the wine press of the fierceness of the wrath of God, the Almighty. He has on his garment and on his thigh a name written, "KING OF KINGS, AND LORD OF LORDS."

This return will display the greatest violence perpetrated on the earth by any group of individuals. The Lord and His saints will come to take the world for His possession and will kill millions. We must make no mistake of His intentions and His action which will be terribly violent.

Revelation 19:17-21
I saw an angel standing in the sun. He cried with a loud voice, saying to all the birds that fly in the sky, "Come! Be gathered together to the great supper of God, that you may eat the flesh of kings, the flesh of captains, the flesh of mighty men, and the flesh of horses and of those who sit on them, and the flesh of all men, both free and slave, small and great." I saw the beast, and the kings of the earth, and their armies, gathered together to make war against him

who sat on the horse, and against his army.... The rest were killed with the sword of him who sat on the horse, the sword which came out of his mouth. So all the birds were filled with their flesh.

Jesus was a "lamb led to slaughter" not because He was a pacifist; instead, it was due to the fact that He was the Son of God (divine) and a man (human) who came to die.

Isaiah 53:4-6
Surely he has borne our sickness and carried our suffering; yet we considered him plagued, struck by God, and afflicted. But he was pierced for our transgressions. He was crushed for our iniquities. The punishment that brought our peace was on him; and by his wounds we are healed. All we like sheep have gone astray. Everyone has turned to his own way; and Yahweh has laid on him the iniquity of us all.

The Father was in control and by the Father's sovereignty and power, His Son went to the cross. The Father offered the Son to Himself as a sacrifice. Jesus was not practicing pacifism as a way of transforming society. Though these "believers" think they should never defend themselves against their enemies and only love them, this pacifistic understanding of our faith is not biblical. Pacifism is the world's way, not God's way.

In summary, we have now discovered that self-defense, the defense of those we love, and the innocent are clearly distinguishable from killing intentionally, accidentally, and for justice. Self-defense and the defense of others is the best way to love our neighbor and enemies. It is not inconsistent with turning the other cheek, forgiveness, or the silence of Jesus. Finally, we learned that it does not have to be consistent with pacifism because this concept is not biblical.

In this chapter, we learned that we may defend ourselves, those we love, and the innocent against aggressors whether they are attempting to physically hurt us for our faith or any other reason. We looked carefully at the reasons people do not believe in self-defense and the defense of others and none of them were valid biblically.

The Defense Against Enemies

Some believe that we should not defend ourselves against our enemies. I make a distinction here between strangers and known enemies because Jesus' reference to "enemies" would have been known enemies. These would not necessarily have been ones who desired their deaths; instead, they would have been those with a mutual dislike for one another for a variety of reasons. They were "neighbors" who had wronged them and became "enemies." Jesus gave various commands about how we were to treat our enemies based on how God treats His enemies. These people will contend that we should not become violent to our enemies because Jesus taught us to love and forgive our enemies. The objections are in no particular order.

The Love of Enemies

Now we must consider, the perpetrator of harm and evil as our enemy or the enemy of the ones we are attempting to defend. Some might say, "I thought we were supposed to love our enemies, bless them, pray for, and do good to them?"

Matthew 5:43-46
You have heard that it was said, "You shall love your neighbor and hate your enemy." But I tell you, love your enemies, bless those who curse you, do good to those who hate you, and pray for those who mistreat you and persecute you, that you may be children of your Father who is in heaven. For he makes his sun to rise on the evil and the good, and sends rain on the just and the unjust. For if you love

those who love you, what reward do you have? Don't even the tax collectors do the same?

The answer comes from the previous discussion. Ponder this question, "What better way, to love, bless, pray for, and do good to someone than preventing them from murdering another human being?" Since a person is judged for every wicked deed that they do, the defender will keep that person from committing a more grievous act of murder. If we defend our innocent enemy from harm, then this would even be better.

The Turning of the Other Cheek

Often, when a discussion of self-defense arises, someone will say, "Aren't we supposed to turn the other cheek in any violence?" Or one might ask, "Aren't we supposed to take the attack in the name of our Lord?" The answer to both these questions is "No!" The concept of turning the other cheek has nothing to do with someone attempting to harm us.

The passage that is being referred to is in Matthew 5, there is a similar passage in Luke 6 also.

Matthew 5:38-42
You have heard that it was said, "An eye for an eye, and a tooth for a tooth. But I tell you, don't resist him who is evil; but whoever strikes you on your right cheek, turn to him the other also. If anyone sues you to take away your coat, let him have your cloak also. Whoever compels you to go one mile, go with him two. Give to him who asks you, and don't turn away him who desires to borrow....

This simply means that the saints of God should not resist helping their needy but hostile enemies.   0000

We know this because in Matthew 5:42, after providing three examples of not resisting enemies, Jesus presents a general guiding principle. His followers are to give to every person who asks or wants to borrow. They should not oppose them because they are enemies. When people need something that the saints have, they should generously provide it for them, even if they are enemies.

He is contrasting this to their misunderstanding of "take an eye for an eye and a tooth for a tooth." This would dictate that when enemies ask, Christians should resist them or deprive them of what they need, because they do not deserve it. This is not what God does. He provides for the needs of all men.

Therefore, as an illustration, the Lord Jesus provides three extreme cases that would illicit a strong response from His audience. The first illustration involves the disrespect of believers who have offended enemies. A strike on the right cheek would indicate the believer was hit backhanded with the enemy's right hand. This was not an act of violence, but a challenge to a believer. The man was not punching him in the face but demanding a response. It was not a slap that would injure the face, but it would injure the pride. The slapping of the right cheek was really a backhanded slap to humiliate someone because he had offended him.

The Old Testament provides an example of this concerning the prophecy of Micaiah. In 2 Chronicles 18, Ahab of Israel and Jehoshaphat of Judah made an agreement to go to war against Syria, a long-time enemy. Evil King Ahab brought all his prophets together to inquire of God as to whether they would have victory in the battle. To impress the king, all of them agreed that they would have a great victory.

2 Chronicles 18:5
Then the king of Israel gathered the prophets together, four hundred

men, and said to them, "Shall we go to Ramoth Gilead to battle, or shall I forbear?" They said, "Go up; for God will deliver it into the hand of the king."

Being a man of God, Jehoshaphat, was suspicious of their motives and asked Ahab if there was another prophet in the land. Ahab suggested Micaiah but he did not like him because Micaiah was always prophesying doom to Ahab. Of course, we know from other Scriptures that Ahab was an idolator and treacherous with his people. When Micaiah was summoned, without a hesitation, he mockingly agreed with the others.

2 Chronicles 18:14
When he had come to the king, the king said to him, "Micaiah, shall we go to Ramoth Gilead to battle, or shall I forbear?" He said, "Go up, and prosper. They shall be delivered into your hand."

The king knew what he was up to, and he demanded that Micaiah tell Him what God really said. So, the prophet told him that he would die in the battle because God had sent a lying spirit to his prophets to encourage him to engage in the battle as a judgment against him. When the prophets heard this, they were insulted and humiliated Micaiah.

2 Chronicles 18:22-24
"Now therefore, behold, Yahweh has put a lying spirit in the mouth of these your prophets; and Yahweh has spoken evil concerning you." Then Zedekiah the son of Chenaanah came near, and struck Micaiah on the cheek, and said, "Which way did Yahweh's Spirit go from me to speak to you?" Micaiah said, "Behold, you shall see on that day, when you go into an inner room to hide yourself."

The author did not say "strike on the face." Zedekiah was offended and gave Micaiah a sign of that offense which was a backhanded slap. Then, their humiliation by Micaiah led to a gesture that also would humiliate Micaiah.

HOW CHRISTIANS MAY DEFEND THEMSELVES AGAINST ATTACK

In Lamentations 3, Jeremiah is bewailing the fact that God is judging His people with a coming defeat by the Chaldeans.

Lamentations 3:30-32
Let him give his cheek to him who strikes him. Let him be filled full of reproach. For the Lord will not cast off forever. For though he causes grief, yet he will have compassion...of his loving kindnesses.

Here, using the "slap on the cheek" as an analogy, the prophet is exhorting the people to accept the humiliation of the defeat because it is God's chastisement.

As we can clearly see, the words of the Lord concerning "turning the other cheek" has nothing to do with self-defense but entails our response to a shaming or humiliating word or action against us. We do not have to retaliate. Since this has to do with the meeting of needs, then most likely this enemy wanted something the believer had and was upset that he would not give it to him.

So, he thought the best way to get it was to humiliate the believer. The child of God will accept it without retaliation. In fact, he may even go to the extent of turning his other cheek to let him have it again. The Father experiences this from his enemies and does not strike them back.

The second illustration involves an enemy who thinks a Christian possesses what he needs, so he sues the believer in court. In this example, the enemy needs the inner garment of the saint, so he sues the saint for it. Someone does not sue another unless he needs something that the other possesses and thinks he deserves it. Jesus says that he should just give him the inner garment and the outer as well. The Christian is not to retaliate or get angry. This saint should relinquish and give up his most essential garment, the cloak. Saints should not resist these enemies who feel they need whatever the saints possess.

The third illustration involved soldiers who were in need of help. These military men did not need objects from others, but physical help. By law, soldiers could ask regular citizens to carry their pack for a mile. This hated Roman soldier asks a Jew to walk a mile with his pack. He is to take it two miles. As an example, Simon the Cyrene was required to carry the cross of Jesus because the Lord struggled with it. The Roman soldiers were hated by the Jews and considered enemies. The implication was powerful.

So, when an enemy is in need of physical help, a believer should give him twice as much as he needs. The point of the Lord is extremely clear. His followers are nothing like their unbelieving counterparts. They will go out of their way and beyond their comfort zone to meet the needs of people.

Does someone need something a believer has and tries to disrespect him to get it? There is no need to challenge him because he can have it. Does someone sue a believer because he needs something the believer might be wearing? He should not bother, because he will give him two articles of clothing. Does someone need a believer to help him carry something some distance? There is no problem because he will carry it twice as far. Believers are not like any other people. Christians will not retaliate against their enemies by refusing to help them; instead, they will love them by meeting their needs.

Therefore, the striking on the cheek had nothing to do with physical violence. This means it cannot be utilized as a tool by individuals who want to turn Christians into pacifists or non-violent, passive preachers who only speak of love and grace and refuse to speak of violence of any kind.

The Forgiveness of Enemies

Some will argue that self-defense and the defense of others shows a lack of forgiveness. Yet, self-defense and forgiveness are not mutually exclusive. In fact, they complement one another. Forgiveness for an action is completely separate from the consequences of that action. As parents, we forgive our children for lying to us, but we still give them consequences. In each of the structures God has provided to deal with violence, there are consequences. Briefly, as we have seen, these consequences stop the violence and then deter it from happening again. Without these being in place, violence and murder could and would reign throughout the world more than it does. The fear of these consequences deters violence and should not be eliminated entirely.

Let us remember that the flood prevented the violence that would ultimately destroy the human race because there were only eight righteous people left. It stopped the violence that was occurring or would occur by drowning. The dispersion separated the people so each resulting nation could keep other nations in check. If one nation brought violence upon the other, that nation would fight back. This would deter nations from attacking. The conscience badgers the heart when it wants violence thus preventing it. The conscience will provoke the victim or others to defend against the attacker and this will stop the attack and prevent those watching from considering violent actions themselves. The preventative and defensive actions of parents, family, and governments do the same. What would happen if violence were forgiven without consequences?

Consequences for wrong actions are critical to stopping and preventing those wrong actions again. They also prevent those from escalating into ones that are even worse. This goes for believers and unbelievers though this can be seen from different perspectives. Let us begin with all believers. If we refuse to accept the consequences for our sins or even allow other believers not to accept theirs, we are circumventing the divine learning and training process. Because God is a loving Father, He trains and disciplines us to act like Him and live in a holy way. This is called "sanctification."

Hebrews 12:7
It is for discipline that you endure. God deals with you as with children, for what son is there whom his father doesn't discipline?

God brings trials, which include consequences for actions, into the lives of His children (some self-imposed) to train them. This is what a loving father will do. The Greek word translated "discipline" means "instruction, learning, teaching, or training."

Then in verse 8, the author continues with the results of not being disciplined by God.

Hebrews 12:8-9
But if you are without discipline, of which all have been made partakers, then are you illegitimate, and not children. Furthermore, we had...fathers of our flesh to chasten us, and...paid them respect. Shall we not...be in subjection to the Father of spirits, and live?

True believers are always disciplined by their Father. People who claim that they are Christians but are never disciplined for their sin cannot be true children of God.

Hebrews 12:10
For they indeed, for a few days, punished us as seemed good to them. But he for our profit, that we may be partakers of his holiness.

Earthly fathers discipline us for a few days to help us be good in this life, but God has something greater in mind. He adds that God trains His children to partake of His own holiness.

HOW CHRISTIANS MAY DEFEND THEMSELVES AGAINST ATTACK

We are provided this chance though His discipline process.

Hebrews 12:11
All chastening seems for the present to be not joyous, but grievous. Yet afterward it yields the peaceful fruit of righteousness to those who have been exercised thereby.

Christians do not like God's discipline. It can be extremely unpleasant. Yet, the results are so powerful. The training is for righteous living which brings forth peace.

How do the consequences of our actions fit into God's discipline? The consequences for actions are often the very discipline the Lord God uses to keep us on the right path. The consequences make us say to ourselves, "I better not do that again. That was too painful! I never want to experience that again!" Yet, God has already forgiven us on the cross.

Accepting the consequences of our sins is a portion of the repentance process and not forgiveness. Of course, God uses the many structures He has established to bring the difficult consequences. Occasionally He intervenes Himself. There are numerous examples of this truth in both the Old and New Testaments. For example, the leader of Israel, Moses, was not allowed to enter the Promised Land because he struck the rock two times while he rebuked the people in anger. This was in direct defiance of the Lord's command (numbers 20). David lost his son from his adulterous relationship with Bathsheba and his murder of her husband Uriah (2 Samuel 12). There were many saints at Corinth who were sick and some dead due to their improper observance of communion (1 Corinthians 11:30). Regarding murder, we must forgive but also allow the consequences for the attacker's sin.

Now, let us consider unbelievers. First, the Lord God uses consequences to bring unbelievers to Christ. The classic example is the Prodigal Son. In this story, he loses everything before he will bend his knee to our God. In the story, a son demanded his inheritance from his wealthy father and ran off. He had quite a time living in the luxury and sin, that money could buy. When he spent all he had, he became desperate.

Then a famine hit the land, and it was so severe that he attached himself to a successful farmer and began tending to his pigs. He was so hungry that he was even willing to eat the pods that the pigs were eating, but no one would allow even this. He was completely alone and in deep trouble. Finally, he was so defeated and desperate that he looked upward for a solution. In Luke 15, Luke records this moment.

Luke 15:17-19
But when he came to himself [his senses] he said, "How many hired servants of my father's have bread enough to spare, and I'm dying with hunger!" I will get up and go to my father, and will tell him, "Father, I have sinned against heaven, and in your sight. I am no more worthy to be called your son. Make me...your hired servants."

Notice the son can no longer rely upon himself and his own resources but must look up. When he finally did, he found his solution in his father.

Notice, after his money had run out, then a famine came. Who brought the famine? The Lord God did. Both of these events put him into the perfect circumstances that would bring him right to his knees before God. This is what God He does to bring people to His Son.

Then Jesus continues by describing the father in the story standing day after day at the edge of town waiting for his son to come home. God is waiting for men to come to Him. When he did arrive in humility and repentance, the Father [God] welcomed him with open arms.

HOW CHRISTIANS MAY DEFEND THEMSELVES AGAINST ATTACK

Luke 15:20
He arose, and came to his father. But while he was still far off, his father saw him, and was moved with compassion, and ran, and fell on his neck, and kissed him.

Then, the two men went home and celebrated. Through this difficulty, he knew that God was calling him to come to Him.

What if the father had found his son, forgave him, and then rescued him? Would he have looked up? No, he would still be in his spiritually dead condition. The son would not have looked upward unless his own problems had become so overwhelming that he finally had to ask for divine help from God (represented by his father).

So, though we should forgive unbelievers for their violent actions upon us or others, we must allow the consequences of their actions to bring them to their knees before God. You may say, "Wouldn't forgiveness do it?" Most likely, the murderer would see the forgiveness without the consequences as an opportunity to kill again.

To him it would most likely mean that we were weak and foolish, and he could get away with murder again and again. He would consider our God as weak and foolish also. We must remember that the strong God of the Old Testament is the same God as in the New Testament.

Second, we must forgive unbelievers but allow them to receive the consequences of their violence because it is God's wrathful punishment upon them. This is the "blood for blood" of Genesis chapter nine, the "eye for an eye" of the law, and the "avenging of wrath" of Romans 13. In this punishment comes prevention and the stopping of the violence! Others will also see this happen and it will deter them from also being violent when they get incensed about something.

The Defense Against Persecutors

Some believe that we should not defend ourselves against persecutors. This mistaken notion is based on a variety of passages and other reasons which we will now consider. These objections and the passages that accompany them are in no particular order.

The Priority of Avoidance

Many who think Christians should not defend themselves and others against persecutors object to this because they think this would be the believer's primary response to violent persecution, but it is not. In fact, in the companion book, we discovered that the most typical response to persecution was avoidance with some type of misleading words or behavior. This is the normal response by those in both the Old and New Testaments. Though some periodically faced the persecution with great courage and boldness, this only occurred when believers were surrounded, seized, captured, or arrested. The response of physical self-defense and the defense of others may occur when lives are threatened, there is no escape, and death is at the door.

Some of the greatest acts of faith came when God's people avoided persecution through misleading words and actions. This is one of the reasons that there are few examples of their physical defense because they usually avoided confrontation. When threatened physically, we learned that believers and even Jesus used some of these methods to avoid persecution. There were quick escapes, traveling alternate routes, meeting in different locations than the danger, movements in secret, staying in the public eye so as not to be seized, remaining reclusive, nightly voyages, the escort of brethren to protect, rescue by family, and using disguises among other methods. This is a key reason why we do not see many examples of defense against persecutors.

The Divine Instruction

Some will say that Jesus never addressed the issue of self-defense or the defense of others and rejected it. By way of review, the Lord Jesus did command His disciples to defend themselves and each other. He told them that it was time to purchase a sword for their protection now that He was about to leave them. The staff was sufficient for small day to day dangers and difficulties while under His presence and care, but it would no longer suffice when He was gone. They would have to purchase swords to protect themselves against the coming persecutors.

These were His original instructions.

Matthew 10:9-10
Don't acquire, purchase, or obtain any extra gold, silver, or brass and put it in your money belts. Acquire, obtain, or purchase no extra bag for your journey, neither two coats, nor shoes, nor staff: for the laborer is worthy of his food [his support].

These were His new instructions.

Luke 22:36
Then he said to them, "But now, whoever has a purse, let him take it, and likewise a wallet. Whoever has none, let him sell his cloak, and buy a sword."

Here, we see a definite change in instructions. It would be ludicrous to think that the disciples would need swords because man or animal would become more dangerous due to the Lord's absence as some have suggested. Instead, they would need swords because of the increased violence that would ensue when they began proclaiming the good news of Christ and His resurrection. Therefore, persecutors as well as other attackers can be defended against.

The Silent Suffering of Jesus

When a discussion of self-defense arises often Christians will bring up the fact that Jesus did not defend Himself as He was mocked, scourged, and then crucified on the cross. Then, they refer to Peter's discussion of Christ's submission in his exhortation to house servants. Peter told them to submit though violent and Christians should do the same.

1 Peter 2:18-25
Servants, be in subjection to your masters with all respect: not only to the good and gentle, but also to the wicked. For it is commendable if someone endures pain, suffering unjustly, because of conscience toward God. For what glory is it if, when you sin, you patiently endure beating? But if, when you do well, you patiently endure suffering, this is commendable with God. For you were called to this, because Christ also suffered for us, leaving you an example, that you should follow his steps, who didn't sin, "neither was deceit found in his mouth." When he was cursed, he didn't curse back. When he suffered, he didn't threaten, but committed himself to him who judges righteously. He himself bore our sins in his body on the tree, that we, having died to sins, might live to righteousness. You were healed by his wounds. For you were going astray like sheep; but now you have returned to the Shepherd and Overseer of your souls.

Some will use this passage to teach that the Lord Jesus Christ never defended Himself when persecuted and we should not defend ourselves either. As we saw, Jesus did not defend Himself because it was His time determined by the

HOW CHRISTIANS MAY DEFEND THEMSELVES AGAINST ATTACK

Father to sacrifice for the sins of others. He did not resist because the Lord Jesus knew it was the Father's will. This is revealed by Him in several passages.

Matthew 26:45
Then he came to his disciples and said to them, "Are you still sleeping and resting? Behold, the hour is at hand, and the Son of Man is betrayed into the hands of sinners."

Mark 14:41
He came the third time, and said to them, "Sleep on now, and take your rest. It is enough. The hour has come. Behold, the Son of Man is betrayed into the hands of sinners.

John 7:30
They sought therefore to take him; but no one laid a hand on him, because his hour had not yet come.

When the apostle Peter drew his sword and defended the Lord by striking the ear of the servant of the high priest, Jesus stopped it.

John 18:10-11
Simon Peter therefore, having a sword, drew it. Jesus therefore said to Peter, "Put the sword into its sheath. The cup which the Father has given me, shall I not surely drink it?"

Jesus explained that His time had come.

Here, Peter is addressing the suffering of house slaves with masters who treat them poorly. They are bound before their masters and Christ was bound before the Jews. When this occurs, we must accept the suffering without evil comments. This is how Peter encouraged them. He did this by drawing upon the picture of Christ's unjust suffering at the hands of the Jews. The Lord did not deserve to be treated that way and these slaves do not either. Yet, Jesus did not curse back when cursed or threaten when threatened but instead trusted in His Father to judge them. They were to behave in the same way.

So, Peter is not applying the actions of Jesus to Christians at any time but to those who are compelled to obey a master or those in a situation in which they cannot escape like prison. If they do not obey, they will suffer great consequences. Peter knew that defending themselves would have led to their own death. As we will see, this is the reason why Jesus told Peter to put his sword back.

So, he explains that Jesus was also in a situation which He could escape and rather than curse, he complied. There is a time and place for quiet suffering. The Lord Jesus did not behave this way throughout His ministry. Often, He indicted his adversaries and compared them too vipers, whitewashed tombs with dead men's bones, and other harsh analogies.

The Lack of New Testament Examples

Some will say that there are no examples of self-defense and the defense of others by Christians in the New Testament.

The purpose of the New Testament was to deliver the final revelation to God's people, not to teach self-defense and the defense of others which had already been taught and was practiced throughout the Old Testament into the New.

Jude 1:3-4
Beloved, while I was very eager to write to you about our common salvation, I was constrained to write to you exhorting you to contend earnestly for the faith which was once for all delivered to the saints. For there are certain men who crept in secretly, even those who were long ago written about for this condemnation: ungodly

men, turning the grace of our God into indecency, and denying our only Master, God, and Lord, Jesus Christ.

The Lack of Self-Defense in Paul's Ministry

Often people will cite the lack of self-defense by the twelve apostles as an example of not using force against those who intend violence in persecution. This is a misunderstanding of the many situations in which the apostles and others found themselves. As we saw, the main response to persecution and the violent actions that came with it was avoidance. This is the normal response by those in both Testaments.

When we think of persecution, our thoughts immediately go to the apostles in Jerusalem and how they yelled, "We will obey God rather than men." Yet was this the normal response of believers throughout the Old and New Testaments? Was it even the normal response of Jesus and the apostles, including Paul? It was not. Instead, they continually attempted to avoid all violent encounters. Why? Avoidance was the norm.

Finally, when persecution did come upon them, they were usually outnumbered. When the Jews would attempt to seize Paul, they would gather a mob of people together to take him violently. He could not defend himself without his blood and the blood of his companions. In fact, when arrested, Paul saw it as an evangelistic opportunity as with the jailor in Philippi.

The Mob Assault in Pisidian Antioch

In his first missionary journey, the apostle entered Pisidian Antioch to preach the gospel. When the Jews found out, they stirred up a mob and threw him out of their borders.

Acts 13:50
But the Jews stirred up the devout and prominent women and the chief men of the city, and stirred up a persecution against Paul and Barnabas, and threw them out of their borders.

How could he defend himself?

The Mob Assault in Iconium

In Paul's first missionary journey, he preached the gospel in Iconium, a mob of Jews, Gentiles, and rulers attempted to stone Him, so he fled.

Acts 14:2-7
But the disbelieving Jews stirred up and embittered the souls of the Gentiles against the brothers. Therefore they stayed there a long time, speaking boldly in the Lord, who testified to the word of his grace, granting signs and wonders to be done by their hands. But the multitude of the city was divided. Part sided with the Jews, and part with the apostles. When some of both the Gentiles and the Jews, with their rulers, made a violent attempt to mistreat and stone them, they became aware of it and fled...the surrounding region....

How could he defend himself?

The Mob Assault in Lystra

In Lystra, Jews from two other cities came, stirred up the people, and stoned the apostle Paul. He was outnumbered, stoned, and left for dead.

Acts 14:18-19
Even saying these things, they hardly stopped the multitudes from making a sacrifice to them. But some...from Antioch and Iconium

HOW CHRISTIANS MAY DEFEND THEMSELVES AGAINST ATTACK

came there, and having persuaded the multitudes, they stoned Paul, and dragged him out of the city, supposing that he was dead.

How could he defend himself?

The Mob Assault in Philippi

When Paul was in the city of Philippi, he cast a demon out of a fortune telling slave girl and she lost her demonic powers. This agitated the merchants who owned her, and they went after Paul by stirring up a multitude of people and dragged him to the government officials of the cities.

Acts 16:19-24
But when her masters saw that the hope of their gain was gone, they seized Paul and Silas, and dragged them into the marketplace before the rulers. When they had brought them to the magistrates, they said, "These men, being Jews, are agitating our city and advocate customs which it is not lawful for us to accept or to observe, being Romans." The multitude rose up together against them and the magistrates tore their clothes from them, then commanded them to be beaten with rods. When they had laid many stripes on them, they threw them into prison, charging the jailer to keep them safely, who, having received such a command, threw them into the inner prison, and secured their feet in the stocks.

How could he defend himself?

The Mob scene in Thessalonica

After this, Paul went to Thessalonica to preach the gospel and some came to Christ, but others were angered. They gathered a group of seedy individuals to lay hands on Paul. Even the rulers were swayed.

Acts 17:5-10
But the unpersuaded Jews took along some wicked men from the marketplace, and gathering a crowd, set the city in an uproar. Assaulting the house of Jason, they sought to bring them out to the people. When they didn't find them, they dragged Jason and certain brothers before the rulers of the city, crying, "These who have turned the world upside down have come here also, whom Jason has received. These all act contrary to the decrees of Caesar, saying that there is another king, Jesus!" The multitude and the rulers of the city were troubled when they heard these things. When they had taken security from Jason and the rest, they let them go. The brothers immediately sent Paul and Silas away by night to Berea. When they arrived, they went into the Jewish synagogue.

How could he defend himself?

The Mob Scene in Berea

After Paul began preaching the good news in Berea, the Jews from the previous city came and aroused a multitude of people. So, Paul left.

Acts 17:13-14
But when the Jews of Thessalonica had knowledge that the word of God was proclaimed by Paul at Berea also, they came there likewise, agitating the multitudes. Then the brothers immediately sent out Paul to go as far as to the sea...Silas and Timothy still stayed there.

How could he defend himself?

The Mob Scene in Corinth

In Corinth the Jews of the city agreed that Paul had to be stopped and beat Sosthenes before the ruler. He did not care.

HOW CHRISTIANS MAY DEFEND THEMSELVES AGAINST ATTACK

Acts 18:12-13
But when Gallio was proconsul...the Jews with one accord rose up against Paul and brought him before the judgment seat, saying, "This man persuades men to worship God contrary to the law."

Acts 18:16-17
So he drove them from the judgment seat. Then all the Greeks seized Sosthenes, the ruler of the synagogue, and beat him before the judgment seat. Gallio didn't care about any of these things.

How could Paul defend himself?

The Mob Scene in Ephesus

Paul's preaching in Ephesus had caused the people who believed to renounce their idol worship. The silver merchants who created objects for the worship became outraged when they started losing money. They stirred the city into a frenzy.

Acts 19:25-32
Whom he gathered together, with the workmen of like occupation, and said, "Sirs, you know that by this business we have our wealth. You see and hear that not at Ephesus alone, but almost throughout all Asia, this Paul has persuaded and turned away many people.... the temple of the great goddess Artemis will be counted as nothing and her majesty destroyed.... When they heard this they were filled with anger...cried out, saying, "Great is Artemis of the Ephesians!" The whole city was filled with confusion, and they rushed with one accord into the theater, having seized Gaius and Aristarchus, men of Macedonia, Paul's companions in travel. When Paul wanted to enter into the people, the disciples didn't allow him...the Asiarchs, being his friends, sent to him and begged him not to venture into the theater. Some therefore cried one thing, and some another, for the assembly was in confusion.

How could he defend himself?

The Mob Scene in Jerusalem

When Paul attempted to appease the Jews by making a special offering in the temple, they accused him of bringing a Gentile into an area of the temple he did not belong. The apostle was literally mobbed, beaten, and would have been murdered had not the Roman soldiers intervened. They came storming into the crowd.

Acts 21:27-32
When the seven days were almost completed, the Jews from Asia, when they saw him in the temple, stirred up all the multitude and laid hands on him, crying out, "Men of Israel, help! This is the man who teaches all men everywhere against the people, and the law, and this place. Moreover, he also brought Greeks into the temple, and has defiled this holy place!" For they had seen Trophimus, the Ephesian, with him in the city, and they supposed that Paul had brought him into the temple. All the city was moved and the people ran together. They seized Paul and dragged him out of the temple. Immediately the doors were shut. As they were trying to kill him, news came up to the commanding officer of the regiment that all Jerusalem was in an uproar. Immediately he took soldiers and centurions and ran down to them...stopped beating Paul.

How could he defend himself?

The Mob in Jerusalem After the Speech

Paul asked the Roman centurion if he could address the crowd which Paul did. Unfortunately, his words only stirred up the people more, so the Romans had to whisk him away.

Acts 22:19-25
"I said, 'Lord, they themselves know that I imprisoned and beat in every synagogue those who believed in you. When the blood of

HOW CHRISTIANS MAY DEFEND THEMSELVES AGAINST ATTACK

Stephen, your witness, was shed, I also was standing by, consenting to his death, and guarding the cloaks of those who killed him.' "He said to me, 'Depart, for I will send you out far from here to the Gentiles.'" They listened to him until he said that; then they lifted up their voice and said, "Rid the earth of this fellow, for he isn't fit to live!" As they cried out, threw off their cloaks, and threw dust into the air, the commanding officer commanded...to be brought into the barracks, ordering him to be examined by scourging, that he might know for what crime they shouted against him like that. When they had tied him up with thongs, Paul asked the centurion who stood by, "Is it lawful for you to scourge a man who is a Roman, and not found guilty?"

How could he defend himself?

The Mob of Pharisees and Sadducees

When Paul spoke before the Sanhedrin, he theologically divided the two sects and threw them into chaos. They began to act like a mob and the Romans once again had to intervene. This time, they had to grab him and quickly whisp him away from the danger of the mob.

Acts 23:7-10
When he had said this, an argument arose between the Pharisees and Sadducees, and the crowd was divided. For the Sadducees say that there is no resurrection, nor angel, nor spirit; but the Pharisees confess all of these. A great clamor arose, and some of the scribes of the Pharisees' part stood up, and contended, saying, "We find no evil in this man. But if a spirit or angel has spoken to him, let's not fight against God!" When a great argument arose, the commanding officer, fearing...Paul would be torn in pieces by them, commanded the soldiers to go down and take him by force from among them, and bring him into the barracks.

How could he defend himself?

The Mob of Assassins

After this incident, the Jews had had enough with Paul. Forty of them bound themselves with an oath to assassinate Paul and were give the consent of the Sanhedrin which was the Jewish government.

Acts 23:12-15
When it was day, some of the Jews banded together, and bound themselves under a curse, saying that they would neither eat nor drink until they had killed Paul. There were more than forty people who had made this conspiracy. They came to the chief priests and the elders, and said, "We have bound ourselves under a great curse to taste nothing until we have killed Paul. Now therefore, you with the council inform the commanding officer that he should bring him down to you tomorrow, as though you were going to judge his case more exactly. We are ready to kill him before he comes near."

How could he defend himself?

The Protection from The Mob

This assassination plot worried the Romans, and they gave him a large escort to the governor.

Acts 23:22-24
So the commanding officer let the young man go, charging him, "Tell no one that you have revealed these things to me." He called to himself two of the centurions, and said, "Prepare two hundred soldiers to go as far as Caesarea, with seventy horsemen, and two hundred men armed with spears, at the third hour of the night." He asked them to provide animals, that they might set Paul on one, and bring him safely to Felix the governor.

Here, there was no need to defend himself.

HOW CHRISTIANS MAY DEFEND THEMSELVES AGAINST ATTACK

The Veiled Warning to Persecutors

Though Jesus did not defend Himself directly against His persecutors because His hour had come, he did threaten them physically. Jesus came to earth the first time to die for our sins and to save the lost. This involved accepting the worst kind of punishment for His teachings and their results. The second time, he would judge the wicked. This would involve Him coming to defend Himself and His brethren. Though He had not come to defend Himself the first time, He nevertheless, warned them that He would come again and defend Himself even against those who were killing Him (on judgment day).

When Jesus spoke to Judas at the moment of His betrayal, the entire crowd of Jewish leaders, Roman soldiers, various onlookers, and the mob that accompanied them fell as dead men.

John 18:4-7
Jesus therefore, knowing all the things that were happening to him, went out, and said to them, "Who are you looking for?" They answered him, "Jesus of Nazareth." Jesus said to them, "I am he." Judas...who betrayed him, was standing with them. When therefore he said to them, "I am he," they went backward, and fell to the ground. Again therefore he asked them, "Who are you looking for?" They said, "Jesus of Nazareth."

This was a display of His power and a message to all that at any moment, He could stop them.

This is a powerful testimony to God's powerful design of self-defense and the defense of others. Had Jesus not come to die for man's sin, His defense would have quickly come and no one would be able to stand against Him. This will happen at the second coming. This was a simple display of the power Jesus could have used to defend Himself.

The Reaction to Pilate

Some may say, "We should not defend ourselves against persecutors because God's kingdom is not of this world as Christ said to Pilate." When Pilate asked Jesus if He was a king, Jesus explained that His kingdom was not of this world. If it were, legions of angels would have come to defend Him.

John 18:36
Jesus answered, "My Kingdom is not of this world. If my Kingdom were of this world, then my servants would fight, that I wouldn't be delivered to the Jews. But now my Kingdom is not from here."

What did He mean by this? He was the rightful heir to the throne of David. He was the King of the Jews. Herod was not the rightful heir, but Jesus did not come to take His throne from him. He came to save sinners and take the power of death from the Devil. As a result, His kingdom was not a physical kingdom at the time due to the rejection of Jews of their Messiah and God's closing of their hearts. This passage cannot be used to teach that Jesus does not want us to defend ourselves because we are in a spiritual kingdom. This is not in view in this passage.

The Lack of a Legal Distinction

We are commanded to obey the laws of government.

Romans 13:1-4
Let every soul be in subjection to the higher authorities, for there is no authority except from God, and those who exist are ordained by God. Therefore he...resists the authority withstands the ordinance of God...those who withstand will receive to themselves judgment. For rulers are not a terror to the good work, but to the evil. Do you desire to have no fear of the authority? Do that which is good, and

you will have praise from the authority, for he is a servant of God to you for good. But if you do that which is evil, be afraid, for he doesn't bear the sword in vain; for he is a servant of God, an avenger for wrath to him who does evil.

The fact that the legal authorities do not make religious distinctions in any of its laws on self-defense demonstrates its legitimacy. It does not matter to the government whether we are attacked for our faith or not, we may defend ourselves. These authorities are not going to explain to us that we could only defend ourselves if it was not for our faith. In fact, people committing violence upon religious people for their beliefs is usually considered a hate crime and with it comes a greater judgment.

The Diverse and Hidden Motivations

Some think that we must be passive when violence comes our way due to persecution but not due to other motives. For example, if someone desires to hurt us because we are saints, we are supposed to just stand there and take it. If someone wants to hurt us for something that has nothing to do with our faith, then we are able to defend ourselves. This position is false and is utterly impractical in real life. Most of all, it is without biblical proof.

If this were true, then we would have to rely on discerning whether it was for persecution or for another reason before we could take action. In real life situations, we cannot always discern the motive of the people. For example, there is a loud knock on our front door. We look through the peep hole and see two men in tee shirts and jeans with guns. Are we, as Christians, supposed to shout, "Are you two here to hurt us because we are followers of Christ, or for a different reason?" The understanding would be that if it were for our faith in

Christ, then we would let them in and kill us. If the two were not persecutors, we could escape or defend ourselves. This would be ridiculous.

Second, this does not match the numerous illustrations of persecution in the Bible. Often, the motives for persecution were not necessarily because the people were preaching the gospel or because they were Christians directly but often due to the results of their preaching or ministry. A careful study of the journey of Christ to the cross, the ministry of the apostles through their initial persecution, and Paul in his evangelism to the bitter end, we will find many different reasons for their persecution. It was ultimately because of Christ but not always directly. Often, persecutors lied. Sometimes, the accusations and charges would change if they did not work and at other times, they would change because the reaction of the people they were listening to changed. This makes the true motive difficult to discern at any given time.

In Luke 23, Jesus was accused of something other than His proclamation of the gospel. Notice, the Jewish leaders' initial accusation before Pilate.

Luke 23:1-2
The whole company of them rose up and brought him before Pilate. They began to accuse him, saying, "We found this man perverting the nation, forbidding paying taxes to Caesar, and saying that he himself is Christ, a king."

When verses 3-5, Pilate was not at all satisfied with these charges and desired to release Jesus, so they added others.

Luke 23:4-6
Pilate said to the chief priests and the multitudes, "I find no basis for a charge against this man." But they insisted, saying, "He stirs up...people...throughout all Judea, beginning from Galilee even to

this place." But when Pilate heard Galilee mentioned, he asked if the man was a Galilean.

None of their charges included a definite statement that they were persecuting Him for His declaration that He was the Son of God. Though we know this was the real reason, they had to come up with other accusations because he would not care about this understanding.

In Acts 5, the apostles were healing people, gathering large crowds, and then were arrested. Luke records that it was jealousy that caused their incarceration.

Acts 5:17-18
But the high priest rose up, and all those who were with him (which is the sect of the Sadducees), and they were filled with jealousy and laid hands on the apostles, then put them in public custody.

This motive of jealousy had little to do with their theology but much to do with their popularity.

After they were released by an angel, they went out and preached again. When they were arrested, the charges given were something different than jealousy.

Acts 5:27-28
When they had brought them, they set them before the council. The high priest questioned them, saying, "Didn't we strictly command you not to teach in this name? Behold, you have filled Jerusalem with your teaching, and intend to bring this man's blood on us."

The point is that persecutors attempt to harm or even kill us, as believers, for many reasons not just our faith. It would be foolish to think that we would have to discern the real reasons every time someone would desire to be violent with us before we could defend ourselves.

In Acts 16, Paul was seized in Ephesus by businessmen who made idols. His conversion of a demon-possessed slave girl was ruining their fortune telling business. When these merchants brought him before the legal magistrates, they accused him of something different than the real reason that they grabbed him. This was for their loss of income from the idol selling businesses that he had caused. He was essentially putting them and others out of business.

Acts 16:20-21
When they had brought them to the magistrates, they said, "These men, being Jews, are agitating our city and advocate customs which it is not lawful for us to accept or to observe, being Romans."

To have him imprisoned, they accused him of encouraging others to follow customs against Rome. Obviously, these were not the real motives behind their actions but the ones they verbalized. How are believers to discern motives with this kind of complexity?

Why would we expect a direct attack from Lucifer? This fallen angel did not tempt Adam and Eve directly, but he appeared to them as a serpent and questioned God's motives.

Genesis 3:1
Now the serpent was more subtle than any animal of the field which Yahweh God had made. He said to the woman, "Has God really said, 'You shall not eat of any tree of the garden?'"

In fact, Paul states that this serpent from old will appear as an angel of light.

2 Corinthians 11:14
And no wonder, for even Satan masquerades as an angel of light.

So, we must not rely on the discernment of motives for self-defense and the defense of others but simply the violence that someone is about to commit.

The Absurd Discernment

Some might say that we must discern whether a violent act is due to persecution for our faith. If it is, we should not defend ourselves. The truths from Scripture are amazing in their application to real life. We never see principles that are confusing or put the believer into a dilemma as to what they should do in a situation. Paul indicates God is a God of order.

1 Corinthians 14:33
for God is not a God of confusion, but of peace, as in all the assemblies of the saints.

1 Corinthians 14:40
Let all things be done decently and in order.

We saw God's order in the structures of self-defense He put into society.

Another reason that self-defense and the defense of others is a valid action whether people are attempting violence upon us for our Christian faith or not is the absolute chaos it would bring in the midst of a very violent situation. Consider the following scenario. Several men come to our door and have weapons in their hands. They are intent on harming us. In a split second, we must decide what to do. Is it reasonable to ask them through the peep hole if they are going to harm us because we are Christians? Then, if they are, we do not defend ourselves but allow them to kill us. If they aren't, we pick up weapons and defend ourselves. This is utterly ludicrous. We defend ourselves and other against attack no matter what the intentions are because they cannot often be discerned.

The Satanic Immobilization

Another reason we cannot attempt to discover intentions of people before they try and harm us is the deception of Satan. Lucifer in the garden did not use a direct attack with Eve; instead, he appeared as a serpent. Since this is the case, why would we expect a direct attack from persecution rather than a deceptive one?

Genesis 3:1-3
Now the serpent was more subtle than any animal of the field which Yahweh God had made. He said to the woman, "Has God really said, 'You shall not eat of any tree of the garden'?" The woman said to the serpent, "We may eat fruit from the trees of the garden, but not the fruit of the tree which is in the middle of the garden. God has said, 'You shall not eat of it. You shall not touch it, lest you die.'"

Revelation 12:9
The great dragon was thrown down, the old serpent, he who is called the devil and Satan, the deceiver of the whole world. He was thrown down to the earth, and his angels were thrown down with him.

Eve thought she was doing something good for herself while Adam rebelled. This killed Eve spiritually, led to very painful curses, the death of her firstborn, and her eventual physical death. God would not allow His people to have to make a split-second decision to defend or not to defend where they could be deceived and physically die. If someone acts to hurt us, we defend ourselves.

We must be aware that Satan comes as a truth bearer but only lies.

2 Corinthians 11:13-15
But I am afraid that somehow, as the serpent deceived Eve in his craftiness, so your minds might be corrupted...And no wonder, for

even Satan masquerades as an angel of light. It is no great thing therefore...servants also masquerade as servants of righteousness, whose end will be according to their works.

He has deceived some into believing that they should just let someone kill them in the name of Christ. There is absolutely no command to stand and die if it is possible to defend.

The Demonic Confusion

Another reason we cannot attempt to discover intentions of people before they try and harm us is the deception of his evil angels. Demons work in the arena of false beliefs and doctrines. In 1 Timothy 4, Paul explains to Timothy that those disturbing the brethren in his church are following doctrines of demons.

1 Timothy 4:1
But the Spirit says expressly that in later times some will fall away from the faith, paying attention to seducing spirits and doctrines of demons.

Why would we not expect these evil angels to infiltrate the Lord's church and convince people that believers must accept persecution by simply trusting and praying? They do not want us to defend ourselves. Why? So, we can be controlled either through our own submission, imprisonment, or death. They must stop our witness. The easiest way is to convince us to submit.

There are many ways to do this. They can create a "hippie" Jesus who seeks peace and never defends Himself and would never tell His disciples to defend themselves. Or they leave the righteous, just, and holy God in the Old Testament and focus on the loving, gracious, merciful Jesus God in the New

Testament. How could the followers of a loving, gracious, merciful God hurt people even if they are trying to hurt them? They might say. "My goodness, Jesus would never do that!" Yet, when He returns, he comes with a sword not a bundle of flowers and a basket of muffins.

Revelation 19:11-16
I saw the heaven opened, and behold, a white horse, and he who sat on it is called Faithful and True. In righteousness he judges and makes war. His eyes are a flame of fire, and on his head are many crowns. He has names written and a name written which no one knows but he himself. He is clothed in a garment sprinkled with blood. His name is called "The Word of God." The armies which are in heaven followed him on white horses, clothed in white, pure, fine linen. Out of his mouth proceeds a sharp, double-edged sword, that with it he should strike the nations. He will rule them with an iron rod. He treads the wine press of the fierceness of the wrath of God, the Almighty. He has on his garment and on his thigh a name written, "KING OF KINGS, AND LORD OF LORDS."

Others might respond with, "two wrongs don't make a right." This is a lie because defending oneself is not "a wrong."

The idea of "two wrongs do not make a right" might work on a school yard but not in real life. This is presented to children because we cannot have young children deciding when to defend themselves and when not to because they do not have the discernment. Instead, they must get an adult to help but real life is not a school yard, and the police may not come in time. In fact, it may be the police acting outside their God given responsibility that bring the persecution.

Christians may take the appropriate action to stop violence against them and end the threat. We cannot let the lies of the devil and his minions fool us into becoming passive and willing to put up with any kind of violent attack to silence us.

HOW CHRISTIANS MAY DEFEND THEMSELVES AGAINST ATTACK

The Testing of the Lord

In the companion book, we discussed numerous responses to persecution. Christians could submit, take legal action, defy the law, avoid with words and actions, or present a strong gospel. In this critical book, we discussed the physical response of self-defense. These are all biblical.

The Devil and His demons want us to believe that no action is necessary except to trust God and pray. If we just "trust and pray" without taking defensive actions, then we might be actually "testing the Lord" as the Devil asked Christ to do.

Matthew 4:1-7
Then Jesus was led up by the Spirit into the wilderness to be tempted by the devil. When he had fasted forty days and forty nights, he was hungry afterward. The tempter came and said to him [Jesus], "If you are the Son of God, command that these stones become bread." Then Jesus was led up by the Spirit into the wilderness to be tempted by the devil. Then the devil took him into the holy city. He set him on the pinnacle of the temple, and said to him, "If you are the Son of God, throw yourself down, for it is written, 'He [God] will command his angels concerning you,' and, 'On their hands they will bear you up, so that you don't dash your foot against a stone.'" Jesus said to him, "Again, it is written, 'You shall not test the Lord, your God." Again, the devil took him to an exceedingly high mountain, and showed him all the kingdoms of the world and their glory.

We have established throughout the book that the Lord God's normal method for defending his people is by aiding them in their own defense. Telling believers not to defend themselves in persecution is like telling people not to jump out of the way in front of a speeding car. This false belief is a powerful tool in stopping Christians. We cannot believe this horrifying lie. It puts all believers and those they love at great risk and will stop the spread of the gospel.

The World's Deception

The World desires to uphold many values contrary to the Christian faith. They see Christians as standing in their way. In Romans 1, Paul describes the characteristics of the societies around us. The terms he uses speak of many sins that lead to deception.

Romans 1:28-32
Even as they refused to have God in their knowledge, God gave them up to a reprobate mind, to do those things which are not fitting; being filled with...unrighteousness, sexual immorality, wickedness, covetousness, malice; full of envy, murder, strife, deceit, evil habits, secret slanderers, backbiters, hateful to God, insolent, arrogant, boastful, inventors of evil things, disobedient to parents, without understanding, untrustworthy, unloving, unforgiving, unmerciful; who, knowing the ordinance of God, that those who practice such things are worthy of death, not only do the same, but also approve of those who practice them (DEJ).

They not only desire to commit every kind of sin but want to encourage others to do the same.

One important way this is accomplished is by silencing the holy words and behavior of Christians. This is accomplished by making the saints believe that they should trust and pray and let God work when the world speaks or takes action against them. This will put a cover over our lights.

When we disagree with the values they are propagating, they merely have to come after us for our Christian faith, and we melt into a slumbering body of people who just trust and pray without taking action. True believers throughout the centuries have always acted, if possible. What would have happened to the nation of Israel if Abraham, Moses, David, Isaiah or others had just trusted and prayed without action?

HOW CHRISTIANS MAY DEFEND THEMSELVES AGAINST ATTACK

As we learned in our study of 2 Timothy 3 in the companion book, the world is growing in their evil and ungodliness. This pours forth into every kind of chicanery to influence all to participate in their evil and wickedness.

2 Timothy 3:1-5
But know this: that in the last days, grievous times will come. For men will be lovers of self, lovers of money, boastful, arrogant, blasphemers, disobedient to parents, unthankful, unholy, without natural affection, unforgiving, slanderers, without self-control, fierce, not lovers of good, traitors, headstrong, conceited, lovers of pleasure rather than lovers of God, holding a form of godliness, but having denied its power. Turn away from these, also.

Making self-defense for persecution a sin allows them to go unchecked because believers in Jesus will become nothing but immobilized, imprisoned, or dead.

The False Religious Examples

Not only will Satan, His demons, and the world deceive us into becoming passive, so will false prophets. The Lord Jesus and His apostles continually warned saints in the church about many false prophets would come in among them and sow seeds of error.

John 10:1-3
Most certainly, I tell you, one who doesn't enter by the door into the sheep fold, but climbs up some other way, is a thief and a robber. But one who enters in by the door is the shepherd of the sheep. The gatekeeper opens the gate for him, and the sheep listen to his voice. He calls his own sheep by name, and leads them out.

The apostle and inspired writer Paul also warned of these false teachers entering the flock.

Acts 20:29-30
For I know that after my departure, vicious wolves will enter in among you, not sparing the flock. Men will arise from among your own selves, speaking perverse things, to draw away the disciples after them.

These could be non-Christians with the cloak of pastor or true Christians who have believed these false pastors and leaders.

Either way, for the Devil to be successful in his schemes to protect his domain of darkness until eventually the whole world worships and is controlled by a man he has possessed, he must immobilize Christians. What better way than to convince them they should not resist?

How wickedly clever it is to use the Lord Jesus as his pawn in the deception. They would say that Jesus did not resist nor should we. This is a direct lie. We know from our study in the companion book that Jesus avoided capture by His enemies both naturally and even supernaturally. He only allowed Himself to be arrested when the Father determined that it was the right time for Him to die.

The Blind Following of the Heart

Some people might come along and say something like this, "self-defense against persecutors just seems wrong." One of the reasons this occurs is due to these perpetrators of error (Satan, demons, the world, false prophets) who constantly barrage believers with unholy attitudes. They desire to fool us into becoming passive to further their own sinful agenda which is against everything believers stand for.

They bombard us with their lies and deceptions until our values get turned upside down as Israel's did.

HOW CHRISTIANS MAY DEFEND THEMSELVES AGAINST ATTACK

Isaiah 5:20-21
Woe to those who call evil good, and good evil; who put darkness for light, and light for darkness; who put bitter for sweet, and sweet for bitter! Woe to those who are wise in their own eyes, and prudent in their own sight!

They will tell us to "follow our hearts" when our hearts can deceive us greatly.

Jeremiah 17:9
The heart is deceitful above all things and it is exceedingly corrupt. Who can know it?

They encourage us to do "what we think is best" when this only leads to sin and corruption as the people of Israel found in the book of Judges.

Judges 17:6
In those days there was no king in Israel. Everyone did that which was right in his own eyes.

They explain that we should ask the question, "What would Jesus do?" when most believers today do not know enough about the Lord to know what He would do.

Matthew 22:29
But Jesus answered them, "You are mistaken, not knowing the Scriptures, nor the power of God."

The only reliable source of knowledge is the Bible and a careful study as I have demonstrated leads to only one conclusion: Is it right to defend ourselves, those we love, and the innocent from harm even as God does.

DEFENDING YOUR LIFE

Conclusion

As we conclude this book, I would like to leave us with some final thoughts about persecution and belief in Christ. First, if you have received Jesus as Savior and Lord, you now have the spiritual tools needed to stand your ground. If we follow the principles that we have discovered in the Holy Scriptures concerning persecution, then whatever we do we will glorify God.

Second, if you read this entire book and realized that you do not understand salvation or have never received Christ as Lord and Savior, then I would like to encourage you to seek Him. Please do not skip this critical section; it may be the most important in your life.

From all outward appearances, humans seem "good" and attempt to live decent lives. This is man's concept of himself. This is not God's concept. The Almighty's view is that people all over the world and throughout the ages sin, sin, and sin again (Romans 3:23). This is a terrible and utterly destructive condition. Yet, they have ramifications that are much worse. These sins condemn us to everlasting divine retribution. We will live for eternity without God in His condemnation. This means forever and ever and ever and ever.

Though described briefly in the Old Testament, the Lord Jesus Christ clearly announced and proclaimed the future punishment to come. Contrary to popular belief, Jesus did not only speak of love, grace, and mercy, He also spoke of the coming judgment for sin. He declared that the judgment of sin would be everlasting punishment in a place He called "Hell." The Lord portrayed this place as an eternal inferno (Matthew 18:8) where there would be the weeping (from the sorrow) and gnashing of teeth (from the agony and anguish of suffering) continually into eternity (Matthew 8:12; 13:42, 50; 22:13; 24:51; 25:30; Luke 13:28).

Why must people face this horrific punishment? Though God is a God of love, grace, and mercy, He is also a God of great holiness, righteousness, and justice (Psalm 89:14,18). These attributes are just as much a part of His divine nature as His love, grace, and mercy. You have broken God's law as we all have, and the penalty must be paid. This began with the first man Adam (Genesis 3:1-7). When this occurred, His love, grace, and mercy surfaced, and a provision was made. Someone else would have to take man's place and pay the penalty. Someone who had never transgressed Him, who would never deserve punishment, and would fulfill all of God's Laws, would be substituted in man's place. This was the Son of God, Jesus Christ.

As the God-Man, He would pay the penalty for our sins in His death on the cross. Once done, the Lord God made only one provision for people to appropriate what His Son had done on the cross for them. This provision is receiving Jesus Christ as Savior and Lord. Though I cannot possibly share with you this good news in the confines of this book, I would love for you to consider purchasing my book entitled *Finding the Light: The Kingdom of Heaven and How to Enter It.* It can be found on Amazon.com. It is inexpensive and contains the full gospel message for your consideration. This message is so important and extensive that it cannot be presented in a few pages at the end of a book. May you discover through the Lord Jesus Christ the joy only found in Him.

ABOUT THE AUTHOR

Dr. Donald Jones is currently a Christian Pastoral Counselor with thirty-eight years of experience in the fields of pastoral ministry, public education, and Christian counseling. He carries degrees and certificates from four major universities and from a variety of educational institutions. He has been a professor of Languages and Bible, a television commentator, and a featured speaker at a variety of events and seminars at churches, schools, and other organizations across the United States. He is a member in good standing of several secular and Christian professional organizations. Dr. Jones has been a published author since 1976. For further information view his website at www.donjonesphd.com.

www.ingramcontent.com/pod-product-compliance
Lightning Source LLC
Chambersburg PA
CBHW030327240426
43661CB00052B/1558